The Therapy of the Christian Body

The Therapy of the Christian Body

A Theological Exposition of Paul's First Letter to the Corinthians, Volume 2

Brian Brock
AND
Bernd Wannenwetsch

FOREWORD BY
Douglas Campbell

CASCADE *Books* · Eugene, Oregon

THE THERAPY OF THE CHRISTIAN BODY
A Theological Exposition of Paul's First Letter to the Corinthians, Volume 2

Copyright © 2018 Brian Brock and Bernd Wannenwetsch. All rights reserved. Except for brief quotations in critical publications or reviews, no part of this book may be reproduced in any manner without prior written permission from the publisher. Write: Permissions, Wipf and Stock Publishers, 199 W. 8th Ave., Suite 3, Eugene, OR 97401.

Cascade Books
An Imprint of Wipf and Stock Publishers
199 W. 8th Ave., Suite 3
Eugene, OR 97401

www.wipfandstock.com

PAPERBACK ISBN: 978-1-4982-3352-1
HARDCOVER ISBN: 978-1-4982-3354-5
EBOOK ISBN: 978-1-4982-3353-8

Cataloguing-in-Publication data:

Names: Brock, Brian, 1970–, author. | Wannenwetsch, Bernd, 1959–, author. | Campbell, Douglas A. (Douglas Atchison), 1961–, foreword.

Title: The therapy of the Christian body : a theological exposition of Paul's first letter to the Corinthians, volume 2 / Brian Brock and Bernd Wannenwetsch ; foreword by Douglas Campbell.

Description: Eugene, OR : Cascade Books, 2018 | Includes bibliographical references and index(es).

Identifiers: ISBN 978-1-4982-3352-1 (paperback) | ISBN 978-1-4982-3354-5 (hardcover) | ISBN 978-1-4982-3353-8 (ebook)

Subjects: LCSH: Bible.—Corinthians, 1st—Commentaries. | Bible.—Corinthians, 1st—Theology. | Bible.—Corinthians, 1st.

Classification: BS2675.53 .B76 2018 (print) | BS2675.53 .B76 (ebook)

Manufactured in the U.S.A.   09/25/18

An earlier version of a portion of this manuscript was published as:

Brian Brock, "Theologizing Inclusion: 1 Corinthians 12 and the Politics of the Body of Christ," *Journal of Religion, Disability, and Health* 15 (2011) 351–76.

Contents

Foreword by Douglas Campbell | vii

Abbreviations | xi

1 Corinthians 10 | 1

Types in the Old Testament · 1
De-moralizing Old Testament Types · 5
Beyond the Pedagogical God · 6
Flight into Trusting Communion · 13
Eucharist beyond Religious Ritual · 16
Idolatry and the Sociality of Christian Conscience · 19
Love Displacing Idolatry and Flattery · 25

1 Corinthians 11 | 27

Excursus: Bodies and Their Communicative Surfaces · 28
Bodily Semiotics and the Embarrassments of Power · 33
Distinguishing Church from Mere Physical Gathering · 48
Confusing Apostles and Patrons · 51
"Broken Loaf" Betrayal · 56
Life Open to Divine Judgment · 61
A Worldly Eucharist · 65

1 Corinthians 12 | 72

Clearing the Spiritual Haze · 73
Upbuilding Gifts of an Active Spirit · 76
Allocated to Each, for the Whole · 81
Living into Bodily Being as Given · 85
Absorbing the Many Gifts into One · 100
Honor for Outsiders—the Same Care for All · 110
Ministries and Ministers · 120
Excursus: Exegesis and Pastoral Application · 126

1 Corinthians 13 | 128

    Beyond the "Double Love Command" to Love's Aesthetic · 128
    Love as Fruitful Communication · 130
    The One Who Loves · 139
    Loving Knowledge and Being Known by Love · 143
    Excursus: Theology and God Talk · 144
    Abiding in the Love of the One · 148

1 Corinthians 14 | 150

    Distinguishing Private and Public Edification · 150
    Immediate Ecstasy and Mediated Speech · 166
    Desiring vs. Coveting Spiritual Gifts · 170
    Manufactured Comprehension vs. Gospel Understanding · 174
    The Dynamism of the Prophetic Spirit · 178

1 Corinthians 15 | 192

    Scripture and Resurrection: Mutual Vindication · 195
    Pitiful Christians · 202
    Queuing for Heaven · 204
    The Practicalities of Fighting Death · 209
    Will I Be "Me" in the Resurrection · 212
    Two Deaths, Two Resurrections · 220
    Changed in the Lord's Work · 224

1 Corinthians 16 | 228

    Traveling as Carrying Generosity · 228
    On Reading Other People's Mail · 230
    Exercising Authority Together · 233
    Staying with the Gospel's Enemies · 236
    Refreshed by Present Believers · 240
    Saying Goodbye to Paul · 243

Bibliography | 247

Name Index | 255

Subject Index | 261

Scripture Index | 277

Foreword

PAULINE SCHOLARS LIKE ME, who yearn for a deeper, richer theological conversation when Paul's texts are being expounded, will, on reading this book, feel a bit like a deer panting for water that comes upon a burbling mountain stream.

The professional guild of Pauline exegetes is dominated by historical-critical exegesis. This is, putting things summarily but hopefully not completely inaccurately, an approach that assumes a broad liberal democratic framework for conversation, which excludes God from the public square. Given these rules, conversations about the Bible can take place in state-run and financed institutions, and in academic conferences between very different parties—say Christian, Jews, and atheists—because any confessional claims and personal loyalties that might elicit conflict have been removed from the discussion by definition. It follows from these presuppositions, however—these liberal rules of engagement—that history is a closed causal nexus, and that the supernatural should be treated with suspicion, if not excluded. (If interpreters are in fact personally committed to God (et cetera) then these views should be bracketed for a time, but this amounts to the same thing.) Hence, statements *about* God in relation to the text, in the sense of a *living* God—as against the notion of God that the writers and readers of the text think in terms of—are to be excluded. The result of all this is a collapse of biblical interpretation from its rich diversification and function within the life of a community of faith, where it is supposed that God is at work, back into an original moment of composition and delivery, which is itself carefully sanitized. A suitably sober, modern view of people, causality, and reality is introduced where the text makes more extravagant claims, and any later discussions and concerns from a faith-community are vigilantly and emphatically repudiated.

Now, a lot can still be said in these terms about the Bible more broadly and about Paul more narrowly. Indeed, even this limited, liberal conversation never needs to end (a critical element within any modern scholarly method). It is always possible to find another detail within a complex original moment that needs to be illuminated, and there are always further delicate connections to be made between ancient sources and artifacts and our primary texts, as our understanding of the original world of the Bible continues to deepen. We do learn things from this method. And it certainly teaches its practitioners to read closely and carefully. But there is clearly a degree of artificiality about this whole business as well, especially when it is recalled that texts like the Bible are *Scripture*.

Texts like Paul's letters to the Corinthians are historically part of a community that is oriented toward God, and so they are supposed to support and enrich that orientation by delivering information and material that is normative and norming. They are texts that in some sense are not merely about God, or about what ancient people thought about God, but are *from* God. And I suspect that it is really only as interpretation presses into this dimension that it becomes useful to the members of faith communities, and is, moreover, ultimately very interesting. We could read Paul's texts as instructions from someone who lived a very long time ago, and had a number of very quaint beliefs that we now need to move rapidly and firmly beyond—things like "miracles," and "angels," and "Satan" (and "sin"?). Or we can read them as texts from someone summoned by God to shape and to form the first generations of the most significant movement in human history, which is the Christian church, and who consequently still, even read in a historical mode, has things of great value to say to it. God spoke through them, and still does. But even if we grasp that something therefore needs to be added to historical-critical reading—its careful focus on an original moment (or two) of meaning-creation and reception should not be lost—there is still the difficult matter of knowing just what that looks like, and this is where biblical scholars who are interested in this journey will learn so much from Brian Brock and Bernd Wannenwetsch.

Elsewhere I have suggested that this richer sort of interpretation is a complicated matter.[1] There is a sense in which a traditional historical reading is still the base of the broader interpretation. (Certainly it must be, for example, insofar as one wants to reconstruct what a person called "Paul" thought.) Scholars should therefore still attend carefully to the form of the text, and to its responsible translation in lexicographical and grammatical terms. Moreover, careful attention should be paid to any cues being supplied by genre. Paul's texts are fundamentally *rhetorical* in the sense that he is trying to persuade people of certain things. Moreover, they are *letters*, and ancient letters had various conventions. And they are usually *arguments*. Paul frequently persuades by teasing out the implications of Christian notions and warrants. All these dimensions in the text need to be explicated carefully. Moreover, historical interpreters will want construals of these in-

---

1. See "The Recognition of a Discourse," in *The Deliverance of God*, 221-46, and endnotes, pp. 989-96.

terpretative dimensions to be framed appropriately. Do the lexicographical claims (et cetera) make sense in terms of the linguistic options available at that time? Can we supply a plausible account of Paul's biography for what his given text seems to be concerned about? And is our reading of any localized parts of a letter really plausible when it is viewed in relation to the concerns and textual movements of the letter as a whole?

However, in the case of Paul in particular, another layer of reading is also quite important, even in these basic historical terms, although not all Pauline interpreters like to tackle it. We should ask how his basic conceptual structure for the analysis of God's work through Jesus—put more traditionally, his theology—compares with the structure that is revealed by his other letters. There is a systematic dimension to Paul's thinking, without which he would be simply incoherent, which is self-evidently not the case, although he is also clearly a circumstantial writer and very much a practical theologian. He is *theorizing* and so we need to try to recover as much of his theory as we can.

But interpretation must not stop here, after we have pressed through four interpretation dimensions and their associated frames, where historical interpreters tend to pause and content themselves with small and ofttimes nervous gestures towards ecclesial and political matters. *This is where things start to get really interesting.* From this point onward, several more important conversations need to be introduced, *and these are different types of conversation that require different conversation partners.*

We must attend to the sense in which Paul's thought is *paradigmatic*. Paradigms, using this term in Kuhn's sense, are especially important theories that set various fascinating interpretative dynamics in motion. Moreover, Paul's paradigmatic thinking is bound up with a long and highly politicized history of interpretation within the church. This great cloud of witnesses accompanies any reading of his work. We are shaped by a pre-existing set of readings that are often highly skilled and, themselves, resonantly paradigmatic. Who can read Paul without feeling the impress of Augustine, or Luther, or even of Barth?

In a similar vein, we all bring powerful explanatory categories to the text inherited from our modern cultural, political, and ideological locations. We have a deep-rooted sense of what a person is, what history is, what an appropriate political organization is, and so on. We seldom examine these notions self-critically, so they tend to operate subliminally, out of our purview, *which makes their influence all the more dangerous.* What if our modern anthropology is fundamentally different from Paul's (which it is)? We must recognize this part of our modern liberal inheritance and adjust our analysis accordingly, yet without being educated *in* our modern liberal inheritance we will probably miss the influence of these categories.

It is here where Brock and Wannenwetsch help us so profoundly. They read the text carefully and historically, building on the historical work of other conventional scholars. But they engage quite self-consciously, creatively, and responsibly, with the interpretative traditions and questions of the church, ranging across its many major traditions, traditions they are deeply familiar with. They know these questions and know many of the answers, bringing them into a fascinating conversation with the pressures of Paul's thought. Arguably, even more helpfully, however, they are profoundly aware of the pressures and challenges of a modern political, cultural, and conceptual, context. They recognize these too, scrutinizing their influence—critically!—and, where necessary, refusing to let the implications of the text be sanitized or occluded. The result is a Pauline interpretation that speaks through the church to modernity in a way that lives. The historical Paul is not left behind in history but reaches us in a way that is not merely informative but potentially transformative, and surely this is what a really interesting reading is supposed to be.

Every engaged interpreter of Paul—let the reader understand—should interpret 1 Corinthians henceforth with a commentary like Thiselton in the left hand, and a copy of Brock and Wannenwetsch in the right—until, that is, she can generate interpretations of her own that reflect not only a rigorous historical-critical training, but that press beyond those to have the skilled conversations with church history, with sociology, and with modernity that Brock and Wannenwetsch here show us how to have. Until that time, however, they point the way forward, and we are indebted to them.

—Douglas Campbell

The Divinity School
Duke University
October 2017

Abbreviations

The symbol ">" denotes a cross reference, as in (>2:9–10).

The following abbreviations are used for frequently cited works.

ACT	Anthony C. Thiselton, *First Corinthians: A Shorter Exegetical and Pastoral Commentary*
CD	Karl Barth, *Church Dogmatics*, Bromiley and Torrance eds., 14 vols.
CKB	C. K. Barrett, *A Commentary on the First Epistle to the Corinthians*
DBWE	Dietrich Bonhoeffer, Dietrich Bonhoeffer's Works in English, Green ed., 17 vols.
DEG	David E. Garland, *1 Corinthians*
JC	John Calvin, *The First Epistle of Paul the Apostle to the Corinthians*
JK	Judith L. Kovacs, trans. and ed., *1 Corinthians: Interpreted by Early Christian Commentators*
JMO	Jerome Murphy-O'Connor, *Keys to First Corinthians: Revisiting the Major Issues*
JTS	*Journal of Theological Studies*
LW	Martin Luther, *Luther's Works*, American Edition, Pelikan and Lehmann eds., 55 vols.
PG	J. P. Migne, ed., Patrologiae cursus completus: Series graeca, 161 vols.
PL	J. P. Migne, ed., Patrologiae cursus completus: Series latina, 221 vols.
Pusey	E. B. Pusey, ed., A Library of Fathers of the Holy Catholic Church: Anterior to the Division of the East and West, 48 vols.
RBH	Richard B. Hays, *First Corinthians*

RFC	Raymond F. Collins, *First Corinthians*
SC	Sources chrétiennes, 548 vols.
ST	Thomas Aquinas, *The Summa Theologica*, trans. Fathers of the English Dominican Province, 22 vols.
TA	Thomas Aquinas, *Commentary on the First Epistle to the Corinthians*
VPF	Victor Paul Furnish, *The Theology of the First Letter to the Corinthians*
WA	Martin Luther, *D. Martin Luthers Werke*, Kritische Gesamtausgabe, 61 vols.

1 Corinthians 10

Resuming the discussion of idol food Paul opened in chapter 8, he now proceeds to offer an alternative answer addressed to those in particular who might have assumed that the issue had been laid to rest in that chapter. A superficial reading of chapter 8 might easily discern a straightforward argumentative sequence along those lines: "Look what Israel did, and how God punished them accordingly. The Israelites provide a moral lesson for the church, that it ought to avoid any type of behavior prone to defile those who are expected to partake of the Lord's Supper 'with clean sheets.'" It is a reading, however, that quickly unravels upon closer inspection. If Paul's primary concern was with exhorting Christians to prophylactically attend to their moral purity before the Lord's Table: Why should his treatment of Israel's sins contain such an obvious network of references to the Christian sacraments overlaid on the events of the exodus in 10:2 and 4? And what is the purpose of his extending his discouragement of certain types of behavior by opening up the much broader issue of Christians "desiring evil things" (10:6)? As we will discover, with this typological connection of Israel and the church Paul is doing no less than remaking the categories of Christian ethical discernment.

Types in the Old Testament

> ¹I do not want you to be unaware, brothers and sisters, that our ancestors were all under the cloud, and all passed through the sea, ²and all were baptized into Moses in the cloud and in the sea, ³and all ate the same spiritual food, ⁴and all drank the same spiritual drink. For they drank from the spiritual rock that followed them, and the rock was Christ. ⁵Nevertheless, God was not pleased with most of them, and they were struck down in the wilderness.

As we have previously noted (>4:14–21), it is tempting but misguided to read Paul as operating primarily within a pedagogical rationale in which his role as teacher/parent is collapsed into the role of the pedagogue. While the overarching *theological* rationale for his approach in this chapter does include educative aspects, these differ significantly from a strictly pedagogical approach. Already the opening address, **I do not want you to be unaware, brothers and sisters,** signals this difference. This opening is immediately followed by an unfolding of an entire narrative cosmos for his readers by deploying a number of immediately recognizable images: **under the cloud** (Exod 13:21), **passed through the sea** (Exod 14:22), **Moses ate the spiritual food** (Exod 16:4–35), **and drank from the ... rock** (Exod 17:1–7; Num 20:2–13). This approach of the Apostle presents an antithesis to what we could imagine a mystagogue would open his address by stressing: "I can tell you that there is some knowledge that I possess that you do not yet know but will need to in order to progress." The way Paul instead offers this mini-biblical narrative makes it clear that what he will be discussing is integrally connected to the whole sweep of salvation history, including its culmination in **Christ**. He opens by making transparent his fundamental theological presumption that what the faithful need to know in order not to go astray is nothing less than the whole story.

This re-minding of the Corinthians of the historic experiences of Israel is a *locus classicus* in contemporary debates about analogical exegesis, figurative interpretation, and typological reading.[1] As interesting as these contemporary academic debates are, we will neither enter them here nor will we deploy any one of them to explain Paul. Our interest is in coming to terms with the specific manner in which Paul is reading the Old Testament with the Corinthians, though we hope that what we discover might, in another setting, shed some light on the value of these various hermeneutical debates and theories. Given the parameters of the modern debates it may be somewhat provocative to note that the "comparison" that Paul sets up in 10:1–4 blatantly cuts short rather than stimulating the analogical or speculative imagination of his readers. As he points to the recognizable symbols of the pillar of cloud and the passage through the Red Sea, Paul leaves no time or space for his readers to engage in imaginative thought regarding what these symbols stand for in the context of their own time and circumstances. Instead, he almost rushes to settle such questions by immediately indicating that they point to baptism, describing the Israelites as **baptized into Moses in the cloud and in the sea**. The same move is then repeated with regard to the narrative of the **rock** from which Israel **drank**, whose referent is again immediately identified: **and the rock was Christ**.

Why does the Apostle apparently resist letting the analogical imagination of his readers even begin to do the work it is supposed to do, when it

---

1. Renewed interest in this type of "pre-modern" interpretation was triggered through the work of scholars associated with the "Yale School" such as Hans Frei and his influential book *The Eclipse of Biblical Narrative*.

is precisely the task of analogical imagination to help the readers discover their own lives within the strange new world of scripture? Why short-circuit the imaginative engagement of self-convicting discovery that moral-development theorists have found so useful to employ with biblical narrative materials? Within the orbit of contemporary theories of analogical interpretation and moral development Paul's interpretative practice appears as having fallen rather short of the mark. Like the conversationalist who kills a joke by explaining it, Paul is apparently robbing himself of rich opportunities by taking his readers directly to the conclusion of the journey.

The sensation that Paul's approach is deficient according to the standards of contemporary hermeneutic and moral theories might alert us, though, to the possibility that the Apostle is actually pursuing a strategy so different from what we expect that it is simply not detectable within the parameters of these theories. We are forced back onto the basic question of any good reader: What is really going on in Paul's trotting out this string of images only immediately to distill what they "mean"? Our contention is that the noticeable terseness with which Paul presents these images indicates that they are not meant to function as symbols to be deciphered. Were this his approach we would have expected him to name at least some of the typical features that would invite the readers' imagination to discover aspects that they can "throw together" (*symballein*[2]) with their own experience of the world, as does Augustine as he reads this verse: "the rock was Christ because of its firmness, is not the manna also Christ since it is the living bread which came down from heaven . . . And the pillar also because it is straight and firm and supports our infirmity? The sea is red, and likewise our baptism."[3]

Yet with his staccato evocations of Old Testament images, Paul effectively discourages such a symbolic reading. We are hence forced to pay closer attention to how he himself uses the language of τύποι (*typoi*, **examples** [10:6]) or τυπικός (*typikos*—the adjectival form [10:11]) as he deploys these images. Paul, we suggest, is confining himself to concise hints because he expects these *typoi* to evoke in his readers the whole Old Testament narrative in which these types feature prominently as recurring characters. The function of brevity in Paul's references here, then, is not to rev up imaginative speculation to fill out the details of the picture, but to set out these elements as complete and comprehensive types. To take one example: When Moses functions as a type, it is not any of his individual traits that are of interest, such as characteristic types of behavior that might be held up for our

---

2. *Symballein* is the verbal root in the Greek language of "symbol." A symbol is a throwing together of things that are fitting to create meaning. Symbolic reading will therefore demand a search for shared features.

3. Augustine, *Reply to Faustus* 12.29, PL 42:269–70, in JK 162.

emulation, but his character as a whole, which can only be grasped by evoking the rich narrative context in which that character is developed. "Moses," as he is being referred to in this way, is therefore not to be understood as an exemplar to be emulated but as a character who has played a specific and irreducible role in the story God has with humanity.

To use types in this manner only works if characters are thought of as whole and complete units, and this depends in turn on the viewpoint of a narrator who can speak in the third person. In distinction from first-person perspectives, third-person narratives not only make bold to tell us the intentions of an agent, but describe the main character's intentional acts as engagements with actions and judgments that originate from other, separate, centers of agency. The obvious literary fact that biblical narratives are never framed as first-person perspectives reflects the assumption that a character can only fully be described as a coalescence of human agency with what the human agent receives from other agents, most importantly from divine action, whether judgment or blessing.[4]

When biblical figures are characterized in this way they are presented as existing within a complex interwovenness of human and divine agencies that goes far beyond all depictions of humans as passive victims buffeted by fate. David, for example, is a biblical *typos* not as the stereotypical courageous man that medieval kings, for instance, praised for his skill in governing and military prowess; as a biblical *typos* David is rather the one whose courage showed precisely in his willingness to repent before God instead of killing the prophet who confronted him with his transgression (2 Sam 12:13).[5] In the context of our chapter Paul seems to even go one step further in this direction in that the *typoi* that he offers to the Corinthians out of the tradition of the Old Testament narratives are not even human agents or persons, but **things** that **occurred as examples** (10:6) or **things** that **happened to them to serve as an example** (10:11). This insight is especially important if we are to make sense of the Apostle's crucial emphasis late in the chapter that the blessing, sharing, and breaking of bread are all *actions* that these

---

4. The inset poetry that occasionally punctuates these third person narratives does interject a role for the first-person accounts while not over determining how the third-person narratives are to be read, as important as these interjections are for interpreting those narratives. See Brock, *Singing the Ethos*, 19–34, 272–73.

5. McClendon, "Narrative Ethics and Christian Ethics." As Murphy also points out, biblical characters are sometimes depicted in scripture as discovering themselves within those types. Referring to 1 Samuel 17, Murphy comments, "Saul need no longer hunt David, and David retaliate by stalking Saul, because of their mutual recognition that David is not a killer of God's kings. For Saul to recognize David as merciful and cease his pursuit David had to recognize *himself* as having the magnanimity of a king" (*1 Samuel*, 246).

types make intelligible. A *typos* is thus succinctly defined as a *pattern of action* in distinction from a historical analogue, a recurring image, or a point of conceptual overlap.

De-moralizing Old Testament Types

> ⁶Now these things occurred as examples for us, so that we might not desire evil as they did. ⁷Do not become idolaters as some of them did; as it is written, "The people sat down to eat and drink, and they rose up to play." ⁸We must not indulge in sexual immorality as some of them did, and twenty-three thousand fell in a single day. ⁹We must not put Christ to the test, as some of them did, and were destroyed by serpents. ¹⁰And do not complain as some of them did, and were destroyed by the destroyer.

To understand how "examples" (as the NRSV translates τύποι/*typoi*) are supposed to work within Paul's argument we must face the second interpretative stumbling block in this chapter. In a chapter in which these Old Testament figures and stories are intended to provide moral instruction for the Corinthians, why is the consecutive phrase in 10:6 so obviously overcomplicated: **so that we might not desire evil as they did**? Would it not have been more straightforward and sufficient to say, "These things occurred as examples for us so that we might not *do* as they did"? What is the purpose of introducing the language of *desire* in this context? Verse 10:6 is apparently meant to summarize the import of the list of biblical recollections offered in verses 1–5. Paul now moves to direct his readers's attention away from the phenotype of Israel's deeds and toward an understanding of what lay underneath in terms of the complex motivational patterns denoted by the language of ἐπιθυμία (*epithymia*/**desire**). This is where Paul's usage of *typoi*, deployed to indicate concrete cases of Israel's transgressions, comes clear as a set of references designed to trigger a recollection of the full story. Such recollection, insofar as it follows the lines laid out in the biblical accounts, will also include those inner aspects of a given character's actions that underlie and precede externally observable deeds.

A closer look at one of the *typoi* will indicate how Paul's argument is working. In 10:9 the moral exhortation **We must not put Christ to the test** is offered as the conclusion of a narrative recollection of the events recounted in Numbers 21. There, first, "the people became impatient on the way." Then their inner movement was translated into a verbal utterance: "The people spoke against God and against Moses." This utterance was then converted into an explicit motion of mistrust expressed in speech, "why have you brought us up out of Egypt to die in the wilderness?" Finally, by way of divine intervention, their posture was transformed back into confiding reliance when the people were offered the opportunity to trust the bronze serpent lifted up on a pole as a symbol of God's faithfulness.

It will be important for our later argument that we note here what the Numbers account directly states, that "the Lord sent poisonous serpents among the people and they bit the people so that many died." As he recounts the tale here, though, Paul uses a passive construction that allows him explicitly to avoid the claim that God was the agent meting out punishment. This changing of grammatical *modus* occurs several times in this section when Paul's retells Old Testament stories: **twenty-three thousand fell, were destroyed by serpents**, and **were destroyed by the destroyer**. Our noting of this softening of the ascription of divine agency is not a reflex of our modern instinct to shy away from associating the loving God with harsh punishments. What is important to note here is the way the divine subject recedes as sole causal agent in Paul's rendition of these stories, because doing so provides an insight into the way in which Paul's argument sets the stage for a very precisely calibrated type of moral exhortation to be offered later. Despite mentioning the punishment of the Israelites, Paul refuses the violence inherent in the attempt to utilize the fear of punishment to force his readers into following his moral instructions.

Beyond the Pedagogical God

> **¹¹These things happened to them to serve as an example, and they were written down to instruct us, on whom the ends of the ages have come. ¹²So if you think you are standing, watch out that you do not fall. ¹³No testing has overtaken you that is not common to everyone. God is faithful, and he will not let you be tested beyond your strength, but with the testing he will also provide the way out so that you may be able to endure it.**

If he is not engaged in the straightforward moral pedagogy that displays examples of how immoral behaviors receive corresponding punishments, what then is Paul doing? The answer lies in 10:13 in which a palpable shift in tone occurs that could be described as a movement from exhortation to consolation: **No testing has overtaken you that is not common to everyone. God is faithful, and he will not let you be tested beyond your strength, but with the testing he will also provide the way out so that**

you may be able to endure it. Paul comforts those who threaten to fall or have fallen by shifting their attention away from their own capacities, including their "capacity to be moral," and toward God's faithfulness, which has been so amply dispensed in the past and which can therefore be trusted in the future. As the Apostle presents this word of consolation, however, he insists that it be rightly understood: the consolation being offered is not that we can trust the divine pedagogue to achieve good results whenever he puts us to the test. The reading that understands **let you be tested** as pedagogical language does adequately translate the Greek root term that Paul uses here, πειρασμός (*peirasmos*). But the question is how such testing is to be understood. The crucial point to notice is that testing is described with a passive voice that denies definitive knowledge of who the agent is that is administering the test. Instead, Paul points to a different role for God's agency in this testing, explicitly defining God as the one who *limits* it and can be trusted to provide an escape: **God is faithful, and he will not let you be tested beyond your strength, but with the testing he will also provide the way out.** Insofar as Paul offers us an account of God's agency in this passage it is definitely not that of the pedagogue who sets up a regime of edifying *peirasmos*, but as a deliverer who can be counted on to *rescue* from temptation through his own unambiguous action.

Unfortunately, this insight has often been inverted in the Christian tradition. Origen provides a typical example in his taking consolation in the thought that God can be trusted to fine tune his tempting of men and women by not allowing temptations to exceed the individual's capacity to endure. As athletes gain strength by undertaking more arduous training regimes, so Origin understood God to be progressively making believers stronger by putting them in the position to defeat ever greater temptations.[6] Contemporary versions of this approach find the measure that limits divine temptation by pointing to the human limits of individuals, based on a reading of what is translated in 10:13 as **common to everyone** (εἰ μὴ ἀνθρώπινος/*ei mē anthrōpinos*), which is more literally translated as "humanlike." According to this interpretation, Christians can safely assume that there will always be a way to escape or skirt a temptation, because temptations are "simply part of being human, alongside all misplaced desires, misdirected passions,

---

6. So Origen: "Those who are in charge of athletic contests do not allow entrants to compete indiscriminately or by chance, but after careful examination of their physique and age they join them in proper pairings . . . so we must understand that divine providence arranges with most righteous care all who enter the contests of this life, taking account of each one's virtue . . . God allows us to be tempted, but not beyond our strength: we are tempted in proportion to our strength" (*On First Principles* 3.2.1–3, SC 268:152, in JK, 167).

self-deceptions, and illusions" and are sent by God "for Christians to attain maturity by bearing up under temptation."[7]

We think it more plausible to read Paul's claim that there is a "human-like" limit to the testing visited on humans as an expression of his trust that God will not allow the tempting of humans to escalate to the level of the superhuman or demonic. Such a reading has the advantage of emphasizing the comfort the believer receives through the hope for a divine intervention with a "way of escape" instead of positioning Christian trust as the hope that escape from temptation is always somehow already within reach because God has limited temptation to the measure of *our* human capacities.

Such a reading, however, also forces us further to clarify how we understand the language of **enduring** used here. The English equivalent to what the German *Einheitsübersetzung* reads here would be, "so that you can prove yourself in it." "Passing a test," however, is quite different from "enduring an examination." The more we emphasize that what is in view is the passing of a test, the wider we are opening the gate to retrospectively reading back moral failure into the disasters that have afflicted people, a gesture exemplified by Job's self-righteous friends. Furthermore, to read "enduring" as passing a test also complicates the reading of ἔκβασις (*ekbasis*), the **way out**, or **exit**, in undermining Paul's emphasis on this being *God's* provision when the time is right. Paul's own accent is laid on the divine *limitation* of trials rather than on the human passing of a divinely set test. Strictly speaking, this latter familiar interpretation of *ekbasis* would render unintelligible the language of *enduring* temptation, since there is nothing to endure if one is in principle already in possession of an exit strategy that can be known to be effective if only sufficient willpower can be mustered.

Taken on their own, any one of these subtle linguistic points may not seem to amount to much, but taken together they prepare us for an important insight. The comfort that Paul provides in 10:13 is in fact tied to a discrimination between what needs to be known and what does not need to be known. What we really need to know in the midst of temptation is that God knows us and our particular contingent capacities, and promises to be faithful to limit the time of temptation and rescue us. The point is that there can be types of knowledge that we may be tempted to rely upon for comfort even though, structurally speaking, they are inimical to it. A pedagogical account of divine action presupposes that insight can be gained into the operational pattern of divine providence, understood as a teleological system of purposes and ends, from which (self-)comfort can be drawn in the

---

7. Thiselton, ACT, 154.

time of temptation if we will simply recall that the divine plan for our moral progress is in fact guiding the process as a whole.

In offering us an updated version of the reasoning patterns of Job's friends, the theodicy tradition is well-known for diving deep into the intellectual task of sorting out the respective powers and responsibilities implicated in instances of suffering or testing. Within this approach a God who is somehow involved with humans who suffer temptation can only be vindicated when it has been demonstrated that what has been happening is for the good or has produced growth. Philosophically put, in such thinking God is only vindicated when a benign proportionality is discovered between his causing or tolerating the suffering that *peirasmos* entails and the contribution he has made towards its overcoming by having provided endowments already in the believer's possession—as proved in the actual betterment of the human protagonist's situation or character. The sheer complexity and scope any such intellectual explanation will demand makes for endless and eternally fruitless inquiries that seek to "justify" the ways of God in times of human trial.

Furthermore, a pedagogical reading assumes that everything Paul says here about testing and enduring is addressed to individual believers. So strong is our desire to be able to claim the promise of rescue that we comfortably overlook the fact that Paul throughout stubbornly uses the plural, not the singular address. The expectation that the apportioned degree of strength will always be enough to carry individuals through their trials is thus set up for a rude awakening. Not only will the individualist reading lead to disappointment in one's own life when, once again, God appears not to have lived up to his promise to make all trials morally productive, it also paves the way for the pious pastoral insensitivity that takes the form of judging fallen brothers and sisters. Such judgmental attitude easily rests on the conclusion that if Paul is correct in his assertion in 10:13 that God has not ever tempted humans beyond their capacities, then their falling must be due to the weakness of human willing.

When confronted with someone in the throes of dire marital problems, the loss of a loved one, or the overwhelming new duties and anxieties of parenthood, many is the pastor or Christian friend who has reached for the elixir they assume Paul is setting out here: "rest assured, God will not allow this difficult experience to go beyond your personal strength." But what may not dawn on such well-meaning Christians is that such individualist consolation might well falsify the hope Paul is in fact offering. Such gestures can be ready-made surrogates for what might really be needed here, such as proactive inquiries in search of help among the church community for the person in the midst of trial who may indeed be stressed and tempted beyond her own individual strength. Without denying the freedom of God directly to intervene, especially at those moments when the church fails to suffer with the suffering, we detect in Paul's reminder not to discount the strength of Christ's body an echo here of Jesus's momentous promise to Peter that this communion will not be overcome by the gates of hell (Matthew 16:18). In short: Paul's promise that you (plural) will not be tested beyond your (plural) strength is best understood as a promise that reveals the burden-sharing capacity of the *ekklesia*. This is to insist that the strength to which the believer can cling in the midst of temptation has been divinely provided through the body of Christ, in which our individual weaknesses can be met and upheld by the faithful love of others who with us pursue the fruit of the Spirit to "bear one another" (Gal 6:2).

Our reason for resisting a pedagogical reading of 10:13 is that such a reading masks the genuinely comforting character of the overall passage.[8] A pedagogical reading displaces the comfort Paul is offering—that God can be trusted to keep faith with us and to personally intervene to rescue us—with a false security that bases itself on its presumed insight into providential patterns of action. The fatal nature of this substitution is exposed in sharp relief by Paul's suggestion that self-manufactured security is the fundamental weakness underlying all the forms of individual transgression that he has indicated throughout 10:6–10. The point is particularly emphasized with the sharp warning, **if you think you are standing, watch out that you do not fall.** This observation further bolsters our claim that Paul cannot have been offering the Old Testament examples simply to set out a list of problematic patterns of behavior he hopes to discourage. His main concern lies with "habits of the heart"—the misdirected desires that underlie and generate these types of behavior. But which of the Corinthians' habits triggered the Apostle's decision to finger precisely the issue of self-assurance as the crucial problem?

The two expressions Paul uses in 10:3–4 offer us an important clue in speaking of **spiritual food** and **spiritual drink**. The Old Testament narratives being invoked here are obvious, the stories of manna from heaven and of the water from the rock; equally obvious is the warning Paul sees in the fact that having received this divinely mediated nourishment did not stop the Israelites from falling into sin. It is far less obvious, however, what the meaning of 10:3–4 might be, which we have not yet discussed: **all ate the same**, and **all drank the same** spiritual food and drink. The repeated emphasis on "all" functions as an intensifier of the warning, since in most

---

8. Against both Hays (RBH, 165) and Barrett (CKB, 228), who suggest that this verse offers the chapter's "moral."

of the concrete examples to which Paul alludes (golden calf, Moabite wives, moaning), a majority was led astray with only a minority of faithful ones remaining (sometimes Moses alone), despite the fact that all had partaken of the divine nourishments in equal measure.

The formulaic repetition of the modifier "spiritual" (which does not recur elsewhere in Paul's discussions of the practices we call church sacraments[9]) makes it likely that the Apostle is using these expressions as slogans that he either heard from the Corinthians or by which he meant to encapsulate a cluster of opinions and attitudes he discerns amongst his addressees. It is clear from Paul's pointers in 10:2 and 4 (**baptized into Moses; and the rock was Christ**) that he wishes his readers to understand Israel's provision and dealings with *their* spiritual food and *their* spiritual drink (alongside God's judgment) as illuminating the Corinthians' attitudes (and predicament) toward the Christian sacraments. Seen from the perspective of the summative exhortation in 10:12, it now appears that it must have been the Corinthians' mistaken understanding of the sacraments on which their ill-fated false sense of security rested, a security that solidified their pretentious sense of immunity from "those petty moral disputes" that Paul will simply not leave well enough alone.

What we know of Hellenistic religiosity in general and more specifically of that sub-grouping now called the "mystery cults" allows us to imagine that those habituated in the atmosphere of such a religious context would instinctively bring a particular set of expectations, understandings, and corresponding practices to the Eucharist. Drinking and eating the eucharistic elements could easily be understood as an act providing the worshipper with some form of protection, perhaps rendering partakers immune to the vagaries of fate or the malign influences of rival spiritual forces. The famous later characterization of the Eucharist as a *pharmakon athanasias* (Ignatius of Antioch), literally the "medicine of immortality," may even be a distant echo of such a mentality. Paul's drawing attention to spiritual food and drink

---

9. Paul's avoidance of these formulaic expressions ("spiritual") in his own constructive exposition of the Eucharist from 10:17 onward indicates his aim to overcome the set of assumptions he associates with these slogans. He could have followed his regular practice of adopting slogans in order eventually to subvert them, but his abstention from employing this rhetorical strategy could be seen as shedding light on the theological priorities Paul seeks to honor as he carefully positions the rhetorical form of this passage. While he regards it as entirely appropriate to deploy an ironic communicative mode in many spheres of communication, the holy meal might have represented a sphere for him where such modes of communication were deemed inappropriate. His refusal to use ironic speech in conjunction with the Eucharist would then be understood as a mark of deep respect for it paralleling his high respect for the language of being "in Christ" (>4:10).

can certainly be read as a challenge to the Corinthians' desire for a more immediate, perhaps magical form of protection for the individual than the Christian proclamation associates with the eucharistic union with Christ. Once again, then, we detect another outcropping of the pragmatist version of Christianity Paul was warding off as early as 1:22–28.

The typological reading Paul sets before us rests on an identification of the church with Israel. Yet, as the conclusion of 10:11 indicates, if this identification is to be morally instructive it must presuppose differences that resist being dissolved into a false homogeneity: **these things were written down to instruct us, on whom the ends of the ages have come**. The heightened historical awareness characteristic of modern Christians makes it quite natural to be aware of the ways in which our historical, moral, cultural and geographical distance from ancient Israel distinguishes us from "them" as we read what is **written down**. Nor is Paul overriding the legitimate distinctions between Israel and the church by positing a simple homogeneity of the two. The crucial thing to notice is how the Apostle locates what the two social bodies share. Rather than developing an analysis of unity and discontinuity between the patterns of *human* action that comprise Israel and church respectively, Paul simply asserts that what unites the two is the sameness of *God* and of his faithfulness in dealing with his people, whether Israel or the church.

Identifying Paul's core target to lie with the misguided sense of security that the Corinthians attached to the sacraments as a sort of magic potion now begins to make the thrust of the whole chapter much more transparent. The Apostle is using the typology he has presented to dispel a rival typology that is ordering the Corinthians' misconceived understanding of the sacraments. Having had their desires and understanding of all things spiritual influenced in direct and indirect ways by the Hellenistic cults, which situated religion as a quest for spiritual insurance and individual enhancement,[10] the Corinthians would naturally have approached Christian worship and its ritual intake of food and drink with such Hellenized expectations. *Pagan* images thus functioned as the *typoi* through which they perceived and performed the Christian sacraments.

Recognizing the inevitable existence and operational force of typological modes of comprehension in human life—we are always prone to

---

10. There is some debate among historical critics as to the plausibility of the contamination of Corinthian worship by the logic of the mystery cults we have suggested here. The debate is surveyed in Garland, DEG, 453–54. Our reading, though, rests on theological not a historical premise: that Christian faith and life are always a process of coming to understand how idolatrous logics overlay and subvert the traditions we embraced in our baptism.

understand new things according to the patterns of understanding that we have previously developed—Paul realizes that only a powerful rival typology could ever shake the Corinthians out of their misconceived patterning via inappropriate *typoi*. These considerations help us see a reason for Paul's directness in his opening presentation to them of their real and legitimate ancestry, Israel: **I do not want you to be unaware, brothers and sisters, that our ancestors were all . . .** In summary: the false attitude Paul seeks to overcome is one that seeks *knowledge* that brings *security* in the midst of trials, primarily by way of trusting that we already possess all we need to weather any trial that might come our way. What the Apostle wishes his addressees to incorporate is that knowledge can never offer the *comfort* that comes only as we *trust* in the activity of a God who is faithful and do so as members of the tangible and supportive community that faithfulness has brought into being.

Flight into Trusting Communion

> ¹⁴**Therefore, my dear friends, flee from the worship of idols.**
> ¹⁵**I speak as to sensible people; judge for yourselves what I say.**

We would be ill-advised to take 10:14 as changing the subject, as if Paul is abruptly resuming a topic dealt with in chapter 8, the worship of idols. The opening conjunction **Therefore** (διόπερ/*dioper*) connects the discussion of idolatry with the immediately preceding paragraphs of this chapter. But how far does this linkage reach? Does it refer to the consolation in 10:13 only? Or does it also include the moral exhortations in 10:7–10? Perhaps it refers to the whole discussion, including the biblical typology? The imperative mode of 10:14, **Therefore . . . flee from**, has led us to expect the answer to the question of the extent of the matter Paul wishes to include in the "therefore" to be given in the form of an inquiry into what it takes to flee from idol worship. In keeping with the strong consecutive stress in this "therefore," we suggest that the appropriate reading of **worship of idols** has to be one that embraces the entirety of the discussion in 10:1–13, and therefore the whole list of *typoi* that Paul sees as falling under this description, from the obvious case of the golden calf down to the Israelites succumbing to sexual immorality and complaining. If Paul's use of the types is meant to invoke the whole narrative context, then such a reading makes sense, for example, of the complaints of the people as an expression of their *idolatrous* craving for the sensual satisfaction and the sense of security associated with the fleshpots of Egypt (Exod 16:3; Num 11:5). As Psalm 78:18 puts it, "They tested God in their heart by demanding the food they craved." The way in which Paul invokes Israel's exemplary history now appears an attempt to help the Corinthians recognize that idol worship is by no means confined to a material surface of detectable and exhaustively categorizable types of action such as bending the knee in front of alien altars, but is rather to be understood in terms of identifiable types of utterances of the heart.[11] By the phrase "utterances of the heart" we mean to conceptually describe what Paul calls **desire** for **evil** and the misdirected sense of security associated with cultic practices as a means of ascertaining spiritual goods *ex opere operato*. Idolatry is not first an act, but a type of gaze.[12]

In the final analysis, then, the basic moral imperative of the whole of chapter 10 is deceptively simple: **flee**. On the basis of this wider understanding of the inward chambers in which temptations to idolatry resonate, it becomes less surprising that in his material exhortation Paul resorts to the language of fleeing. The language of "flight" only makes sense if we understand the worship of idols as a sphere of power, whose extent is not clearly defined, as distinguished from a mere set of practices from which one can (decide to) abstain. Recall that Paul's description in chapter 8 of the habituation of those with a weak conscience in pagan religious cults was best explained by reference to the cults as exerting a continuous sphere of influence on the lives of Christians, even after conversion. Likewise, the language of flight is also prominent in chapter 6, "flee *porneia*." In our comments on chapter 6 we suggested that the Eucharist is the distinct place from which to flee from the apparently all-embracing sphere of *porneia* (>6:18). The reading we offered there is supported by Paul's making a similar move here. Though the exit metaphor might be understood in terms of deliverance *out of* a dangerous region, and so not necessarily *into* some other sphere, in conjunction with the promise of 10:13 that God will rescue from temptation by limiting it, 10:14 suggests that this divine limit is not offering a simple escape hatch but holds out a stronger sphere of influence with contours genuinely different from the sphere of temptation and idol worship.

It is on this basis that the Apostle can move from the one moral imperative, "flee," directly to the Eucharist. The Eucharist is offered as the divinely provided exit from temptation that 10:13 holds out to those facing trials. Fundamentally, fleeing must be understood as a genuinely spiritual exercise in being structurally different from (if not juxtaposed to) all pedagogical approaches. Flight is an act of human desperation rather than one

---

11. On the principled relation of idolatry and desire, see Wannenwetsch, "The Desire of Desire," 315–30.

12. Marion, *God Without Being*, ch. 1, secs. 1–2.

that is cool, calm and firmly willed. It is, as we have seen, a human activity that runs toward God's steady faithfulness for consolation rather than seeking to steady itself with an intellectual grasp of God's identifiable patterns of action or a sense of one's own human capacities and limits. One who is aware that a walk of faith can break into flight from danger at any moment is one who knows the necessity of living in hope of God's provision of an exit whenever needed.

Since the pedagogical reading is focused on the "what *for*" of all temptations, the improvements that accrue are presumed to result from bearing up under it, thus sidetracking the question of "what are we tempted *by*." Paul, in contrast, puts the emphasis on specifying what it is that must be fled in every instance: idolatry. It is true that verses 10:7–10 name a number of sinful activities that could be read as a comprehensive list of temptations. But Paul's point is that these divergent potential activities are temptations only insofar as they are occasions for worshipping a different God. Correspondingly, to understand the Eucharist as an exit from temptation is to know it precisely as a rescue from idol worship. This insight, however, further complicates the Corinthians' situation, because as we have seen, what God was holding out to them as their appropriate exit from temptation, eucharistic celebration, was being obscured by their understanding it by way of yet another idolatrous *typos*.

Paul discusses temptation not as the common human experience of being drawn to some activity that the intellect knows as unhealthy. For the Christian temptation is not an inclination to doing things they think they should not, but towards idolatry. The one temptation to idol worship can take a variety of forms that can be flushed out into the open by the test question: "What would it mean to worship another god?" It is as if Paul was sensing that the debates about eating idol food, when pursued as a *moral* discourse, could be pursued in a way that in effect took the question of idol worship off the table. What Paul is demonstrating to the Corinthians in this chapter is that the issue of idol food is not *one* moral issue amongst other moral issues but concerns the *one* moral issue that counts for the Christian life: discerning in any type of action whether it might in fact be a covert worshipping of powers other than the Trinity.

The rhetoric of flight thus opens a window into what we might label Paul's moral psychology. If there is any mileage in our reading of this verse, based as it is on a distinction between a spiritual and a pedagogical rationale for human suffering, its power will be proven by its ability to link the discussion here with prominent debates from Attic Greek philosophy to Reformation theology and further about the nature and scope of natural moral capacities. If desire is taken to be the decisive forum in which human behavior and actions are given direction, the self-designated strong and spiritually minded members of the Corinthian church must have been misled in their assumption that all it takes to extricate oneself from temptation is reason's insight into the realities at stake and the corresponding orientation of the will. The link between the apparent mindset amongst the Corinthians of Paul's day with capacity-oriented philosophical and theological traditions before and after their time is the assumption that once the metaphysical situation has been made clear, the will can be oriented accordingly, and right action will follow.[13] But in turning his account of responding to temptation toward the Eucharist, and then defining Eucharist as a divinely provided exit, Paul gestures toward the renewal of the whole human being as *animal desiderans*, including the affective powers. For Paul the Eucharist is the paradigmatic location in which right appetites are given and formed.

I speak as to sensible people; judge for yourselves what I say (10:15). This seemingly superfluous rhetorical gesture has a serious purpose: to effect a break in the Corinthians' assurance that their "sensible" knowledge is in fact Christian, or "necessary knowledge" (8:2). By breaking down their understanding of the problem of idol food as a moral question into deeper and different, though related topics, Paul forces what appears to be a "merely" moral problem out into questions at several seemingly unrelated conceptual levels. He will now explain why this widening and deepening of their merely moral inquiry is theologically unavoidable.

Eucharist beyond Religious Ritual

> [16]The cup of blessing that we bless, is it not a sharing in the blood of Christ? The bread that we break, is it not a sharing in the body of Christ? [17]Because there is one bread, we who are many are one body, for we all partake of the one bread. [18]Consider the people of Israel; are not those who eat the sacrifices partners in the altar? [19]What do I imply then? That food sacrificed to idols is anything, or that an idol is anything? [20]No, I imply that what pagans sacrifice, they sacrifice to demons and not to God. I do not want you to be partners with demons. [21]You cannot drink the cup of the Lord and the cup of demons. You cannot partake of the table of the Lord and the table of demons. [22]Or are we provoking the Lord to jealousy? Are we stronger than he?

---

13. On the theological mistake that grounds such widespread anthropological assumptions, see Melanchthon, *Loci Communes* 1521, chs. 1 (*de hominis viribus*) and 2 (*de peccato*); see also Wannenwetsch, "Affekt und Gebot."

Having initially prepared his central claim—to flee idolatry—by emphasizing the problem of disordered desire, Paul now lays out his underlying theological assumptions more explicitly. The focus in the following sections is on the practices that *represent* and, in so doing, *create* spheres of power that envelop those who engage in them. Paul begins by turning to a discussion of activities with overt religious coding—**blessing, breaking** and **sharing**—to widen the scope of the discussion beyond the restricted interest of the Corinthians on spiritual food and drink understood as attributes of the sheer materiality of the eucharistic elements. Paul makes it abundantly clear in 10:19–20 that what matters in this context is not food or idols *per se*, that is, what they *are* in themselves, but rather what the Corinthians *do* with them: **I imply that what pagans sacrifice, they sacrifice to demons and not to God.** This framing of the discussion places the emphasis on the *koinonia* established by all such ritual undertakings.

This approach appears to mesh nicely with the insights of modern philosophy or sociology of religion, namely that religious rituals inevitably generate a sort of liturgical union in being communicative activities in which people become communally embedded at a deeper spiritual level. In our view, however, to follow this approach will make it rather more difficult to comprehend the thrust of Paul's engagement. We are skeptical of claims that Paul is drawing on general assumptions about the power of religious rites to foster community cohesion. Had this been his intent, the Apostle would have been better served by first explaining how pagan sacrifices work and then moving to demonstrate the parallels to the sacrifices of Israel or the Eucharist of the church. Paul makes no such effort and instead works from a positive and material portrayal of the Eucharist. There is a further hint indicating Paul's resistance to narrating the Eucharist as an exemplar displaying how powerfully religious rites operate. In 10:21, the statement toward which the whole argument is developing, he preempts any such conclusion by declaring the eucharistic celebration incompatible with all other religious rites, and so, by definition, not properly understood if taken as an exemplar of a wider category.

The subtlety of the argument becomes more apparent when we pause to imagine the educated Hellenist's response: "Why do you think your rite is so different in kind from ours? Why should my participation in the Eucharist rule out other religious commitments or sharing in other religious activities of a similar kind? I accept that every rite entails commitments peculiar to it and the community that maintains it, but why should these conflict with other rites that create different commitments? Why understand religious activities in such exclusivist and mutually intolerant terms?" As questions of this kind have recently resurfaced we do well to pay close attention to the components of Paul's response. Commentators who have appreciated the structural differentiation between pluralistic religion and monotheism have still sometimes failed to see the significance of Paul's basing the distinction between the two precisely on the *unity* of the one body, as opposed to a simple *repudiation* of all other worship.[14] To draw on the contrast between polytheism and monotheism as historical entities tends to read the Corinthians' problem as not yet having come to terms with the conceptual difference between paganism and Christianity.

Throughout his treatment Paul works from a thick description of what the Eucharist is in itself, uniquely, by emphasizing the oneness of the body and its anchorage in the church's sharing of the one bread: **Because there is one bread, we who are many are one body, for we all partake of the one bread.** Notice that here Paul speaks of one bread, not one loaf (in contrast to 11:23). While a "one loaf" account might function very well within a general rationale of the religious rite as a symbol of communal unity, the one bread is, for Paul, none other than the bread of life (Matt 6:35), the one Christ who is Lord of all. The oneness of "bread" is thus sharply defined christologically, ecclesiologically, and cosmologically (Col 1:15–20). It represents the Lord's "jealousy" (10:22) in a structural rather than temperamental way. Unlike the Greek gods who were portrayed as constantly quarrelling amongst themselves, displaying jealous behaviors not only toward other deities but even toward humans, the God of the Eucharist is jealous for the uniqueness of the Eucharist as an entailment of God's oneness.

It is illuminating to imagine Hellenistic flexibility with regard to cultic participation as a sort of proto-Enlightenment attitude that culminated (and still culminates today) in a sense of moral superiority over the gods whose jealous behavior only demonstrates their lack of maturity and, worse, lack of tolerance. Against this backdrop 10:22 need not be read as a threatening gesture towards the Corinthians that they had better clean up their act or risk the wrath of a jealous God. As we have previously noted, Paul takes great grammatical pains not to specify that God must be the center of agency behind the painful events that befell sinners in Israel. In a similar vein, he allows us to understand the jealousy of the Lord as an immediate implication of his oneness, paradigmatically stated by Jesus in the saying, "You cannot serve two masters" (Matt 6:24).

Hence the question, **are we provoking the Lord to jealousy?**, is revealed as a rhetorical formulation implying the brisk answer, "of course not!" This is so not because God *should not* be provoked to jealousy (a moral injunction), but because he *cannot* be provoked (a metaphysical claim),

---

14. Such as Hays, RBH, 170.

precisely because he is the one Lord without any peer or natural rival (of the same kind). "Provoking the Lord to jealousy" must therefore be understood as naming what God's people are doing when they follow after other gods. Although the Lord cannot be provoked to jealousy, such provocation can nevertheless be *undertaken* by means of serving another lord. As in the slogan "food does not take us before God" (8:8), the Corinthians are flirting with the human desire to coerce divine attention. Paul is thus stating what is true, that God is a jealous God, while at the same time forcing his interlocutors into revising their definitions of the relation between "provoking" God and divine jealousy.

The way the NRSV translates 10:22b, **Are we stronger than he?**, could therefore be seen as addressing those for whom a person-specific bricolage of religious beliefs (familiar to inhabitants of modern liberal societies) is taken to be pragmatically and morally superior to the mass of "simple" believers with traditional faith commitments. It is at this point that the light shed by Paul's theologically framed critique of idolatry illumines the strong resonances between our modern pluralistic sensibilities and Hellenistic polytheism. We moderns tend to feel squeamish about the unseemliness of the so-called Jealous God. The most common presumption in our late modern society is that religion is only good if venerating an irenic deity, whereas belief in a God who judges is taken to be intrinsically linked to deadly zealotries of all types.[15] The modern liberal mindset stands strikingly close to the stance of the Corinthian "strong" ones in its linkage of the pragmatic heresy—religion must be useful, in this case, to create social harmony—with a sense of moral superiority over traditional, exclusive, religious communities.

Idolatry and the Sociality of Christian Conscience

> [23]"All things are lawful," but not all things are beneficial. "All things are lawful," but not all things build up. [24]Do not seek your own advantage, but that of the other. [25]Eat whatever is sold in the meat market without raising any question on the ground of conscience, [26]for "the earth and its fullness are the Lord's." [27]If an unbeliever invites you to a meal and you are disposed to go, eat whatever is set before you without raising any question on the ground of conscience. [28]But if someone says to you, "This has been offered in sacrifice," then do not

---

15. A common thesis recently defended in a scholarly forum by Sloterdijk in his *God's Zeal*, but which has been endlessly repeated in popular media by the likes of Peter Hitchens and Richard Dawkins.

> eat it, out of consideration for the one who informed you, and for the sake of conscience— ²⁹I mean the other's conscience, not your own. For why should my liberty be subject to the judgment of someone else's conscience? ³⁰If I partake with thankfulness, why should I be denounced because of that for which I give thanks?

10:23–24 sets up the final movement of Paul's argument in this chapter by recalling positions he has already developed in some detail. 10:23 can be read as a restatement of 8:1 ("Knowledge puffs up, but love builds up") in the form of two tight antitheses between the attitude of the Corinthians that he wishes to transform and the *oikodome* imperative that constitutes the crucial component of this transformation: **"All things are lawful," but not all things are beneficial. "All things are lawful," but not all things build up.** Next an *inclusio* is opened that signals he will be pursuing a single theme until 10:33, **Do not seek your own advantage, but that of the other.** This single injunction summarizes the message of the remainder of the chapter, in which Paul will take pains to explain what he means in enjoining it.

From 10:25 through to verse 30 or perhaps verse 31, Paul discusses a single case scenario that includes several interesting variants. There is some controversy as to what those variants are, and in what follows we will discuss two main alternatives, each of which can claim a fair degree of plausibility despite their different emphases. 10:25 and 10:27 provide the least complicated initial access point. The challenge envisioned here is for the Christian who accepts the invitation of a non-Christian to dinner but wonders what sort of food is being put before him. Paul diffuses this question by recommending an "eat, don't ask" policy; **eat whatever is set before you without raising any question on the ground of conscience.** On the surface this recommendation appears to turn on its head the one Paul made in chapter 8 where he summoned the believers not to eat for the sake of the other's conscience. Nevertheless, it is not too difficult to understand this concrete resolution here as being based on a set of principled considerations very similar to the ones orienting Paul's recommendations in chapter 8. The axiomatic assumption driving his response in both cases is the social constitution of conscience. It is for this reason that Paul discourages any course of action that is likely to result in provoking a situation in which actions will be undertaken that enact a sort of "statement" prone to harming other people's consciences, understood as the locus of the individual's coming to be embedded in communal life (>8:1–3).

We have presumed that in this whole discussion Paul continues to address the self-proclaimed strong ones in the congregation, leaving us reading **on the ground of conscience** as again referring to the conscience of a "weak" brother or sister also present at the meal. It would be theoretically possible to assume that an uncertain Christian is being addressed, for whom not raising a question about the provenance of the food would mean protecting his or her *own* conscience. But such a scenario makes little sense, since any insecurity about the status or potential harmfulness of idol food would only be exacerbated by not asking about its source.[16] Assuming the scenario as we have described it has the additional benefit of allowing a plausible reading of 10:28–30, in which **someone**, presumably another guest, another Christian, and more specifically, one whose conscience would be described as weak (in the language of chapter 8), points out the religiously dubious provenance of the meal. Paul's response to this scenario is in keeping with his reasoning to this point: **then do not eat it, out of consideration for the one who informed you, and for the sake of conscience.** The additional clarification, **I mean the other's conscience, not your own,** is equally self-explanatory on the basis of our reading.

The interpretative difficulty begins with the following phrase, **For why should my liberty be subject to the judgment of someone else's conscience?** It is at this point that decisions about whose voice we are hearing induce different readings of the next section, primarily 10:29–30. The main alternatives are either to hear Paul's voice straight through these verses, or to hear Paul responding to certain slogans and the theological rationales one can assume stand behind them.[17] The first option takes 10:29b "**For why . . .**" as Paul's explanation for what is clarified in 26—that the strong Christian's liberty to eat in principle rests on her doctrinally correct understanding of creation.[18] On this reading, the emphasis on the phrase be subject **to the judgment of someone else** is crucial, since abstention from eating for the "strong" Christian is assumed not to be an expression of subjection to a heteronymous authority, but an expression of faithfulness to the principle of not defiling another's conscience. 10:30 would then follow as a rhetorical question since, for the so-called strong Christian, it is again but a reminder of the correctness, both of his certain, correct beliefs and his considerate behavior towards the weak, neither of which would provide any basis for denunciation. Paul's statement, **If I partake with thankfulness,** which grants

---

16. We find this imagined situation more plausible than the main conceptual alternative, which is to engage in an archaeological debate about whether or not there was food available in the marketplace that definitively had not been offered to or blessed in the context of idol worship, a position we find both difficult to substantiate and less plausible than our reading (defended by Garland, DEG, 490–92).

17. For a survey of the interpretative options, see Garland, DEG, 497–500.

18. Barrett, CKB, 243.

the Christian an allowance to eat everything as a basis for any abstention if morally appropriate, seems to resonate with the passage in 1 Tim 4:4: "For everything is created by God, and nothing is to be rejected provided it is received with thanksgiving."

Although this reading appears thoroughly plausible, it leaves us with one disconcerting question: does it essentially present us with a foreign Paul? Although it cannot be denied that Paul affirms the *doctrinal* claims of the "strong," an impression confirmed if we compare his treatment of this theme in Romans 14, we cannot but feel uneasy about a reading presenting Paul as proffering a wholesale commendation of the supposed strength of the "strong." On that reading the weakness of the other would only be allowed to influence the *behavior* of the strong one, but not the strong one's *conscience*, again rendering conscience as an asocial human moral faculty. What motivated the strong Christian to not eat on that reading was, strictly speaking, the weakness of the other and not a concern for the other as a person. The inherently condescending nature of this way of taking the other's weakness into account is precisely matched with a palpable preoccupation with his own integrity that such a reading would put in the Christian's mouth, **why should I be denounced**? Is this not the kind of question that we expect from one who wishes to preserve his strength even in his bending down to the weak brother? How could the same Paul who famously professed to be "strong when I am weak" (2 Cor 12:10) commend the Corinthians to take up such a "why should I?" attitude to back up his exhortation? We sense here a parallel with the Apostle's previous argument that the understanding of the strong about the goodness of all *creation* is eclipsing what the work of the *redeeming* God means for how the goodness of creation is to be appropriated within a social matrix (>8:8–13).

As we remain unconvinced by any reading that sacrifices the folly of the cross on the altar of a smoothly unfolding argument, we propose an alternative reading that is prepared to reckon with a somewhat more complicated dialogical structure to Paul's argument here.[19] We suggest that 10:29b and 30 present slogans that Paul found in the Corinthians' letters, or which

---

19. Irrespective of the inner plausibility that we are convinced our reading possesses, there is one complicating factor worth mentioning. 10:29b uses the Greek conjunction γὰρ (*gar*) which is typically understood to emphasize the consecutive character of the phrase it introduces and would therefore seem to suggest the same voice is being used in the whole verse (see Barrett, CKB, 243). 10:26, however, also employs this conjunction to introduce a quotation (of Ps 89:12). Watson takes the line we prefer ("I Cor. 10:23—11:1," 1–18, in Thiselton, ACT, 165), and suggests *gar* can be seen as a rhetorical device to signal a conjunction but also the introduction of a quotation. Such a reading underlies Thiselton's translation, "For why [you ask] is my freedom being subjected to another's awareness."

he takes to aptly characterize their mindset, and to which he critically responds in 10:31–33. **Why should my liberty be subject to the judgment of someone else's conscience?** This question would then be read as representing the "strong" Christians's objection to Paul's summons in the preceding sentence to abstain from eating out of consideration for the other. To those attuned to the predominant patterns of contemporary thought in Western societies this sounds curiously like the most influential expression of the liberal spirit.[20] Those driven by this spirit pass all moral thinking through the filter of their individual liberty. While they can take consideration of the same liberty granted to others, they could never be *subject* to a judgment that is not their own.

This more philosophical formulation of the objection in 10:29 is bolstered in verse 30 with a structurally parallel theological objection: what could be wrong with a course of action that is explicitly carried out as an expression of gratitude to the creator God? Paul answers this question by suggesting that thankfulness is no quasi-magical gesture having the capacity to sanctify an act that is not good in itself. The objection we hear Paul offering here operates within the same grammar as his questioning of Corinthians' misguided expectation that the spiritual food or spiritual drink they ingest can be expected automatically to work as a sort of salvation potion regardless of their consideration for each other.

The problem that arises if thanksgiving is used by Christians to justify a course of action that lay outside the limits of any traditional form of Christian morality can be illustrated with an anecdote. A colleague of ours told us about a conversation he'd had during an elevator ride one morning at a North American seminary. A handsome couple entered the elevator and lovingly embraced in the way we have come to expect from those who have recently fallen in love. The only slight marring of the picture was that he was a visiting scholar with four children back home as well as a wife—who was not the woman in the elevator. And this woman was a faculty member teaching theology at the seminary.

Although rumors of their liaison had already reached our unsuspecting friend, the proximity of the situation accentuated by the intimacy of the elevator provoked a consternated silence on his side. For a reason that our

---

20. Kant's opening of his "Religion within the boundaries of mere reason" might have come straight out of the Corinthian playbook in its rejection of the binding of human consciences being either by God or other humans: "So far as morality is based on the conception of the human being as one who is free but who also, just because of that, binds himself through his reason to unconditional laws, it is in need neither of the idea of another being above him in order that he recognize his duty, nor, that he observe it, of an incentive other than the law itself. At least it is the human being's own fault if such a need is found in him . . . " in *Religion and Rational Theology*, 57.

friend never fully understood, his silence elicited an explanation of their behavior to him, and they began to let him in on the spiritual subtleties of their quest to come to terms with what had happened to them. By the time they had reached the upper floors of the tower they confessed that their evangelical consciences had initially been disturbed by the dissonance of their affair with their traditional assumptions about marital fidelity. After long and searching prayer they were relieved eventually to be given peace of mind and were now able to thank God for their newfound love in spite of the unlikely context in which it had been discovered. How then to respond to such a revelation during the time left as the elevator neared the end of its ascent into the heights of a theological seminary? Our cornered colleague, unable to say much, simply answered, "If your God tells you so, well, it must be a different one than mine."

What are we to make of such a brusque and apparently loveless response in the light of Paul's discussion with the Corinthians about Christians with troubled consciences? Interesting light is shed on this question in the parallel discussion in Romans 14, in which the very same issue of idol food and conscience is addressed. Without adding any new material that discussion does apparently clarify his intentions here: "Those who eat must not despise those who abstain, and those who abstain must not pass judgment on those who eat: for God has welcomed them. Who are you to pass judgment on servants of another? It is before their own lord that they stand or fall" (Rom 14:3–4a). Despite the unforgiving time limits left to our friend to formulate a response, shouldn't we conclude that his brief statement contravened Paul's summons to not judge another?

The way we read the term "another" in Paul's formulation in Romans makes all the difference: one cannot pass judgment "on servants of another" who, it is clear, live by commands that differ from those of the one Lord. When we follow the Apostle's shifting of the focus of analysis, away from the idea of judging behavior from a generalizable vantage point to one that considers decisive for any judgment the question of *who* the one under judgment is actually serving ("It is before *their own* lord that they stand or fall"), our friend's reply appears rather astute. It is Paul's insistence on this shift in the level of analysis that drives the formulation of his recommendations about idol food. What formerly appeared to be yet another question about appropriate moral behavior has been pulled up by Paul to the level of discussion of idolatry: Which God? Whose worship?

Love Displacing Idolatry and Flattery

> ³¹ So, whether you eat or drink, or whatever you do, do everything for the glory of God. ³² Give no offense to Jews or to Greeks or to the church of God, ³³ just as I try to please everyone in everything I do, not seeking my own advantage, but that of many, so that they may be saved. ¹¹:¹ Be imitators of me, as I am of Christ.

It now becomes clear that 10:31 is Paul's response and rebuke to the "strong" ones's objections to his summons not to seek personal advantage, but to be solicitous toward the conscience of the other: **So, whether you eat or drink, or whatever you do, do everything for the glory of God.** There is a further reason for presuming 10:31 not to be a continuation of the Corinthian slogan. In 10:30 the emphasis is on *my* thanks, and by implication its efficacy in justifying behavior, while the focus of 10:31 is on the glory of *God*. It may well be possible to give thanks while giving offense to others, but it is impossible to glorify *God* while doing so. Giving glory to God is therefore presented as the perfect antithesis to idol worship. In his letter to the Romans, the parameters of the antithesis set out here are clarified by reference to another set of theological terms. Whereas here Paul speaks of "craving evil" in its connection with idolatry and its opposition to giving God glory, in Romans 14:23 he uses the terms "doubt" and "sin" in contrast to their opposite, "faith": "But those who have doubts are condemned if they eat, because they do not act from faith; for whatever does not proceed from faith is sin." Both formulations of this antithesis appear in greater clarity if we note the ways Paul is deploying what are usually considered quite distinct conceptual packages to explicate his enduring theological and pastoral point.

Whether you eat or drink, or whatever you do . . . Once again Paul reiterates his central emphasis in this train of argument, that glorifying God is the opposite of idol worship. Idol worship is a *typos* that can assume a wide variety of forms. This is why both eating and not eating can, in principle, be instances of either glorifying God or idol worship. Though an endlessly perplexing hall of moral mirrors seems to be opening up here, we hope to have demonstrated that Paul has not finally left the Corinthians in a state of heightened confusion but has offered them a clear criterion for judgment: they must become aware of the importance of resisting evil desires while distinguishing this active resistance from the exit provided by God's faithfulness as coalescing in the eucharistic encounter. The ending of the chapter fine-tunes this point by turning the Corinthians' attention away from the quest to *protect* their freedom and reputation to the quite different quest to *love* in such a way that the world is known differently.

I try to please everyone in everything I do. Paul ends this cycle of his argument by presenting his own example as worth emulation. We must not overlook his one qualification: **as I try to** ("I seek to"). The various scenarios the Apostle invoked in discussing the case of idol food in this chapter would have served as a salutary reminder that it is not always possible to please everyone or be at peace with everyone.[21] It is easy to imagine how a situation might arise in which abstention from eating for the sake of the brother's weak conscience both might be the right thing to do and also not please everyone, not least the host. The denunciations that were only hypothetically mentioned in the slogan of the "strong ones'" (10:30) could very well become real consequences for those willing to embrace Paul's summons.

Bearing this complexity in mind, we commend Theodoret's observation that this desire to please everyone is in the final analysis quite different from flattery in that its stated aim is for the stated reason: **so that they may be saved.**[22] As every Christian knows, this is something that can be hoped for only from God's own salvific activity that believers recognize in the Christ who was willing to suffer denunciation, though undeserved, in order to save those he loved. It therefore seems wise to draw the first verse of chapter 11 together with Paul's culminating argument in chapter 10,[23] since Paul's example cannot be emulated by emulating individual trains of action, but only insofar as it emulates Christ's *typos* of self-sacrificial love: **Take me as your pattern as I take Christ for mine.**[24]

---

21. "If it is possible, *so far as it depends on you*, live peaceably with all" (Rom 12:18).

22. Theodoret, *Commentary*, PG 82, 308–9, in JK, 173.

23. This chapter division is not only assumed by most contemporary exegetes, but by many earlier commentators in the tradition including Calvin, Conzelmann, William F. Orr and James Arthur Walter (Fitzmeyer, *1 Corinthians*). The textual reasons for this placement are discussed in Collins, RFC, 390–91.

24. Thiselton's translation.

1 Corinthians 11

The fact that this chapter has borne subheadings such as "On the impropriety of women appearing in public unveiled,"[1] "The Veiling of Women in Public Worship,"[2] or "Headdresses of Women"[3] indicates why most modern Christians find the first part of this chapter (vv. 2–16) hopelessly culturally dated.[4] Sighs of relief are audible all around at the palpable moral progress made in subsequent centuries of Christianity. It is therefore mildly irritating to notice that this chapter also sets out the "words of institution" for the Lord's Supper used verbatim in most present-day churches. And any relief that might have remained fully evaporates when thinking this question through to the remarkable quandary this chapter places us in: how can one half of this chapter be deemed historically outdated and ignored in most churches while the other is assumed to be constitutive of church practice for all times?[5]

Part of the issue here is that the dominant lines of Christian interpretation of the first part of the chapter have in various ways understood Paul to be pushing back the disorder in the Corinthian community by

1. Hodge, *1 & 2 Corinthians*.
2. Robertson-Plummer.
3. New American Bible. Cited in Murphy-O'Connor, JMO, 142 n. 2.
4. "More than any other passage in this letter, 1 Corinthians 11:2–16 presents severe problems for the interpreter ... We can neither understand it entirely nor accept it entirely." Hays, RBH, 190. Peppiatt offers the most theologically sophisticated analysis of these verses to date, and though resisting her suggestion that some of the pivotal verses should be read as Corinthian slogans Paul is refuting (for reasons discussed in the excursus "Moral dimensions of characterization and scripture's plain sense"), we do so in agreement with her overarching interpretative trajectory: "we should at least explore the possibility that Paul's approach to how women should be treated 'in the Lord' was far more radical than we might allow, and that he might actually have been concerned to release the women from a patriarchal and theologically flawed practice designed to keep women in their proper place" (*Women and Worship*, 76).
5. "Since it is impossible, on the basis of traditional readings, to argue against the fact that Paul makes a link between dressings for the head and eternal spiritual truths, one would expect this passage to remain binding upon the church. Of course, very few churches do observe the instructions apparently issued in this passage, yet I have not come across an adequate account of why we are now at liberty to ignore this ruling altogether." Peppiatt, *Women and Worship*, 65.

reinscribing a preferred social order; Paul the cultural conservative is trying to suppress and channel ecstatic behavior. If we find Paul the "law and order" theologian distasteful, as we indeed do, we will need to try to discern *why* Paul positions his interventions into the different types of disorder as he does, accounting as we do so for the fact that both parts of the chapter seem evidently to contain "apostolic rulings."[6] Instead of assuming Paul to be offering a bit of gentle (or not so gentle) riot control to a community suffering with a bad case of anarchy or disorganization, we will need to discern how Paul's whole argument might be an expression of his proclaimed goal to further a new kind of peace rather than merely intervening in order to restore order. We will suggest that the distinctive contours of his alertness to occasions for abuse in the church (such as drunkenness or sexual titillation) flows directly from his understanding of the essential dynamics of Christian worship and the risks that he perceives as concomitant with the bodily proximity intrinsic to the church's practices of eating and gathered worship. If approached from this angle, the chapter's discussions of how best to negotiate fashion choices in mixed-gender and class-differentiated public worship will provoke critical questions about how the reconciliation brought about by Christ summons Christians in every age to resist and displace the war of the sexes and class warfare. Such are the implications of Paul's understanding of worship as the prime forum in which we learn to negotiate the concreteness of our material lives.

Our exposition thus aims to demonstrate how the chapter's two parts are unified by a single question: "How does cultural decorum relate to liturgical practice?" We use the term "decorum" to draw attention to the level of detail Paul engages as he describes the progress of the redeeming work of Christ as it breaks in on and reformulates the cultural encodings in which human life is lived. Resisting the temptation to let the contentious-hairstyle discussion drift free from the overarching theme of the chapter ("so then, my brothers and sisters, when you come together . . . wait for one another" 11:33), we set out in this first part of the chapter to discover how Paul's regulating affirmation in 14:33 (that God "is not a God of disorder, but of peace") is being practically cashed out.

Excursus: Bodies and Their Communicative Surfaces

Before proceeding it is worth acknowledging the particular vantage point from which modern Western readers will inevitably approach such a text.

---

6. "There is a clear agreement among commentators that this passage [11:2–16] contains within it an 'apostolic ruling.'" Peppiatt, *Women and Worship*, 108.

We need to face the reasons why we wish to keep the difficult opening section of this chapter at arm's length. The familiar Christian dismissal of arguments of biblical authors as "culturally determined" rests on an assumption that it is possible to sift out the culturally specific claims made in the text from those of universal relevance. But the challenge of 11:1–16 is that, as we will demonstrate, Paul makes his case using a range of argumentative strategies that are far from culturally dependent.

Four types of argument are discernible. In verses 2–6 we find Paul arguing in what might be anachronistically termed *doctrinal* fashion by invoking the hierarchical order of the cosmos as morally authoritative. In verses 7–9 the Apostle develops an *argument from scripture*, emphasizing the binding significance of creation. While verses 10–13 are not easily categorized as a single type of argument, verses 14–15 constitute a classic *argument from nature*. A concluding verse (16) presents special challenges for rhetorical classification since it seems to present an express argument from culture, insofar as Paul appeals to the authority of custom. We will eventually label this an ecumenical argument, however, since it is not the custom itself that bears the weight; rather what makes the appeal authoritative is the fact that these customs are practices of all the Pauline churches and of the universal church.

This cursory survey of the types of argument deployed in these sixteen verses undermines any easy presumption that the first part of the chapter can be dismissed as culturally outdated. True, Paul is writing to a specific congregation in a particular cultural-geographic context to address a uniquely enculturated conflict. But what really matters for Paul's argument is that the cultural currents under discussion are the very material he will theologically negotiate. The clichéd assumption that Paul's arguments cannot be binding today because they are culturally conditioned is now exposed to be a conflation of the *validity* of argument with its inevitably *contextualized* nature. Paul is not as grudgingly allowing himself to be dragged "down" from sublime Christian truth into the nether regions of mundane and tedious debates about appropriate hairstyles in worship but is harnessing some of his most weighty theological ideas to negotiate what look to us a relatively trivial issue of decorum. That the Apostle does so we understand to be another indicator of the detail, concreteness and moral seriousness of his theological commitment to become a gentile to the gentiles (>ch. 9).[7]

The convention of the day for Jews prescribed head covering for men as a symbol of the reverence due to God in prayer, a practice paralleled on

---

7. "Paul . . . was not in the habit of teaching in a merely formal way, but made use of everything which he realized was suitable for helping and furthering his teaching." Calvin, JC, 193.

very different grounds in Roman worship.⁸ Greek habit was more variable.⁹ If the Apostle is going to seriously engage the respective cultures shaping the conflict in this local church he is going to have to bracket his inherited Jewish cultural sensitivities about the moral connotations of head coverings. This observation offers us a first point of analytical purchase on the chapter: Paul is not taking the obvious route here—imposing Jewish practice on gentiles. No "one size fits all" response will be proffered to dampen the culturally complex turbulence in the Corinthian practice of worship. Instead the Apostle embarks on a theologically dense negotiation of the cultural signals that head coverings were sending out in his given context.

It is worth pausing at this point to consider whether the so-called sexual revolution of the late 1960s, which so deeply shaped contemporary Western sensibilities, presents pertinent parallels with the situation Paul is renegotiating in 11:2–16. Both were moments of cultural liberation in which people expressed a sense of freedom from oppressive patterns of authority and social order by rejecting established conventions of bodily presentation that were felt to be representative of the old order. Along with the instantly recognizable iconic fashion trends that we associate with the cultural revolution of the late 1960s came the then-shocking embrace of longhaired men and shorthaired women. Those of us on the other side of this revolution have inherited a sensibility birthed in that era to the ways in which hair can communicate liberation, the malleability of gender, and the inescapability of the socially communicative function of any hairstyle we might choose.

Like the placenta or fingernails, hair is a physically liminal part of the human body: part of but not wholly flesh. Like clothing, hair can be "styled," and is therefore especially suited for communicative purposes, since constant decisions must be made about how it will be tended. How we attend to it communicates not only that we are male or female, but also that we are trustworthy or edgy, careful or sloppy. The hair that we will see to interest Paul is not in the first instance the hair we *have* but the hair that we *do*, our hairdo. In Greek the expression for having one's hair long is a single word, κομάω (*komaō*), a verbal form condensing the material substrate and the form of its arrangement into one expression. That one term used (in verses

---

8. "Archaeological evidence ... gives ample evidence of [Roman] men wearing a headdress while at prayer ... but it is not unlikely that the Roman practice was also customary in imperial Corinth." Collins, RFC, 400.

9. The latter half of this claim is less certain than the former. "The Jewish custom, to be sure, can be unequivocally ascertained, and corresponds to Paul's regulation: a Jewess may appear in public only with her head covered. On the other hand, the Greek practice in regard to headgear and hairstyle cannot be unequivocally stated for the simple reason that the fashion varies." Conzelmann, *1 Corinthians*, 185. See also Taylor, "The Woman Ought to Have Control," 9–53.

14–15 and nowhere else in scripture) serves as a linguistic reminder that in doing our hair we are manipulating our bodily appearance in a way that is inevitably socially communicative. Paul is concerned with hair because he is convinced that through it the body "preaches."

The church fathers were highly attuned to this reality. In the course of a detailed discussion of appropriate and inappropriate forms of Christian dress and self-presentation, Clement of Alexandria displays an essentially theological interest in the communicative semantics of the body as he explains why Christians might resist dying their hair.

> Neither is the hair to be dyed, nor grey hair to have its color changed ... Above all, old age, which conciliates trust, is not to be concealed. But God's mark of honour is to be shown in the light of day, to win the reverence of the young. For sometimes, when they have been behaving shamefully, the appearance of hoary hairs, arriving like an instructor, has changed them to sobriety, and paralyzed juvenile lust with the splendor of the sight.[10]

The reality that human bodies have a communicative surface inescapably generates discussions of culturally appropriate and inappropriate modes of self-presentation; Clement's insight is to read the communicative traffic between the signaler (the one who does his or her hair in a particular way) and the receiver of signals to be governed by their respective relationships to God. He determines the appropriate behavior of the Christian in this three-way relationship according to the rule that bodily signaling is to have a morally salutary effect on others.

Rather than assuming this to be a historically outmoded line of reasoning, we are better served asking whether these dynamics have been intensified by modern and postmodern understandings of the body. Modern and postmodern discourses have increasingly led Westerners to understand their bodies as a projection screen on which a "self" can be displayed or performed. Made famous for the fanatical attention he paid to bodily surfaces of all sorts, one of the fathers of postmodern art just as famously wore grey wigs at a relatively young age. What is fascinating for our purposes is how Andy Warhol's explanation for his "fashion choice" unconsciously recapitulates but inverts Clement's third-century observations:

> I decided to go grey so nobody would know how old I was and I would look younger to them than how old they thought I was. I would gain a lot by going grey: (1) I would have old problems, which were easier to take than young problems, (2) everyone

---

10. *Pedagoge* III.XI, in *The Ante-Nicene Fathers*, vol. 2, 286.

would be impressed by how young I looked, and (3) I would be relieved of the responsibility of acting young—I could occasionally lapse into eccentricity or senility and no one would think anything of it because of my grey hair. When you've got grey hair, every move you make seems "young" and "spry," instead of just being normally active. It's like you're getting a new talent.[11]

Warhol cannot imagine the three-agent moral hermeneutic of bodily semantics presumed by Clement. He thus indicates how our inescapable enmeshment in particularly enculturated orders of bodily appearance and social expectation can allow our desire to increase the scope of our social power or moral license to rule decisions about self-presentation. Warhol also obsessively worried about his skin. The rise of elective cosmetic surgery is yet another extension of what is considered the canvass for such social signaling into and through the skin, with conditions like anorexia being deforming internalizations of such norms.

While the extent of the liberation of the cultural icons of the 1960s could be judged by how many inches their hair grew over the tops of their ears, their contemporary equivalents indicate how far we have travelled along this cultural trajectory in the radicalism with which their very bodies are remade. These considerations suggest that, whatever cultural configuration we might describe, we have not outgrown the scope of Paul's discussion, nor will we. No detour is needed through contemporary debates about the permissibility of what the mainstream Westerner sees as "anachronistic" forms of dress to re-introduce us to the main question Paul is raising in this first part of the chapter. From Islamic forms of veiling women to neo-primitivist movements in which individuals scarify and stretch their skins to the hyper-modernism of popular performers like Lady Gaga with her raw meat couture, all such forms of explicit body-preaching in our late-modern societies testify that the ways we stylize our bodily appearance projects our sense of belonging and the social alliances we seek (with subcultures, ethnic groups, liberation movements, etc.). And the belonging we seek always entails wider religious or philosophical commitments of which we may or may not be consciously aware.

In this chapter we understand Paul to be extending his overarching quest to incite the Corinthians to attend more closely to the practices that make up their lives as Christians and the way that these practices are situated within the conventions of various subcultures. This line of criticism was already obvious in Paul's discussion of the problem of going to prostitutes at the end of chapter 6. There the problem was that the new sense of liberation

11. Quoted in Dillon, *Tormented Hope*, 243.

experienced by Christians had fostered an assumption in some believers that their true self somehow rose above the mundane level of bodily activities. The brothel represented a subcultural domain in which the communicative nature of the body was basically denied. It is not surprising that an overheated spirituality that has rendered bodily semantics peripheral in the one case is accompanied by tensions around how worshippers's bodies are presented in Christian worship.

Bodily Semiotics and the Embarrassments of Power

> ²I commend you because you remember me in everything and maintain the traditions just as I handed them on to you. ³But I want you to understand that Christ is the head of every man, and the husband is the head of his wife, and God is the head of Christ. ⁴Any man who prays or prophesies with something on his head disgraces his head, ⁵but any woman who prays or prophesies with her head unveiled disgraces her head—it is one and the same thing as having her head shaved. ⁶For if a woman will not veil herself, then she should cut off her hair; but if it is disgraceful for a woman to have her hair cut off or to be shaved, she should wear a veil. ⁷For a man ought not to have his head veiled, since he is the image and reflection of God; but woman is the reflection of man. ⁸Indeed, man was not made from woman, but woman from man. ⁹Neither was man created for the sake of woman, but woman for the sake of man. ¹⁰For this reason a woman ought to have a symbol of authority on her head, because of the angels. ¹¹Nevertheless, in the Lord woman is not independent of man or man independent of woman. ¹²For just as woman came from man, so man comes through woman; but all things come from God. ¹³Judge for yourselves: is it proper for a woman to pray to God with her head unveiled? ¹⁴Does not nature itself teach you that if a man wears long hair, it is degrading to him, ¹⁵but if a woman has long hair, it is her glory? For her hair is given to her for a covering. ¹⁶But if anyone is disposed to be contentious—we have no such custom, nor do the churches of God.

It has never escaped commentators how uneasily Paul's praising of the Corinthians for holding on to the παράδοσες (*paradoses*/**traditions**) **just as I [Paul] handed them on to you** (11:2) sits with the detailed criticisms of their ways set out in the remainder of the chapter, not least because Paul draws attention to this tension by means of the **but** of verse 3. Some commentators ancient and modern have suggested that this is another instance of Paul using ironic speech to set up a contrast with the unfaithfulness he discerns in the Corinthians' practices of worship. Aquinas, for example, takes this opening as ironic and also assumes that because only males can be priests who speak in public worship, Paul's concern here must be some disgraceful behavior in women's private prayer groups.[12]

We will take the opposite route and understand Paul's praise of the Corinthians for maintaining the traditions as he handed them down as genuine, also assuming that both men and women spoke in early Christian worship. In this we converge with the current consensus among historical-critical scholars that it is most likely that Paul is addressing a community practicing gender-inclusive worship unheard of in the cultural context of his day.[13] Our presumption is that the Corinthians correctly grasped Pauline teaching that gender inclusive worship appropriately characterizes the church as a community of the reconciled.[14] In living out a form of worship beyond gender segregation and male-only ministry, however, the conditions emerge for new types of disorder to arise that the Apostle feels need further address.

We imagine something like the following scenario: the Corinthian believers have embraced full ecclesial participation of either sex, which was certainly a new experience for those who came from a Jewish background. It is clear from a wide range of testimonies about the practices of early Christian worship, including the Pauline letters, that it was taken for granted that women would not only participate in the various activities of the public performance of the liturgy, but would also routinely perform functions that involved addressing the congregation as a whole.[15] Paul explicitly mentions the **praying** and **prophesying** of women in the context of his present discussion. While it is obvious that he finds no fault in principle

---

12. Aquinas, TA, secs. 585–87, 596. Modern interpreters (as will we) tend to take the opposite line, highlighting the problem of the relation of the public and private spheres: "Were it only some private gathering among the family or among only women, [the womens'] attire would not have been an issue." Garland, DEG, 518.

13. Gundry-Volf, "Beyond Difference" 8–36; Hays, RBH, 183.

14. Wannenwetsch, *Political Worship*, ch. 6.

15. "In Romans the names Mary, Tryphaena, Tryphosa, and Persis are mentioned (Rom 16:6, 12). [Paul] was happy with women as leaders of house churches (Lydia in Acts 16:14-15 and Phoebe in Rom 16:1). We know of Priscilla and Aquila, who were both leaders and who both disciplined Apollos in the faith (Acts 18:26), and Phoebe, who led a church at Cenchreae (Rom 16:1). Paul refers to his friend and co-worker Junia as an apostle (Rom 16:17). Furthermore, he is clearly happy with women prophesying and praying in public in Corinth, and obviously approving of Philip's four daughters, who were known as prophets (Acts 21:9)." Peppiatt, *Women and Worship*, 12.

with the engagement of women in public worship, it does appear that he had worries about how some of these activities were being carried out. As women stepped into novel cultural roles and into the limelight by performing speaking roles in worship, questions of appearance and its semiotic connotations inevitably followed.

Some of the new issues to be negotiated related to sexuality. Sexual attraction is a two way street, and men in ministerial roles are by no means immune from being trapped in its dynamics. It is easily observed in a wide range of contexts that this attraction can be intensified from either side in various ways. But few would dispute the generic claim that sexual tension can be quickly and easily intensified by visual signals sent out by the female sex. This unwanted but often unavoidable erotic charging of public appearance, particularly sensitive as it is for female representatives ministering to their respective social bodies, would naturally have been intensified given the particularities of early Christian teachings and practices in which was emphasized the brother- and sisterhood of all believers on the one hand, and the bodily and even sensual character of their central ritual on the other.

What is indisputable is that from the very beginning of Jesus's ministry the release of women from social expectations is easily detectable. Nowhere is the breadth and power to scandalize of this liberation more powerfully portrayed than in in the washing of Jesus's feet (an extremely intimate act) by Lazarus's sister Mary. For reasons we will soon discuss, the scandalous nature of the act was compounded by her wiping of his feet with her unbounded hair (John 12:2–3). We therefore think it plausible to assume that many Christian women were inspired by the magnitude of Christ's triumphant success in gathering a church whose peace and unity would overcome the antagonisms that once characterized human societies, including those between the sexes, a triumph pithily encapsulated in Paul's teaching, "There is neither Jew nor Greek, there is neither slave nor free, there is neither male nor female; for you are all one in Christ Jesus" (Gal 3:28). Embracing this new spiritual reality of the church's universal brother- and sisterhood must have been a liberating experience for women, whether coming from a Jewish background that had kept them outside of the center of public worship, or from the opposite experience of Greco-Roman ecstatic cults in which the presence of women in leading roles turned precisely on the exploitation of the erotic power of their femininity.[16]

---

16. Chrysostom relates an understanding of women/gender relations in Corinthian pagan temples that is largely in line with subsequent historical research: "We are told that this Pythia, who is a woman, sits on the tripod of Apollo with her legs spread. Then a wicked spirit, sent up from below, slips through her genitals and fills her with madness. Loosening her hair, she goes into bacchic frenzy and foams at the

We thus have good reason to imagine that Paul's concern about Christian women breaching decorum in literally letting their hair down was neither a rebuke of arrogant or overbearing men who were suppressing the gifts of women nor was targeting a group of selfish women who were exploiting their public functions to evoke admiration or attention. On the contrary, it was on account of the very traditions that Paul had handed down, including gender inclusivity and brotherly patterns of interaction in the church "family," that we must expect women were genuinely liberated to "care less" about the decorum of personal appearance that is accompanied by constant internal banter ("Is this dress too revealing? Will people think I'm seeking attention if I wear this?").

Our suggestion, then, is that Paul is addressing a relaxation of decorum resulting from a genuine spiritual freedom but which has begun to show signs of spilling over into a form of libertarianism.[17] It is true that the worship celebrated in Pauline churches was intentionally desexualized in comparison with previous pagan experiences.[18] But the effect of this

---

mouth. Thus intoxicated, she utters frenzied words." *Homily* 29, PG 61:239–42, in JK, 197. This rather unattractive image raises an important philosophical question that we cannot address in any detail here: How is sexual "capital" accrued and deployed? It must suffice simply to note that the Old Testament struggles around the sexualized gods of Baal and Ashtoroth may well have represented deployments of sexual power (perhaps through ideas of fertility) that did not operate by direct mechanism of visual attraction. This is to allow that the law of human sexual existence afoot in Corinth may have operated through practices such as ritually suggestive displays of hair, posture or clothing, and not necessarily directly through the "siren-voyeur" dynamics. Our use of this language should thus be understood as an assertion that sexual "capital" may be accrued by both genders as well as deployed to manipulate the other gender in ways other than the siren-voyeur mode, though this game is perhaps only the most obvious and therefore immediately intelligible version of all such illegitimate exploitations of the law of sexual attraction.

17. For Jewish converts, the mere fact of joining this Christian sect would have appeared as a case of libertinism, which would naturally have exacerbated the problems that would have been created by women appearing before the congregation with their hair down. "If a female Prophet led in worship (in that Jewish-Roman culture) with her head bare, all eyes would be on her (unlike the women seated in the congregation). Her bared head would be seen by some as inappropriate exposure. The Babylonian Talmud records a saying of Rabbi Shesheth (third to fourth century) that reads, 'a woman's hair is a sexual incitement, as it says, *Thy hair is as a flock of goats* [Song 4:1].' Such attitudes are of great antiquity and they persist across the Middle East, in conservative areas, to this day." Bailey, *Paul through Mediterranean Eyes*, 305.

18. "Civic religion was dominated by men. This partly accounts for the growing popularity of the mystery religions ... For those who were on the margins of civil life, especially women and slaves, these cults offered religious recognition. ... One of the characteristics of a good Dionysiac session was the wild screaming and yelling of the women ... If the Corinthian women had come to think that this was all part of a proper religious celebration then it would explain why eucharists at Corinth were quite so

desexualization appears to have created a situation open to a resexualization having very different contours. Given the cultural context, the liberation of women to "let their hair down" while prophesying could hardly avoid evoking deeply imbedded cultural imagery of cult priestesses if not even of other categories of sexually available women. Nor it is impossible to imagine that this flirting with the semiotics of sexual availability was being encouraged by men used to the erotic charge associated with such performances or, on the other side, provoking men to heavy-handed and authoritarian attempts to shut it down.[19]

Paul is therefore best understood as resisting the encroachment of several cultural habits on Christian worship at once. Ecstatic cults in Greek culture were normally situated in private homes, so prophetic utterance made it easy to conflate the public and private. In addition, in the culture of the day the very notion of a woman letting her hair down belonged to the private sphere and therefore, for Christians, to the decency of a Christian marriage. By reaffirming the public character of the Christian assembly Paul is locating the dispute in question as in the first instance being one of establishing Christian worship as a *public* gathering.

At the same time the Apostle is resisting another potential misunderstanding we might term the carnival principle. Carnival is a routine in which the traditional boundaries of a society are playfully dissolved or renegotiated within the limited and liminal space of ritual practice as an outlet for affective energies suppressed in the normal course of a society's daily routines. Paul's argumentation is certainly far from implying that Christian liturgy is a kind a carnival, not being a playful suspension of the decorum patterns that normally hold in order to return to them later. Yet he is also far from suggesting that Christianity simply authorizes given cultural patterns. The Apostle is aware that the gospel sometimes suspends the decorum laws of given cultures, a break that can become an actual inversion of the ways in which societies structure themselves.[20] Part of the reason why we today find it difficult to discern the precise challenge Paul is trying to levy in this passage has to do with the fact that the real suspension of several types of decorum

---

chaotic. . . . One of the characteristics of the cult of Dionysus was a fascination with the reversal of sexual identities; men dressed up as women and women as men" (Radcliffe, "Paul and Sexual Identity," 63–64).

19. Peppiatt (*Women and Worship*, 98) is therefore right to point out that if this latter scenario is envisaged, then Paul should also be understood as rebuking attempts by men in authority to suppress women's behavior according to the grammar of the factions with their subtle but proud and authoritarian claims to pre-eminence—a critique that she rightly points out strikes at the heart of the main lines of traditional Christian interpretation of this passage.

20. Forbes, *Prophecy and Inspired Speech*, ch. 6.

rules that we see being negotiated here has now been accomplished and long ago been established as the common sense of the Western world.

We have explained the reasons why we might take as read Paul's commendation of the Corinthians for having continued to worship as he taught them. There is, however, one specific exception. What sort of speech act is introduced in 11:3 by the conjunction **but**? On our reading, what Paul is concerned with here and wishes the congregation to **know** is that the spiritual embrace of the new reality inaugurated by Christ, which genuinely liberates Christians from preoccupation with questions of decorum, must still be understood as a *creaturely* existence with its own limitations. While the laws of sexual attraction are certainly put into perspective under the one reign of Christ, this is not to suggest that they need no longer be reckoned with. They continue to present challenges to the proper ordering of the church's worship.

At this point it is important to notice yet again that Paul's intervention is not a narrow attempt to sort out this one "ethical problem" of Christian conduct in church. Again he is using the practical question in view to offer the Corinthians a *theological* insight about the relationship of two "laws" whose proper order must be kept in view. To speak of a "law" of sexual attraction is to acknowledge that we encounter the created world as a structured space, marked, for instance, by expected patterns of repeated cyclical activity, while at the same time also recognizing that any such law can become tyrannical if isolated or coming to rule inappropriate domains.

This reading is suggested by Paul's foregrounding in 11:3 of the cosmological hierarchy of all such laws over which the Christian confesses the law of Christ to have precedence. This invocation of divine rule apparently assumes that Christ's law proves its power not by annihilating or displacing the laws of the created order, but by permeating their sphere in order to make them fit for the new world that the gospel has begun to open up. The Apostle needs to make this point in order to negotiate the problems of a church that appears to have forgotten that the kingdom has not yet been consummated and that their worship is still a *foretaste* of heaven. It therefore makes good sense when Paul reminds his readers in 11:7–9 that in Genesis the "image" is linked with sexual differentiation despite the fact that he focuses this chapter very precisely on *worship* rather than what we think of as a more general account of sexual ethics.

Having emphasized the turn Paul performs between 11:2 and 11:3—in his reminder for those who enthusiastically embraced the new status of being under the "law of Christ" that Christ's law does not do away with but transforms the laws written into the created reality (including of sexual attraction)—we are now in a better position to grasp the detail of 11:3. Here

Paul conceives a series of three elemental relationships that are all characterized by a particular type of headship: **Christ is the head of every man, and the husband is the head of his wife, and God is the head of Christ**. The exegetical literature bulges with heated discussions as to how κεφαλή (*kephalē*) is appropriately rendered, with suggestions ranging from "head" to "preeminence" or "source,"[21] and it is obvious that the main protagonists of the modern discussion are driven by a desire to either unmask or defend Paul as an outspoken representative of patriarchal gender hierarchy.

On our reading this preoccupation with the correct translation of *kephalē* easily overlooks the way in which the series is set up and operates within the overall train of Paul's thought. The expression **the husband is the head of his wife** (which absorbs many a contemporary exegete's energies) is framed by the formal paralleling of the headship of Christ over man and of God over Christ. This framing alone should remind us that what is at stake in this series is not primarily the ordering of domestic life and the relationship of the sexes but the ordering of the domestic order by the more overarching ordering of human life as a whole within the cosmic ordering that is defined by Christ's rule within God's reign. While the notion of *kephalē* certainly entails the notion of authority, it is not easily translated into an ontological hierarchy.[22] The last member in this series makes this point plain, for Christ's subjection to God the Father is not implying an ontological inferiority of any kind, but is a missiological expression. The Father is the head of the Son in the sense that the Son is obedient to the Father in the context of the Son's lowering himself to be "all things to all people."

We therefore seem best advised to take the language of *kephalē* as indicating three specific spheres within which one respective member is expected by the "head" to act in a certain way and who therefore has the capacity to bring either shame or honor on that head. It is not inappropriate to see already at work here the logic of decorum, which Paul will be explicitly discussing in terms of the concrete issues arising between the sexes in the church from 11:4 onwards. The crucial and productively disconcerting

---

21. For a systematic understanding in historical perspective, see Wannenwetsch, "Head: Christianity Medieval Times, Reformation Era, and Modern Europe."

22. "Whatever κεφαλή does mean, it does *not* mean that as God rules over Christ, Christ rules over man, and man rules over woman, because we cannot claim that God rules over Christ in the first place . . . So whereas his teaching could be open to the interpretation that woman is the last in the chain of submission . . . in this letter he is framing the language of *kephale* to *prevent the concept from being understood in this way*. If it is used in this way, it becomes clear that it can then be used to undermine a woman's full participation in public worship and to convince her that she should be under her husband's or a man's authority." Peppiatt, *Women and Worship*, 91, 96, emphasis original.

point is the vulnerability of the "head" to the actions of someone else who is in the position to bring either honor or shame on both parties. To "disgrace the head" is to bring shame on a loved one with whom one is in inextricable relationship. Headship conceived in this way points to a complex economy of power that cannot be reduced to the terms of a unilateral flow. Put in the simplest terms, this series names those agents who are in the position to shame the ones designated as "heads," here portrayed not as actors but as hostages to the actions of others.

Throughout Paul's letter to the Corinthians we have seen how the logic of witness reveals in manifold ways that it is not only the church that is at the mercy of individual members whose conduct will either disgrace or bring honor to it, but even Christ himself. By taking up the role of the head of the church, Christ puts himself at the mercy of its members in their concrete dealings with the world. In a similar manner, the New Testament traditions have portrayed the complexity of the economic power relations between Christ and the Father as ones in which the Father completely "entrusts" his dealings with creation to the Son, thus putting himself at the mercy of the Son's faithfulness who, in turn, as evidenced in his resurrection from the dead (the Son now being at the mercy of the Spirit), is given reign over the cosmos that he will eventually hand back to the Father (>15:23).

Given this cosmological-Trinitarian framing of Paul's portrayal of the relationship of the sexes through the notion of *kephalē*, it should be clear that Paul's overarching interest is that the conduct of individual members or groups in the church does not bring shame on the respective others, and most importantly, not on Christ's body, and thus the Lord himself. Within this scheme of shame and honor what Paul is asking of the Corinthians now appears plausible and certainly less offensive to one sex in particular. It is a summons to the potentially over-enthusiastic group of women in the Corinthian church to keep to the decorum of appearance as it relates to the "head" associated with the other sex, so as not to bring shame on them. While it might certainly be possible to envision scenarios in which the conduct of **wives** would disgrace their **husbands**, we are not convinced that this translation, which the NRSV uses for ἀνήρ (*anēr*) and γυναικός (*gynaikos*) only in 11:3, is helpful. It seems more in keeping with the wider scheme Paul set out in 11:2 that the sort of shame the women who let their hair down while prophesying in public worship bring on others is to be understood with respect not to each one's spouse, but to "men" in general (in the congregation).

There is no doubt that Paul is drawing on biblical and rabbinic traditions when, in verses 8–9, he cites the Genesis account of the origin of the sexes as establishing sexual difference as important and to be maintained; **man was not made from woman, but woman from man. Neither was**

man created for the sake of woman, but woman for the sake of man. Nevertheless, as 11:11 indicates, Paul is working with this tradition in order not to reinscribe a general rule of patriarchal supremacy but in order to clarify the *significance* of sexual difference in terms of the mutual commissioning of the sexes for each other.[23] The key move in 11:11-12 is his use of the term χωρὶς (*chōris*), "without" or "**independent of**": **in the Lord woman is not independent of man or man independent of woman. For just as woman came from man, so man comes through woman; but all things come from God.** The absurdity of an individualistic reading of "man" and "woman" now becomes apparent in that this verse would have to be read as levying a near-demand that every man and woman marry so as not to be without his or her own spouse. Although rabbinic interpretations of the creation tradition could sometimes come close to such an imperative, the Christian church always honored the celibate life as at least an equally valid alternative way of living out the gospel. If, therefore, we are to understand 11:11 in generic terms, it will be as the mutual commission of all members of both sexes to serve the respective other in the various ways appropriate to the many circumstances of life in which they meet.

Once again Paul commends a theologically configured image of gender equality and distinguishes it from reductionist readings in which domestic hierarchy might be defended by appeal to the biblical narratives of the origin of the sexes. At the same time he reinforces the centrality of authority and service as the matrix within which appropriate decorum is to be negotiated in the relationship of the sexes. Just as Christ's mission is to serve the Father, so every believer's mission is to serve Christ, including between the sexes. In a non-trivial sense, women are created to "serve" men, and men to "serve" women. As the author of Ephesians understood so well, the summons of one sex to serve the other (Eph 5:24) as "head" (Eph 5:23) is firmly located within the prior call for mutual submission to Christ (Eph 5:21).

The key to the first part of chapter 11 as a whole thus turns on a theologically precise and christologically ordered understanding of the logic of submission. Paul is certainly resisting the pharisaic tradition of

---

23. The reference here is to Gen 2:18. "It was not *Eve* who was lonely, unable to manage and needing help . . . Women, for Paul, are not created 'for men,' that is, for their bed and board. Rather women, as descendants of Eve, are placed by God in the human scene as the strong who come to help/save the needy (the men). In this reading of the text, Paul the Middle Eastern male chauvinist disappears. In its place Paul emerges as a compassionate figure who boldly affirms the equality and mutual interdependency of men and women in the new covenant . . . This reading of the text helps explain why Greek women of high standing were attracted to Paul's message and why they joined the movement he represented." Bailey, *Paul through Mediterranean Eyes*, 310.

interpretation in which the Genesis account of the origin of the sexes was taken to establish an ontological hierarchy between them. But he is also concerned with another equally important task—to make sense of the ways in which the embrace of gender equality might be legitimately worked out in concrete expressions of the mutual commissioning of the sexes toward each other. In short: any theologically appropriate approach to the concrete "moral" issue of female hairstyle in Corinthian public worship will have to be alert to how this mutual service was to shape an awareness of *both* the law of sexual attraction *and* of the new law of the church's de-sexualized brother- and sisterhood.

Paul's moral summons can therefore be understood as an invitation to women and men both to abstain from employing the culturally specific semiotics of erotic attraction in a manner that will have the effect of eventually bringing shame on both sexes.[24] Christian women who are attentive to the problem of not shaming men are respecting and honoring the male members of the congregation in their particular bodiliness, including the bio-psychological constitution of male sexuality with its close linkage of the visual to the erotic. To be committed to not shaming men is to refuse to deploy any semiotics that places men in the "game" of siren and voyeur, whether they desire or resist this emplacement. Caring for one's hair is therefore a way of respecting the law of nature by respecting the way in which sexual attraction operates in the other sex.

The cultural attentiveness we are enjoining has often been short circuited in the exegetical tradition in one of three ways. The first is to circumscribe the problem along the lines suggested by Aquinas, by disputing the claim that women can be in ministerial positions at all. The most familiar way to set up this conclusion begins from a set of disembedded texts (most often drawn from this chapter in combination with 1 Cor 14:34 and 1 Tim 2:12) that establish that the burden of proof is on those who would argue that women should teach men in the church or be ordained. On our reading this disembedding of "proof" texts from their canonical context has the effect not only of misreading them, but of lending them far more weight than

---

24. This is a point with significantly wider implications than we can address here, which are especially important for the Western church to grapple with given the regularity with which it has constructed its account of normative sexual expression by way of simply anathematizing the impure transgressor. It is not going too far to suggest that this injunction to "not shame" one another in the domain of sexuality amounts to a deep challenge to the familiar sentimental construction of heterosexual marriage as a safe domain of especially pure relationship with God and the human neighbor. See Rees, *Romance of Innocent Sexuality*, ch. 4. This call to "not shame" can thus be read as another iteration of what we understand to be one of the epistle's key injunctions, to "wait for one another" (>11:33).

they warrant in relation to other obviously relevant tracts of scripture. In relation to 1 Corinthians, taking this line commits the reader either to finding a way to explain how we can know that women are barred from having certain charismatic giftings (a limitation we think unwarranted based on the detailed account of spiritual gifts developed in chapter 12) or to deny the account of church offices as a *recognition* rather than *bestowal* of the gifts of the Spirit that we have understood as fundamental to Paul's account of church ministry in chapters three and four (>12:27–29).

There are also two lower-level strategies that attempt to escape the cultural negotiation we take Paul to be enjoining in this chapter, either by denying the law of attraction altogether or by assuming static and stereotyped accounts of sexual difference. This latter approach is most often linked with "mechanical" proposals for inter-gender decorum in Christian community, such as teaching men not to watch, or addressing women alone with the demand not to dress provocatively. A properly two-sided rendering of the relation between the sexes insists that either sex can set up the social realm of the voyeurism-titillation game, so forcing everyone else either to delight in or to be uncomfortably subjected to it.

A long history of attempts to prescribe a decorum that will diffuse the creaturely laws of sexual attraction can be glimpsed in those traditions that espouse the concealment of anything that could invite sexual attraction, be it a nun's habit, the hijab, or Victorian dress codes. In the end, the best such projects can do is push the semiotics of bodily communication toward more refined or narrowed triggers for sexual attraction. If literary representations are anything to go on, the Victorians were as titillated by an exposed ankle as moderns apparently are by full frontal nudity. Aquinas's discussion of the practice of nuns having shaved heads under their habits provides a case in point. Commenting on 11:6—**For if a woman will not veil herself, then she should cut off her hair; but if it is disgraceful for a woman to have her hair cut off or to be shaved, she should wear a veil**—his Aristotelian account of nature removes Paul's culturally sensitive **if** to assert that it is universally unnatural for a woman to shave her head. This puts him in the position of having to offer a defense of the practice, apparently common at the time, of nuns having shaved heads covered by habits. The route he takes in this defense presents us with a classic example of how in these discussions eschatology can easily efface creation: "from the very fact that they take a vow of virginity or widowhood with Christ as their spouse, they are promoted to the dignity of men, being freed from subjection to men and joined to Christ Himself."[25]

---

25. Aquinas, TA, sec. 600. "This symbolic function of the head covering is vividly

With the eviction of Paul's "if" from 11:6, Aquinas also loses the subtle interplay apparent in Paul's theological understanding of the relation of culture and worship. Because he has appealed first to the doctrines of God and the work of Christ and only then to creation as recounted in Genesis, Paul offers an account of sexual difference that is intentionally not bound to one culturally specific configuration of the semiotics of the sexual difference. Paul's claim is that *if* it is disgraceful for a woman (by the cultural standards of her time and place) to have her hair cut off or to be shaved, *then* she should wear a veil. The clear implication is that if this concrete moment of bodily semiotics does not exist in a given culture, another semiotic may be imagined, but no semiotic is available that is immune from the law of attraction between the sexes. The bodily semiotics of our own culture has made the inescapability of the law of attraction particularly visible in that those women who regularly and gladly appear in public with "shaved" heads are by no means considered unnatural or unattractive in doing so. Whether a woman or man strives for the androgynous look, the hyper-masculinization of the body-builder, or the hyper-femininity of enhanced conformity to the faddish shapes of pinup models, Paul is suggesting that any attempt to escape or exploit the semiotics of sexual attraction finally boils down to forms of disrespecting the legitimate powers of attraction that exist between the sexes.[26]

The phrase, **For this reason a woman ought to have a symbol of authority on her head** (11:10) should therefore be read as paralleling verse 4, **Any man who prays or prophesies with something on his head disgraces his head**. Both equally reflect cultural habits of Paul's age that may not be as distant from our own as they appear at first glance. From the medieval knight's lowering of his helmet as a mark of subjection to a lord, to John Wayne's iconic lowering of his Stetson on entering a church in the convention of western movies, to the bowing of heads in prayer before Christ as Lord; all are culturally encoded versions of the same gesture of subjection and vulnerability. In the ancient cultural context in which the Corinthian

---

expressed in the Hellenistic Jewish narrative *Joseph and Aseneth* (written sometime in the first century BCE or the first or second century CE): after her conversion to Judaism, the young woman Aseneth is ordered by an angel to remove her head covering, 'because you are a holy virgin today and your head is as that of a young man' (*Joseph and Aseneth* 15:1–2)." Hays, RBH, 184. Our emphasis on the universality of the problem of cultural negotiation, on which our construal of the enduringly binding apostolic pronouncement about how it should be negotiated rests, is lost in Peppiatt's decision to read this verse as a Corinthian slogan being refuted by Paul in a manner more in tune with the sensibilities of contemporary modern biblical scholarship. Peppiatt, *Women and Worship*, 99.

26. Barth, *CD* 3/4:167–68.

church worshipped, citizens and nobles wore hats, slaves went bareheaded.[27] In conceptual terms, then, authority is a form of power (ἐξουσία/*exousia*), and to show deference is to lay down the symbol of one's own power.

This matrix of ritualized gestures allows us at last to see what precisely is at stake in the problem of how one styles one's hair in Corinthian worship. If in the cultural matrix of that time and place the semiotic power of the women in Corinthian society had come to be concentrated in the way hair is bound or unbound, then for women to "cover" their heads by plaiting their hair and wrapping it around their heads into a sort of a hat[28] would appear to be a disciplined act of laying down one's social power in deference to a higher one. Given the cultural context, a man's taking his hat off may precisely parallel a woman putting her hair up in carefully arranged braids in that both perform a ritualized laying aside of public symbols of certain forms of power. In a similar manner to the gestures by which the British queen today shows her subjection as the holder of civic and military power to the rule of Jesus Christ, by being crowned in church, in this ancient context the braiding of the hair was a gesture of surrendering erotic power. What needs to be attended to in a specific cultural context are the gestures that one makes in a given forum in order to bring others under subjection. It is for these reasons that we have understood Paul's interest not to be in establishing or reasserting the *limits* of decorous behavior but in bringing into view the essentially *theological concerns* that orient the Christian negotiation of the unending problem of decorum.

We have understood Paul to be seeking a valid way to challenge the ontological hierarchies some had perceived the Genesis accounts of the origin of the sexes to sustain, along with the assumption that long hair is universally degrading to men (Ezek 44:20) by setting these claims within his new understanding of the egalitarian freedom for both sexes characteristic of the reign of Christ. 11:7–9 displays the sensitivity of Paul, the cultural Pharisee, to Jewish traditions about sexual order as he simultaneously validates their emphasis on maintaining sexual difference while at the same time resisting any hint of ontological subordination. It makes sense in this light to read 11:7 as part of Paul's effort to synchronize the creation account

---

27. The reasons for this are clearly related to the discussion at hand, as the following citation from Plutarch illustrates: "Men cover their heads when they worship the gods ... For they uncover their heads in the presence of men more influential than they: it is not to invest these men with additional honor, but rather to avert from them the jealousy of the gods, that these men may not seem to demand the same honors as the gods, nor to tolerate an attention like that bestowed on the gods, nor to rejoice therein." From his *Moralia*, quoted in Collins, RFC, 401.

28. Murphy-O'Connor, JMO, 146–49.

with this egalitarian vision: **For a man ought not to have his head veiled, since he is the image and reflection of God; but woman is the reflection of man.** Having offered a theological account of egalitarian Christian worship, Paul refuses to deny the significance of sexual differentiation, and deploys a non-hierarchical asymmetric imagery that pictures man as the image of God, but woman as the glory of that image. We need only think of the implications of the departure of the glory of the Lord from the tabernacle to see that what is being emphasized with this comparison is not a reinscription of an ontological hierarchy but the mutual dependence of men and women in imaging their creator. Even when the ark of the covenant remained in it, Israel's tabernacle was decisively diminished by the departure of the glory of the Lord.[29]

We are left with the enigmatic phrase, **because of the angels**. An incredible variety of interpretations of this phrase have been proposed. Some ancient interpreters understood this as a reference to those creaturely beings who are appropriately veiled in the presence of God,[30] and others to representatives of divine judgment on laxity in worship.[31] Modern authors have struggled mightily and come up with a wide range of solutions including the idea that what is being implied here is the messenger function of those members of the congregation who have reported to Paul the goings on in the Corinthian community[32] or that an appeal to the angels was being used to justify female prophetic behavior.[33] Our admittedly speculative suggestion is that Paul's reference to the angels means to indicate that when sexualizing human habits encroach on the eschatological space of worship, the angels, who the early church understood to be present in that space, are justifiably scandalized by the problems and confusions that characterize the realm of sexualized law in which they do not participate as wholly eschatological creatures.[34]

29. See Macaskill, *Union with Christ*, ch. 5.

30. Drawing on Augustine's *uti-frui* distinction and the demonology and angelology he develops in the *City of God*, Thomas argues that demons are attracted to sensual display, which is why women should keep their heads covered, as they should for the same reasons to protect the "angels" in the church, the priests. TA section 613-614.

31. "Therefore this phrase is given by way of amplification, as if he had said: 'If women do away with their veils, it is not only Christ, but all the angels as well, who will be witnesses of the ruinous result.'" Calvin, JC, 233.

32. Murphy-O'Connor, JMO, 164, 176–77.

33. Taylor, "Woman Ought to Have Control," 41–42.

34. This proposal draws on biblical hints such as the theme of angelic "watchers" (Dan 4:17; 2 Pet 2:11) whom first-century sects like the Qumran community understood as participants in worship conceived as an outpost of heaven. These traditions may be drawn together with biblical hints that angels are properly asexual (Matt 22:30),

Paul begins to draw his discussion of this theme to a close by saying **Judge for yourselves**, a rhetorical move aptly characterized by Aquinas: "he submits to his hearers to judge what he has said after the manner of one who is confident that he has sufficiently proved his point."[35] The argument is now concluded, and the reader invited to discern its worth. Why then does the Apostle proceed to add yet another type of argument? **Does not nature itself teach you that if a man wears long hair, it is degrading to him, but if a woman has long hair, it is her glory? For her hair is given to her for a covering.** It is tempting to understand this last argument as an afterthought: "doesn't nature tell us just what we read in scripture?" Such a reading, however, underestimates the rhetorical placement of the argument while overestimating the weight of the argument itself. It is obvious that Paul has not saved the best argument for last, but this does not mean it can be dismissed as a mere appendix bearing no weight. Rather, Paul's placing of this argument from nature after the arguments from doctrine and from scripture have been comprehensively unfolded should be understood as significant in its own right, indicating something useful about the way in which natural law and theological law relate to each other.

"Perhaps," comments Chrysostom, "someone might see another difficulty here and ask what offense there is in woman's baring their heads or for men to cover theirs?"[36] The term Paul uses for "nature" here is not κτίσις (*ktisis*/creation), but φύσις (*physis*), which in the context really means biology. In effect, he is pointing out that the different type, luster, weight and durability of hair does in fact make discriminating between the sexes possible, and in this context female hair presents a more flexible palette for semiotic display. There is not much heft to such a "natural theology," which amounts to little more than a practical observation available to anyone who has ever had his or her hair cut or styled, as all of us must. This argument from biology allows us to see the sense in which Paul understands long hair to degrade a man—the given or "natural" palette simply cannot support much styling. We therefore understand Paul's suggestion more at the level of a practical observation than an ontological assertion: long hair is degrading to men in

---

are offended by sexual immorality (Jude 8), and if acceding to the law of sexual attraction, become mortal (Gen 6:2).

35. Aquinas, TA, section 619.

36. Chrysostom's account is sensitive to the nuances of the relation between arguments from scripture and nature, setting arguments from nature within doctrinal arguments: "Now the laws about garments [in the Old Testament] were legislated by man, even if God later ratified them. But the business of whether to cover one's head was legislated by nature. When I say 'nature,' I mean 'God.' For he is the one who created nature." *Homily* 26, PG 61:214 and 216, in JK, 180.

the way a ponytail embarrasses rather then makes attractive an aging rock star in its futile attempts to make a mountain of the molehill that nature has left. But no warrant is supplied here for absolute statements about long hair on males being degrading in every imaginable culture.

When not understood within in the wider framework of *ktisis*, "creation," biological facts do not by themselves teach us anything. If arguments from nature are to have a role within Christian discourse, they can never be self-contained. The theological horizon opened by the creation that Christians confess is also an affirmation that the moral "message" of nature is never available on the surface, but must be heard by those who have ears to hear, that is, those who have been schooled in sustained listening to the divine Word.[37] But if they are placed in such a subordinate place alongside theological arguments, arguments from nature can indeed add their own supporting weight.

Our contention is that both parts of this chapter deal with the question of how cultural decency or indecency is to be understood as shaping ecclesial practice. To this point Paul has been concerned theologically to articulate how the church is disgraced in the way it is carrying out its legitimate *refusal* to adhere to cultural standards of decency in ecclesial life. He now turns to the inverted problem, behaviors in which the church disgraces itself precisely in its illegitimate *adherence* to cultural patterns of decorum.

Distinguishing Church from Mere Physical Gathering

> [17]Now in the following instructions I do not commend you, because when you come together it is not for the better but for the worse. [18]For, to begin with, when you come together as a church, I hear that there are divisions among you; and to some extent I believe it. [19]Indeed, there have to be factions among you, for only so will it become clear who among you are genuine.

Paul begins his **following instructions** by indicating the parallels and distinctions between the chapter's two main topics. His discussion of hairstyling and worship began by commending the congregation for maintaining his traditions and only then proceeded into the critical discussion of a specific respect in which their faithfulness fell short of the full scope of these traditions. In 11:17, in contrast, Paul begins his discussion of eucharistic behavior in Corinth by immediately telling them **I do not commend**

---

37. For a fuller account of the significance and difference between arguments from nature, creation, and scripture, see Wannenwetsch, "Creation and Ethics."

you. The inversion of the rhetoric in this introduction of the second part is significant in helping us understand why Paul speaks of their coming together as **not for the better but for the worse**. The Greek notion of συνέρχεσθαι/*synerchesthai* (which the NRSV aptly translates **come together as a church**) literally indicates a coming together, a "congregating," but would soon become a formalized expression by which the Christian tradition came to denote the liturgical eucharistic worship of the church as a whole in distinction from other *ad hoc* gatherings of believers.[38] We will only fully understand how Paul approaches this discussion if we keep in mind that he is playing with the linguistic polyvalence of the term *synerchesthai* at this historical juncture. In this light, the question that orients this whole discussion can be summarized as an inquiry into what sort of "coming together" the Corinthian celebration actually is: is their gathering a proper eucharistic celebration or a partial Eucharist, a pseudo-Eucharist, or perhaps even an anti-Eucharist?

A first hint towards an answer we discover in 11:18: **For, to begin with, when you come together as a church, I hear that there are divisions among you**. Here, we must again take issue with the NRSV translation. Taken literally, it is important to realize that Paul does not speak of their gathering "**as**" a church, but uses the preposition "**in**": ἐν (*en*). Ecclesiologically this makes a vast difference, since if what is going on in Corinth is a gathering *as* church, the implication would be that a church gathering is the mere result of the sociological phenomenon of people congregating. But the Corinthians find themselves at the receiving end of a highly critical discussion in which Paul charges that as they are gathering in a sociological sense they do not in fact *do* church in a theological or true sense; they do not live and celebrate according to the gospel. For the Apostle, a church that does not *do* church cannot *be* the church.

What is it then about the *en* expression Paul uses in conjunction with their gathering "in" church that offers the clue to his precise criticism? Despite *en* being a spatial signifier, it cannot be taken here to mean entering a church building for the simple reason that there were no such distinct purpose-built buildings available for the earliest Christians. What the "in" construction does, however, is to place the emphasis on entering—the entering of a place that God has prepared for the believers to be church in their celebrating and receiving the sacramental gifts. The theologically decisive question, therefore, as opened up by the combined semantics of *synerchesthai* and *en*, is whether or not the type of gathering that happens

---

38. More commonly termed *synaxis*. Dix, *Shape of the Liturgy*, 20–21.

when the Corinthians come together is to be a genuine mode of entering *into* that place which is "church."

As we shall soon see, Paul's conceptualization of this point will eventually turn on the language of **discerning the body**. Is the Corinthians' coming together a discerning of the body of Christ and hence a genuine case of *synerchesthai* in the qualified sense that the later tradition would reserve for this term? Is it, in short, a moment of coming together in the ecclesia as a whole as opposed to mere gatherings of various subgroups within it? Paul's verdict on the Corinthians' current worship practices is resoundingly negative. While the Corinthians do come together (sociologically speaking), their actual practices of table fellowship constitute a deplorable anti-teleology of *synerchesthai*: for all the phenotypical resemblances that might indicate that they gather for a genuine eucharistic celebration, they remain literally stuck in the entrance portal.

Indeed, there have to be factions among you, for only so will it become clear who among you are genuine. We have commented on this passage in several earlier contexts (>1:2–3, 17), and have taken this as straight speech rather than a quotation of Corinthian slogans—those "sentiments with which Paul could not possibly agree."[39] Without recapitulating the various reasons we have put forward for why this sentence is completely plausible as non-ironic speech within the overall flow of Paul's letter, it suffices at this point to note only one such reason that is immediately evident within the present context of Paul's discussion. Given the way he sets up an ecclesiological self-examination and the decisive role the call to discernment plays throughout the remainder of his discussion, it seems plausible to understand 11:19 as pointing to a sort of self-discernment of the body of Christ. Paul's overall communicative aim is to overcome the internal divisions within the Corinthian church. But it is precisely in this overcoming that it will **become clear who among you are genuine**, and therefore even the divisions that occur **have to be**, are bound to play a role in this process. If the body is to find its divinely given unity, those divisions that are in need of healing in order that this unity be achieved will come via specific discernments of which rifts genuinely need healing to result in a real rather than a superficial unity. Rifts are not thereby divinized in a Hegelian fashion, as if sin was necessary in order for maturity to be achieved; Paul is simply noting that in a fallen world they are the presenting occasion that provokes the crucial exercise of discernment by which the body of Christ is built up.

---

39. Murphy-O'Connor here is responding affirmatively to Thiselton's translation, which puts this comment in quotation marks. JMO, 219.

Confusing Apostles and Patrons

> ²⁰When you come together, it is not really to eat the Lord's supper. ²¹For when the time comes to eat, each of you goes ahead with your own supper, and one goes hungry and another becomes drunk. ²²What! Do you not have homes to eat and drink in? Or do you show contempt for the church of God and humiliate those who have nothing? What should I say to you? Should I commend you? In this matter I do not commend you!

In the discussion that follows Paul is obviously trying to put right what he perceives to be a deplorable situation in the Corinthians' habits of celebrating Eucharist, but in order to do so he will need to answer the much broader question of what type of activity the Eucharist actually is. This question he answers by clarifying how the Eucharist is situated in the space between human and divine action.

Problems in the translation of 11:20 are thrown up by what we will call the "mental operation" reading that has marked many contemporary appropriations of the remaining verses in this chapter. The NRSV translation emphasizes the constitutive role of human intentionality: **When you come together, it is** not really **to eat the Lord's supper**. This is to hear Paul saying, "You Corinthians don't really reach the level of a true eucharistic celebration because your intentions are marred." This translation suggests that what is wrong with the Corinthians' approach to the Eucharist is that their gathering is not even intentionally directed to becoming a full eucharistic gathering. Such a reading indicates that Paul was telling them "you may call it the Lord's Supper, but what you are really after is something else, a bit of edifying fellowship with your Christian friends, perhaps, if not an excuse for getting drunk." We will discover that this mental operation reading has important implications at several other sensitive spots in this chapter. For instance, in such a reading the commendation of 11:28–31 to "examine/judge yourself" is imagined as a preparatory examination of conscience preceding eucharistic celebration in which each believer contributes to the Eucharist coming off by making sure that they harbor correct intentions. Correspondingly, the summons "remember me" in 11:24–25 is then construed as the act of calling up an image or memory in one's mind.

An alternative translation such as the one offered by Luther—"hält man da nicht das Abendmahl"—avoids the mistake of the NRSV, which imports an emphasis on intentionality not present in the Greek, but pushes too far in the opposite direction by stressing the objective quality of what is happening. The effect could be to suggest a ceremonialist reading along the lines that, "you gather and celebrate, but you do it so incorrectly that a Eucharist is not achieved." We suggest a much simpler and more literal reading here, even if its meaning is less immediately clear: "You Corinthians are coming together, but it is not eating the Lord's Supper." A more expansive translation that hews closer to the literal Greek would be "but your celebration is not an eating of the dominical meal." In Paul's presentation the Eucharist is neither a voluntarist concept whose coming into existence in each instance depends on the purity of the intentions of those gathering nor an *ex opere* mechanism that functions irrespective of what is happening between the participants if the ritual is performed accurately. It is the other plank of Paul's two-pronged critical engagement with the Corinthians that rules out these two accounts of the Lord's Supper, as becomes clear in 11:27.

Whoever, therefore, eats the bread or drinks the cup of the Lord ... Notice that Paul does not shy away from describing the material consumed by the Corinthians **in an unworthy manner** as **the cup of the Lord**. Given his earlier portrayal of the Corinthian celebration as "not eating the dominical meal" we would have expected Paul not to speak so unambiguously of the cup of the Lord in this context. The crucial theological question is, then: How can it be that in drinking the real **cup of the Lord** there can still be a failure to celebrate the Eucharist? In our view the most plausible explanation is that there is something about the material aspects of eucharistic celebration that withstands the arbitrary ways in which the congregation might wish to define or redefine what is happening in it. This is to understand Paul's approach here as another iteration of the position he developed in his discussion of the body as temple of the Holy Spirit. Like the human body, the body that is the eucharistic elements has a teleology that cannot be willfully bent towards whatever meaning people might wish to give it: either when engaging in what is taken to be "merely casual" sex or eating idol food but insisting that doing so is of no relevance to the ecclesial body (>6:13–17).

We have represented the intentionalist account as a misunderstanding, in which the constitutive component of the Eucharist is taken to be the intentions of the one who receives, as well as its opposite, the quasi-mechanist incantation account in which it is assumed that the enactment of an accurate ritual sequence is the central component constitutive of communion. The latter account is, however, onto something. Paul's reference to the so-called words of institution in conjunction with the sharing of bread and wine apparently assumes an as-yet-unspecified objective quality of this undertaking. Those who take the bread and drink the wine are summoned by the Apostle to take seriously the objective quality of this happening that adheres in a stubborn way to the material elements and the ritual forms associated with them. Because the elements have been *given* by Christ in their own material *solidity*, they are "object-ive" (Lat. *obicere*, "throw in the way") in the sense of literally putting an object in the way of the Corinthians to which they can cling and which is not reducible to or dependent on their will to "get it right."

Paul is apparently insistent that the combination of material artifacts, bread and wine, with the words of institution that name their connection to Jesus, their referent and giver, can somehow literally "withstand" the arbitrariness of the community's desires to define or redefine the semiotics of what is happening in their midst. Venturing a more fulsome paraphrase of Paul's point, we suggest: "You may think that you cannot spoil something that has not even happened, but I tell you that whatever your intention, you are still dealing with the cup of the Lord and the Lord's own words, and therefore you are engaged with a reality that will have an effect on you one way or another, as either a cup of blessing or of judgment." Calvin picks up the salient point here: if you come together and are not made better by the Eucharist, that is, are not growing together in it, you are made worse by it.[40] The Eucharist is either the staff of life or a deadly meal.

The precise problem with the Corinthians' table fellowship is diagnosed in 11:21: **For when the time comes to eat, each of you goes ahead with your own supper, and one goes hungry and another becomes drunk.** The drastic nature of the scenario envisioned makes it easy to overlook that the theological heart of the matter does not rest in its morally appalling surface (some hungry, others drunk) but in the characterization of their meal as ἴδιον δεῖπνον (*idion deipnon*): "each has his or her own meal." As we know from the wider context of contemporary usage in profane Greek, *idion* (his own) is most regularly used to indicate a matter of the private sphere. There are several key texts in the apostolic tradition in which *idion* and *koinon* are explicitly juxtaposed as a way of describing the distinguishing particularity of the church as a social entity organized not around that which everyone has for his or her own but around exactly those things that they have in common.[41] This suggests that for Paul the core mistake underlying the problems visible in the Corinthans' celebration of the Lord's Supper did not lie with their behaviors but in what these exposed about their conflating of the public gathering of the church with a private meeting.

---

40. He does so, of course, within a strongly intentionalist reading: "If we derive no benefit from the gatherings for worship, and we are not made better men as a result of them, it is our ingratitude that is to blame, and therefore we deserve to be reproached." Calvin, JC, 237.

41. See Acts. 2:44-46, and further on this point, Wannenwetsch, *Political Worship*, 133-59.

It was a conflation that was almost bound to occur given the apparent need for the juvenile church to meet in the private homes of congregants whose houses were big enough to accommodate the whole local ecclesia. As Murphy-O'Connor observes, it must have seemed like an incredible stroke of luck for Paul to have converted any of the tiny numbers of wealthy elite who lived in this large Hellenistic seaport. The social stratification typical of the northern shores of the Mediterranean must have been particularly stark in that time, as the wealth of the wealthy rested on plentiful slave labor.[42] If one of the wealthy members of the congregation (perhaps Gaius, mentioned in Rom 16:23) hosted the whole church in his private home, it would have been all too easy to conceive the church's special liturgical gathering, with its table fellowship, as something to be arranged according to the expected patterns of the patron's hosting clients, friends or slaves.

Historical scholarship informs us that the typical pattern for these private functions reflected status differences between guests through fine-tuned seating arrangement and graded food service. Architectural features of Hellenistic stately homes would further reinforce those patterns by allowing only a limited number of guests to gather around the main table in the triclinium (typically no more than nine), while lesser guests would be treated to lower quality food and drink in the adjacent atrium that would accommodate a larger number (probably between thirty and fifty) but without comparable levels of comfort.[43] Pliny the Younger provides us with a striking account of the procedures of caste reinforcement in the Greco-Roman context:

> I happened to be dining with a man . . . whose elegant economy, as he called it, seemed to me a sort of stingy extravagance. The best dishes were set in front of himself and a select few, and cheap scraps of food before the rest of the company. He had even put the wine into tiny little flasks, divided into three categories, not with the idea of giving his guests the opportunity of choosing, but to make it impossible for them to refuse what they were given. One lot was intended for himself and for us, another

---

42. Murphy-O'Connor goes on to note that we can get some sense of the size of gap between the rich and the working classes by way of a fourth-century official description of Rome which found there to be 1,797 "houses" against 46,602 apartments. JMO, 188. Recent archeological evidence suggests that there were equal numbers of slaves and free men and women in the city of Corinth, which, as a trading city, was heavily reliant on slave labor for transporting goods over land and sea.

43. Murphy-O'Connor, JMO, 183.

for his lesser friends (all his friends are graded), and the third for his and our freed men.[44]

Given this cultural and material context, we understand Paul's expression **when the time comes to eat** as referring to the way in which those who the Roman standards of hospitality would expect to dine at the main table in the triclinium would also be those who would have the leisure to arrive early and begin their meal first. These patterns of decorum would also make them feel entitled to begin their meal without waiting for those other members whose working conditions would not allow them to arrive until later. The time lag this arrangement would have set up goes some way in explaining how it was that some could be drunk and others (arriving at the last minute) could end up hungry.

Paul couches his verdict on their behavior in the form of a rhetorical question: **What! Do you not have homes to eat and drink in? Or do you show contempt for the church of God and humiliate those who have nothing?** By thus conflating the church's Eucharist with a private meal the true confusion among the Corinthian believers is exposed: the unique forms of churchly authority have been displaced by the rule of local decorum and oversight held by a *pater familias* (patron). Because a Christian patron owned the space in which worship was being held he might easily have assumed that it is his patterns of fellowship, and thus the laws of oligarchic precedence, that are to define the shape of their coming together to share at Christ's table. When the eucharistic rite is performed as a rich man's feast, what is displaced is the law of Christ, as evidenced by the Corinthians having come to "look down" (καταφρονέω/*kataphroneō*) on the church in the act of shaming its poorer members. With the surprising return of the chapter's earlier motif of shaming we are given a solid linkage of this discussion with the earlier considerations of appropriate appearance in the public worship of the church and the shame a particular type of behavior brings on its head.

---

44. Pliny, *Letters* 2:6, quoted in Murphy-O'Connor, JMO, 185. Paul was not the only author of the time to notice how these decorum patterns had the effect of turning what was ostensibly a genuinely communal affair into its opposite: a performance in which individual meals were eaten in merely physical proximity. After one meal in which a rather less privileged Roman had been denied full participation in a meal that had favored the rich guests, Martial complains, "Why do I dine without you, Ponticus, though I dine with you?" Quoted in Murphy-O'Connor, JMO, 185.

"Broken Loaf" Betrayal

> ²³For I received from the Lord what I also handed on to you, that the Lord Jesus on the night when he was betrayed took a loaf of bread, ²⁴and when he had given thanks, he broke it and said, "This is my body that is for you. Do this in remembrance of me." ²⁵In the same way he took the cup also, after supper, saying, "This cup is the new covenant in my blood. Do this, as often as you drink it, in remembrance of me." ²⁶For as often as you eat this bread and drink the cup, you proclaim the Lord's death until he comes.

We embrace here the consensus view that in these oft-cited verses Paul is quoting an early tradition that has found its way into and given shape to early Christian eucharistic celebration and that later Christian generations have termed the "words of institution." What we would like to investigate, however, is the *significance* of the Apostle's decision to quote this traditional block as a whole. How does he understand the individual expressions contained within it to advance the case he is making to Corinthian believers?

The two expressions **I received** (παρέλαβον/*parelabon*) and **handed on** (παρέδωκα/*paredōka*) are technical terms that, taken together, describe the core actions that constitute any tradition. Whatever the biographical details were of Paul's receiving these words **from the Lord**, he is not appealing to that experience as the ground of his authority in the discussion that follows. He is deploying semantic signifiers not unlike those sometimes employed by the holders of the Holy See at Rome as they demarcate particular propositions as spoken in the highest authority *ex cathedra*. Paul speaks here as one commissioned by the Lord to direct the church's attention to the tradition of that same Lord. It is that activity—"traditioning" his churches in the gospel—in which he is engaged here when addressing the problems of eucharistic practice in Corinth.

The first thing we can say about the inclusion of the traditional words of institution here is that such a familiar quotation would have functioned as a leveling gesture in the context of Corinthian factionalism, putting every Corinthian believer on the same ground. Drawing attention to this symbol of unity would not only remind the Corinthians of their embeddedness in the wider ecumenical church, but also, more specifically, of the words of Christ's passion. "Symbol" is the language later Christian traditions would use to denote ecumenical confessional points of agreement, such as the Nicene Creed. The metaphorical background of the term captured in the verb *sym-ballein*, which literally means "to toss together," nicely explains why a "symbol" unifies people. The basic image is of a stick or a pot shard which has been broken into two halves that have been given to different parties so that, if brought together at a later time, as in the context of the verification of messengers in a diplomatic context, the messenger could be proved to be genuine.[45] Paul's invocation of the words of institution as a "symbol" of Christian unity would therefore function as a point toward which Paul could gather this fragmented church.

As important as it is to understand the undeniably unifying effect of Paul's deploying the words of tradition to draw people together, we must not allow this formal point to overshadow the concrete ways in which the *content* of these traditional formulations provides the essential insights that will fund Paul's work of untangling the knots visible in the Corinthian church. The evidence that Paul sees the traditional formulations addressing the concrete predicament of the Corinthian church is indicated by his interweaving the words of institution with his material discussion in this chapter with the use of linguistic signifiers such as γὰρ (*gar*/for). **In this matter I do not commend you** he says, for **I received what I also handed on to you**. This is to say that, "*because* I have received this tradition, I cannot abide your divisions." The Apostle makes the same careful linking gesture after his quotation of the *paradosis*, linking it in 11:27 with his conclusions through the term **therefore**, "ὥστε (*hōste*).

Indeed, on closer observation it becomes obvious that Paul pulls several key ideas from the traditional material more or less explicitly out into the wider argument that he advances in this chapter. It is important to emphasize this link to the argument of the chapter as a whole since it is easy when approaching a passage as familiar as this one to overlook the deftness with which Paul has woven the whole chapter together. As we will see, terms and ideas that appear at pivotal points in the traditional liturgical formula have been drawn outward to shed light on the mundane exigencies of the Corinthians' local worship practices. An entirely fresh vista opens up when we begin to investigate Paul's concern to show how the one universal institution of the Lord's Supper has within its very structure what is needed to enlighten and heal the cramped situation into which the Corinthians have maneuvered themselves.[46]

The first hint that Paul is directly linking the traditional saying to the Corinthian situation appears in a linguistic play in 11:23: **For I received from the Lord what I also handed on to you, that the Lord Jesus on the night when he was betrayed . . .** What the NRSV translation conceals from us here is that the same expression by which Paul earlier signaled what he

---

45. Chauvet, *Symbol and Sacrament*, 112.
46. Wannenwetsch, *Political Worship*, 146–48.

handed on to the church of the **tradition he received** is also being invoked to denote the circumstances of the **night** in which the activities of the Last Supper occurred. What is translated as **he was betrayed** is, literally, "he was handed over," παρεδίδετο (*paredideto*). What Paul seems to be suggesting by repeating this term is that those who have been handing on the words of the eucharistic institution in perverted ways are thus "handing over" the body of Christ for a second time. The Corinthians are guilty of a misappropriation of the words of institution whose gravity is revealed by calling it a recapitulation of Judas's betrayal.

That said, there are also good theological reasons to defend the non-literal translation of "betraying" instead of "handing over" by the translators of the NRSV, who were in the company of a long tradition of translation in a variety of languages that has made "betrayal" a fixture of the eucharistic liturgy. So while it is true that this established translation tends to conceal an important theological point, from our perspective its prevalence in the liturgical formulations of the global church allows it also to be understood as a testimony that the lesson Paul aimed at the Corinthian church was in fact heard by the global church and taken to heart. While the notion of "handing over" tends to draw attention to the agents outside Jesus's inner circle who came to fetch Jesus and hand him over in turn to the Roman authorities, the language of betrayal makes a different point and without any ambiguity: a precise question is being levied at those who quote these words week by week. A message is being sent to the Corinthians: "You quote these words in your liturgies to make them work for you, imagining yourselves alongside the faithful disciples who are the beneficiaries of Christ's self-giving. But be alert! In quoting these words you may well be posing questions about your own act of betrayal."

An analogous linguistic parallel appears in 11:23–24, where the same point is reiterated. Whereas the NRSV has **when he was betrayed he took a loaf of bread . . . and . . . broke it**, Thiselton aptly points out that the Greek first has a generic term (bread) and then a particularizing term (loaf), and translates, "in the night on which he was handed over he took bread and . . . broke the loaf." Paul's formulation emphasizes that the one heavenly bread breaks one particular loaf and hands it out to the disciples, and in so doing binds them to himself. The salient point is that Paul is drawing attention to this distinction in the context of a Corinthian church that very much resembles a "broken loaf" to the extent that its practices defy its unity given in and through the one heavenly bread. The central concern Paul raises yet again concerns the manner in which reliance on the one loaf that the *Lord* breaks—and the Lord *alone*—is the only way to be drawn back into the unity that is given the church as a divine provision. Though dissensions in the church are unavoidable, the one loaf provided by the church's Lord is sufficient to draw this fractious crowd back into a unity in him. When the church breaks bread together in the fashion of, say, a patron's feast, it has no reason to expect that its breaking will yield unity; rather, the religious valorization of social stratification will instead only reflect and deepen existing factionalism.

The betrayal that Paul wishes the Corinthians to understand in light of the dominical tradition is one that he couches in the language of **contempt for the church** and **humiliating those who have nothing**. We think it unlikely that Paul, the highly theologically educated Jew, would not hear evoked in the traditional expression **this cup is the new covenant in my blood** (11:25) the whole complex of biblical traditions through which Israel was constantly reminded of the coincidence of the vertical with the horizontal dimension in the covenant.[47] Israelites were never to forget that covenantal fidelity (as paradigmatically celebrated in the Passover meal) was demonstrated in their treatment of widows and orphans.[48] The litmus test revealing whether Israel had betrayed the vertical bonds of the covenant was most visible in how they negotiated the horizontal links formed or broken in their dealings with those at the social margins.

It is on the basis of our alertness to the intricate way in which Paul sees the historical betrayal of Jesus on that **night** being related to the repetition of such a betrayal in this day of the Corinthians' eucharistic gatherings that we are offered a better handle on the meaning of his conclusion that those who participate in the Eucharist are **answerable for the body and blood of the Lord**. The Greek ἔνοχος (*enochos*) is much stronger than the NRSV's rendition as **answerable** or even "accountable," and is more appropriately rendered "guilty." On the grounds of their eucharistic malpractice, the Corinthians are guilty with regards to the body of the Lord. Paul's notion of the double betrayal is being articulated here once again, based on what we might call a performative understanding of the dominical words as something that inevitably draws those who quote them inside the plot that those words narrate.[49] At last Paul has made it clear in what the "objective"

---

47. "I will lay your cities waste, will make your sanctuaries desolate, and I will not smell your pleasing odors." Lev 26:31.

48. "Therefore, because you trample on the poor and take from them levies of grain, you have built houses of hewn stone, but you shall not live in them . . . For I know how many are your transgressions, and how great are your sins—you who afflict the righteous, who take a bribe, and push aside the needy in the gate." Amos 5:11a–12.

49. Oswald Bayer has demonstrated how the speech act performed through the words of institution is best understood as a form of *promissio*, a promise that becomes reality in the moment of its utterance by virtue of the divine power of its originator. Bayer, *Martin Luther's Theology*, 50–54.

character of the **cup of the Lord** and the liturgical dealings with it consist, and why they cannot be redefined at will.

For as often as you eat this bread and drink the cup, **you proclaim the Lord's death until he comes.** Why does Paul now suggest that partaking in Eucharist is a proclamation of Christ's **death**? Recall that for Paul, especially in chapter 9, the core of his mission is to proclaim a "free" gospel.

Our suggestion is that Paul emphasizes the linkage of the Eucharist with the death of Christ because this death is the moment in the life of Christ in which the human and material aspects of the hypostatic union are most clearly on display. To proclaim Jesus Christ's death is Paul's way of drawing the story of creation into the narrative of the gospels. Within the whole narrative of Jesus Christ recounted in the gospels, it is this moment that most unambiguously reveals the full depth of the immaterial God's investment in materiality, and so in creation as a whole. Because God has so invested Godself in creation through Jesus Christ, we can know that the material world is made by the Father, and therefore can trust that all its contingent particularities have a christologically grounded tangibility. It is because Christ died, therefore, that we can affirm that the very materiality of the bread of the Eucharist matters in the body of Christ—as do hairstyling and architecture and the quality and distribution of food. Such things are not *adiaphora* but the *mise en scène*, the material condition in which all human life and worship are carried out.

This death that is being proclaimed is thus the premise on which Paul can exhort the Corinthians to **discern the body**, to come to terms with the materiality of its presence to them. Paul is not here just adding one more argument to the ones already developed, as the eucharistic discussion is finally the one that anchors the whole and exposes the universal reach of the work of Christ. The cosmological argument about nested sequences of subordination with which Paul opened the chapter now emerges as one facet of the whole, though not its definitive form. Despite its grand scope it is in fact a sub-argument designed to establish a theological understanding of subordination within the context of the question of hairstyles for worship. In Paul's order of thought, this cosmological argument cannot reach all the way down into the many material questions that constitute the moral life, though it does advance the Corinthians' understanding of the one issue at hand. The discussion of the Lord's Supper, on the other hand, has a far more encompassing reach precisely because it is a gospel that can only reveal its power by breaking in on life-worlds already shaped by given rules of social decorum. What we have here is a *theologia crucis*, of sorts, but one that does not, as some versions do, redirect attention away from the materiality of our lives by focusing on the individual benefits that can be reached by Christ's death or by securing a place in heaven by focusing finally not on death but resurrection. Instead, it exposes how Christ's work is to embed us more firmly and coherently in the created world in all its proper fullness.

Life Open to Divine Judgment

> ²⁷Whoever, therefore, eats the bread or drinks the cup of the Lord in an unworthy manner will be answerable for the body and blood of the Lord. ²⁸Examine yourselves, and only then eat of the bread and drink of the cup. ²⁹For all who eat and drink without discerning the body, eat and drink judgment against themselves. ³⁰For this reason many of you are weak and ill, and some have died. ³¹But if we judged ourselves, we would not be judged. ³²But when we are judged by the Lord, we are disciplined so that we may not be condemned along with the world.

These verses have provoked a reception history that is deplorable in many respects. The way in which the NRSV renders 11:28 is already a case in point: **Examine yourselves, and only then eat of the bread and drink of the cup.** This translation moralizes the Eucharist in a manner that disastrously inverts the genuine moral dimension of the Eucharist Paul has set before the Corinthians. Two aspects of the poisoned chalice this reading offers us must be directly refuted: its invitation to *moral self-examination* understood as preceding eucharistic participation, and the status of this examination as a *prerequisite* for achieving a state in which one is not *unworthy* to take communion. What we earlier (and briefly) referred to as the "mental operation" mode of reading is unfortunately the default among contemporary interpreters, who, as a result, tend to overlook details pointing in a very different direction. This can be explained to a certain extent by the way in which the three ideas highlighted above form a compound that is both very familiar and also compellingly coherent. The reading it yields runs something like: "*examine* your conscience by admitting your sins to God, know thyself honestly and thoroughly so that you know whether you can approach the table *worthily*, that is, with a clean conscience. *Only then* should you proceed to communion having before achieved some warranted certainty that it will be to your benefit."

The first problem with this reading is that the Greek in 11:28 does not in fact suggest a temporal or sequential logic, let alone the expansion of this logic assumed in the NRSV translation that seems to yield a criteriological stipulation: **only then**. Καὶ οὕτως (*Kai houtōs*) literally means "and so," which links the "eating" with what precedes it—δοκιμαζέτω (*dokimazetō*, "prove yourself"). Paul is not linking the two moments to suggest that the testing or proving is a *prerequisite* of the eating but is rather characterizing the appropriate *mode* in which the eating is to happen. Setting aside temporal or sequential readings allows us to see how *dokimazetō* entails a much wider linguistic scope. While it does connote a sense of testing (transitive), and hence a critical moment, in general Paul's theological usage of the term throughout his corpus is geared more toward the (intransitive) notion of proving the value of entities within the context of the activities to which they should be suited (see 1 Cor 3:13; Gal 6:4; Rom 12:2).

The activity in which the Christian congregation is to "prove" themselves within the wider context of eucharistic practice is specifically the activity of discerning the body: Christians prove themselves by going about their business in ways that *suit* the peculiar phenomenon that is the church. They are proved, therefore, as they actively "recognize what characterizes" the church (Thiselton). So describing what it is that needs to be proven, namely, the discerning of the suitability of any church practice to the very being of the church, explains in turn why the translation of **unworthy** in 11:27 is also misleading. The unworthiness in view is not immediately a moral category since the Greek term ἀναξίως (*anaxiōs*) is more appropriately rendered as "unsuitable" or "unfitting." The unworthiness of the church is not discerned by measuring actions against an abstract standard of moral decency, but the very concrete standard demanded by the given and proximate particularities of the church as Christ's body.

The temporal or sequential reading that has grounded the familiar misinterpretation just refuted is also unhelpful in suggesting that a similar temporal logic prevails in 11:29: **For all who eat and drink without discerning the body, eat and drink judgment against themselves.** A two-step sequence introduced by the temporal matrix of much modern interpretation tends to be associated with a problematic account of judgment yielding a reading along these lines: "you eat and drink in a defective fashion, pointing back to the preceding failure of self-inspection, and this defective mode of celebrating summons up the one who sits in judgment over you, resulting in your eventual condemnation." In spite of the familiarity and widespread diffusion of this two-step account of judgment, it is nevertheless incapable of making sense of Paul's expression to **eat and drink judgment against themselves.** This formulation suggests the simultaneity of practice (or malpractice) and its concomitant effects. To cite a familiar contemporary example, Paul's warning here is like the ones found on cigarette packages: "smoking kills." Engaging in act A you discover yourself as being in state B. The formal parallel to "smoking kills" should not make us overlook, though, how profoundly Paul's invocation of the judgment they will **drink ... against themselves** differs from the moralizing connotations we associate with the former. His warning to the Corinthians does not follow the simple logic of act and consequence, as if Paul's central concern was to ensure the members of the congregation are aware that if they get drunk in the celebration they might well wake up the next morning with a hangover. Neither is he portentously warning them that because they have not been diligent in rooting out their moral deficiencies they should expect to one day to find themselves punished by God.

The nature of the judgment Paul names as the immediate connotation of the perverted eating and drinking of the congregation is rather that the same poor members that failed to be properly fed at the table will correspondingly be left out of the diaconal care of the church with the unsurprising result that **many of you ... are sick and ill and some have died**. The refusal to discern the body that is the church called to mutual care and love provides the explanation for why Paul can link "drinking yourself judgment" (**against themselves** is yet another unfortunate bit of translation by the NRSV, which again fails to account for the simultaneity of drinking and judgment) and the deplorable state of health care in the Corinthian community with the expression **for this reason**.[50] In addition, our reading with its emphasis on the self-judgment taking place in the Corinthian community also offers a plausible way to understand Paul's insistence that they are despising the church by humiliating "the least of these." This humiliating now becomes intelligible as a very tangible shaming insofar as the church's neglect to care for others in table fellowship indicates its lack of interest in taking the full diaconal responsibility for the wellbeing of their brethren's bodies. While offering them a gospel of new life, they are leaving some brethren to languish in all sorts of deforming and life-threatening conditions. Again it is the very materiality of the connections between Christians, and Paul's speaking to them in terms of shaming one another, that reveals that we are still developing the discussion about bodily semiotics that organized the first part of the chapter. While there Paul was concerned with the appropriate appearance of female bodies that were desirably healthy and beautiful, in the second half of this chapter he directs attention to the shame inducing actions in worship that disfigure the bodies of potentially underfed and under-provisioned members.

To speak of judgment that is not only self-inflicted but even in a way self-executing with regard to the life of the whole (ecclesial) body is not, of

---

50. Garland affirms the substance of this interpretation (DEG, 552), but admits that he resists fully embracing it in not having found a way to interpret *dokimazetō* ("prove yourself") as we think we have successfully done by way of a fully theological account.

course, a denial of a judgment to be reckoned with that remains God's alone. Yet it seems crucial to us not to conflate these two types of judgment—that which is self-inflicted and that which is divinely meted out—a conflation that dogs the NRSV's translation of 11:31: **But if we judged ourselves, we would not be judged.** Such a translation obscures the fact that the Greek employs two different terms for what is rendered here with the single term **judged**: διακρίνειν (*diakrinein*) and κρίνειν (*krinein*). While the latter term always denotes juridical judgment, the former term, used in conjunction with **ourselves**, is the same that Paul uses in 11:29, where it is appropriately translated as "discerning the body." Acknowledging that the Apostle is setting up parallel expressions suggests that 11:31 would appropriately be read, "if we discerned ourselves, we would not be condemned." This, in turn, would also explain why Paul introduces **the judgment of the Lord** in the next verse with a contrasting **but**. Paul is describing a reality marked by two totally different but not unrelated judgments that must not be conflated. The whole complex of terms Paul discusses in 11:31–32 is best paraphrased along these lines. "Make sure to eat and drink in a discerning way, which means to communicate amongst yourselves in forms that suit the reality that is the church. Doing so will avoid the self-inflicted and self-enacting judgment that brings disease and death (destroying the body in both senses of the word) and will put you in a position to genuinely meet the judgment that is due from God." In other words, what we have here is the call to a discerning life that understands its activities of discernment not as directed toward prophylactically heading off divine judgment, but as a giving up of those forms of human judgment that are self-inflicted and self-enacting.

This is to suggest that the discernment Paul is calling for is one that does not attempt to surmount the truth that genuine judgment is always God's. Such discernment reveals the Corinthians' activity as in fact a lack of discernment in that its intent is to anticipate or stave off God's judgment through practices of self-examination that preventatively speak judgment on their own selves. In sum, for Paul discernment is the form Christian life takes when continually leaving itself open to divine judgment.[51] To so live is to exist as a living antithesis to the culture of moral self-evaluation that essentially usurps divine judgment (however unwittingly). If discerning is an openness to the ongoing judgment of the Lord, which always entails the "setting right" of our ways, then this divine disciplining and setting right will enact judgments in an entirely different register from the judgment that will come through the human usurpation of divine judgment. Those en-

---

51. Bonhoeffer, "God's Love and the Disintegration of the World," in *Ethics* (DBWE 6), 319–26.

meshed in avoiding a final condemnation by some external power through a sustained culture of moral self-examination and self-judgment, however rigorous or pious it may be, will no more avoid the fitting judgments of their faith in their own activity than will unbelievers.

A Worldly Eucharist

> ³³ So then, my brothers and sisters, when you come together to eat, wait for one another. ³⁴ If you are hungry, eat at home, so that when you come together, it will not be for your condemnation. About the other things I will give instructions when I come.

Paul is determined eventually to eradicate the pathogen that is killing the Corinthian church. But for the time being he concludes this chapter with the concession that the pressures creating drunkenness for some and hunger for others ought to be immediately addressed with a pragmatic measure: **If you are hungry, eat at home, so that when you come together, it will not be for your condemnation.** To this concession he adds that there is more to be said that is not appropriate for inclusion in a public letter: about these **other things**, Paul says, **I will give instructions when I come.** In a future unforeseeable to the Apostle the problem presented to the Corinthian church by the intersection of the forces of patronage culture and domestic architecture would be resolved by the building of basilicas—buildings whose design was oriented around serving the worship of the church rather than the dinner parties of wealthy Roman citizens. But at this point in time Paul thinks it wisest not publicly to rebuke the patron, demanding, perhaps, that he knock down his walls to create a single dining area for the eucharistic feast.

As the story was to unfold that begins in this chapter, what would eventually become clear is that the tensions between the physical arrangement of space and the corporate life that was to be lived out in it were in fact building up a Christian sensibility that the church's worship exerts a pressure for the space in which it happens be *theologically* ordered. We must therefore credit Paul with raising a rather profound and influential question: What is it about liturgical space that facilitates *the discerning of the body*? The sensibilities evoked among early Christians that this was an important question are evident in the fact that the first basilicas were not just big barns designed to hold more people than could fit into the stately home, nor were they all-purpose rooms in which the furniture could be cleared away for recreational activities. When they were built, it was not to address a pragmatic matter of accommodating greater numbers, but to express a richer theology of worship learned, not least, from 1 Corinthians.

We can credit the design of the earliest basilicas as an inheritance of the apostolic teaching of 1 Corinthians 11 in the sense that their very floor plan was theologically schematized. Many of the earliest churches were ordered around the font, with the rest of the space radiating out from it to yield a circular building in which everyone is equidistant from their source in baptism. As churches moved out of the stately homes of Hellenistic culture with their emphases on refined dining and the maintenance of social stratification, the effect was to codify Paul's closing pragmatic advice to "eat at home" by rendering it more of a practical necessity. With the movement of Christian gatherings out of the stately homes of rich patrons into the basilicas as unambiguously public places of worship, the problematics generated by the linkage of the Eucharist with communal meals that is acute in this chapter falls into the background, as the separation of the two activities eventually became the norm, for better or worse. This is not to suggest that the core problem Paul was targeting in this discussion of eucharistic community disappeared with the change of venue. The new cultural settings that came into existence in the era of Christendom only shifted the matrices for the discernment of the body that Paul enjoins in this chapter. When Christianity had become a mass phenomenon the sheer size of the new venues raised again with new urgency the question of celebrating the Eucharist in such a way as to correspond to the nature of the Church as a body in which every member is to be visible and visibly engaged.

In the end we must read chapter 11 as presenting a single thought: the Eucharist is not a subject for discussion in one particular sphere, but rather a point of culmination of the overall rationale that grounds the whole chapter. The chapter sets before our eyes the inescapable and perennial need for the Christian church to negotiate decorum in the light of the gospel's reign. Paul's emphasis that eucharistic practice is but a mode of proclaiming Christ's death presses the church continually to grapple with the challenge of the materiality of the Christian life. The two parts of the chapter must thus be understood as expressing a single imperative: "Don't give in to any form of spiritualizing belief in the surmounting of the creaturely condition of Christian existence in the world (as exemplified in hairstyling or eating)." The Christian life always finds itself within a given host culture and is never in a position to invent its own conditions of life from scratch, not even by developing into a "Christian culture" or "Christendom." The task of negotiating the logics of cultural decorum and the reconciling gospel is always a messy one; such discernment does not expect to arrive at permanent solutions or even long for timeless blueprints for such solutions.

Instead, it requires patience and the willingness to formulate *ad hoc* solutions and venture provisional judgments in attention to the law of Jesus's reign. Given the complicated yet modest nature of this task of continually negotiating the way of the gospel around ever changing sets of local and temporal standards of decorum, we easily understand the multiform drift in the history of Christian thought to circumvent these negotiations by seeking a more stable grounding. But we now also understand why Paul portrays this as a temptation.

Recall Aquinas's defense of the shaved heads of nuns. Women who let their hair down in worship in Corinth did so, we saw, because they might have felt themselves "beyond sex." Aquinas's reading of this chapter presented a curious parallel in explicitly stating that women who have become brides of Christ "are elevated to the status of men" and so are also beyond sex. In light of the whole chapter, though, our analysis of Paul's argument has suggested that either form of such spiritual transcendence of the creaturely bounds of human sexed existence amounts to forgetting that in the Eucharist we "proclaim Christ's *death*," that aspect of Christ's passion which most sharply exposes the materiality of the Eucharist, and with it of all creaturely relations (>15:1–50).

Notice also that Aquinas's discussion is not limited to hair, but moves out into wider circles of material culture by considering the habit that covers the nun's shaved head. Habits and uniforms are meant to release those who wear them from having to negotiate the question of decorum that organizes human societies. Because nuns and monks are really citizens of heaven, the logic goes, they can wear the same clothes in every society. They are freed from the cultural requirement to think about which fashion trends are appropriate and which are not. Luther's rather harsh dismissal of that form of life as parasitic and arrogant[52] is probably unfair as a sweeping judgment on the monastic tradition as a whole, but it points to a very real temptation for every period. The spiritualizing urge can be extended through many individual features of the monastic ideal that seem to be principled ways of avoiding the necessity of negotiating decorum: the "self-sustaining" ideal of the monasteries allows an escape from the contaminated sphere of commerce, for instance. Thus, the challenge of negotiating secular space can be circumvented by living within walls. Political negotiation can be avoided with rules and vows of obedience, and the decorum of conversation with vows of silence. As the rich literary tradition of reflecting on these problems in Christian monastic culture certainly indicates, Christian monasticism

---

52. Circular disputation on Matt 19:21, "Concerning the Three Hierarchies" (1539), in WA 39II:39–91. See also Bayer, *Luther's Theology*, 296–99.

cannot finally be judged simply a form of escapism. Yet the question remains critical as to when and to what extent the eschatological exception from the necessity to negotiate local cultures itself threatens to become a culture. Nor do we have to look far to observe strands of Protestant Christianity that are attracted to the avoidance of church-world negotiation. One powerful contemporary attempt along these lines is visible in evangelical and charismatic communities that go so far as to attempt a "world-free" parallel Christian culture with its own separate schools, music and clothing industry,[53] even civil communities and towns.[54]

Does a more this-worldly Protestantism exist that displays more substantive resources for resisting this evasion of cultural negotiation? Where would we look to see a Protestant Christianity whose eucharistic practice anchors a form of life that "proclaims Christ's death"? As just indicated, it is easy enough to spot forms of Protestantism that revel in the proclamation of Christ "until he comes" and that have very little entrée into whether or how the church, *as* church, might name and resist the patterns of decorum that stratify and separate. Protestants, especially cultural Protestants who take the progress of culture to be a prime mark of the church's influence and effect on it, have often ended up refusing critically to negotiate the decorum of their societies in precisely the opposite way to the monastic culture: by deciding largely to embrace the given decorum of their time. In this vein, living out a gospel that is all about the "resurrection" *rather than* the "death" of Jesus Christ renders discussions of material culture a tangential concern. The freedom of the gospel is presumed to be best ensured not by attending to the material practices that shame and place barriers in the church, but by "mental operations" that keep intentions pure and minds elevated. Here eucharistic practice is considered "commemorative" in the sense of being disconnected from the material and cultural matrix within which any local church celebrates it. Nevertheless, to believe that the Lord's Supper is protected by "introspection and repentance" rather than by discerning the material and cultural habits by which the decorum of our age presses to impregnate our eucharistic practice means that Christians will

---

53. Christian clothing stores like C28 very well grasp that clothing "preaches" and explicitly present their wares as exploiting this possibility (http://www.c28.com/message.asp). The contemporary Christian music business more often implicitly draws on an anti-contamination logic, as do many of the most popular rationales given for running Christian schools.

54. Interestingly, the most recent attempt along these lines is Roman Catholic in inspiration. The town of Ave Maria in Florida is a new-build town centered around a Roman Catholic church and university and follows the template for such "concept towns" embodied in Celebration, Florida, an earlier Disney experiment along the same lines.

eventually "shame those who have nothing"—as did the rich patrons in the Corinthian church.

Admittedly, there is a degree of irony if we put the parallels between Protestant and Catholic traditions in these terms, since the structural proximities we have drawn out are easily veiled by surface dissimilarities. But structurally speaking, what unites the usually opposed groups of culturally liberal Christians and evangelical Protestants does indeed appear to be their attraction to what we have described as the patriarchal-caste misreading of the Eucharist. The opposite pole seems to be inhabited by another pair of groups also not often presumed to travel together, the hyper-feminine prophetesses in Corinth and nuns in habits. In sum, if today cultural Protestantism recapitulates the segregation the rich were introducing into Corinthian worship by dismissing the importance of Christian criticism of contemporary culture on theological grounds, the Roman conception of monasticism recapitulates the charismatic problem of "loose hair."[55] Thus does our detour to consider Paul's discussion in its significance for a variety of historical contexts come round in a surprising way to offer us a handle on the otherwise perplexing equation Paul makes in this very chapter between "letting their hair down" and "shaving their heads."

The ironic sense in which the farthest poles of phenotypically opposed phenomena appear under theological scrutiny to be two variants of the same misunderstanding prepares the ground for an unambiguous and highly important concluding insight. Precisely because they are ceaseless proclaimers "of the Lord's death until he comes" Christians cannot join the ranks of the cultural warriors for whom Christianity is equated with the rise or fall of some generally defined cultural package, such as "family values" or "Judeo-Christian morality." They cannot because they know the task of negotiating the decorum regime that rules their own time under the reign of the gospel, never ends. One generation's gospel inspired defense of "family values" (against infanticide, as in early Cristian centuries, for instance) can in another be tied up with all sorts of idolatries (such as the contemporary fetish for a "wanted, genetic child").

---

55. In one of his characteristically provocative long footnotes Stanley Hauerwas enters the discussion of the necessity of negotiating culture by discussing the differences between Protestant and Roman Catholic kitsch. While taking the line we do that "Protestantism more reflects a culture than creates a culture," he is also keen to emphasize that there are more bodily strands of Catholicism than the one we have highlighted in our discussion. "I am sure little hangs on rosaries in plastic eggs, but that Catholic hospitals continue to bury fetuses of early miscarriages is a practice that I suspect, if lost, would change the character of Catholic theology." Hauerwas, *Sanctify Them in the Truth*, 165 n. 16.

To refer to a contemporary dispute to which we will return in later chapters, the interminable arguments in the contemporary church about music styles in worship do not reach the level of a genuine *church* dispute as long as they merely recapitulate the world's perplexities and battle lines over the divide between classical and popular music, carried out by people holding church membership cards. What eucharistic existence affords, in contrast, is a genuine sense of utopia, a non-place that is, however, still within the confines of a world defined by competing cultural claims.[56] This principled refuge from the powerful absorption that cultural wars represent is the very opposite, structurally and pastorally, of attempts to create a place that allows Christians to exist outside the need to negotiate the claims laid upon them by the gospel and their particular cultural situatedness.

We conclude with a final integrative insight. Understood in its fullest breadth and scope, the summons to "wait for one another" can be understood as the core invitation held out by the chapter as a whole. We read this exhortation as going beyond the narrow claim that the immediate context obviously suggests that would run something like, "if the poor cannot get here before 7 p.m., don't start before then." Paul seems insistent that *waiting* for one another has a substantial theological weightiness, an insistence that we suspect is intimately connected with several discussions of the problems of the relations of the weak and strong that recur in this letter. The self-confessed strong are those who cannot wait for the weak to arrive at the insight that the strong claim for themselves. Nor can the spiritualist women who have transcended sex wait for the rest of the congregation, including the male constituency, to fully embrace the new reality of brotherhood and sisterhood. Because they cannot wait they subvert the body by loosing an invasive sexual subtext. The rich do not wait for their meal in order that those who live in a dangerous proximity to all sorts of bodily threat, those already or potentially disabled, may join them. What is missing in each case is a discernment prepared to wait so that the differences in pace that are due to all can be taken into account in practice. This is why *discernment* is the determining term in situating Paul's aim to teach the community to seek *peace*, a living together in harmony. This peace has an order, the order not of subordination, but one that arises from fine grained discernments about the needs, capacities and cultural sensitivities of each individual in the community.

Paul's summons "wait" in 11:33 is thus understood as enjoining waiting in order to genuinely discern the body. This would suggest that in 11:34 he is going one step further, a step that is in a different sense also a step

---

56. Wannenwetsch, "Representing the Absent in the City."

back. His pragmatic suggestion offers a discernment about how this waiting might be concretely carried out in the context of the Corinthian eucharistic predicament generated by the *domos* decorum of Hellenistic culture. At the same time the advice to "eat at home" will suggest a rather incoherent string of messages if read as again dematerializing the church by saying that eating together is not a genuine part of Christian worship—eventually leading to a principled decoupling of table fellowship and eucharistic fellowship. What would be left after such a misreading are only a few broken bits of the host as a residue of the very materiality of a social unity of the church.

It might therefore be best to read 11:34a–b very strictly in the light of 34c, **I will give instructions when I come**. The NRSV strikes the wrong note with its **about the other things,** τὰ δὲ λοιπὰ (*ta de loipa*), which actually means "further instructions forthcoming" and so marks the advice in 11:34a–b as of a provisional nature. This rendering sets up the following reading: "live with this advice for the time being, though it might be too high a price to pay in the longer run for a church that has come to terms with the reality that Eucharist is not a private affair. This is a pragmatic rather than programmatic advice, which I will deal with more directly when I, Paul, come in person." Paul intends when he comes in person to explore in further concrete detail what the one principle of waiting for one another might entail for the Corinthians. This would likely be accomplished in face-to-face discussions in which a pastoral coming alongside various believers could be modeled that is both discerning and directive, designed to avoid embarrassing the protagonists while at the same time highlighting the specific concerns of individuals within those affecting the body as a whole.

1 Corinthians 12

Where does the nub of the Corinthians' resistance to the divine working to establish a community of peace finally lie? The overarching purpose of this chapter is to help the Corinthians to grasp the transformed social reality into which they have been called through Christ's reconciliatory work as "brothers and sisters." By creatively reshaping an ancient tradition of describing political life through images of the human body, Paul develops the famous image of the church as the body of Christ in order to communicate with the Corinthians the deleterious effects of their tendency to try to arrange the social body on their own terms. In their misguided attempts to do so they overlook and resist the composition of the body already bestowed by the Trinitarian God.

Paul's main thrust as he emphasizes the non-negotiable reality that is the human physical body is to summon the church to embrace the pneumatological reality of which they have been made part through God's abundant gifting. More precisely, Paul describes for the Corinthians the features he thinks they should expect to find in a functioning church: one characterized by intense sympathetic connections between its members that allow each directly to register the events experienced by any other individual member. Each believer is to be discovering how their own wellbeing is intimately tied to the receipt of the divine gifts given to the church through every believer. As a close examination of Paul's argument will reveal, the image of the body is offered not as a rhetorical strategy by which Paul can draw the Corinthians from the territory of known knowledge (physical organism) into the unknown (spiritual body), but as a finely tuned criticism and restructuring of their current habits of relating to one another as believers.

The flow of chapter 12 is best grasped if we first note the unusually high number of references to divine action. God is described as energizing (6, 11), giving gifts (7, 8) and honoring (24) as he wills (11), placing (18, 24) and appointing (28) the church's members into their proper relationships. This emphasis on the precedence of divine over human action is combined with the imagery of the church as a living body to yield yet another highly instructive displacement of the language of moralism ("you really should not say things like that to other believers") with a quite different theological account of communication in the church.

1 Corinthians 12

Clearing the Spiritual Haze

> ¹Now concerning spiritual gifts, brothers and sisters, I do not want you to be uninformed. ²You know that when you were pagans, you were enticed and led astray to idols that could not speak. ³Therefore I want you to understand that no one speaking by the Spirit of God ever says "Let Jesus be cursed!" and no one can say "Jesus is Lord" except by the Holy Spirit.

It is plausible to hear in Paul's opening expression another response to a question that has arisen in previous communication with the Corinthians: **Now concerning** [περὶ δὲ/*peri de*] **spiritual gifts**. It is worth pausing to consider the linguistic detail that the Greek here has no noun, but only the adjective "spiritual." The underdetermined nature of this expression gives us a hint at the purpose of Paul's following discussion, which aims to clear up the fogginess about "all that spiritual stuff" he detects wafting about the Corinthian community. Paul will soon speak in a very precise way about the *charismata*, the "gifts" of the Spirit to the body. He does so, however, not simply as a lesson on their operation, but as at the same time a critical engagement with the wider anthropological and cosmological presumptions of his addressees about what may be appropriately deemed spiritual or not.

The expression **brothers and sisters, I do not want you to be uninformed** has a formulaic quality that we have encountered before. Identical wordings appear in 10:1 and 2 Cor 1:8. Later in the discussion it will transpire that what Paul is emphasizing by repeating this introductory expression is especially closely tied to the character of his apostolic mission as a divine offer of certainty to his churches. This is *paraklesis*; exhorting consolation, or consoling exhortation about the activity of the Trinitarian God and his provision to his people of everything that they need to live in faithfulness to the gospel. In the light of this particular apostolic mission, to offer certainty to the churches, the translation **I do not want you to be** uninformed seems remarkably unspecific. As his address to the Corinthians as brothers and sisters demonstrates, Paul is consoling and exhorting them by setting before them the reality already imparted to them. Yet this reality is not one that they can or need to be informed about; what they need is a reminder of their divinely given and assigned place within that reality. The critical undertone in ἀγνοεῖν (*agnoein*), translated as "uninformed" in the NRSV, puts the emphasis not so much on a deficit of knowledge understood as a package that one can possess by degrees, but rather on the status or situation of the person in danger of being deformed by his or her attachment to a knowledge that lacks not in degrees, but in truth.

Paul's three uses of the phrase **I do not want you to be uninformed** in the Corinthian correspondence nicely displays the three registers of awareness he wishes to foster amongst the believers of the divine working that is already in operation. In 10:1 he stresses that they are already, with *Israel*, led by one and the same *God*; here in 12:1 he opens a line of instruction in learning to discern the *Spirit's* action in which they are already participants; finally, in 2 Corinthians 1:8 he elaborates the insight that they need to see the reality of these divine activities within their local community as embodied in the Apostle's sufferings that convey a sense of what it means to say that the sufferings of the church are participation in Christ's sufferings.[1] In this chapter Paul is sensitive to the danger of letting there be any appearance that he is offering a treatise on "spirituality" separable from the Trinitarian divine activity, which would make it impossible for genuine spiritual activity to be discerned and so truthfully apprehended.

After having announced that he will provide the Corinthians with what they need to know about spiritual matters in 12:1, verse 4, **Now there are varieties of gifts, but the same Spirit**, would seem organically to follow. Why then does Paul seem to disturb this flow by inserting verses 2 and 3? These verses seem especially obscure, given his opening, which speaks of idols and a strange anti-confession, **"Let Jesus be cursed!"** We may begin to understand why this apparent detour is necessary for Paul if we recall the indeterminate opening expression of 12:1: "spiritual things." If the Corinthians are to be properly informed about the Holy Spirit's ways they will first have to be helped to unlearn and overcome concepts of the spiritual that characterized their life **when [they] were pagans**. Paul needs to engage with the "spirituality" of their previous existence precisely because for him there cannot be an easy equation of "Christian" and "spiritual." His whole treatment of the question aims instead at fostering discernment or discrimination between different spirits (>12:10).

A first step in fostering this discrimination is to begin to set out the rival operational patterns of those spirits. 12:2 characterizes the spirit at work in pagan idol worship as manipulative and silencing at its core: **you were enticed and led astray to idols that could not speak**. The translation "enticed" is a relatively tame rendering of ἀπαγόμενοι (*apagomenoi*); this passive participle form of the verb ἀπάγω (*apagō*) indicates the experience of rapture, being dragged or swept away by an irresistibly powerful force

---

1. "In other words ... the body of Christ could only function as such if the words and actions which purported to be charisms actually expressed the character of Christ's free act of grace on the cross—enacted in the strength of that grace, without selfish subplot, in service to God and for the benefit of others." Dunn, *Theology of Paul the Apostle*, 559.

in a manner characteristic of the variety of ecstatic cults common in the Hellenistic Corinthian environment. Paul's discussion of the ways of the Holy Spirit will develop several contrasts with Hellenistic expectations about the workings of the spirits, the most important being the tendencies of demonic Spirits to draw the whole body into a single sensory realm, whether that of the eye, the nose, the ear, or any other sense. One way of characterizing idol worship in the ecstatic cults of the Hellenistic culture of the day would be to draw attention to their tendency to draw participants into an all absorbing sensual experience conducted in a powerful register, whether it be a visually irresistible feast that made them "all eye," a wall of drum sounds that turned them "all ear," or the irresistible flurry of tactile experiences on offer from temple prostitutes.[2]

Paul associates these irresistible colorful, loud, and verbose pagan cults with muteness. While the image of the mute idol is a stock image in Israel's polemic tradition (Ps 115; Hab 2:18–19), Paul unpacks this tradition with the Hellenistic cults in view with which his gentile readers would be more familiar. These clamorous cults, he says, lack genuine communication because they are organized not by *call* and response but by a ritual that *demands* response because of its irresistible presentation. The first contrast between the spirits and the Spirit, Paul suggests in 12:3, is that the Spirit of God opens *communication*. In the cults there is no back and forth, and therefore no communication, but in the Spirit of Jesus Christ the Christian deity speaks in such a way as to invite genuine communicative response—in the form of a confession. The two rival confessions presented in 12:3 suggest that we must also reckon with idolatrous confessions in which idol worship mimics the communicative dimension of genuine worship by manipulating its participants into forms of life that boil down to the anti-confession **"Let Jesus be cursed!"**

While we will later reflect on implicit ways in which this anti-confession is made, its bald propositional form is best known in the context of Christian exorcism, when the demon that possesses the human sufferer curses Jesus and is resisted by the exorcist with the most primitive Christian claim of all, **"Jesus is Lord."** By drawing attention to this clash of confessions, Paul sets the discussion to follow within the framework of a battle between rival spirits. This indicates yet again why Paul is so keen to remind the Corinthian Christians that their having been claimed for Christ can only be described by an account of the spiritual that is Trinitarian in

---

2. On the problem of a "total" sensory immersion and its characteristic denial of the synaesthetic dimension of human sensuality (when individual sensory perceptions are mediated with one another) as a prime condition for human freedom, see Wannenwetsch, "Plurale Sinnlichkeit."

essence. There is no Christian spirituality to be had in abstraction from the gifts given by the Father through the Spirit of Jesus Christ the Son. This framing of the spiritual import of confessions gives us insight into why, later on in his unfolding of the body metaphor, Paul confronts various confessions by believers that set up rival forms of communication or resist it altogether. Significantly, he will do so in a way that transcends the issuing of merely moral injunctions.

Upbuilding Gifts of an Active Spirit

> ⁴Now there are varieties of gifts, but the same Spirit; ⁵and there are varieties of services, but the same Lord; ⁶and there are varieties of activities, but it is the same God who activates all of them in everyone. ⁷To each is given the manifestation of the Spirit for the common good.

The terms **gifts, services,** and **activities** are now set out in order to develop a supple threefold characterization of the gifts of the Spirit. Before discussing these types individually and the relationships between them, attending to a translation difficulty will give us a provisional indicator of the thrust of Paul's argument. The NRSV translates εἰσίν (*eisin*) as **there are**, which leads the reader to ask questions about the existence of these gifts. This in turn evokes a reading that makes the reader assume that Paul is speaking of three different phenomena. But how could a gift of the Spirit be categorically different from "service" or "efficient power"? Given the flow of Paul's discussion as a whole, it seems obvious that the triadic expression explicates one and the same phenomenon, the spiritual gift, with the triad also apparently providing a hint that a Trinitarian account of the gifts will soon follow.[3]

Paul's main point is that unless it takes the form of actually enacted service, a gift ought not to be associated with the Spirit of Christ at all. By understanding the three expressions as a variegated description of a single phenomenon we are prepared to embrace the perspicuity of Luther's decision to render *eisin* in German simply as *es sind*. In other words, Paul is not beginning an abstract discussion of spiritual gifts that exist "somewhere" but instead is emphasizing the reality of divine provisions that are *already*

---

3. Conzelmann (*1 Corinthians*, 207–8) discusses verses 4–6 in a manner that on the basis of textual analysis arrives at a similar conclusion to the one drawn on theological grounds by Athanasius: "What the Spirit gives to each individual is furnished by the Father through the Word. For everything that belongs to the Father belongs also to the Son. Thus the **spiritual gifts** given by the Son in the Spirit are gifts of the Father. And when the Spirit is in us, the Word who gives the Spirit is also in us, and the Father is in the Word." *Letter to Serapion* 1.30, PG 26:597–600; 3.5–6, PG 26:633, in JK, 200.

present among the very congregation he addresses, present that they may be (more) firmly apprehended and enacted. In so doing Paul again explicitly refutes the Corinthians' hankerings to acquire a set of gifts that can "exist" and can therefore be considered options between which they might choose, ideal talents they might aspire to develop.

It is a well-attested fact that the concept of *charismata* is, if not unique, at least prominent in Paul's theology in a way that distinguishes him among the writers of his age. He can therefore legitimately be labeled the inventor of the Christian concept of the "spiritual gift." *Charisma* occurs only once in the New Testament outside the Pauline corpus, and is extremely rarely used even in extra-biblical literature of the time. The term itself, *charis-ma*, "denotes the result of gracious giving (*charizesthai*, 'give graciously')."[4] The relative novelty and unusual character of this category of *charisma* explains why Paul feels the need to explain in some detail the phenomenon he denotes by it, and he does so by adding these two further descriptors.

We are on safe ground assuming that *diakonia* was as well understood a term in the early church (as "service") as it is today. In a modern context, however, the term *energēma* is almost incomprehensible. Based on the root *energia*, "power," the best translation is probably "efficient power." An efficient power is like the radiating light of the sun that is continually at work as it effectively warms the earth. Such a dynamic, actively working power is to be distinguished from the vast energy that resides within the sun but has not yet emerged from its inner furnace as photons and radiating energy. Paul characterizes the gifts of the Spirit as like the warming rays of the sun, always at work, and never merely a potency that might or might not become activated. The implications of his adding this term to his discussion of the gifts cannot be overstated: spiritual gifts only *are* in the *enactment*. They are gifts because God *has* in fact given them, as opposed to the idea of God's unseen desires to bestow them at some future date. The NRSV translation is thus conceptually unintelligible in speaking of a **variety of activities** that God **activates**. A more suitable translation would speak of a variety of enacted powers, God being at work in every one. Within Paul's account it is improper to characterize God as a the one who has "preloaded" humans with powers that might be accessed by activating one's God-given potential; God always remains the originator of the actual efficient powers that are at work in all their variety in the Christian church.

In characterizing the gifts of the Spirit in this threefold way Paul has set out the parameters within which all further elaborations of the Spirit's work in this chapter will unfold. Within these parameters he has the leverage

---

4. Dunn, *Theology of Paul the Apostle*, 553.

he needs to overturn rival Hellenistic modes of perception within which spiritual gifts would be likely to be conceptualized among the Corinthians. If we attend to Paul's critique we discover a dual background that shaped their understanding of the spiritual. First, he resists a tendency to locate the spiritual in the sphere of extra-human powers "out there"—the world of demons, ghosts, and spirits. Second, he exposes the ill-fated influence of Greek anthropological traditions with the Corinthians, in which it was presumed that a pneumatic dimension was a faculty of the human being. Even when conceived as a human faculty, however, the πνεῦμα (*pneuma*) was typically configured according to the logic of the first background conceptuality, as that aspect of the human closest to the extra human, the "near divine" part of humanity. Paul's approach overcomes these Hellenistic frameworks by categorically disassociating manifestations of the Spirit of God from what we may call a phenomenological proximity to the spiritual world "out there." To learn to perceive the work of the Holy Spirit as the bond of the community is, happily, to have the misperception fall away that there are more and less "spiritual" gifts of the one Spirit. We can see this logic at work in two related moves Paul makes in 12:8–10. He first elevates gifts that at first glance seem to stand at the opposite pole from the spiritual realm, pedestrian activities such as service and organization. These gifts, Paul suggests, are no less spiritual than those typically associated with the spiritual realm by virtue of characteristic features such as excitement or paranormality. And with a move that is characteristically bold, given the Corinthian context, Paul then dethrones and decenters the phenotypically ecstatic spiritual gifts such as prophecy by placing them in a much longer and more diverse list of gifts.

His positioning of the gift of prophecy offers a particularly instructive example in this respect. Placing it in a prominent position on his first list of gifts (12:8), Paul nevertheless makes sure that his hearers do not conflate its importance as a *charisma* with the mistaken idea that its importance lies in it more directly mediating the transcendent into the immanent sphere. For Paul prophesying ranks as a Christian *charisma* only when prepared peacefully to coexist with all the others, whether high or low on the list. What is more, prophesying, for all its natural ambition to be spiritual, is only recognizable as a *charisma* if it is deployed in a manner that embraces the other gifts, including the associated gift of assessing what the prophets speak (a theme that will come into the foreground in chapter 14). It is characteristic of Paul's account that gifts such as prophesying or speaking in tongues that our instincts, informed by a philosophy of religion organized around the features of *fascinosum* and *tremendum*, would immediately recognize as spiritual (as in Rudolph Otto's *The Idea of the Holy*), are teamed up with other seemingly more pedestrian gifts such as discerning and interpreting, which ensure that the former gifts are recognized as varieties of service, and so properly gifts of the Spirit.

The teleology of *charisma* is nicely summarized in the phrase **for the common good** in 12:7. Boldly, yet accurately, the NRSV shows itself sympathetic to the political thrust of Paul's discussion here by using the political coinage "common good" to translate συμφέρον (*sympheron*) "that which is useful," putting on display the essential orientation of the gifts to the good that they bring into the body. This political thrust is obscured, however, in the rendering of *phanerōsis* as **manifestation**, a generic word making no reference to any divine agency. The Greek term, in contrast, literally means "revelation," and places emphasis on the divine working in all sorts of human affairs.

This offers us an exciting and challenging insight within our political rendering. If **every membe**r of the body is not merely a possessor of a portion of the respective gift allotted to him or her through the respective *charisma*, but is rather a *revealer* of the Spirit to the body as a whole, then there can be no central agency that administers the Spirit, arranging and re-arranging the spiritual body. The Spirit alone is the arranger of the gifts that make up the different parts of the body. This notion of revealing is closely connected to the moment of discovery. If respective fruits of the Spirit are meant to reveal the Spirit to the body, we must speak in terms of a *moment of discovery*, since a revelation is never merely a deposit that can be known in advance but is an actual happening, an instance of recognition and reception. A *charisma* thus reveals the Holy Spirit to the body as each respective gift is embraced as God's gift. This is why the gifts are *energēma*—always *enacted* and always needing to be *discerned* in real time.

Such moments of revelation in the embrace of a particular gift might occur in the life of young Christians, for instance, when members of the body help them to discover their proper places and roles in the community. Should a shy teenager be given some form of leadership role in a church's youth work, the discovery of her unique gift to the body as a whole will typically be prepared by an initial tentative grasp of that gift by those who encourage her to step forward in order to allow the full *phanerosis* of the gift to appear. We may also expect moments of the Spirit's revealing new gifts through those whose gifts to the community have been long established, say in a particular ecclesiastical office. The question in such a case then turns on whether the community is prepared to expect to learn new things from the old man, or whether they will rather tie him down to those true insights of his that he so helpfully shared with them in the past.

The significance of Paul's use of a plurality of descriptors for the one phenomenon he wishes the Corinthians to understand can be grasped when asking how the relationship between the *energēmata* and social roles plays out in the concrete life of the Christian church. On one hand, Paul's characterization of spiritual gifts in terms of efficient power reminds his readers that there is no spiritual gift except one that actually *happens*. Yet this emphasis on efficient power, if taken on its own, could not make sense of the more settled political reality indicated by the official ministries of the church. Again, taken on its own, the *energēma* dimension of spiritual gifts could be thought of as a bilateral phenomenon between two people, such as the healer and the healed one. But such an example displays why there is no single *charisma* in the church that is not at the same time political. Paul makes this point unmistakable with his use of the term *diakonia*, denoting service *to others* and combining it with an emphasis on the Spirit's self-revelation *to others* in those gifts.

When we grasp that the notion of *charisma* inevitably designates an enacted and so extant political reality we will understand what was to develop in the subsequent tradition of the Christian churches: the public and formal recognition of enacted gifts. The recognition and embrace of spiritual gifts has been routinized in a range of ways by Christian communities through the centuries, from mere grateful willingness to be on the receiving side of enacted *charismata* to more formal procedures of ecclesial recognition linked to specific codified roles within the community—up to the full development of conceptually and practically elaborated ecclesial offices. In terms of the list of *charismata* that Paul presents in 12:28–30 (which varies somewhat from the list in 8–10), we can assume that in his day certain gifts like those of apostles, prophets, and teachers had already become more or less established as formal offices (1 Tim 3:8–10). Elsewhere in the New Testament we even have a biblical report of the gift of service developing into the full-fledged office of the deacon (Acts 6).

This close reading of Paul helps us to break the stalemate between defenders of charismatic ministry and those who define ministry as "office bearing."[5] To do so we need to insist that the gifts of the Spirit are always to be understood in terms of their dual designation as *energēma* and *diakonia*. It is this dual designation that helps to resist the unhelpful dichotomy modern theology has inherited between a "charismatic" church emphasizing the fruits of the Spirit and a "formalized" church organized around certain established offices. Against this dichotomy we understand Paul's emphasis to be, on the one hand, that both *diakonia* and *energēma* designate qualities *of*

---

5. A particularly sophisticated version of this debate occurred around the turn to the 20th century between Rudolf Sohm and Adolf von Harnack, influencing subsequent sociological accounts of ecclesiastical and political leadership, most notably Max Weber's. See Adair-Toteff, *Fundamental Concepts*.

the Spirit. On the other, Paul seems capable of anticipating some legitimate concerns that cropped up in those later debates in presenting a duality that supplies the church with a theological conceptuality that allows for self-correction. Any one-sided emphasis on *energēma* that wishes to identify the workings of the Spirit with its actual efficient, palpable, and powerful manifestations, needs to be reminded of the political dimension of receipt and valorization by a church rightly concerned that gifts serve others. The critical power of this duality of designators is its capacity critically to work in either direction depending on the circumstances. This seems an important reminder, especially for the structurally differentiated and administered churches of our day in which the temptation seems ever present to assume the holder of an office will automatically manifest the gift that his or her particular ministry represents independently of the power and surprising activity of the Spirit. For those churches, on the other hand, that put all the emphasis on the latter, Paul's dual designator of gifts will serve as a wholesome reminder that this emphasis, when left unbalanced, will be likely to promote structures and power-relations in the congregation that easily become autocratic in eschewing any role for orderly procedures.

Allocated to Each, for the Whole

> ⁸To one is given through the Spirit the utterance of wisdom, and to another the utterance of knowledge according to the same Spirit, ⁹to another faith by the same Spirit, to another gifts of healing by the one Spirit, ¹⁰to another the working of miracles, to another prophecy, to another the discernment of spirits, to another various kinds of tongues, to another the interpretation of tongues. ¹¹All these are activated by one and the same Spirit, who allots to each one individually just as the Spirit chooses.

In the list of *charismata* we find in 12:8–10, a triad not unlike the threefold designation of 12:4–6 is deployed to situate the readers's understanding of the working patterns of the Spirit. Here Paul varies the use of the prepositions by which he identifies the agency of the Holy Spirit in the giving of the gifts. The three prepositions employed are **through**, διά (*dia*, 8a), **in accordance with**, κατά (*kata*, 8b), and **in**, ἐν (*en*, 9a and 9b, unhelpfully translated as **by** in the NRSV). Assuming that this is more than a mere rhetorical variation of terms, what might be the theological significance of this variety of prepositional characterizations of the Spirit's agency?

We do not think it too farfetched to detect here a proto-conciliar pneumatology employing different expressions in order to ward off potential misunderstandings that might arise in conjunction with each respective previous expression. "Through the Spirit" might all too easily be misread in terms of a merely instrumental role for the Spirit conceived as making no personal contribution to the divine life and serving only as a vehicle of the working of the other Trinitarian persons. "In the Spirit," while usefully correcting the latter misunderstanding, might be seen as still prone to sliding into a dynamist understanding in which (to employ a later term) the Spirit is conceived not as a divine *person* but as impersonal *power*. This impression might receive in turn a salutary correction with the preposition *kata*. The expression "in accordance with" occurs elsewhere in scripture but in Paul's writings in particular, most often to indicate that a given person stands in the line of an earlier author such as an evangelist or a tradition. All of these uses presume the Spirit acts personally and in accordance with other persons and is not simply a power.

We think it theologically legitimate to read Paul in the light of later doctrinal disputes whose conceptual distinctions can help us to see subtleties in his writing otherwise easily overlooked. The immediate problem that Paul's triple use of prepositional expressions helps him to clear up is the Corinthians' conceptual confusion regarding the way "spiritualities" have shaped their common life. The clarification presented in these verses is therefore an invitation for them more fully to embrace the particular gift that is his main interest here, namely, spiritual discernment. Paul's emphasis on the multitude of gifts is not an attempt to scoop all sorts of happenings and powers into an undefined catch-all account of the Spirit. Rather, the three prepositional expressions provide the confused Corinthians with a precise and detailed picture of the Spirit's workings: "through the Spirit" ensures they understand the Spirit as originator and giver of gifts that can only be understood as spiritual if they are enacted in such a way as to help their bearer to remain inside (Gk. ἐν) the reign of the Spirit and "in keeping" with the traditional witness of the particularity of the Spirit's ways. The Spirit is, after all, part of a Trinity of persons who have made themselves known through the workings of this same Spirit. The task of discernment rests on understanding how the activity of the third person of the Trinity reveals things that are genuinely new, but never novel or arbitrary.

This second, more developed enumeration of *charismata* is rhythmically structured by a repetitive use of **to another**, ἄλλῳ (*allō*). What is special, unique, and individual about each gift is not merely an expression of qualities held by their individual bearers; it rather lies, Paul insists, in the distinct apportioning of individual gifts to those individual persons **as the**

Spirit chooses (12:11). The individuating agent is the Spirit alone. Even if we affirm that the individual allocation of gifts is a way of honoring the configuration of the human person as an *individuum*, an indivisible whole, we must still resist the conclusion that the individuality of the person is the root of the distinctiveness of the charismata. Following this route would send us down the blind alley of equating the spiritual gifts with natural talents.

Foregoing a detailed explanation of each entry in Paul's list of gifts,[6] our purposes here are best served by looking in more depth at one widely featured in the scriptural witness. This will allow us to demonstrate how the criteria that Paul offers for the discernment of gifts helps us to understand one exemplary gift. The most surprising entry on Paul's list, at least for Protestant readers, has to be **faith**. How can faith be featured on a list as one amongst many listed gifts when the same author elsewhere makes it the central criterion for salvation? While certainly a gift, is faith not rather a "gift of gifts" in establishing the Christian person's fundamental relationship with the Trinity? Furthermore, is faith not by definition the most intimate designator of the Christian's relationship with Christ? How then can it be called a "service" to others? Paul's characterization of any gift of the Spirit as entailing a *diakonic* dimension gets us moving in the right direction in reminding us that there is an aspect of faith that is for others rather than merely or even mainly *pro me*. This is underscored in the gospel narrative in which Jesus praises the acts of faith embodied in the friends of the crippled man who lower him through the roof to be healed by Jesus (Mark 5:19; Luke 2:4). How are we to understand this vicarious dimension of faith more precisely?

Thiselton sensitively grasps the vicarious dimension of faith when he explains: "this gift promotes an ebullient, robust, optimistic acceptance of God's sovereign love and mercy in such a way as to put heart into a troubled church in times of uncertainty."[7] But we would suggest that the vicarious faith Paul is indicating cannot depend in this way on the larger-than-life person of faith whose forward-looking optimism acts as a "morale booster" for those who find it harder to see the light at the end of the tunnel. Vicarious faith as a gift of the Spirit is better understood in terms of a special sort of nerved connection with the body that allows its bearer to detect where faith in another member is beginning to wither. (We will return to the motif of nervous connection shortly, which we take to be central for Paul's account of the church as a body.) Those who are gifted with the distinct *charism* of

---

6. For a much more detailed survey of the discussions about the list of gifts, see Garland, DEG, 579–87.

7. Thiselton, ACT, 199.

faith, as differentiated from the gift of faith in every Christian, vicariously represent the single and foundational faith of the church especially towards, and on behalf of, those that struggle with their faith. In this representative function they might even be able to detect faith even in those who feel they have none or very little. To be clear, we are suggesting that what is different about this *charisma* is not that it establishes the existence of types or degrees of faith, but that one and the same faith can be afforded this different or special nervous connection to other members of the one body. In sum, we see in the example of this especially complex gift that every single gifting is precisely structured in the manner summed up in 12:7: **To each [individual] is given the manifestation of the Spirit for the common good.**

Paul's emphasis on the individual allocation of gifts, as expressed in 12:11, **by one and the same Spirit, who allots to each one individually just as the Spirit chooses**, has an even more intense ring in the Greek. What the NRSV renders as "to each one individually" is expressed with the adjective ἰδίᾳ (*idia*) that would be more literally translated "to each his or her *own*." *Idiōn* has a clear possessive overtone: either mine or yours and not immediately ours. Although the *telos* of each gift is what is **helpful to the body as a whole**, that gifted entirety is always routed through individual gifts to individual persons. The determining factor for the way in which the apportioning actually happens is expressed by Paul in a lapidary phrase, **just as the Spirit chooses**. What new is being indicated in this statement that the Spirit "allots"? Paul seems to find it necessary to make sure that the principle of allotment, the giving to each one what is due, is not being determined by any ideas or capacities that the recipient may possess—either by what she wants, or what her existing talents might seem to request—or the community that may find itself in need of a particular gift that they think God ought to fill by way of the specific person they have chosen for it.

We must be clear on what is apportioned here. Luther, for example, in his commentary on the Gospel of John, refers to this chapter in order to suggest that Paul is speaking of "a divided Spirit" in the community of *charisma*. Only in Christ, Luther declares, is the Spirit complete, whereas for the church this side of the heavenly city, the Spirit is given out in portions.[8] While we can sympathize with Luther's reason for taking this line—since the Spirit is in fact present in and to Christ in a different way than he is present in and for us—the Reformer still overlooks that the description in 12:11 of the Spirit allotting is not a reflexive. What the Spirit allots is not *herself* in small portions, but the *gifts* that come as specific allotments to their

---

8. "To other saints the Holy Spirit was apportioned in part; no one possesses the Holy Spirit wholly, not even Moses. To Christ alone the Holy Spirit is given completely." Luther, *Sermons of the Gospel of St. John, Chapters 1–4*, in LW 22:488–89.

individual bearers, for the third person of the Trinity cannot be divided in her self-giving. It is therefore crucial to understand that Paul's account of the *charismata* conceives the Spirit giving herself wholly in each gift through the individual to the body and as a whole, *toto*, albeit not exhaustively, *in tote*, to borrow a distinction employed in Christological discussion about the Eucharist from the reformation period.

Living into Bodily Being as Given

> ¹²For just as the body is one and has many members, and all the members of the body, though many, are one body, so it is with Christ. ¹³For in the one Spirit we were all baptized into one body—Jews or Greeks, slaves or free—and we were all made to drink of one Spirit.

In 12:12 Paul introduces his famous image of the body. The introductory expression καθάπερ γὰρ (*kathaper gar*), **For just as**, signifies that Paul has understood his argument up to this point as a preparation for the introduction of the organic imagery by which he will advance his instruction about spiritual things. It is striking that Paul turns to the physical sphere to overcome a confusion among the Corinthians about a realm they tended to locate at maximal distance from that sphere. Commentators have noted that Paul was by no means the first or last to invoke the organic image of the body to address the problem of political dissension.[9] Yet this must not cause us to overlook how counter-intuitive a move it is that Paul performs here as his way of clarifying what genuinely can count as spiritual.

It is all too easy to see this turn to an organic image as though it was Paul's attempt to begin his reasoning at a commonsense point of contact with Corinthian natural knowledge. After all, everyone has a body and is supposed to know how the body is arranged and functions. To assume he is proceeding in this way would picture the Apostle building on everyday knowledge of bodily functioning by translating its features analogically into a different realm, in this case a theologico-political account of the church. But if we assume a transition is being made here from a known *analogatum* to a less known *analogans* we will miss the crucial fact that Paul introduces the body metaphor in a manner that immediately contradicts Corinthian presumptions about the body. The Corinthians apparently conceive of the church as a negotiable social "arrangement" built up by way of hierarchies grounded in individuals' respective progress in the various stages

---

9. Kim, *Christ's Body in Corinth*; Käsemann, "The Theological Problem," in *Perspectives on Paul*.

of wisdom. In the face of this attraction to what we moderns might term a kind of managerialist account of political organization, Paul introduces the image of the body as a rival and specifically theological account of the life of the church. The very fact that in 1 Corinthians he draws on a variety of metaphors for the church, such as the activity of building (3:10-15), God's temple (3:16-17), or the organic life of plants (3:6-9), should make it clear enough that Paul is not explicating his whole account of the body of Christ with sole reference to the natural wisdom of the physical body.

All too often the formula "the body of Christ" has been invoked in order to then draw on individual "helpful" features of the organic realm, up to and including using them to defend forms of political existence that directly contradict the form Paul sets out in this chapter. Some of the simpler and more plausible deployments of the image of the body of Christ serve to valorize our normal and innocuous desires to feel close to others, to find ourselves in emotionally warm connection, and so on. If the notion of the body of Christ is not understood as part of Paul's larger attempt in this letter to define the form of the church as a political entity *sui generis*, the image will inevitably invite us to bring all sorts of "common-sense" knowledge that we have about how our bodies function into the analysis. Only a sharp limitation of our reliance on the body image as *one* of Paul's ways of describing the proper form of the Christian community will avoid deploying it in ways that effectively uphold or establish politically manipulative accounts of the church. Victor Furnish suggests this is so because,

> Paul is neither presupposing nor introducing a doctrine of the church as "the body of Christ," but simply asking his congregation to think of itself as a "body" that belongs to Christ. Later writers will elaborate this metaphor by identifying Christ as the "head of the body, the church" (Col. 1:18; see 2:19; Eph. 4:15-16; 5:23), but it is significant that Paul himself does not take this step.[10]

Paul's corpus is rife with metaphorical modes of communicating, but a sensitivity to the Apostle's regular use of metaphor must not, however, blind us to the fact that not every use of an image by Paul is metaphorical. Without becoming overly technical, we cannot avoid asking what form of argument Paul is deploying in his discussion of the body. On this question we take 12:12 to be decisive. The opening **For just as**, (καθάπερ γὰρ/*kathaper gar*), signals that Paul expects his readers to be perfectly well prepared immediately to get the significance of the imagery he now introduces of the

---

10. Furnish, VPF, 90-91.

body that **is one and has many members**. He has already in this chapter drawn attention to the fact that the unity of the church lies in the single origin of the multitude of its gifts in the one Spirit. This will have prepared his readers to now make the mental connection between Paul's discussion of the interrelatedness of the church's members and the interrelations of the members of the physical body.

The reader would have logically expected Paul to conclude 12:12 with the flat statement, "and so it is with the church." To end the verse this way would have ensured that everything he is going to say from that moment on, his portrayal of the communicative structure of the organic body, would be heard for its significance for the self-understanding of the Christian body. By taking this line Paul would have adhered to familiar conventions in the political rhetoric of the day in which the rhetorician knows that when he speaks of the physical body, once he has given the hint, his readers will in every case hear *polis*. It is therefore surprising that Paul resists any such seamless linkage by ending 12:12 not with the expected "and so it is with you, the church." Instead, he says, **so it is with Christ**.

The NRSV translation overreaches at this point. Οὕτως καὶ ὁ Χριστός (*Houtōs kai ho Christos*) has no verb, and literally rendered reads, "for just as the body is one and has many members . . . so too the Christ." It is a disruption we are especially prone to overlook given our long familiarity with the notion of the church as Christ's body, fostering the mistaken assumption that "and so with Christ" is merely shorthand for "and so it is with Christ's body, that is, the church." It is certainly true that in the subsequent verse 12:13 Paul points to baptism and perhaps the Eucharist as the believers entry point **into one body**—a body that cannot but be Christ's. But the leap to assume that in 12:12–13 Paul is offering nothing more than the necessary mental bridge between the physical body and the (community as the) body of Christ is prone to underplay the pivotal theological point: the *unnatural nature* of the church. In whatever ways it might be comparable to an organic body, awareness of these aspects of the church's reality must never override the point that the church is political in a way that is different from all other political bodies.

The metaphorical exploitation of the body image according to whatever any generation might find particularly "helpful" in it, however widespread it might be in Christian literature, breaks faith with Paul's subversion of that pattern in Greek political rhetoric. In particular, such an exploitation of the body image betrays the covenantal tradition that we understand to be the underlying source of Paul's intensive interest in the political form taken by the church's life. For instance, Christian discussions of 12:13, **For in the one Spirit we were all baptized into one body—Jews or Greeks, slaves** or free—**and we were all made to drink of one Spirit**, have tended to be occupied by the question of whether **drink of one Spirit** can or should be seen as pointing to the Eucharist in order to suggest Paul is offering a "full" sacramental grounding of his talk of the one body.

As legitimate as this question is in general terms, it has unfortunately tended to overshadow a different backward reference we detect in Paul's mention of baptizing and drinking. There are strong echoes here of his earlier discussions in which he reminded the Corinthians that Israel as a people "baptized into Moses" also "drank from the supernatural rock which followed them, and the rock was Christ" (10:2–4). For Paul, Christ was featured in the covenant, and the covenant accordingly is to feature in the Christian body through Christ. When gentiles say "Christ," Paul is suggesting, they are intrinsically invoking the grammar of "covenant." While it is clear that in the parenthesis **Jews or Greeks, slaves or free** Paul demarcates the opening up of the traditional boundaries of the covenantal people toward the inclusion of **all**, his invocation of the covenant after his first introduction of the body image holds Israel and the church together under the same emphasis on the political form in which his addressees currently exist. As church, the Corinthians must learn what it means to continue the political form of Israel as a covenantal people in the explicit mode of being the body of Christ.[11]

Tales of conversations between individual body parts were standard fare in the ancient world, as were their deployment to illumine aspects of political relationships.[12] Livy, a writer only a generation older than Paul, provides the best known version of a fable supposedly told in order to subdue a rebellious crowd by the Roman senator Menenius Agrippa.

> In the days when man's members did not all agree among themselves, as is now the case, but had each its own ideas and a voice of its own, the other parts thought it unfair that they should have the worry and the trouble and the labor of providing everything for the belly, while the belly remained quietly in their

---

11. In the Israelite understanding of the covenant, the existence of the covenant itself was taken to be the concrete and material embodiment of God's grace always available to Israel for their inspection. Paul is here exploring for the gentile church the dynamics of conflict resolution within a covenant-shaped political regime, representing knowledge he has imbibed from the long experience of the covenant people, Israel, for whom the divinely assembled collective is simply given, to be received with gratitude, and to which a response must be made.

12. "Lindemann identifies four principal ways the metaphor was applied, referring to passages in the works of Plato, Aristotle, Cicero, Livy (who cites Menenius Agrippa), Seneca, Epictetus, and others." Furnish, VPF, 89 n. 17. The Lindemann article to which Furnish is referring is Lindemann, "Die Kirche als Leib"; he also directs readers to Boring, Berger, and Colpe, *Hellenistic Commentary*, 694–96.

midst with nothing to do but to enjoy the good things which they bestowed upon it. They therefore conspired together that the hands should carry no food to the mouth, nor the mouth accept anything that was given it, nor the teeth grind up what they received. While they sought in this angry spirit to starve the belly into submission, the members themselves and the whole body were reduced to the utmost weakness. Hence it became clear that even the belly had no idle task to perform, and was no more nourished than it nourished the rest, by giving out to all parts of the body that by which we live and thrive, when it has been divided equally amongst the veins and is enriched with digested food—that is, the blood. Drawing on a parallel from this to show how like was the internal dissension of the bodily members to the anger of the plebs against the Fathers, he [Menenius Agrippa] prevailed upon the minds of the hearers.[13]

Notice first what Paul shares with this account: an awareness of the utility of using the image of the body to dramatize particular problems of political dissension. For both Pliny and Paul, communications between body parts become the main trope used to direct attention to the aspects of political converse taken to be most critical in achieving political harmony.[14]

---

13. Livy, *Historia* 2.32.9-12, translated in Dunn, *Theology of Paul the Apostle*, 550 n. 103.

14. It would take us too far afield to argue the case that Western Christian political theory has all along been driven by images of biological harmony orienting accounts of political functioning. It must suffice to offer some telling quotations and to suggest that this whole tradition bears revisiting by those interested in the question of Christian accounts of political life. Augustine famously linked the harmonious quasi-eternal order he imagined between human parts or organs with the ordering of political groupings: "The peace of the body, therefore, lies in the balanced ordering of its parts . . . In this care [of one person/part for another] lies the foundation of domestic peace: that is, of an ordered concord with respect to commanding and obedience among those who dwell together. For commands are given by those who care for the rest—by husband to wife, parents to children, and masters to servants. And those who are cared for obey." Augustine, *City of God*, XIX.13-14, 938, 942. See also XIX.16.

Marsilius of Padua, in *Defensor Pacis*, is arguably the first Christian to deploy an Aristotelian framing of the body image in order to question the drift of an Augustinian politics toward monarchical supremacy. "Let us say that the ruler through his action in accordance with the law and the authority given to him is the standard and measure of every civil act, like the heart in an animal . . . Now if the ruler received no other form beside the law and the authority and the desire to act in accordance with it, he would never perform any action which was wrong or corrigible or measurable by someone else. And therefore he and his action would be the measure of every civil act of men other than himself, in such manner that he would never be measured by others, like the well-formed heart in an animal. For since the heart receives no form that inclines it to an action contrary to the action which has to emerge from its natural virtue and heat, it

Given the marvelous complexity of living things, to draw bodies into the orbit of political rhetoric always demands a selective reduction of complexity. Biological complexity must be reduced or schematized in a manner that lends plausibility to some proposed solution to a political problem that lies buried in the overwhelmingly complex factors that make up political situations. But making things simpler than they are always demands choosing which features are to be highlighted and which ignored.[15] As the Agrippa fable demonstrates, in which a possibly very legitimate sense of rebellion by the underprivileged classes in society is quashed without a hearing, there is a potentially manipulative aspect in choosing which facet of an organic metaphor will be stressed to make a political point. Organic metaphors are powerful means of steering public self-understanding because their sheer and commonsense plausibility evokes the seemingly indisputable functional mechanisms of a well-known physical entity. The reduction of biological complexity through the organic political metaphor allows the rhetorician to borrow a plausibility and stability from biological phenomena to suggest that a political relationship really has a nonnegotiable reality. While allowing that Paul is deploying a simplified picture of the organic body in the same way as these other authors, we will only avoid charging him with the same manipulative and socially conservative intervention into political life if we ignore the crucial Christological disruption that we detected in 12:12b, in which Paul insisted that the church is not *like* Christ's body, but *is* that body.

Despite this important difference in starting points, the use of the body image by Paul and Agrippa do share an ancient understanding of bodies as made up of discrete parts, each of which have their own integrity and even will. Our modern understanding of the human body as an assemblage of organ *systems* can obscure the essential *differentiation* and *discreteness* of the ancient account of bodily parts necessary for understanding the political

---

always does naturally the appropriate action and never the contrary. Hence it regulates and measures, though its influence or action, the other parts of the animal, in such a manner that it is not regulated by them nor does it receive any influence from them. But since the ruler is a human being, he has understanding and appetite, which can receive other forms, like false opinion or perverted desire or both, as a result of which he comes to do the contraries of the things determined by the law. Because of these actions, the ruler is rendered measurable by someone else who has the authority to measure or regulate him, or his unlawful actions, in accordance with the law. For otherwise every government would become despotic." Quoted in O'Donovan and O'Donovan, *From Irenaeus to Grotius*, 435.

15. Alternatives to Western medicine are always based on such rival mapping of the human organism. Chinese acupuncture rests on a different account of the operation of bodily systems, as does the Indian chakra system with its emphasis on internal energy flows.

points both writers are making. For them a body is an entity very like a political community in being made up of parts that must be kept communicating with one another and must actively work to support one another.

On the surface Paul seems, like Agrippa, to be censuring and so trying to silence some citizens of the polity. But on closer inspection his characterizing as impossible utterances that individual body parts might make, which he insists Christians **cannot say**[16] (such as the head telling the feet **"I have no need of you"**), suggest that he is not deploying standard first-century modes of intra-organic bodily communication. What Paul depicts as being communicated between individual parts of the body is more accurately described as a form of negotiation. The biological body can indeed live without certain parts, and there are, for example, situations in which the head does indeed need to inform a limb like the hand or foot that it "needs" to do without it, even though only temporarily. What may appear, therefore, as Paul's own parallel version of the Greek tradition of political rhetoric begins to look very different when we understand it in the context of Paul's overriding concern to keep the Christian church's self-understanding faithful to Israel's covenant-ordered existence. Bearing in mind his overarching interest in the question of political form, we understand the force by which the Apostle marks an utterance—such as "I do not belong"—as "impossible" expresses a political sensitivity he has developed about the nature of the covenant as forming a community in which God alone can ultimately determine who is in and who is out.

As a Jew who we have seen to be well aware of the role played by the body as a means of communication, Paul now shows himself to be equally comfortable working with a Greek tradition of political thought in which images of the organic body were used to communicate political purposes. For both communities, therefore, the body offered a particularly serviceable imagery by which the perennial problem of every political entity, of multitude and unity, could be brought into view and discussed. And being a good Jew also prepared him to subvert the Greek use of body imagery to valorize a politics of force by offering instead a politics of communication. Greeks would have never gone so far as to finally claim that the *polis* itself *was* body and therefore could only exploit individual features of the body metaphor as a way to serve those in the *polis* attempting to overcome specific political difficulties. But this assumption of the irreducibility of the given *polis* had an inherently conservative tendency and thus toward the constant reinscription of a politics of force.

---

16. This is highlighted in the Greek grammar of the sentence, which begins, οὐ δύναται (*ou dynatai*), "cannot."

Because for Paul the covenant was the form of Israel's political existence this was an implication he could never accept.

Covenants did exist in the ancient Near East as instruments for regulating relationships *between* political entities such as tribes or peoples. What is unique about Israel's understanding was that for them the covenant became the very *form of its political existence*. Because Paul perceived the particularity of covenantal existence to be both generated by and sustained through speech acts like that of the covenant formula, "I am your God and you are my people" or in the partners' covenantal vows, he was prepared for the groundbreaking political innovation that is rightly associated with his theology: an understanding of the church itself as Christ's body sustained through the spiritual gifts that keep each individual member connected in a very direct and affectively rich manner with one another and the whole as "in Christ."

Only when we grasp the unique role played by the covenant as the structuring form rather than a side component of Israel's political existence are we are prepared to understand the breathtaking grandeur of Paul's pneumatological ecclesiology. In stark contrast from the Greek exemplars with which he is in dialogue, Paul aims not to help the church to understand politics, but to understand itself *as* Christ's body in its own appropriate political form. What he takes from our knowledge of our own bodies is that they are sheer givens, active and internally communicative in a manner resistant to being negotiated or rearranged at will. The Apostle starts from the assumption that to live life as/in a body is to be presented with the task of coming to terms with the realities that bodily existence demands. His core theological point, then, is that the body of Christ can only have the form that God has given it.[17] The bodily existence of limbs and senses *per se* is not the "real" datum on which the argument rests but the reality that fellow Christians are parts of Christ's actual body (*houtōs kai ho Christos*).

Understanding the church as the body of Christ in this way may, however, also open a variety of avenues of meaning that can and should subsequently be explored in relation to the functioning of biological bodies. The success of any such exploit will rest, however, on the clarity with which it has apprehended the unique characteristics of the body of Christ. Recall that in Menenius Agrippa's version of the body parable a central organ (the stomach) functions as a storehouse for the resources of the community. If deposits are not made disbursements will be withheld, causing the whole community to suffer. We are now in the position to appreciate the surprising fact that for Paul the communal body has no "master organ"—no heart,

---

17. Kittel, *Theological Dictionary of the New Testament*, 4:561–65.

stomach or controlling brain. He avoids any mention of either the digestive or circulatory systems, thereby refusing any valorization of human "political leadership." In his portrayal of the body the organs all communicate directly with each other, a decentralized circulating nervous system wholly constituted by the ongoing activities of connection and service administered from "above" or "outside" the nexus of human interaction—as if the "head" or "brain" were elsewhere.

As we have demonstrated in our discussion of chapters 6, 7, and 11, the Apostle understands the body as fundamentally a *medium* rather than a mere *instrument* of communication, providing its bearers with a communicative surface by which individuals are present to one another. Paul will now explain the theological reasons why he takes communication to be a constitutive part of the definition of the church. He does so by describing the workings of a body as focused exclusively on the limbs and organs primarily responsible for communicating with and reaching out toward the outside world, especially the senses that support the receptive and perceptive capacities of the human body.[18] Despite their prominence as parts of human biology as well as their recurrence in biblical and ancient images of the communicative attributes of the body, there is no mention here, for example, of the digestive system, or even of the heart and the circulatory system. Even the later reference to the less "presentable" members (a reference to the genitalia) presupposes the centrality of the communicative dimension of the body. Having set the emphasis up in this manner, Paul's body appears primarily as one composed of skin (with its embedded senses and its locomotive capacities) and nerves: the communicative body. It now makes complete theological sense for the Apostle to introduce individual organs by describing them as "speaking" to each other. Having its undeniably humorous aspect, this image nevertheless rests on a serious theological conviction about the particular blessing of the human body's capacity to interact with other bodies and the world.

The shift of focus in Paul's use of the body metaphor from Menenius Agrippa's emphasis on the digestive system to the nervous system is thus not theologically insignificant. The political life of the church as Christ's body is characterized by direct sympathetic communication between all the members that moves at the speed of light, unlike the slower and more indirect modes of communication that signal via the digestive/circulatory system as Agrippa depicts it. In the Agrippa tale political dissent is overcome only through slow siege processes that wear resistant members down to produce conforming behavior. For him speech is only the first act of

---

18. Collins, RFC, 460.

more coercive acts of rule, the withdrawal of the necessities of life, food. Resistant to such accounts of politics, in which one individual is able to coerce peace in the secular *polis*, Paul wishes to investigate the fundamental connective bonds that constitute and hold the church together as a political community. The conclusion he will draw from this line of reasoning is crystal clear, though not presented until later in the chapter (12:26): **If one member suffers, all suffer together with it; if one member is honored, all rejoice together with it**.

Having asked, "What has prepared Paul to both embrace and subvert the tradition of using the body metaphor in political rhetoric?" we have rediscovered how ill-equipped we are as modern readers to grasp the initial plausibility and inescapability of the metaphor as it would have appeared in Paul's day. In the wake of the scientific revolution, our understanding of our own body has been largely reduced to physicality. And at the same time our political sensitivities have submitted to an ideal of political union as sustained by a contract for our own best interest that we constantly need to revisit in order to protect those interests. Both trajectories implicitly demand we give up any idea of the givenness of the political body, making it difficult for us to imagine political form as having any meaningful solidity. Hence our inability to follow Paul's moves as he elaborates the image of the church existing *as* the body of Christ.

We must be prepared to return to the basic forms of our relations to others and to rethink them from the ground up if we are to grasp the vision of human relations shaped by an active Spirit that orients Paul's account of the body of Christ. We must ponder, for instance, what difference it makes to understand and live marriage as a covenant rather than a contract. Within a contractual arrangement the deal is good just as long as either one of the parties feel they are being well served by it. Thus in a marriage understood as a contract, divorce is always a real option because either party can always take a rough patch to mean that the utility of the bond is no longer worth the effort. Marriage understood as a covenant, however, situates each party's relation to conflict quite differently, because the vows each has made are unconditional "till death do us part," made before a God and a community who both take an interest in the faithfulness of the partners that goes beyond each partner's own assessments of the utility of the relationship. The difference evident here between the two dynamics of conflict resolution when marriage is practiced as a covenant instead of a contract makes the import of political form more evident. We understand Paul to be exploring these same covenant dynamics at the level of the church as a whole.

The covenant as a political form is most obviously at home in the sphere of the *politeuma*. Precisely because the covenant is the political form in which Israel exists, its discussions about whether or not to have a king are not to be conflated with the question of whether Israel's political form might become a monarchy or not. The various modes of government Israel took on in its long history, whether ruled by charismatic judges, one prophet, one prophet and seventy elders, or one king, has never been as determinative for the political form of Israel as the covenant. The strange and seemingly mutually irreconcilable multitude of opinions about the monarchy that we find in Israel's scriptures, from praises of individual kings to very principled resistance to the idea of the monarchy as a whole, must be seen not as an embarrassment of incoherence, but as a strong testimony for the unbreakable clarity of Israel about its one and true political form, the covenant.[19]

The analogous challenge for the Church is therefore to discern and embrace its genuine political form as the (covenantal) body of Christ within whatever ecclesial governance structure happens to exist. Here again, however, contemporary churches might face even more difficulties than the first century Greeks, for whom the form of the *polis* or republic was clear, and the physical or organic body could serve to highlight problems that arose within any given form. In our age we have become rather less clear what the political form of *our* community actually is, or even if we understand in a more abstract sense what *political form* is as a concept. The expansive and all invasive model of the contract, with its eternal imperative to revision and rearrangement, seems to have pushed us towards an ever-greater indifference to questions of political form. The uniform and principled commitment in Western societies to democracy as the most superior political arrangement does not contravene but rather confirms our suspicion. Insofar as it is based on a more foundational commitment to the contract as the basic political relationship, the Western prerogative for democracy is not *for* any one political form, but for a construal of political arrangement that *defies form* in favor of forming and re-forming according to the type of contractual relation that seems most expedient at any given moment.

Paul's emphasis on keeping communication open suggests that he places a premium on the immediate effect that a suffering or dysfunctional member has for the whole body. This shifts attention away from the symptom, political conflict within the church, to the root of the problem, the loss of sympathetic connection with other Christians that ensures they **have the same care for one another** (25b). This Pauline picture of communication between discrete bodily members contrasts with the habit, prevalent in modern times, of comparing the social body to an ecosystem in which interactions between sub-entities are driven by a tendency

---

19. O'Donovan, *Desire of the Nations*, ch. 2.

toward equilibrium—an tendency that, as Jürgen Habermas has argued, easily entails compromising the ideas of individual responsibility and the meaningfulness of political consensus.[20] Paul's account of the communicative body also contrasts with another prominent idea in modern societies, a positivist picture of the body and the body politic in which the discreetness of individual parts is emphasized by a mechanistic portrayal in which parts are seen as interchangeable and replaceable—the view that spawned, for example, organ-transplant medicine. In light of these rival depictions, Paul's attraction to the picture of a healthy body as made up of discrete organs, each having a voice that demands a hearing, can therefore be understood not just as an archaic view but as a legitimate theological account of political life. It offers a conceptualization of the human organism that is intended to suggest immediately intelligible implications for the political vocation of its bearers.

In sum, for Paul the *charismata* are not skills, possessions, or fixed social functions played by the giver, but rather denote the "message" of service that passes between believers. Whereas the previously cited example of the sun allowed us to depict the nature of the gifts as *energema*, noting how the energy *inside* the sun is not equivalent to the energy that it has *given off*, a different image is needed to depict the circulation of gifts *within* a political body. Here the nervous system offers a more serviceable analogue. A nerve cell is capable of receiving and passing on the electric pulse that constitutes the firing of a nerve, but this electric signal is different in kind from the substance of the nerve cell itself. Nerve impulses are identical and send out generic electric pulses. It is therefore impossible to identify the "signature" of a nerve impulse, as we can do by analyzing the unique light spectrum emitted by each star or the origin codes of internet communications. The nerve cell originates or receives and passes on an entity different in kind from itself; made of organic material, it is made to pass on an electric impulse. The biological structure of the nerve cell is thus entirely configured for the purpose of sensitively receiving and passing on minute fluctuations of energy from adjacent compatriots.

The all-important communicative fluidity that is basic to our account of the gifts within the polity of the church turns on our awareness of the importance of the capacity to receive and hand on the Spirit's gifts. Moreover, the realization that service is an activity that is extended in space and time protects this revelatory reading from the accusation of occasionalism.

---

20. The classic debate about this (controversial) aspect of system-theoretical accounts of human sociality occurred between Habermas and Niklas Luhmann and is sometimes referred to as the "Frankfurt-Bielefeld controversy," which was documented in a joint publication, *Theorie der Gesellschaft oder Sozialtechnologie*.

Enacted works of service must not only benefit the body, but must be continually circulating for there to be a body at all. The body of Christ *is* a circulator of divine gifts, a network that lives by passing on the Spirit's gifts. If such a unique body is going to arise and persist it will only do so as each member serves in a temporally extended manner the giving of the Trinitarian God to the church via each member. The individual believer, concludes James Dunn, is therefore not *simply* an individual, "but the functioning member, the member with his or her charism or charisms. Individuals are members of the body as charismatics."[21] Paul's strategy in this chapter is thus very like Jesus's in the Sermon on the Mount, in which he draws the hearer's attention away from the visible result of sin to raise questions about its initial impulse and its location in the heart, in which one has allowed anger to grow that is then transmitted outward, flowing into the violence of a blow by the hand (Matt 5:21–30). With this interpretation by Jesus of the law an insight is yielded that Paul reproduces here, namely, that the way to tackle a problem together as church is not by condemning violence at its end point but in confronting it at the place where it begins—in the barriers we erect against the circulation of the spiritual gifts.

What are we to make of Paul's parenthetical insertion **Jews or Greeks, slaves or free** into his investigation of the form of unity that should characterize the political multiplicity of Christ's body? It is evident elsewhere in Paul's work (as in Galatians 3:28) that he understands the social, religious and sexual differences that tend to fuel political antagonism in human societies to have been reconciled through Christ and further, that the church is called to represent this reconciliation in its own corporate life.[22] The challenge for Paul in Corinth is to provoke the believers to more fully live up to the reality of this reconciliation and it is to this end that he has addressed specific problems arising from sexual, traditional religious, and economic differences in the church (idol food, hairstyles, table seating). We might therefore conclude that Paul is simply invoking here in a compressed way the sorts of differences that easily inflame the antagonisms that have essentially been surmounted in the kingdom. Though this might be the case, it would still be a reference with a somewhat negative ring that potentially overshadows the sense in which these old, surmounted, differences have become less interesting for the present church—less interesting, that is, than a variety of other differences that positively challenge the church in its new existence: the varieties of gifts, services, and effective powers that the Spirit brings. By noting the common triad of seemingly threatening differences in the context of his discussion

---

21. Dunn, *Theology of Paul the Apostle*, 559–60.
22. Wannenwetsch, *Political Worship*, 136–37.

of spiritual gifts, Paul prepares the Corinthians to see and embrace the far more interesting set of benign differences bestowed as gifts of the Spirit that transfigure these formerly threatening differences by welcoming them as the lifeblood of the church's organism.

Despite their incorporation into the body of Christ, Paul nevertheless finds the Corinthians in a situation in which the embrace of different spiritual gifts has become an occasion for separation and strife that threatens to burst the community apart. Even within the reign of reconciliation and despite being showered with an abundance of gifts, old race, gender, and economic status hierarchies still offer to fallen creatures the germs of dissent. Paul's secure resting in the reconciliatory power that emanates from the cross and that has begun to form a new community of reconciled Jews and Greeks, slaves and free, women and men, sustains his consistent emphasis that it is a new set of differences that calls the Christian community away from any romantic attachments to a community understood as a homogeneous social entity. There is no salvation in homogeneity, which does away with differences in a manner that always threatens to break up the community. There is no difference between people that does not have the potential to produce disruption, even the abundant provision of the most wonderful gifts, which is why Paul's characterization of a spiritual embrace of the *charismata* differs in kind from the perennial quest for homogeneity so characteristic of the manifold "identity discourses" that so dominate the contemporary landscape.

The embrace of difference in the sphere of reconciliation to which Paul summons the Corinthians should therefore be understood as having a *homologous* quality.[23] **No one can say "Jesus is Lord," except by the Holy Spirit.** Political homogeneity is achieved either by reducing or denying difference, typically achieved by silencing the voices of those who are felt to be "too different." A homologous political identity, in contrast, comes into being when different voices chime in to a shared confession. In this identity different voices are understood to be constantly learning to contribute to an orchestration of one identifiable piece of music in which differences are being reconciled to create harmonic sound. For the church, of course, this homologous identity grows from the joining in of every believer in the most fundamental confession, "Jesus is Lord." *Homologein* literally means "to say the same, or speak with one voice," but the ecclesiologically decisive point is that the voice is not the voice of one individual or sub-grouping that makes itself heard by overpowering other voices, but rather the unified voice of a

---

23. On the distinction between homogeneity and homologeneity, see Wannenwetsch, *Political Worship*, 214–18.

choir. A choir can be called good when it presents as one highly complex voice, a task that entails moving beyond the simple aggregation of a number of individual voices. The proof that a group of singers has not achieved the status of a choir is made evident through performances in which one or another singer's voice obtrudes.[24] This is why the aim of every spiritual gift is the work of service that prepares the body to make its confession of its Lord with one (variegated) voice.

To mark yet again the contrast being drawn with modern identity discourses, note how Paul abstains from entering the register of moral assessment in his presentation of paradigmatic utterances that fail to harmonize with the one confessional voice. While he certainly understands it to be wrong to say "I have no need of you," or "I don't belong to the body," he does not quash such confessions of pride or false humility by way of moral exhortation. He could easily have said to the proud, for example, "these others are also part of our community, you should be kind enough to at least grant that." Such a response, however, would itself remain caught within the parameters of the self-identification discourse that Paul is challenging as the precise source of the obsession of this body politic with determining who is in and who is out.

Having noted the tendency of many baptismal and eucharistic debates to swallow Paul's finer points in 12:12–13, we still owe readers an indication of what we take these two verses to suggest along these lines. The context of his discussion in 10:16, **The cup of blessing that we bless, is it not a sharing in the blood of Christ? The bread that we break is it not a sharing in the body of Christ**, has prepared us for a reading that understands the particular eucharistic drink as an entry into a form of enacted bodily belonging. We think a eucharistic reading is most clearly commended by the grammatical form of the related verb. Ἐποτίσθημεν (*Epotisthēmen*) is an aorist passive construction perhaps best rendered by "steeped into." The image of a liquid substance that nourishes the whole body by permeating it strongly echoes the formulation of 10:4: "For they all drank from the spiritual rock that followed them, and the rock was Christ." Whether we understand the drink imagery as an admittedly somewhat more far-fetched explication of baptism or as a eucharistic pointer, what seems fair to assume is that the purpose of 12:13 is to further clarify the sacramental character of Christ's body. While this has certainly become a stock confession for every Christian tradition, different ecclesiological traditions of teaching have emerged that would put the emphasis in their respective readings of 12:13 in a range of rather different ways. We only hint at those questions

---

24. Brock, *Singing the Ethos*, 359.

by raising the question of what it actually means to claim that Christians have been baptized "in" the body. The Greek formulation εἰσ ἓν σῶμα (*eis hen sōma*), literally, "in one body," leaves open the question of whether *en* is better understood as indicating a movement from one place to another, or more specifically as highlighting the teleological nature of a divinely commissioned act that brings a new reality into being. It is therefore textually legitimate for readers in the Roman Catholic tradition to emphasize the former reading, presupposing the always already existence of the church into which new members would be baptized, while those in the Reformation traditions have tended to put the stress on the power of the sacraments to recreate the church over and over again.

Absorbing the Many Gifts into One

> [14]Indeed, the body does not consist of one member but of many. [15]If the foot would say, "Because I am not a hand, I do not belong to the body," that would not make it any less a part of the body. [16]And if the ear would say, "Because I am not an eye, I do not belong to the body," that would not make it any less a part of the body. [17]If the whole body were an eye, where would the hearing be? If the whole body were hearing, where would the sense of smell be? [18]But as it is, God arranged the members in the body, each one of them, as he chose. [19]If all were a single member, where would the body be? [20]As it is, there are many members, yet one body.

From here to the end of the chapter Paul will indicate the concrete entailments of the theological account of the church as Christ's body he has now set out, a procedure that is easily obscured when the message of this chapter is moralized. 12:15 has proved especially problematic in this regard. The renowned fourth-century preacher John Chrysostom falls into this trap by suggesting that Paul is setting out here to soothe "the feelings of the one who has the inferior gift and is troubled by this."[25] His assumption is that the problem being addressed by the Apostle in this section is the pride of the holders of supposedly greater gifts in relation to the envy of those with less. The reading has the merit of having evoked some beautiful commentary on how to overcome envy. "Whatever my brother has," says Augustine, "if I don't envy him but have love, is mine."[26] Thiselton is in good company, therefore, when he concludes, "Verses 14–20 introduce

---

25. Chrysostom, *Homily* 29, PG 61:243, in JK, 201.
26. Augustine, *Sermon* 162A.1–5, in JK, 212.

Paul's appeal to those who feel "inferior" to recognize that they genuinely belong to Christ's body."[27] But is this reading really warranted by the text? To answer yes at this point will commit us to reading the discussion to come in 12:22–24, about less and more honorable members of the body, as an elaboration of the implications of envying other believers's gifts, thus extending the moralization of this chapter.

We will take a different line, however, and will understand Paul's interest in this passage to be conceptual clarification rather than moral exhortation. Instead of imagining him to be making a directly pastoral intervention, our suggestion is that he is displaying in some detail the logical impossibility of certain speech acts. Consider the if-then structure of statements like the following: **If the foot would say, "Because I am not a hand, I do not belong to the body," that would not make it any less a part of the body**. If any believer were to claim that they were not part of the body, for whatever reason, Paul is suggesting that this would be a logical impossibility as the church is constituted by one Spirit. Such a statement might arise for a range of reasons, including the pride-inferiority economy in which someone else's gifts are envied or one's own disdained. But there is no evidence that this is Paul's concern here. Rather, he is drawing attention to the self-cancelling reality of utterances like "I do not belong" in order to emphasize how they break up the body as a communicative entity, no matter what the subjective reasons for uttering it might be. In so doing Paul makes a theological and conceptual point about the sort of thing that the body of Christ is and how certain acts (including speech acts) have the potential to dismember this body.

This is why we insist that a moralistic reading that assumes Paul is trying to reduce peoples's envy and pride by showing how all the gifts are equally valuable misses his core point. We instead understand the Apostle to be clarifying for the Corinthians *how* discerning, fostering, and seeking engagement with the economy of the Spirit's working through individuals generates and sustains the church's nervous connection. The problem with a moralizing reading is that it displaces the question "How do I embrace the giving of the Spirit?" with the identity question "Which gift is mine?" or "What do I get from spiritual gifting?" When the body is alive in its communication of the gifts of the Spirit, its corporate life becomes a shared confession that "Jesus is Lord" (12:3). Thus to utter the phrase "I do not belong" is in effect to say, "Let Jesus be cursed," because such an utterance embodies a servitude to human ideals of success and failure, preeminence and lowliness. The spirit of such identity quests differs irreconcilably from

---

27. Thiselton, ACT, 209.

the Holy Spirit whose work is to endow believers with the desire to provide **the same care for one another**.

Our reading begins from the observation that the pairs of organs that Paul has speaking to each other are of the same type and status in 12:14–20. The foot compares itself to the hand and the ear compares itself to the eye. Discussions between these pairs would not be driven by disputes about functional superiority, but by status differentials. This suggests that Paul's target is false presumptions among his interlocutors such as, "I'm not a full Christian if I don't possess all the gifts or at least some of the more prestigious ones." Whether articulated or not, this is a worry that is fully intelligible in a context in which those taken to be especially gifted have formed cliques. Such cliques would easily generate the assumption that "not belonging," either from those outside who wish that they were more "high performing" or from those inside who would be tempted to think that the rest of the church could only be tolerated but not fully affirmed as "ones with us." Such are the divisive questions that are generated and sustained by the identity discourses that Paul has just been trying to lay bare, and extirpate from among the Corinthians (>12:12–13).

The way Paul develops his treatment also suggests that there is another dynamic afoot. It is one that on first glance seems less obvious and yet subsequent developments in the history of the church have made amply clear how difficult it has been for the church to handle appropriately: the temptation to absorb the church's genuine diversity of gifts into a single agency. The Apostle clearly signals this problem with a pair of rhetorical questions whose potency has rarely been appreciated in the tradition. **If the whole body were an eye, where would the hearing be? If the whole body were hearing, where would the sense of smell be?** (12:17).

Having already noted the selective appearance limbs and senses make in Paul's portrayal of the body, we think it worth considering further why he avoids discussing any organs that might be naturally entitled a central role. The stomach in Agrippa's fable played a starring role in being the storehouse and distributor of the whole body's sustenance, and we do not think it accidental that Paul does not mention it nor any ancient equivalent such as the brain or the heart.[28] The question of absorption of the many into one is so foundational for Paul that the actual existence of the body depends on it. **If all were a single member, where would the body be?** (12:19). With this way of putting the question Paul suggests that the aspiration to absorb the multitude of gifts into a single agency amounts to a nonsensical absorption of

---

28. The head is mentioned in verse 21, not, however, as a ruling member but only as one member of the body among others.

the space the rest of the body is supposed to occupy. Although there are moments in which a body must be "all ear," or others in which it must be "all eye" in order to be appropriately responsive to its environment, the temporary nature of such occasioned focusing is not to be conflated with an ontological claim that one agency could in principle perform in a single brilliant effort that of which only the breadth of individual agencies are capable.

The aim in football (soccer) is scoring goals, to take a simple example. Were the situation to arise in which strikers began to consider themselves the only "real" players, this would not simply *devalue* other types of player, but would in fact represent an *abandonment* of the reality that football is played by a team in favor of an *illusion*. Without a functioning defense and midfield, the striker is precisely nothing. She does not even exist since football is by definition a team sport. Positions can only exist within the political form that is a team in the same way that Christians can only exist as Christ's body. It thus completely misses the point to suggest that Paul is saying something like "midfielders are important too." Rather, Paul wants us to hear "you are deluded if you think you are *anything* on your own or can do *anything* without the others." Thus the question **where would the body be** can only be rhetorical. The absorption of all gifts into a single agency cannot be a development of the life of the body, nor simply a reduction of its proper complexity of giftings; for Paul it amounts to an attempt to annihilate the body of Christ.

Given this reading, we find 12:18 to be highly instructive at the conceptual level in not simply contradicting the paraphrased attitude "I do not belong" in order to correct it ("yes, you do belong"), but in confronting the rationale underlying it. The literal translation of ἔθετο (*etheto*) would be "God *put into place* the members in the body, each one as he chose." All suggestions that the Christian community can be understood as an "arrangement" are therefore to be firmly resisted (despite the NRSV translation of the verb here as **arranged**). Arrangement language presupposes something like interchangeable constituent parts that have been put into an initial order and can later be reordered for optimal effect. If things have been arranged they are always open in principle to re-arrangement and later rearranging. On these grounds we find it extremely counterintuitive to use the notion of arranging with regard to the Christian social body even when such a suggestion was to put the emphasis (referring to 12:18) on God as the "arranger." The reason for our resistance is that it has been precisely the spirit of social arrangement that has hovered over most of the hostile antitheses that Paul has been trying to overcome with his portrayal of the body as a multitude of gifts, each of which has its own respective *telos* and dignity. The fallen (especially modern) political imagination is so easily absorbed in the practical tasks of arranging and re-arranging various social orders that the question with which Paul has been so concerned in this chapter, of the church's appropriate political form, has become totally obscured.

If our reading is correct we can hardly overestimate the seriousness of the threat hanging over the church that gives in to the temptation to absorb the multitude of giftings into single agencies. Though we cannot here go into a detailed discussion of the development of formal offices in the church(es), it is difficult entirely to defer the question of whether the development toward the so-called monarchic episcopate should be understood as one such centralization. In *The Shape of the Liturgy* Dom Gregory Dix offers a seminal account of the development of this political form in critical terms and in some detail, and suggests that early Christian liturgies were much more finely tuned and balanced as joint ventures of a multitude of ministries. Initially characterized by the broad contributions made by the ministries of the people, and reflected in the name taken from pagan political contexts and applied to the Christian practice of worship (*leitourgia*, a composite of *laos*, "people," and *ourgia*, "public work"), such liturgies of the people were eventually obliterated as the one ministry of the priest or bishop gradually absorbed liturgical tasks and responsibilities that once belonged to other discrete ministries.[29]

In light of the sternness with which Paul warns against this trajectory in our chapter it ought not come as a surprise that the tendency towards the monarchic episcopate occurred when the church sought to mimic worldly political forms of governance and its "pragmatically superior" wisdom of centralizing power.[30] Once it is forgotten that the church has its own unique and theologically describable political form it is inevitable that believers will find themselves trapped in the dead ends of political imaginaries and languages such as the constitutional discourse in which the constant question can always and only be which arrangement of political governance is most efficient.

Later in the chapter, though, Paul will allow one agency within the church to represents all the *charismata*: the apostle, a role that, accordingly, will appear at the top of one of his list of gifts. By virtue of representing the multitude of gifts to the body apostles can indeed be said to legitimately represent the body in their one ministry. Because the apostolic ministry belongs to the church as a whole, its particularity and uniqueness ensures that no other ecclesial role or office can claim to be such a complete representative of the body. It is on the basis of this claim that Paul, *as* an apostle,

---

29. Dix, *Shape of the Liturgy*, ch. 2.
30. The *locus classicus* for this point is 1 Sam 8. See Murphy, *1 Samuel*, 58–71.

can definitively state that any structure of governance built around the idea of agents who completely represent the respective bodies for which they are responsible must be called worldly. In 1:11–13 Paul has already confronted this very problematic in the factions, whom he accused of dividing Christ by breaking the Christian community up into subgroups organized around their loyalty to specific iconic leaders.

Paul's discussion should press us towards self-critical assessment of developments in our churches that are easily evaded by the premature conclusion that the only phenomena Paul could have in his crosshairs today is the papal office. After all, Roman Catholic ecclesiology has had the good theological sense to characterize the papal claim to represent the whole of the (Western) church precisely as a representation/continuation of the apostolic office, the seat of Peter. There might well be good reasons critically to scrutinize such accounts of the papal claim in the light of Paul's warning but there is not the slightest reason for Protestant writers to presume that the all-in-one absorption problem is exclusive to or even a peculiar problem of the Roman church. On the contrary, if there is a prototype of that syndrome, it would more appropriately be the Protestant ideal of the omnicompetent pastor who is expected to cover the complete range of ministries in the church with the force of his or her personal *charisma* or at least professional expertise. The iconic Protestant jack-of-all-trades pastor mimics on a local scale the problematic development in the Western church toward one central priestly ministry that came to absorb a multitude of the body's other liturgical ministries and pastoral gifts. If anything, the Protestant version intensifies the tragedy precisely to the degree that it assumes an indisputable sense of superiority to the Roman Catholic priest, whose personality is in fact not expected to carry his office, but the other way around. We must notice that the closest equivalent to the modern pastorate in Paul's list of charismata, the gift of the κυβερνήτης (*kybernētēs*, "navigator"), is featured as only one gift among many; it is not even high up on that list and by no means to be conflated with the apostolate, which is the sole legitimate claimant to represent the multitude of gifts to the body.

In response to what is perceived as the Roman overreliance on the ontological effectiveness of the office (*ex opere operato*) Protestants have tended to assume that every pastor is expected to fill the otherwise empty forms of the ministry with "real" life by investing all the capacities he or she has developed through training in erudition, leadership, and people management skills, as well as pastoral empathy. All these "gifts" that the pastor is expected to invest in his or her ministry could be summed up under the notion of "personal charisma." The Protestant quest to find new pastors who have "so much to give," therefore, becomes a way of supplanting Paul's emphasis on the importance of the breadth of the gifts across the church. There is a spiritual immaturity evident in the gesture of congregations to hold wide open the mantle of the many-gifts-in-one for candidates who dare to believe they can wear it. This leads to a well-known pathetic symbiosis between immature congregations that want to be represented in a dominating manner and pastors who find it impossible to refuse the flattering offer. When disaster strikes, what is typically lamented is the burnout of the functionary, which is quickly followed with efforts then commencing to restore him or her back to his or her capacity once again to fulfill the very same overbearing demands.

Rarely does the analysis of such disasters transcend the psychological level (overworked, overwhelmed, undersupported) to include theological scrutiny of the misshapen ecclesiological premise that kick-started this vicious circle and keeps it in motion. In one sense the problem could be said to have found an initial recognition by the megachurch movement, though again the non-theological form of the response is indicated by the management nomenclature through which the political imagination of its proponents is revealed. In these churches the "executive pastor" takes responsibility for arranging the personnel on multiple sites and "site pastors" are then tasked with pastoral care on "satellite campuses"—satellite because the preaching on such sites is done by "teaching pastors" given to produce highly polished sermons that can be projected to several sites. Such an understanding of the relation between the gifts that sustains the body of Christ seems a far cry from Paul's imagination.

There is an equally disturbing parallel to the rise of the monarchic episcopate (whether Protestant or Roman Catholic) in the evolution of church music that in the eighteenth and nineteenth centuries increasingly came under the sway of one overwhelming instrument, the pipe organ—an instrument capable of absorbing (and replacing) all other voices of musical instruments into one. From its heyday in the Baroque era, when it had evolved into the multi-pedaled and multi-voiced instrument as we know it today, it did not take long for the organ—the *"organ,"* the sole voice of the body—to take over what roles there were for musically embellishing the liturgy. The pretentiousness that has surrounded the pipe organ from its inception is nicely captured by the ecstatic rhapsodies this "prince of instruments" evoked in churchmen. A good example appears in Henry Ward Beecher's Yale lectures on preaching, delivered in the early 1870s.

> It is the most complex of all instruments, it is the most harmonious of all, it is the grandest of them all ... It has come to stand, I think, immeasurably, transcendently, above every

other instrument, and not only that, but above every combination of instruments ... No orchestra that ever existed had the breadth, the majesty, the grandeur, that belong to the prince of instruments.[31]

The maritime metaphor Beecher uses to describe how the pipe organ relates to the congregation is especially revealing: "The organ is the flood, and the people are the boats ... There is this power that comes upon people, that encircles them, that fills them, this great, mighty ocean tone."[32] The rise of the organ as the main and even sole musical accompaniment to Christian hymn singing thus displays in a particularly clear way the characteristic feature of all attempts to represent an all-in-one gifting: the overpowering and overwhelming of other actors that produces in the end a silencing of political homology.

Traces of a healthy and playfully ironic suspicion of the all-in-one ideal built into this musical instrument can be found in a legendary tale about the invention of the *vox humana* at the St. Martin Basilica in Weingarten. Joseph Gabler, a famous organ builder, attempted to create for this church an instrument that would perfectly represent and combine not only (like other organs) the sounds made by any other musical instrument but the human voice in all its pluriformity. After a string of unsuccessful attempts Gabler is said to have sold his soul for the magic piece of metal that could successfully mimic the sound of the human voice. When presenting his creation to the congregation of monks whose worship it was meant to accompany they were so overwhelmed and distracted from the actual purpose of worship that the abbot ordered both the creator and his creation to be given over to the fire.[33]

Just as Paul opened the chapter by reminding the Corinthians of the connection of idols and the silencing of the multitude of gifts, so we must understand the claim to complete representation as displayed in the development of Christian worship under the tyranny of the "prince of instruments" as an idolatrous development precisely because it mutes the voices of the body. The pipe organ as an icon/idol of church music has not only proven to be effective at replacing other instruments and at overpowering with its "ocean tone" the singing voices of the congregation. The instrument does not demand but has certainly catalyzed a culture of worship in which the tempo of hymns is dictated by the organist "playing ahead"

---

31. Beecher, *Yale Lectures on Preaching*, 118–19.

32. Ibid., 121–22.

33. https://en.wikipedia.org/wiki/Organ_of_the_Basilica_of_St._Martin_%28Weingarten%29.

of the congregation. This characteristic feature rests on the assumption, widespread amongst organists, that congregations always sing too slowly, and that it is therefore necessary for the master of pipes to play ahead and "wash over" the congregation. The result is to remove from the congregation the right and need to find its own tempo and voice. Having noted the structural parallel of this instrument with the charismatic pastor, it is unsurprising that the worst imaginable combination of the organ-playing pastor has in fact arisen in some traditions that not only absorbs the other roles in the congregation, but also the moment of truth displayed through the battle for supremacy that often rages between the two, rival, all-in-one agents in many of our churches.

Those readers who find themselves amused by our portrayal of these tragedies in traditionalist Protestant churches, being members of churches that have long abandoned the organ for a modern praise band, might perhaps not too quickly indulge a sense of superiority here. Is it not, after all, just another variant of the all-in-one absorption if the music team feels it has to occupy every second during worship with a breezy tapestry of sound underneath any traditional liturgical function, be it prayer, reading of the scripture lesson, or indeed what might have been necessary moments of silence? Aside from many individual parallels to the organ (volume, inescapability, prescription of emotional tone), there are equally worrying parallels here with the idol-pastor as well. Where the personal *charisma* of the pastor is thought to enliven the potentially empty or at least boring liturgical functions and offices, the function of the musical underlay to prayers, testimonies, or even confessions arguably betrays a sensitivity owing more to the logic of marketing psychology than to genuinely pastoral considerations. Instead of understanding the congregation to come to worship bearing a multitude of gifts, the Christian body is assumed to be composed of dumb, lethargic and inert customers who need first to be brought into the mood by the manipulative use of sound in order to be made ready to receive the gospel.

In many modern congregations the worship band is given the responsibility for providing a kind of "soundtrack" that will ensure continuous affective motion in the congregants and, like a movie soundtrack, produce a specific sequence of uniform emotional states and responses that prepare the audience for the next move in the plot. The better the soundtrack, the more it is capable of creating those same responses with ever-greater independence of the quality of the plot. These dynamics have eventually led to a "liturgy" entirely dominated by the charisma, usually delivered through routines, of the worship leader who provides the verbal cues for this emotional ebb and flow of the whole service by deciding when a repeated chorus or prayer is appropriate. It is no surprise that pastors in such traditions often perceive decisions taken by the worship leader to be competitors to the message they want to get across.

It is true that the newer phenomenon of worship teams and praise bands, unlike the organ and the organist, do employ a multitude of instruments played by a number of players and singers, a development that is to be thoroughly welcomed for the ecclesiological reasons we have outlined. But there is a feature of this new culture that threatens to undermine precisely what is gained. In most cases, all individual instruments and voices are amplified and routed through the unifying sound board. It is this arrangement that contains more than a germ of the aspiration to all-in-oneness that once propelled the invention of the organ. The soundboard too, along with amplification, was developed in the context of concert performance and only later caught the attention of the Protestant worship leader, though not necessarily of worshippers who in recent memory were typically found complaining that the "drums are too loud." The tragedy here again is how quickly a theologically defensible impulse to replace the monocratic organ with multi-voiced musical *charismata* has been reabsorbed into the one ill-fated paradigm that fueled the organ's successful colonization of Christian worship in the first place. Even if there seems to be an obvious cultural divide between organ and praise-band churches, their unity is more fundamental as it is problematic. The same tragic confrontation of two ill-conceived ministries entraps both cultures as displayed by the battle lines that inevitably lay between the pastor and music leader. If all were a single instrument, where would the body be? If all were a single office, where would the body be?

Is it possible to take to heart Paul's suggestion that Christians stay away from creating these all-absorbing agencies? Could we really afford to turn off the amplification both of worship bands and pastor personalities? Were we to do so we would probably discover that strange zone of silence created by the switching off of these overweening ministries. What we would undoubtedly at first experience as eerily empty could turn out to be a void that fans into greater life the promised and indeed present, if muffled, multitude of gifts. It is no small irony that many a congregation that run into the "ill fate" of finding its organ in need of a lengthy and costly repair went through a period of amazing discoveries of "hidden" musical talent in their midst that flowered in the "interim" period—only to be suppressed once again—when the 200,000 dollar organ repair had been completed and its old regime reinstated, if only to legitimate the expenditure.

It is God's grace to intervene in the human lives that have become trapped in the silence of idolatry so memorably portrayed in the story of the tower of Babel in Genesis 11. Humans, having successfully banded together to create a gigantic cultic union around the Promethean desire to divinize the race, are reintroduced by God to the importance of the many voices by having their relations fundamentally reordered through the confusion of speech. Having their idol silenced, they have been given an invitation, once again, to hear the multitude, and with it the one creator God.

Honor for Outsiders—the Same Care for All

> [21] The eye cannot say to the hand, "I have no need of you," nor again the head to the feet, "I have no need of you." [22] On the contrary, the members of the body that seem to be weaker are indispensable, [23] and those members of the body that we think less honorable we clothe with greater honor, and our less respectable members are treated with greater respect; [24] whereas our more respectable members do not need this. But God has so arranged the body, giving the greater honor to the inferior member, [25] that there may be no dissension within the body, but the members may have the same care for one another. [26] If one member suffers, all suffer together with it; if one member is honored, all rejoice together with it.

Paul signals the theme of 12:21–27 by shifting the conversants in the discussions between bodily members in verse 21. Whereas 12:14–16 opened with limbs and organs speaking to their equals (hand to foot, ear to eye), in 12:21–27 preeminent members are depicted as "speaking down" to another: **I have no need of you**. The eye tells the hand that depends on it that it does not need it, and the head, the member at the top of the body, tells those on the ground, the feet, that they are superfluous. Paul replies, **On the contrary, the members of the body that seem to be weaker are indispensable**.

Assumptions of inferiority and superiority among body parts immediately strikes us as misguided in violating our highly tuned modern sense of the equal worth of every person. Paul, however, does not challenge hierarchical views of staggered political worth on the basis of some preconceived inclination for universal social equality. He begins, rather, with the given social reality of all human life, which presents each human generation with a particular code of honor and decency within which inferiority and superiority is determined, including of individual bodily parts and functions. The three adjectives by which Paul characterizes the ranking of individual body parts demonstrate this point. His use in 12:22 of the expression **to be weaker** (ἀσθενέστερα/*asthenestera*) emphasizes the conventional nature of any such hierarchical assessments, which is again signaled with the expression ἀτιμότερα (*atimotera*), rendered by the NRSV **less honorable**. This comparative literally means "more disgusting/despised." In 12:24 the passive construction ὑστερουμένῳ (*hysteroumenō*) might best be translated as "disadvantaged" or "those who bring up the rear." The semantic drift of the language Paul is using here is in some tension with the NRSV rendering **inferior**, which points precisely in the wrong direction by putting an ontological slant on Paul's expression. The Apostle is in fact suggesting that the starting point for discerning the Spirit's gifts must be an engagement with *socially constructed* realities—the codes of honor and decency thrown up by every human generation. It is within such codes that inferiority and superiority—even of individual bodily parts and functions—are determined in ways that negate and demean what God has **so arranged**.[34]

With this refusal to ontologize the status quo of conventional status polarities Paul is keeping faith with the core Judeo-Christian doctrine of God's creation, which was declared "very good." Yet to take Paul as merely reminding the Corinthians of the egalitarianism of God's original creation ("We're all the same after all") can stop short of noticing the most exciting theological move in this section—his speaking of God's composition of the body as **giving the greater honor to the inferior member**. This divine lifting up of the lowly cannot be derived from the original act of creation. Paul has to be speaking of God's intervention into the twisted dynamics of fallen human history. Those who take some gifts of the Spirit to be inferior, he suggests, are enacting the common mistake of allowing worldly assessments of stations and natural capacity also to determine the order of divine gifts. When this happens the body of Christ is dissipated into yet another human community responsible for arranging human skill sets that are already known and understood. Paul's church, in contrast, is one that is learning to perceive the spiritual communication of the *charismata*. It learns this receptivity by refusing to reintroduce the ordering of social hierarchies learned in the world, and does so through the empathetic practices of caring for one another.

Since important contemporary theological debates about this passage center on how best to understand Paul's language of the "unpresentable"

---

34. Having already indicated in this chapter the theological centrality of the work of the divine emplacing in determining the shape of the church's life, and that the whole body metaphor falls apart if organs, like persons, are not understood as being fundamentally discrete individuals, we must likewise resist the insertion of the logic of blending at every turn. Garland's reintroduction of the theme here is symptomatic of the difficulty of resisting this tendency: "God 'composed' (*synekerasen*), implying mixing and blending, deliberately so." Garland, DEG, 596.

member,[35] it seems helpful to give an unambiguous account of our reading at this sensitive point. An intertextual inference can help to clarify the specific sense in which the risky language Paul deploys here of "weakness" can be legitimately applied to supposedly unsightly or infirm people. We assume that Paul is making reference here to the dynamics of shame and exclusion unleashed in the Fall. The Genesis narrative (Gen 3:1–18) offers the first couple's betrayal as the origin of all schemes of honor and decency in human history. Adam and Eve's motion of mistrust toward God yields a corresponding mistrust toward the created order that the biblical authors highlight by indicating the novelty of the post-lapsarian awareness that "they were naked." Having repudiated their communication with God, Adam and Eve's immanent communications are ruptured with each other and with their own bodies. Sin is presented here as broken communication, and broken communication as the origin of a culture of scapegoating that demands the designation of "shameful ones" on whom individual and collective shame is then projected.

In this light God's intervention to give the first human couple proper protection to cover their pudenda appears as a harbinger of the gospel in **giving the greater honor to the inferior member**. It is a divine act of redemption that helped the first couple to understand that though they are ashamed of some body parts, these still legitimately belong to the body. When this shame is formalized in human cultures a tyrannous reign over physicality emerges based on an ontologized ranking of individual body parts up to and including fantasies of dismembering and declaring some ("those") parts of us to be sub-human or "not me."[36] It is by no means theologically irrelevant that the body parts first disowned by Adam and Eve are the ones through whom the human race is sustained and so, despite being shunned, are in reality glorious members.[37]

---

35. Reynolds, *Vulnerable Communion*, 237–38; Webb-Mitchell, *Beyond Accessibility*, 64–65; Yong, *Bible, Disability, and the Church*, 92–93, and *Theology and Down Syndrome*, 222; Monteith, *Epistles of Inclusion*, 73, 77–78, 84. Our reading comes closest to that of Young, *Brokenness and Blessing*, 98–100, and Vanier, *Community and Growth*, 47–49.

36. See Dillon, *Tormented Hope*.

37. "Adam and Eve not only were ashamed because of their nakedness, which previously was most honorable and the unique adornment of man, but they also made girdles for themselves, as though it were something most shameful, that part of the body which by its nature was most honorable and noble. What in all nature is nobler than the work of procreation?" Luther, *Lectures on Genesis, Chapters 1–5*, comment on Gen 3:7, in LW 1:167. Luther is expressing a patristic commonplace. "The less honorable parts are useful for procreation and the propagation of our race. Consequently, even Roman legislators punish those who mutilate these organs and make men eunuchs; such people harm the whole race and insult nature itself. But a curse be on all dissolute people who slander the handiwork of God!" Chrysostom, *Homily* 30, PG 61:253–55, in JK, 209.

As the Genesis plot unfolds God again and again gives greater honor to the inferior member as in the story of the mark of Cain (Gen 4:16). Here the one who betrayed the social bond that holds him within human community is protected from becoming dismembered and rejected from the body of human society through God's own provision of an indelible mark on his forehead. What is engraved on the first murderer's countenance is the divine imperative to all other members of the human community to, as it were, not ontologize Cain's self-inflicted fugitive existence with a declaration that he is "out" of the body. As if to reiterate and emphasize this point, the son that is subsequently born to Cain and his wife will bear the name of Enosh, which appropriately means "human being" (Gen 4:26). What we have in this narrative is something like a political iteration of the divine provision of the first couple's redemptive clothing in order that their "less honorable" members not be repudiated. God's refusal to allow the mechanics of inclusion and exclusion to determine the matrix of political formation is a foreshadowing of the form of political ordering that God had in store for Israel, the fully elaborated political form of the covenant community that Paul is offering to gentile Christians in this chapter's articulation of the image of the body of Christ. It is this same dynamic of redemptive care that gives life to the church, Paul suggests, as God assembles the ecclesial body from those the world considers unpresentable or outcasts, but who are nevertheless clothed with honor by God.

With this argument Paul is apparently retracing and concretizing Jesus's subversively free attitude toward human honor codes, which was one of the most striking characteristics of his earthly ministry. Jesus proposed scandalous inversions of the seating order at a feast (Luke 14:7–14); he redefined greatness not as excelling over others but as that service which allows others to grow rather than shrink in one's presence (Matt 23:11–12); and he blessed the persecuted, the sufferers of injustice, and the poor (Matt 5:3–4, 10–12). It is clear from the first chapter of 1 Corinthians that Paul considers himself to be carrying this teaching forward for the community that is Christ's body: "God chose what is foolish in the world to shame the wise, God chose what is weak in the world to shame the strong; God chose what is low and despised in the world, things that are not, to reduce to nothing things that are" (1:27–28).

Observing that Paul is working within this covenantal and gospel tradition prepares us to appreciate his central conceptual point in this discussion: that *charisma* and vocation must be dissociated from worldly status. The engine of ranking processes, even of the gifts that Paul lists as spiritual, is their close association with social status according to the respective phenotypical weight of individual gifts. Why should the Corinthians be tempted to overrate, say, speaking in tongues or other particularly flashy gifts if not for their experience in the world, where the great rhetorician is counted a more valuable member of human society than the maid? Even though the Christian church has been built from the beginning on the foundation of a new and different "divine honor code" that keeps faith with the subversive mission of Jesus, the close association if not conflation of the *charismata* and ministries in the church with worldly roles and status as they are typically adjoined to specific natural capacities or acquired skills has remained a perennial temptation.

To illustrate the difficulties of finding a way for the church to concretely live out the vision of "greater honor to the lesser member," consider the way in which the early church defined its stance toward the poorest of the poor, the class of beggars. The patristic church's care for beggars must certainly be understood as an attempt to take Paul's account of the subversive political unity of Christ's body with full seriousness. From very early on Christians considered the poor as emblematic of the church's very existence, a badge of honor to be carried up front, for example, by making a group of beggars a visible part of the travelling entourage of the bishop.[38] Testimony to this alertness appears in John Chrysostom's commentary on these verses, in which he speaks of beggars as the "fixtures and splendid adornment at the doors of the sanctuary," without which the church "would not attain its full stature."[39] The preacher whose eloquence earned him the name "golden mouth" proves very sensitive to Paul's agenda in even granting beggars their own embodied "proclamation" that appropriately seconds that of the preacher and even surpasses the preacher's voice in clarity and urgency: "While we preachers sit before you and recommend what will do you good, the one who sits before the doors of the church addresses you no less than we do, by his mere appearance, without saying a word."[40] There is no doubt in Chrysostom's mind that the poor provide a special gift and ministry to the church, the work of Jesus Christ lending those with no worldly power a voice of their own that the church needs to hear.

A closer look at the way in which the preacher characterizes the particularity of that gift, however, recalls the difficulty outlined above, the temptation to equate gift and role, vocation and natural talent. Chrysostom goes on to explain in the sermon that he understands Christian beggars to preach can be boiled down to a warning to the established members of the church that "man's life is a shifting and precarious thing . . . Our condition is

---

38. See discussion in Johnson, *Fear of Beggars*, ch. 1.
39. Chrysostom, *Homily 30*, in JK, 208.
40. Ibid.

like a swift river that never wants to stand still but always rushes downhill."[41] While this assault on the pride of those who assume themselves to be "normal" and secure is a theologically important one, what remains problematic in it is that it depends on and so solidifies the equivalence of social stations and spiritual gifts. Chrysostom does not ask his congregation to expect from the beggar one of the gifts Paul has enumerated and so effectively forecloses such waiting in calling his poor dress and outstretched hand his gift to the community. He thus collapses these believer's spiritual gifting into their poverty.

Those still forced to ask for money on the streets have largely disappeared from contemporary churches, notwithstanding their remaining presence in most urban environments even in the rich nations of the West. Though many churches are engaged in charity work on behalf of the poor, the poor have long ceased to be thought of as a visible badge of honor that the churches wish to keep as "fixtures and splendid adornment at the doors of the sanctuary." Jean Vanier's retention of the traditional linkage of the plight of the disabled with the plight of the poor is illuminating in expanding the reach of the "problem of the poor" into the moral perplexities of our own age. Both the disabled and the poor carry the burden of a *socially constructed* inferiority. Every church would wish today to think of itself as having one or even two people with disabilities in their midst (although three or more might become uncomfortable), and would be happy to suffer (to a degree) the disturbance those members of the body might cause, say, in the hour of worship. The further parallel with the poor is unfortunately the perception that what people with disabilities are expected to contribute to ecclesial life so often approximates what Chrysostom allows them to "preach." The way they appear in public is taken to be the gift they bring to the body—their apparent poverty/disability. Thus the church today, like that of the fourth century, too often fails to expect a surprising divine contribution from those at the bottom of the social order precisely to the degree in which they have predetermined the type and scope of their contribution to the gathered body.

Paul is asking us to look again, to expect that the gifts that those with disabilities reveal to the church may be manifold and not reducible to the "message" of their disability. The easy equation of gift and socially constructed appearance deprives the church of what seems to be the implicit matrix in Paul's discussion for genuinely embracing the *charismata*, that is, of surprise, wonder, and discovery about what sort of gift the Spirit might be attempting to give through the life of any individual member of Christ's body. The gift

---

41. Ibid.

that someone we think of as disabled might bring to the Christian body cannot simply be said to rest with that individual (his or her disability), nor is it appropriate to say that it rests with those who receive it, as suggested in the patronizing gesture so common in liberal societies that, "*even* the disabled should have a place." To speak of the need for gifts to be *discovered* means, rather, to understand them as situated "in between" the bearer and recipient, neither simply *expressed* through the exercising of natural capacities nor *bestowed* by the church's need for some role to be filled (as they are when "seeking individuals with leadership qualities, management experience" . . . etc.). This in-between is the particular theater of operations of the Spirit who does not only *originate* the gifts, but needs actively to *donate* them right into the middle of interpersonal relational space.

What might such a discovery of the gifting of the Spirit look like today? Here the witness of those who have been recipients of such discoveries are especially illuminating. As the father of a young child with intellectual disabilities has testified, he sometimes grasps the gift that God gives through his son in a particularly intense way:

> When I come home from a trip, Adam beams with joy at the simple presence of his father, which makes me happy too. I have long given up bringing him toys or other gifts from my travels as I have realized that not only does he not notice them, but if he does, they add absolutely nothing to what is the greatest gift for him, the sheer presence of a formerly absent father. He delights simply in the recovery of nervous connection. Learning this took my admitting my disappointment that though my other children loved presents, Adam never even noticed them. What I have discovered is a gift that is so rare that it needed some time fully to break through my much less rich, and conventional, vision of what our relationship should be.[42]

On our reading of Paul, what this father had to learn in order to experience the relationship that exists with this other member of the body, is to discover the relationship with his son *as it actually is*. Especially in a social context that has become so deeply aware of the multiple layers that are constantly negotiated in human relationships, including their presumed enrichment by gift exchange, the father's experience of this relationship could be said to be of almost shocking simplicity, thus revealing the essence of Paul's definition of the church as characterized by empathetic communication.

To mark the contrast once more with the problematic twist in the initially promising account of Chrysostom of the sermon preached by the

---

42. Brock, "Theologizing Inclusion," 370.

poor, this father eventually learned to recognize the Spirit's gift that his son bore by relinquishing his socially constructed expectations that his son should show some *extra* joy in being given toys. The arrival of the real gift, a unique experience of the purity of relationship, was one that broke in on previous expectations of how father-son, or able-disabled relationships should function. Until the father was weaned off the cultural codes that led him to expect that a good father would bring home a gift and a good child would be excited to receive it, he was unable to really perceive the depth and purity of "rejoicing together," already on offer from his son. The father could not have adduced in advance what was already on offer by examining the phenomenological configuration of his son's disability, nor is what he discovered in the context of this relationship deemed true and good because he "taught me something."

The path of thinking down which Paul has been leading us in this chapter makes us bold to suggest that it is appropriate for such a father to confess that it is through his son that Christ is remaking him. We can further affirm that because there is an increase in "nervous connection" between these two baptized members of the body of Christ that we can also narrate the moments of enlightenment on both sides as the Spirit's donation in the "in between" space that existed between them. This is an enlivening donation that can now be handed on to others in turn. This is but one concrete example of the sort of discovery Paul associates with the church's fundamental task of recognizing and embracing the Spirit's gifts.

The gift given by the disabled person, the poor person, the recovering addict, all those of low esteem to the world, emerges only through the spiritual discernment that is utterly certain that there is even in these unexpected places—unexpected in the perceptions of fallen humanity—a *charisma* to be received.[43] We might even say that the inability to grasp this point is the fundamental problem of the modern church, often characterized by a forgetfulness that Christians as gentiles, themselves the impoverished ones grafted on to the true vine, are the unsightly ones being added to Israel. But thanks to the work of Jesus Christ, the church is that community learning what it means that our genetic, national, and religious status is not all there is to us.[44]

Not only should the strong not look down on the less honored, but the latter should even be given special honor, Paul insists. God has a preference for revealing himself more luminously through the weaker members.

---

43. Stringfellow, *My People Is the Enemy*, 28–32, 43, 47–49.

44. "Colonialism" is one of the most revealing names for what happens when the church forgets that it lives off the crumbs from Israel's table and chooses instead to think "we" are the basic entity to which others must be joined and made to fit. See Jennings, *Christian Imagination*, ch. 6.

If the honor being talked about in this chapter is being a conduit of the Spirit's gifts, then the church would have reason to attend to those the world considers poor not because they have a better perspective on the world, although they very well may, but because there we find out what God's honoring reveals. Because God is partisan for them, they cannot be their own avengers. The "view from below"[45] means that nobody, even the lesser members, need assume that only if they fight for their minority rights will they force the acknowledgment society has so long denied them.

If testimonies such as that of the father and his disabled son are plausible examples of how God's **giving the greater honor to the inferior member** might look in our world,[46] it will at the same time prepare us to follow Paul's next move in 12:24–26. Again an image drawing on the nervous system is deployed, this time to highlight the way the whole body is immediately jolted by the pain of a single part. It is sympathetic connections that allow the members of the Christian body to suffer and rejoice together: **If one member suffers, all suffer together with it; if one member is honored, all rejoice together with it.** The organic body transmits sympathetic reactions through a connective nervous system that must be intact if the living organism is to function. As is well known, conditions like leprosy that affect the nervous unity of the body lead to inevitable loss of extremities and finally limbs. Putting the matter this way helps us see that Paul is not telling the Corinthians they "should" suffer or rejoice together, setting out on the project of engendering a culture of compassion or sympathy. As at several earlier points in this letter we must consciously resist slipping into reading Paul as entering the register of moral exhortation here. What is being presented to the Corinthians is no ideal to be achieved but the reality of the body in which they already exist and which **God has so arranged**. This is to preserve the critical edge of the Apostle' presentation by being especially aware of its sharp emphasis on what we might call the seismographic dimension of co-suffering and co-rejoicing. The presence or absence of this phenomenon tells us what sort of people we are. We know that we are a body when co-suffering and co-rejoicing are actually happening in our midst. When it is not, we likewise know that we are not a body or at least that we are in a situation in which dissension/split (*schisma*) has somehow severed the nerves that were supposed to maintain connectivity.

---

45. Bonhoeffer qualifies any uncritical "preferential option" by stating that "this perspective from below must not lead us to become advocates for those who are perpetually dissatisfied. Rather, out of a higher satisfaction, which in its essence is grounded beyond what is below and above, we do justice to life in all its dimensions and in this way affirm it." Bonhoeffer, *Letters and Papers from Prison* (DBWE 8), 52.

46. See also Williams, *The Shaming of the Strong*.

We have introduced the example of the role and vocation of the poor then and now (as represented by those with disabilities) in order to highlight the problems that come with associating worldly status with spiritual vocation, the confusion of natural talent or social roles with Spirit-given *charismata*. On the basis of these observations we contend that even well-meaning attempts to reserve a place for the poor and disabled in the church and society have often failed to transcend a patronizing register in failing to properly disassociate status and vocation. A typical form that this association takes in contemporary church life is the habit of skill-matching: appointing the professional accountant treasurer in the church, the schoolteacher the teacher of children's Sunday school, and so on. *Charismata*, however, are not simply baptized natural capacities that can be identified, for instance, by arranging a personality test or by looking to see what skills or expertise people have already gained. It is a conflation that breeds frustration and a sense of exploitation in our churches: instead of people enjoying their ministries in service of the church, what they are appointed *to do* there, feels like more of the same old drag that is their professional life. When real curiosity about what gifts God actually wants to bring to the body through the service of individual believers withers in a church, it is inevitable that its members will be sorted and arranged according to the gifts that people assume have already been discerned by some other community, the school or company that has taught them to wear their skill set visibly to all on their sleeves. Where there should be spiritual discernment of gifts, the church all too often looks for nothing more from its members than what the sorting dictates of social status have long before decreed.

Having emphasized the moment of discovery as a marker of the work of discerning the spiritual gifts as well as the continual need to affect a principled dissociation of the *charisma* from social role and status, we must add a final clarification that spiritual gifts and natural skills must not be understood in principle as absolutely independent. The *independence* of the Spirit's gifts from our individual capacities needs to be underlined in order to mark out the appropriate space for the Holy Spirit's operation to actively donate instead of merely provide. But it is a *relative* independence, because giving the Spirit room to work may well entail discoveries of natural capacities that might have been suppressed or hidden from others and even the person herself, but which now become the occasion for God to give the body what it needs through the bearer of these capacities. Such discoveries have been pleasant surprises for many who have realized, for instance, an aptitude for languages by studying scripture, their speaking ability by being asked to address the church, or their musical aptitude after being invited to join the choir, to take three of an almost infinite range of potential examples.

It would be foolish to stress the principled independence of professional roles from spiritual gifts, up to and including a dogmatic account of non-convergence that would disallow, for instance, an accountant becoming the church treasurer and would perhaps even flirt with the idea of appointing a person who notoriously underperforms in all things numerical (>6:4). Any decision made in principle and in advance about whether or not someone's spiritual gifts will align with their worldly roles ignores the most important factor, which is whether the communicative sensitivity a member has to the body and to other members is either hampered or nourished by their activities. To take a different example, the spirit of pragmatic arrangement that tightly links the natural capacities that have already been revealed by social training or role with *charismata* would intuitively put forward the busy young teacher of the local kindergarten as the ideal leader of the church's crèche. But it might well be not her but the grumpy old lady who has attended every Sunday without fail, due to her "nervous connection" to the church and the children in its midst, who might be the actual bearer of the gift that really matters for this peculiar ministry in this time and place.

Ministries and Ministers

> **[27] Now you are the body of Christ and individually members of it. [28] And God has appointed in the church first apostles, second prophets, third teachers; then deeds of power, then gifts of healing, forms of assistance, forms of leadership, various kinds of tongues.**

The list that Paul presents in 12:28 not only differs somewhat in content from the other enumeration of the *charismata* in 12:8–10, but also betrays clear signs of a structural organization that goes beyond mere listing to presume an order to the *charismata*. The language of **first, second** and **third** identifies the specific ministries of **apostles, prophets** and **teachers**, setting them apart from the other members in the list. How is the first list of gifts related to the acts and offices set out here in this order of precedence? How are the two portions of the list related? We can get at this problem by asking why **apostles** appear first on the list. The most plausible answer is that apostolic ministry is distinguished from any other gift in that it represents all the others in one. The accounts that the book of Acts give us of the apostles's mission more than amply demonstrate how it was marked by the amazing plurality of gifts enacted in their exploits. We suggest that the primacy of the apostles should not be taken as an abstract claim to a higher status but rather as representing a divinely provided order that ensures that the church has everything it needs.

The ministry of the apostle therefore represents a special moment in the church's history in which the rich plurality of gifts given to the whole church is combined with a unique demonstration of how all these gifts work together within the compass of a very small group of people. The apostles are a bounded set, divinely chosen so that all the legitimate gifts of the body could be displayed in a manner that would become normative for the church as well as modeling how their plurality of gifts should properly be negotiated under the reign of Christ. It is in this sharply delimited sense that apostles represent the whole body, not by each one displaying all the gifts in a complete and rounded manner, but by being part of a group in which all the gifts are clearly present in abundance and false gifts excluded. Paul's own life and ministry illustrates this point by making unambiguously clear what it means for leadership to be exhaustively discharged as service, a designation by which it can then be appropriately ranked as exemplary. It is on the basis of this all-important representative role of the apostolate that we see why Paul is legitimately and especially concerned in the whole Corinthian correspondence about their perception and embrace of him *as an apostle*. This is not a sign of personal pride but of his fatherly care for the Corinthian body that he knows to be in dire need of an exemplar demonstrating how all the *charismata* properly fit together in love.

Does this account of the apostolic vocation clarify the two other offices named in Paul's list? The way into this question is to ask what service these named office holders provide to the church. We understand the gifting of prophets and teachers to serve the *knowledge* of the church, edifying it towards the *certainty of faith*. Paul is an apostle because Christ has come to him and shown him the relation between the Father as source, the Son as suffering servant, and the Spirit as the conveyer of divine love, as well as what this divine reality means for the body of people who have been made partakers in it. By dint of his apostolic office Paul is uniquely qualified to make the connections clear in 12:4–7 that anchor this chapter's talk of the diversity of gifts in the unity of the three Trinitarian persons. The church can be certain that *every* spiritual gift is *only* a gift if it is from *this* God. All the other roles are discerned by becoming attentive to the one *through whom* God is doing works of service. In the *charismata* Jesus Christ hands on the love of the Father by personally appearing through the Spirit to every believer. These gifts thus convey to each member Jesus Christ's real appearance and presence.

In discerning the relation of the spiritual gifts to Jesus Christ the church is reliant on the work of the Apostle and the certainty he offers through providing criteria by which true gifts can be discerned, as the opening of this chapter demonstrates (12:2–3). Put in summary form, the **apostles** offer certainty to the whole church about the *unity* of the living body in the sufficient, sustaining, ongoing, and diverse works of the Trinitarian God. The **prophets** offer certainty to the whole about the *present* works of the Trinitarian God in both world and church so that the church is enabled to respond to them. **Teachers** offer the church *instruction* about the God who creates, leads, and feeds the church, knowledge gleaned from the preserved canonical stories of past leading, in order that the church can be *responsive* to its apostles and prophets. The remaining gifts sustain the mobility of the body as a responsive whole.

The two-tiered fashion in which Paul discusses the whole list of *charismata* and ministries in 12:28 demands further consideration. While all the other gifts are simply listed ("then . . . then") the top three stand out not only on the basis of a numerical ranking, but also in being described not by verbs but nouns. Does this suggest that while some gifts were considered more free-floating in the body, others were in greater need of permanently structured recognition—a recognition that would soon lead to the development of regular offices in the church? It is a question not so easily answered. On the one hand, the process of solidifying ministries into offices does not seem to be exclusive to the three ministries mentioned in Paul's A-list. Even in the New Testament period we can observe other ministries, such as *diakonia*, developing into fully fledged ecclesial offices when the need arose (Acts 6:1–7). At the same time it does seem that the way in which the three ministries that Paul highlights interlock must somehow indicate their special significance. As we have repeatedly noted, the particularity of the apostolate lies in its unrepeatable capacity to represent all the spiritual gifts to the body. Only on the basis of such a complete representation of the totality of gifts would an individual ranking of them is not be misleading. We think that what we see here is a structural parallel to the discussions in chapter 11, in which individual members of a social unit under consideration—in this case some women and patrons—are singled out for exhortation only after the overriding framework of mutual submission has been established (>11:3).

Only once the multiform *charisma* of the apostolate has been discharged, providing certainty to the body about God's sufficient and abundant provision of gifts, does it then make sense for the prophet to appear in the order of gifting. The peculiar gift of the prophet is to preserve in the community an awareness of the priority of proclaiming and listening that corresponds to the nature of the Trinity as communication and address. Because the prophet's ministry appropriately witnesses to the priority of the divine word by assuming the risky, unsettling, and particularly anarchic task of becoming God's mouthpiece, a place is made for the teacher to offer more settled and didactic instruction about the God to whom the prophet witnesses. Where the prophet concerns himself with *proclaiming* the word, the teacher is concerned with its *exposition* as the necessary attempt to summarize, structure, and partition the content of this word so that its catechetic distribution can resource all the other gifts.

Our portrayal of the interrelationship among the offices Paul highlights in a short cascading series represents an attempt to draw out the sequential logic of his presentation. In doing so, however, we do not mean to suggest that this cascading structure exhausts the potentially more multifaceted and multi-directional exploration of how individual *charismata* relate to one another. As the hint in our portrayal of the teaching office already suggested, we should not only expect Christian prophecy to resource teaching in a manner that solidifies and administers it, but also that teaching in turn is a resource of prophecy. Although Paul's resistance to all attempts to create an all-absorbing ministry or agency is indisputable and ignored only to the church's peril, and although colonizing claims of individual ministries to even partly absorb the peculiar task of another should be resisted, it is nevertheless the case that the enactment of individual gifts sometimes creates benign forms of overlap with others. It has been observed of particularly good teachers in the church, for example, that at times their work assumes a certain prophetic quality.

Having talked about the unique character of the apostle's ministry as representing the fullness of *charisma* in such a way as to make superfluous or impossible any other claim toward an all-in-one agency in any other individual ministry, we are not surprised to see Paul drawing his discussion together by emphasizing this point once again with a final sequence of rhetorical questions.

> [29] **Are all apostles? Are all prophets? Are all teachers? Do all work miracles? [30] Do all possess gifts of healing? Do all speak in tongues? Do all interpret? [31] But strive for the greater gifts. And I will show you a still more excellent way.**

Paul's closing string of questions directs attention to the empirical implications of the conceptual points he has just set out. He in effect goads the Corinthians to look at the church members with whom they worship with the question ringing in their ears, "If all were a single member, where would the body be?" (12:19). The chapter thus ends with an exhortation to practical behavior that we suggest glossing like this: "Realizing that it is inappropriate for a Christian believer to aspire to be the greatest or to possess all the gifts as well as to despair because of the seeming inferiority of the gifts you have received, passionately pursue instead that which the Spirit is giving to you."

The concluding verse, 12:31, has often puzzled modern interpreters: **But strive for the greater gifts. And I will show you a still more excellent way.**[47] While it is obvious that Paul's announcement of his demonstration of a **more excellent way** should be understood as a preparation for his discussion of love in the chapter to come by indicating the entrance he compares to a high mountain path,[48] some take the further step of reading the **greater gifts** indicated in 12:31b as referring to that one particular gift, love. But the use of the plural "gifts" as well as the comparative form "greater" should rather discourage this reading. Love is presented by Paul not as a comparatively greater gift, but in superlative terms as the greatest gift of all. We therefore conclude that his summons to strive for the greater gifts refers backwards to this chapter's discussion of individual *charismata* and ministries, and suggests that after having crested the summit of this path the gifts will not only reappear in a totally new light but should be zealously pursued (14:1).

The Greek term for **striving**, ζηλοῦτε (*zēloute*), which can be more literally rendered as "desire zealously," is such a strong expression that it cannot but make the reader wonder if there is an ironic concluding note being struck. After all, the greatest gift on Paul's second list, the apostolate, is out of reach to the Corinthians since it is only open to those who have personally been called to it by the resurrected Christ. But even if we think of the first attainable gift on the list as prophecy, the biblical narrative begun in the Old Testament makes it abundantly clear that this too is not exactly the sort of ministry for which anyone would zealously strive. As Jeremiah most clearly articulated—in good company with his peers Isaiah, Hosea, and Jonah—being a prophet is probably a job assignment

---

47. The interpretative debates are summarized in Garland, DEG, 600–604.

48. "The word *huperbolen* produced the English word *hyperbole*, which like the Greek word is ethically neutral. In Greek, this word has to do with some form of excess, good or bad. It is a compound word made up of *huper* (over) and *ballo* (to throw). The root meaning has to do with 'overshooting' and 'throwing beyond.' Paul is the only New Testament author to use this word, and he does so (as a verb and as a noun) a total of twelve times ... In each of these cases something, *positive or negative*, is being *intensified*. But in the case of a 'way,' you can start with a 'crooked way,' add *huperbole* and have 'a *very* crooked way.' Or, you can begin with 'a straight way,' attach *huperbole* to the sentence and describe 'an *extremely* straight way.' But you cannot make sense out of 'an extremely way' ... Translators have traditionally turned the 'way' into an 'excellent way' and read *huperbole hodon* as 'a more excellent way.' But there is another option. *Huperbole* can also refer to 'a mountain pass.' This language describes a way that goes up, over and beyond other ways; *the high road* (not the *low road*) is the *huperbole hodon*." Bailey, *Paul through Mediterranean Eyes*, 357, italics original.

best resisted. It marks an extremely exhausting, risky, and fragile life always lived on the brink because it unsettles not only the community the prophets were supposed to address, but also the prophets' lives and that of their peers and families. We may assume that the majority of the Corinthians, being gentile, did not have this Old Testament tradition in mind, and instead associated prophets with exciting center-stage oracular performances, thus making pursuit of this gift an apparently rather attractive prospect. Nevertheless, the main reason Paul can actually commend this zeal rests on its essential contribution to the overall composition of his teaching of the body's gifts. It is possible to strive to be a Christian prophet and to do so for the right reasons only because this particularly bold and fragile gift is buttressed from two sides. It is anchored through the apostolic authority that precedes it on one hand, and through the Spirit's gift of discernment on the other. As Paul will later make clear, prophecy is teamed up with discernment in a particular symbiosis, similar to the way in which the other "high-risk / fragile" *charisma*, speaking in tongues, is grounded by its fellow *charisma* of interpretation (>14:13–20).

Rather than going into a full-blown analysis of how Paul's *charismata* feature or fail to feature in the lives of contemporary churches, we will content ourselves with a single observation, prompted by the obvious contemporary dearth of the gift of prophecy in most mainline churches today. If this absence is not simply embraced and made a badge of honor, perhaps by way of dispensationalist or modernist presumptions, churches have often assumed that much of the essence of early Christian prophecy has been absorbed into the ministry of preaching. While there are a number of structural parallels between the two phenomena, the problem with this equation is not only that the office of preaching has never fully absorbed or covered all aspects of prophecy but that preaching, in turn, has often tended to become a form of teaching to make it a less risky undertaking than the situated application of the divine word to a particular congregation. The question that might fuel a healthy process of self-scrutiny in our churches today therefore is not only whether a particular structure of offices that developed over time are hospitable to the whole host of spiritual gifts that Paul recognizes, but is also where the concrete shape of *individual* offices has led to the domestication or absorption of individual gifts.

Excursus: Exegesis and Pastoral Application

Several of the more pastorally oriented modern commentary series conclude the treatment of each chapter with a list of "Reflections for Teachers and Preachers" (Hays), or "Suggestions for Possible Reflection" (Thiselton). Though we warmly welcome such concern from biblical commentators we have until now deferred explanation for why we have not adopted this kind of procedure ourselves. We feel that it projects, however unwitting, the suggestion that pastoral reflections properly follow more foundational exegetical or theological work. It is a model that rests on the apparent assumption that after the strata of basic theological or historical exploration has been accomplished the results that have been achieved can then be applied to the multitude of pastoral questions faced by the contemporary church. While granting that authors in such books may well be pushed into this format by the demands of series editors chafing at the seemingly yawning gap between academic biblical studies and the pulpit, the sequencing of exegesis in this way remains highly significant. They are always more than an "uninterested" issue of formatting by which material is arranged as they also express and even demand specific methodological assumptions. The best an author working within this pattern can do is to keep pastoral questions in mind while doing the more basic "objective" work of historical and theological exegesis, knowing she will have to produce a concluding section on practical "impact."

In contrast to such an approach, we have methodologically allowed pastoral considerations to enter our reflections at a much earlier stage as a trigger or mediating matrix within which exegetical insights can emerge. We have taken a chapter like the one before us, with its abounding connections to pastoral questions, to be most fruitfully read in something like a double looping procedure. Beginning with the text, we find that it spurs reflections on pastoral concerns we had not initially considered relevant but which are provoked as we are attending to the text. At this point simply bringing these pastoral problems to mind is by no means to engage or settle all the evident practical questions that surround them. But to read the text as scripture is to be sent out into the life of the church in the world having been provoked to look at it a certain way. Considering these pastoral questions drives us back again to the text with fresh questions that act as a probe and give us deeper access to the text, typically revealing much more than we had seen on first reading. In this double looping reflection pastoral concerns thus function as triggers for deeper investigations of a text that facilitate in turn the Apostle's unleashing of a much wider scope of his concerns to us. In our experience this happens with such regularity and potency that a strictly applied exegesis-theology-application model seems to foreclose. It is Scripture itself, we have discovered, that continually corrodes any such dividing and sequencing of the exegetical task, inviting its readers instead into a continual meditation.[49]

---

49. Ps 1:1–2, Brock, *Singing the Ethos*, ch. 5.

1 Corinthians 13

Beyond the "Double Love Command" to Love's Aesthetic

Chapter 13 sees Paul switching into a very different literary register by taking up a poetic form—often given the labels "hymn" or "encomium"—in which something, or more often someone's, praises are sung. The label itself tells us as little as the question that consumes many modern commentators as to whether Paul is drawing on material that was composed independently prior to this occasion for his correspondence with the Corinthians. Our concern is to get to the bottom of what this adoption of a poetic form of speech in which "rhetorical and ethical melodies are played together harmoniously"[1] was meant to convey. The switch into a noticeably different rhetorical register is an unambiguous signal that Paul is asking his readers to pay especially close attention to the material that follows. The shift into the form of praise is Paul's attempt to mark the centrality of love in the Christian form of life that it warrants.

Because love is being presented here as the core and summit of the Christian life, we assume it likely that in this chapter Paul is offering his own re-presentation of Jesus's double love command. That command has come to occupy a prominent place in Christian thought. Subsequent readers have looked to Jesus's own summary of the law and the prophets (Mark 12:28–34 par.) or sometimes taken their starting point from Paul's peculiar use of the available Greek terms for love,[2] to come up with interpretations of the commands to love as "an exemplification of the virtues of love and justice,"[3] or

---

1. Bailey, *Paul through Mediterranean Eyes*, 359.
2. "The verb Paul uses for *love* is *agapeo*. The Greek language of his day had two primary words for love. The first was *eros*, which had to do with passionate love, either religious or sexual. The second was *phileo*, which was used to describe love between friends and the kind of love that is shared in a healthy family. But neither of these words was adequate for what Paul and the other writers of the New Testament wanted to describe . . . In the Greek Old Testament *agape*, as a noun, appears only in the Song of Songs. It is rare in classical Greek, and when used it has to do with 'inclining toward' something. Paul and his friends selected this word that had no clear footprint in the Greek language, and filled it with new meaning." Bailey, *Paul through Mediterranean Eyes*, 349.
3. Stout, *Democracy and Tradition*, 173.

even a universal "theorem of the militant."[4] On our reading Paul's praise of love in this chapter complicates this interpretative tradition that has sought to find in the biblical love command(s) an answer to the quest for a single unified concept of Christian morality. A main problem of such account is that the search for conceptual schematization tends to screen out the poetic presentation of love that the language of this chapter makes so obvious.

If instead we take seriously Paul's employment of the poetic form we begin to see that he is not presenting a *definition* of love, but a highly orchestrated *praise* and *appraisal* that must be understood in the context of his announcement in 12:31b that he is now to show us a "higher way." This is to suggest that in chapter 13 Paul is not offering us an enthronment of love as the highest of the spiritual gifts but a portrayal of the ways in which love saturates every other gift so that it genuinely builds up the community (*oikodome*). What we watch in operation here is not Paul the chemical analyst, isolating the essence of love by defining it in ever more narrow terms and showing how Christian love differs from other moral principles, values, or concepts. We are instead invited to listen to Paul the composer orchestrating an account of love that triggers a harmonic experience in the hearer that communicates by way of complex resonances set up between the 15 descriptors of love that the Apostle offers. The variety of instruments of different pitch and tonal color he deploys bring to life a cosmos of sound that is identifiable as an articulate musical experience so pleasing to the ear that it invites the hearer to add their own voice in praise of love.

The harmonic reading of Paul's hymn to love offers us a way to see why his employment of a whole range of adjectives to characterize love's ways has not just set up an intellectual puzzle we have to solve (and why not be more clear?), but a purposeful and necessary strategy he has consciously embraced in taking up this particular form of writing. The wealth of expression offered in this chapter can only appear as imprecise, labored, and unwieldy if they are subjected to the demands of a conceptual analysis characterized by the quest for summation, definition and distillation. How, precisely, such a tradition insists, is kindness different from love? If love is so many things—indeed, if love is everything—is it not nothing? We will see in the course of our discussion of the chapter that Paul is sympathetic to a different version of this question and has his own illuminating way of raising this question of "what comes to nothing" with respect to love.

Having already suggested that this chapter offers Paul's take on Jesus's double love command, we can now add that the narrative context in which Jesus's teaching appears (Matt 22:37–40) makes it seem plausible to us that

---

4. Badiou, *Saint Paul*, 90.

Paul understands his poetic orchestration of the command is his way of being faithful to Jesus's teaching. In this chapter we will attempt to show why this attempt should be understood as being *more* faithful to Jesus's command than the modern tendency to distill it to an ethical principle. According to the gospel tradition Jesus offers his formulation of the double love command in response to the question of the Pharisee, "Which is the greatest commandment?"—a question that foreshadows the modern quest for a single, all-embracing ethical first principle. It is critical to note here that Jesus's critical response forces a broadening of the Pharisee's own question by offering *two* instantiations of the love command, thereby already indicating that these cannot be absorbed into a single one, no more than "law *and* prophets" can be reduced a singular source of canonical authority.

The label "the double love command" is a misnomer. What Jesus actually offers is a duality that has unfortunately been entangled in an endless negotiation of the possible or perceived tensions between its two parts in the subsequent tradition of interpretation. Jesus offers a dual foci in an answer to the question "which one," and in so doing indicates that for all the centrality of love, it never exists per se, never as an abstract principle. The love embodied in Jesus Christ is always and exhaustively defined by the variety of objects to which it turns and is appropriately destined to turn. On our reading, in the radiating, multipolar exposition of love that follows Paul must be understood as developing a particularly astute elaboration of Jesus's precedent.

If Paul's orchestration of the love theme in this chapter is by no means a mere embellishment but a genuine sign of his faithfulness to the Jesus tradition, it is so in one more important way. That Paul adopts the poetic form at this point in his communications with the Corinthian church signals that this famous chapter *on* love is at the same time one *of* love—a love letter from the Apostle to his church. As such, as theorists of poetry have emphasized, the literary form he has chosen is operative in drawing the first and all subsequent hearers into the very world the poetic constellation is setting before them.[5]

Love as Fruitful Communication

> [1]If I speak in the tongues of mortals and of angels, but do not have love, I am a noisy gong or a clanging cymbal. [2]And if I have prophetic powers, and understand all mysteries and all knowledge, and if I have all faith, so as to remove mountains,

---

5. Ricoeur, "Toward a Hermeneutic."

> but do not have love, I am nothing. ³If I give away all my possessions, and if I hand over my body so that I may boast, but do not have love, I gain nothing.

In addition to his shifting into the rhetoric of hymnody it is also significant that Paul shifts to first-person address. Not telling his readers what to do or not to do, not even "to love," by taking up the first-person address he invites them to consider whether they can or even must embrace the poetic I as their own, to see the superiority of love as a way that they can enter themselves. In order to function as such an invitation to embrace, the poetic I must preserve a certain rhetorical distinction from Paul's biographical "I." It would be misleading and indeed impossible to read the first three verses as Paul's depiction of his own experience of himself. This is true even were we to suggest that these verses describe possibilities that the Apostle has come to know in the form of temptations that he has successfully overcome. A blending of the poetic "I" with the biographical "I" begins to seem less wildly implausible when we get to the characterization of love's ways from verse 4 onwards, where adjectives such as patient, kind, non-boastful, not self-inflated could be seen as resembling Paul's own characterization of his mission and practice. But especially when held up against Paul's own biographical self-characterization, it becomes all too evident that the poetic "I" presented in 13:1–3 is a portrayal of "nothingness" dressed up as something. Rather than resembling Paul's own life and attributes, the "I" who we first meet at the opening of this chapter is presented in a way that plausibly resembles (many in) the Corinthian congregation. But it is positioned in a manner that will allow Paul to reveal in a carefully staged way that the amazing gifts to which this "I" aspires are in fact like the emperor's new clothes.

A consistent rhetorical pattern in these first three verses signals that the poetic "I" is being presented as an impossible possibility. The self that will come to know its own nothingness is marked by a characteristic maximalism, in this case the desire for all spiritual gifts: "all **mysteries**, all **faith**, **give away** all **possessions**." Paul's positive account of love's ways counters this fatal maximalism not by calling for moderation or renunciation, but by initiating a shifting of the desire for the gifts that it expresses toward the different plane where it appropriately belongs. The "higher way" that Paul commends differs from the maximalist pursuit for spiritual gifts in that it is characterized by a freedom to allow love's own agency to do whatever love aspires to in an unreserved and non-inhibiting fashion: love "bears all things, believes all things, hopes all things, endures all things" (13:7). In what we have taken to be a faithful extension of Jesus's response to the reductionist tradition *in statu nascendi*, Paul is seeking to redirect the spiritually ill-fated maximalism of the Corinthians towards a very different type of maximalism that is at the root of Jesus's adoption of the Torah's command to love God "with *all* your heart, and with *all* your soul, and with *all* your mind" (Matt 22:37).

With this interpretative trajectory in mind, we suggest reading the expression "as yourself" to be a liberating release from the natural tendency toward self-concern, a release that invites a love for the neighbor characterized by a delightful lack of reserve. While it is characteristic of modern discussions of the "double love command" to spend immense efforts to demonstrate how the "problem" of relating love of self and love of neighbor can be solved in a manner that allows self-concern as legitimate, this "problem" is strikingly absent for Paul, even inconceivable, a discussion not worth having.[6] To the extent that the Apostle's identity is determined by his vocation, the love he expresses for the confused brethren in Corinth is but a form of loving *himself* as one who has "been fully known" by God (13:12). It is in this way that the apostolic self stands as a paradigm of the self that we are commanded to love (>1:2–3).

Putting things in this way is reminiscent of Paul's famous expression in Galatians 2:20, "it is no longer I who live, but it is Christ who lives in me." Although this is a perfectly viable English translation, Luther's German translation appears to be especially sensitive in putting a comma between ζῶ and δὲ οὐκέτι ἐγώ (*zō* and *de ouketi egō*), to yield the rendering, "I live, but no longer I." This formulation emphasizes the reality of the life of the self against a possible misreading of it being completely absorbed into Christ's life, while at the same time allowing the emphasis to fall on the new form of existence as *fieri*: "becoming"—in the constant process of being conformed to Christ.

Having identified this chapter as a distinctive type of Apostolic speech act, in which a poetic composition *on* love is rendered *in the mode of* a love letter by the Apostle to his church, suggests that we can gain further purchase on the text by attending to the contextual bearings by which Paul is orienting himself as he composes this hymn. We would be ill advised to read the main theme of the chapter, love, in a manner that abstracts from the communicative situation of ongoing discussions in which Paul is engaged with the community in Corinth in mind. Taking this into account will allow us better to grasp how a love letter to a particular community is "addressing" love rather than "describing" it in general terms. It will also bar us from any

---

6. See Nygren, *Agape and Eros*; Outka, *Agape*; O'Donovan, *The Problem of Self-Love*. The alternative we are suggesting here is developed in more detail in Brock, "Dischipelschap: Waarom het volgen van Jezus betekent dat ik mijzelf moet vergeten" [Discipleship: Why following Jesus means forgetting myself], 31–54.

initial assumption that this song of love could be assessed in terms of some independent aesthetic value and slotted into a host of possible occasions as a standalone piece of universally edifying poetry. There is nothing wrong in principle with quoting these words in nuptial sermons or, say, at the conclusion of a film exploring the Enlightenment triad liberty, equality, fraternity, when the director sensed a need to deepen the range of ideas we associate with political liberty.[7] Nor does anything stand in the way of believers and secular humanists alike acknowledging that this chapter sets out an attractive constellation of ideas that are plausibly designated a core contribution of Christian thought to modernity.[8]

But what is given up by any such extraction and distillation processes is what we take to be the beating heart of the chapter. The "higher way" is not a love that can be separated from other Christian virtues, but is *love in and through all other gifts*. Paul is not saying "all you need is love," but rather "without love for concrete others leavening everything you do, all you have is meaningless, wasted activity, alienating rather than creating community." We need all of the Spirit's gifts as depicted in such rich detail in the previous chapter—teamed with the addition Paul makes in this current chapter—to reiterate with the necessary force that all the gifts of the body *must* be infused with love. It would be a mistake to read the chapter backwards from the conclusion, where love is designated as the "greatest" of these gifts, and conflate the "higher way" that Paul announces at the beginning of the chapter with love simply. There may be some scope for the discussion of an ordering of love, hope, and faith, but it is significant that this comes only at the end of Paul's discussion and does not structure it from the beginning.

Commentators throughout the ages have been puzzled about how to reconstruct the subjects Paul is indicating in verses 1–3. For example, what is the faith that could exist without love? Augustine answers this question by linking it with the odd narrative in 1 Sam 19:18–20, which he takes to exemplify the possibility of there being prophecy without love,[9] while Calvin renames it "particular faith ... which does not lay hold of Christ in His Wholeness."[10] Additional alternative readings are proposed by Luther: Paul could be speaking here of a general belief in God, not the Christian faith, or of a Christian faith corrupted by pride and therefore in a state of decomposition. His preferred reading, though, is that "with these words Saint Paul makes love so necessary that he proposes an impossible

---

7. Kieslowski's *Trois couleurs: Bleu/Three Colors: Blue*.
8. Badiou, *Saint Paul*, ch. 8, "Love as Universal Power."
9. Augustine, *Sermon* 162A.1–4, in JK, 217–18.
10. Calvin, JC 275.

example."[11] Luther goes on to suggest that the impossibility of these examples is marked by the fact that no human being is capable of speaking in angelic language. Once again we find Luther's instinct astute. We do not need to enter into speculation about the possibility or impossibility of speaking angelic language, however, to note the more fundamental point that any straightforwardly realist reading would have to proceed on the assumption that it is indeed possible to express the gifts of the Spirit independently of the power of love. This would be to understand love as coming in as an addition that "tops up" and so perfects or fully rounds an entity that is nevertheless real and present without it.

If we jump off from verse 1 and follow the thread of the traditional argument that insisted on the impossibility of human access to angelic speech we will begin to see how Paul uses structural parallelisms to set up contrasts in each case between a resulting "nothing" (am nothing, gain nothing, nothing but inarticulate noise) on one hand and an encompassing "all" on the other. On this reading we should not see Paul as retreading the territory already covered in his discussion of chapter 11, but rather as indicating through hyperbolic speech the aspiration to claim linguistic omni-competence in every conceivable language. Each of these equations in the first three verses can then be seen to "rhyme" nicely, each being a hyperbolic representation of aspirations displacing particular types of impossibility. The coherence offered by this reading is particularly palpable in verse 2. It is as presumptuous as it is impossible for a human being to aspire to possess understanding of **all mysteries** and **all knowledge**. That the Apostle is employing hyperbolic speech is even more obviously evident in verse 3, given the sheer impossibility of success of any attempt to **give away all possessions**. The fierce thirteenth-century debates between Franciscans and Dominicans about whether it is even possible to divest one's self *entirely* of property rested on a controversy about the permissibility of this aspiration among Christians. The current phenomenon of sheer ungovernability of modern corporations reveals the foresight of the Dominican side in the argument. The theological leaders of the *ordo predicatorum* insisted that the distinction between possession *per se* and *usu-fructus*, mere "consumptive use," by which Franciscan thinkers sought to defend the viability of the Franciscan ideal of "giving away all possessions," in effect only corroborated the impossibility of the (Franciscan) construal of the "higher (supererogatory) way."[12]

The theological gain of highlighting the link we think Paul is making between presumptuousness and impossibility is the clearer perception it

---

11. Luther, *Luthers Epistel-Auslegung*, 2:176–77 (authors' translation).
12. Black, *The Theology of the Corporation*.

gives us of the *type* of speech act Paul is performing in 13:1–3. The Apostle is criticizing a series of presumptuous attitudes not because they are morally wrong (e.g., boasting), but because they fail to correspond with reality. In each case the missing component does not render the respective aspiration morally deficient but literally non-existent as the thing it purports to be. What is lost to any such aspiration to possess spiritual gifts to the maximal degree is precisely the twofold emphasis that characterized Paul's account of the *charismata*: their measured quality as individually apportioned according to respective callings on the one hand, and their ecclesiastical purposefulness in the process of building up the community as a whole, on the other. It is this qualitative difference that Paul understands love to bring to bear on the manner in which spiritual gifts are understood and practiced. It is love that ensures the gifts are not held as individual possessions that can nicely be lined up in a quantitative ranking within the logic of "the more the better," but as calibrated works (*energema*) that each believer receives to the degree and in the fashion that it takes to further the commonweal (>12:4–7). Love as the Apostle understands it never merely adds something to something else but becomes operative in a process of curbing, pruning, and helping to let go, depending on what it will take to allow the up-building and communicative purposes of each individual gift to come to full fruition.

Pretentious aspirations misshapen by a lack of love are therefore properly understood as enacted nothingness. Having detected the structural parallelism of the three "I" iterations in verses 1–3 it now becomes fruitful to look more closely at the specific features of the individual equations. If, as we have suggested, the expression **tongues of mortals and of angels** depicts a hyperbolic claim to linguistic omni-competence, Paul's particular characterization of the resultant enacted nothingness as having the quality of **a noisy gong or a clanging cymbal** rests on the positive recognition that tongues or languages are in fact geared toward human communication. What the lack of love undermines is the peculiar purpose of language, *communication*. Paul's claim that language will become distressingly uncommunicative without love becomes more transparent when we track the metaphor he uses to describe speech turned to "nothing." If we understand music as a particularly pleasing form of communication, the pretentious claim to linguistic omnipotence will, ironically, resemble noise. By drawing attention to the peculiar features associated with the types of percussive musical instruments Paul mentions, namely, volume and inarticulateness, we perceive him to be pointing out the fact that at the very moment when those who strive for gifts in themselves ("without love") attempt to communicate, not only are they unloving but also render themselves unintelligible.

The manner in which Paul has characterized what is problematic about the pretentious claim to possess utter communicative competence suggests an inner linkage with his resistance to any form of rhetorical manipulation that he has flagged up earlier as a constitutive feature of his apostolic ministry (>1:17, 9:15–17). Such communicative gestures are self-deceived in the same way as the siren call of the idols that Paul has portrayed as mute in 12:2. Later on in chapter 14 he will further elaborate his critical account of pseudo-speech by comparing speaking in tongues without interpretation to musical instruments that produce sound but "do not give distinct notes"—which will have only the effect of leaving all in earshot with the question, "How will anyone know what is being played?" (14:7b). Here the Apostle is providing us with a detailed specification of *how* love makes all the difference between inarticulate noise and music. Love seeks the consummation of any act of communication not because it strives for maximum projection but because it seeks to calibrate itself to all the variables that must be taken into account if the message is genuinely to be received. Communicative activity is thus not replaced or surmounted but re*tuned* by love.

As in verses 1–2, verse 3 again assumes a hypothetical scenario that should not send us too quickly past the realities on which the description is based. Paul characterizes the nihilistic character of human action lacking love as an activity that can **gain nothing**. In 2 Corinthians (9:12–14) Paul indicates a direct correlation between the giving up of possessions and love between Christians. Commending the collection he is organizing among the Macedonian churches on behalf of the Jerusalem mother church, the Apostle asks his fellow believers not only to give, but precisely to give *as a work of love*.

> The rendering of this ministry not only supplies the needs of the saints but also overflows with many thanksgivings to God. Through the testing of this ministry you glorify God by your obedience to the confession of the gospel of Christ and by the generosity of your sharing with them and with all others, while they long for you and pray for you because of the surpassing grace of God that he has given you.

The gain that Paul associates with giving in a loving manner is real. It might appear that material possessions are given and immaterial ones received when those who give money become the subject of the thanksgiving prayers of the recipients. Theologically speaking, however, the gain that accrues through such acts is only properly understood when we take into account what Paul calls the "longing" (2 Cor 9:14) of the recipients for the givers. Only a recipient can make the equation of a gift having been given with a giving of the self, and it is the presumptuous aspiration to take this equation under control that Paul characterizes as boasting. The presumption that characterizes the aspiration to give up all possessions or to hand over one's body to be burned[13] lies in its usurpation of what is up to the recipient to determine: that the giving of something is at the same time a loving gift of one's self.

This gain that accrues through uncorrupted forms of giving is never a private gain for the giver (in, for instance, reputation or enhanced self-respect) nor for the receiver. In genuine acts of love what is gained is always of a communal nature and so must be understood as *their* gain in being precisely a strengthening of the bond between two sides. If this account of the gain that accrues to those who act in love seems to underplay the vertical context of a horizontal inter-human relationship, this appearance could only be sustained by overlooking that any act of inter-Christian giving rests on the joint recognition of the preexistence of the bond between believers that has been established by Jesus Christ. This is why giving can be understood as primordially an act of loving gratitude for that bond, an act of praise to the God who first created it together with his creatures and restored it through the reconciliatory ministry of the Son. "Through the testing of this ministry you glorify God by your obedience to the confession of the gospel of Christ," Paul states, "and by the generosity of your sharing with them and with all others."

Again it is these connections that help us to even more precisely locate the problem to which Paul is trying to draw attention with the hypothetical scenarios he is picturing. What he has in view are not imaginary thought experiments but actually existing yet corrupted realities. By highlighting these "impossible possibilities" the Apostle is describing the actual predicament of believers who deceive themselves about their real situation. They assume that because they speak they really communicate. Because they believe they have real faith and give alms they believe they are accomplishing works of love. But Paul reveals to them that their aspirations amount to nothing, precisely because they lack love, the one thing that makes these activities real and substantial over against the *nihil*. In putting things this way it becomes clearer what it means when we say that the aspirations Paul highlights are real, though corrupted. Such presumptuous aspirations are

---

13. This reading would also make sense of the textual variants of verse 3, the earlier attested ἵνα καυχήσωμαι (*hina kauchēsōmai*) **that I may boast** and the later wording that appears in many Western texts, ἵνα καυθήσωμαι (*hina kauthēsōmai*) "that I should be burned." Both variants reinforce the point that the aspiration in view is a maximalist one, either for maximum glory or for maximum giving away of all possessions, up to and including giving away one's body.

corrosive of the generative forms of the activities they seek to represent such as the language-communication nexus or the giving-receiving bond. Since these realities cannot be dissolved (language will always exist, and always be geared to communication), the "attempt" to do so must eventually deflate into nothingness. The one who is engaged in such a self-deceptive enterprise is thus formally and essentially self-annulling.

It is love that makes the difference between the genuine and the fake, because the one who loves gratefully embraces both the multifaceted givenness of creation and its redemption (>3:11–13). Love in its communicative power not only attends to the receiver and his or her peculiar circumstances, but at the same time "loves" language by living up to its own particular *telos* to communicate. Loving language in this sense differs from the aspiration to linguistic competence. Paul's desire to "become a Jew to the Jews, and a gentile to the gentiles" provides a very different impetus for learning other languages than the aspiration to acquire such languages in order to increase one's stature as a polyglot. The repeated qualifier "without love" is thus directing our attention not to a *deficiency* but to a *state of alienation*. Unlike a deficiency, a state of alienation could no more be rectified by the addition of more words or greater affective engagement than noise is silenced by turning up the volume. The failure to embrace the realities that God has created as well as the gifts donated into inter-creaturely relations must be addressed. Love alone provides the bond that can keep us connected with other creatures in their contingency and prevent us from being alienated.[14] As Paul has previously emphasized, to confess that humans are creatures is to affirm that they are always embedded in communicative matrices: without love, they misuse and ignore the effects of their constant communication on others (>6:13–17, *Excursus: Bodies and Their Communicative Surfaces*).

In keeping with our reading of Paul's anchoring of the three opening scenarios in this chapter in a particular *relatio realitatis*, 13:2 presents a particular challenge in its suggestion that prophecy and faith without love also result in existential nothingness. Here a particular type of alienation from reality is not merely characterized as *gaining* nothing (13:3), but as *being* nothing: I **am nothing** (13:2). What positive reality is being presumed in this verse in which prophecy and faith rightly give being? Luther's account of faith as existential rather than a mere cognitive or volitional phenomenon comes to mind here (>8:8–13). In the perspective he suggests, faith without love would then appear as something short of such existential investment, something less intense than a passionate clinging of the heart to its savior, a mere cognitive ("belief") or volitional thing that can always keep the heart

---

14. This point is developed in more detail in Brock, "On Being Creatures."

at some distance. In a similar vein, the gift of prophecy could be said to be never less than existentially involving in the sense displayed by figures like Jeremiah and his peers. These biblical figures who are properly called prophets all found, at least for a specific period of time, that their lives had been completely absorbed into their vocation to witness to God's love for his people in announcing redemption or judgment.

In this sense, one can certainly find it possible to encounter prophecy, like faith, in the form of mere semblances, irrespective of whether one resolves to still call these phenomena by the name of the respective "real thing" their appearance resembles or not.

The One Who Loves

> [4]Love is patient; love is kind; love is not envious or boastful or arrogant [5]or rude. It does not insist on its own way; it is not irritable or resentful; [6]it does not rejoice in wrongdoing, but rejoices in the truth. [7]It bears all things, believes all things, hopes all things, endures all things.

In 13:4–7 Paul begins to describe the positive features of love, even if some formulations are still formally negative. Before looking directly at that positive account it is important to ask what it means to "describe" love? Is it really sufficient simply to list its features as Paul appears to be doing here? Can we know we have love if we see in our acting features that we typically associate with this concept? Were we to ask a variety of people to come up with a list of the features that define love, we could expect a good deal of diversity in the descriptions. And were we to undertake a comparison of Paul's list with features we might reasonably expect to find on other such lists, the features enlisted by the Apostle would appear just as selective as any other list, irrespective of the overlaps we would likely find. The critical aspect to note here is that Paul's list is "selective" for a reason peculiar to his vocation as Apostle. It reflects the story he shares with the Corinthian community as testified throughout his letters to them. It might well appear to us that one or another aspect of love is underrepresented in this enumeration. But what matters here is not the balance between the descriptors of love being offered nor their completeness, but rather how well this list offers the Corinthians an account of the love *they* need.

To emphasize the particularity of Paul's concern in this way is not a suggestion that he is eschewing any universalizing language in relation to love. Indeed: love **bears all things, believes all things, hopes all things, endures all things.** This Pauline version of agapeic maximalism is often fingered as a potential threat to personal or communal integrity. What else do these qualifications suggest, some ask, if not a strangely "soft" account of love that cannot but result in a watering down of any clear boundaries—including those set by faith, such as the distinction between orthodox belief and heresy? Could Paul really be commending heresy (**believes all things**), naive optimism (**hopes all things**), political quietism (**bears all things**) or even a masochistic sense of self-sacrifice (**endures all things**)? We take it as a sign of having caught an important drift of Paul's proclamation that Christians have taken this agapeic maximalism with full seriousness as attested in traditions like the Eastern Orthodox holy fool tradition,[15] or in comments like the following from Luther among Western theologians.

> Love is a simple-minded thing. She believes and trusts everyone and . . . allows herself to be deceived and aped and fooled . . . She measures everyone according to their heart and is happy to be wrong in this. This mismeasurement does not ruin her because she knows that God will not let her go. Whoever deceives her, deceives really only himself.[16]

Thus, even if in the final analysis we discover that the love of Jesus Christ is not hopelessly foolish and naive, the central theological question is how it avoids this outcome given the radical openness of its starting point. Even if in the final analysis the answer to the questions just raised turn out to be "no," it is an answer that must not be too quickly proffered.

This problem is complicated by the evident lack of reference to either God or Jesus in this chapter. Paul's decision to speak about love as a personified power in 13:4–8a has been the primary catalyst driving modern speculation as to whether in this chapter Paul has incorporated a poem from another context or source. Commentators inclined to the partition theory of the epistle's composition speculate that Paul has weaved together

---

15. This tradition is memorably depicted by Dostoyevsky. In *The Idiot* the main character is a prince who, though prone to all sorts of breaches of decorum, speaks truth to power: "To attain perfection, one must first of all be able not to understand many things. For if we understand things too quickly, we may perhaps fail to understand them well enough. I'm telling you this, you who have been able to understand so much already and—have failed to understand so much . . . I am a prince of ancient lineage myself, and I am sitting among princes. I am saying this to save you all, so as to prevent our class from vanishing for nothing into utter darkness, without realizing anything, abusing everything and losing everything . . . Let us be servants in order to be leaders." Dostoyevsky, *The Idiot*, 530.

16. Luther, *Luthers Epistel-Auslegungen*, 2:179–80 (authors' translation). The pivotal passages in Kierkegaard's *Works of Love* elaborate precisely this exegesis to illumine the conceptual interdependence of hope and faith and love. See his Second series, chs. 1–6.

a list of accepted virtues to make it intelligible and theologically acceptable.[17] Given the emphasis in the letter that the Corinthians should imitate him, others suggest that his personification of love is a rhetorical device by which Paul can draw attention to the love he has displayed for the Corinthians and invite them to think of him as the one who "shows" them what love is.[18] The end of 13:7 and the beginning of 13:8, however, make it quite clear that there is only one who can be said to embody a love that **never gives up** and **never ends**.[19] Paul's personification of love operates rhetorically like a dangerous pill, which, if swallowed, asks so much of human loving that it eventually makes those who wish truly to love realize that it cannot be had without drinking in the love of Jesus Christ himself.[20] The rhetorical framing of the poem is theologically loaded in inviting the reader to enter Paul's praise of this praiseworthy being and thus to fall for this comely "person." In this manner a love is revealed that is inextricably bound to Christ as the "One who loves."[21] To rejoice in this truth is to gain something *both* communal and individual which does not suffer division according to the logic of particular and universal.

The fulsomeness of the description of love offered in these verses appears to be Paul's response to the very different series of maximalist expressions in 13:1–3 that circumscribed the pretentious aspirations of false love. Having renarrated the Corinthians' claims to individual maximal possession of spiritual gifts as in fact indicative of faith without love, in 13:7 Paul goes on to associate love with a counter-maximalism that contradicts what they have come to expect from the "spiritual" life. The Apostle has already demonstrated in his criticisms of the Corinthians why love's own maximalism is as distant from pretentious loves as it is from a realism that immediately begins to set out limiting conditions for this "all."

The characterization of love as one that **believes all things**, for example, is not to be understood in abstraction from, but precisely in its determination by its other characteristic expression **rejoicing in truth**, which is to say,

---

17. Lietzmann, *An die Korinther I-II*, 67.

18. Garland, DEG 609–10.

19. Thiselton, ACT 226.

20. We therefore agree with Elizabeth Stuart that if Paul in this chapter is doing no more than offering himself as an example to be imitated then he is being highly manipulative in that his "message is that it is only through Paul that the Corinthians can experience the love of God in Christ because only Paul, no other Christian teacher, possesses that love. In short, love is Paul." "Love is . . . Paul," 264–66.

21. This is the key phrase in Kierkegaard's *Works of Love*, which allows him to remind his readers that every time Paul uses the word *love*, he is ultimately invoking the "One who loves."

in Christ. Therefore, to affirm that Christian love believes "all things" is not to specify a set of propositions that are to be believed, because love always turns belief into existential faith, which can only be in a person, Jesus Christ. Analogously, "hopes all things" cannot refer to an all-comprehensive list of things to be hoped for, but to the one who alone can bring about a future in which all things are appropriately ordered. In each case "all" is directing the believer to embrace "all that is Christ's," all that *he* loves.

Paul's discussion of vicarious faith in chapter 12 (>12:9) sheds light on our reading of this hymn on love and reveals a fruitful parallel with hope. Since, like every other gift of the Spirit, faith and hope are apportioned according to individual vocation, there is inevitably the need for some to hold up the faith and hope of others in the church community. Hence "all things" are indeed possible in faith in Christ and in hope for the kingdom, precisely as such faith and hope are always challenged by faithlessness and hopelessness in the church. Such challenges arise not primarily in the form of deficiencies of faith and love in the believers but more seriously through rival forms of belief and hope. The hope in Jesus Christ's love portrayed here by Paul is only truly expressed when it is committed to following the long road of discernment in order properly to love fellow believers prone to believing anything indiscriminately. This is even more difficult when other believers "hope all things" in a naïve manner, unmoored from Christ and so perpetually chase the parade of hopes that course through both the church and other publics (by, for example, investing oneself in pretentious ideologies of progress through routines that promise "results" in one's private piety or "growth" in one's church). Nevertheless, hope in what Christ bears and would yet bear through us remains simultaneously vicarious and fruitful. This is no general hoping that people will eventually reach their highest potential[22] but a fine-grained hope for each individual to find their own "fit" within the economy of the Trinitarian God's loving. Such hope is a form of confident discernment of what Christ has in store for each member and the body as a whole.

Just as hope, when framed by the love and faith of Paul's triplet, is categorically different from the human capacity to form optimistic narratives about the future, so it is with love. Love in this sense is not the natural capacity to desire—*amor* (Augustine) or *appetitus* (Aquinas)—but a gift of the Spirit, *agape*, that *orients the manner in which our natural loves direct us*

---

22. In *God's Zeal* (137–38) Sloterdijk presents a stereotypically modern (Feuerbachian) reification of love. Here God is presented as the personification of all conceivable human perfections, a thought that for him represents the only genuinely novel contribution the monotheisms make to a post-religious world, since they set up a "vertical tension" that constantly expands human aspirations to express their "best self."

to embrace specific objects. The worry that Paul is offering a gullible love that attaches itself indiscriminately to whatever objects is driven by an image of natural desire similar to that of the child who has not yet learned to distrust and hence excitedly embraces all sorts of things, even if it might be to her peril. Because the Apostle has made unambiguously clear that love is a *gift* we can be assured that for him, *agape* is understood as supervening on natural desires, redirecting them into conformity with the love of Christ.

On the basis of this account of the vicarious nature of Christian love, Paul will now break his description down to form a list of the specific attitudes, gestures, and affections that display and convey it, such as patience, kindness, etc. It is a list offered as a direct response to the specific lacks among those he loves, as their Apostle.

Loving Knowledge and Being Known by Love

> **⁸Love never ends. But as for prophecies, they will come to an end; as for tongues, they will cease; as for knowledge, it will come to an end. ⁹For we know only in part, and we prophesy only in part; ¹⁰but when the complete comes, the partial will come to an end. ¹¹When I was a child, I spoke like a child, I thought like a child, I reasoned like a child; when I became an adult, I put an end to childish ways. ¹²For now we see in a mirror, dimly, but then we will see face to face. Now I know only in part; then I will know fully, even as I have been fully known.**

The NRSV translation of ἡ ἀγάπη οὐδέποτε πίπτει (*hē agapē oudepote piptei*) as **Love never ends** is possible, but a more literal rendering gives us a better insight into the logic of Paul's portrayal of the ways of love: "Love never falls" (Thiselton). Since the love that Paul has just been portraying is one that holds or lifts up faith and hope rather than merely having greater temporal duration than these, it matters little whether we understand his description of love as never falling "down" or rather as never falling "apart." Paul elaborates the transformative and perfecting power of this love on spiritual gifts and personal growth by developing a number of polarities in verses 8–12. Several of these are immediately obvious, such as "in part" and "full," or "now" and "then," whereas we can spot some other deeper polarities only by thinking about the examples Paul chooses. By switching to the visual metaphor of the mirror in 13:12a Paul introduces a complication to a discussion of knowledge in order to drive it toward a crucial theological distinction, that between personal and impersonal knowledge. Only when this distinction has been grasped are we in a position to appreciate how all-important the relational distinction is between active knowing and being passively known by God.

By setting up this highly structured cascade of nested distinctions Paul again ensures that God is brought into the discussion of the ways of human love at a rather precise point. In distinction from invocations of God designed to ensure that our claims to knowledge are sufficiently wide and our prophecies sufficiently ambitious, Paul instead suggests that God's transformative involvement in human lives should be detectable by the manner in which love changes perception and knowledge. It is love that changes what we know from the impersonal to the personal, from the merely active to a receptively active phenomenon grounded in God's preceding activity. Love never "falls" because it always exists as a force that "holds up" (13:7), creating lightness. These are the ways of love, the things that love *does*. Love, as Paul is describing it, is not a sentiment or idea but an operation, an activity that "raises" the other from the living death of hopeless and aimless existence—from nothingness into life and communion.

Excursus: Theology and God Talk

This seems an appropriate point to pause and reflect directly on the remarkably uneven distribution of "God language" in this letter. In this chapter the terms *God* and *Jesus* are strikingly absent while elsewhere in the epistle, these names seem almost excessively deployed (a reference to Jesus, for instance, appears in every one of the first ten verses of chapter 1). This unevenness of distribution again raises questions about the theology driving Paul's rhetorical choices. Why does Paul explicitly invoke God in seemingly random places such as greetings, while at this most sensitive point in his argument he eschews speaking directly of God? The fact that we have *both* unabashed use and obvious restraint in Paul's deployment of God's name should at least sensitize us as theologians to the reality that something cannot be quite right when theological approaches embrace only one of these polarities or insist in principle either that theology must always maximize or always minimize God talk.

If anything, Paul's mode of speech in chapter 13 resembles a tendency we associate today with modern theologies of the liberal type that tend to avoid direct God-talk with the aim of offering the substance of religious terms in a more universally acceptable and accessible form. Those who are attracted to this project tend to find this chapter to offer a more "benign" Paul, one that can more easily be meshed with modern discourses than in most of his other writings. According to this logic, the topic of this chapter also seems well chosen for this "other" Paul to emerge. After all, what idea would be better than "love" as a canvass on which God-talk can be transformed into the language of human experience and activity? To round this argument off, it can also be pointed out that the move of absorbing God language into the experiential language of love can even claim an intra-canonical theological justification in form of the Johannine equation of God *as* love (1 John 4:16).

As popular as this translationist agenda has become in the modern era, instead of hitching the Paul of chapter 13 to it we assume it better to reconsider the way in which his love talk actually invites God back into the poetry. By offering an ever-closer description of love's ways, Paul takes the reader on a journey that prepares her to embrace the divine dimension of love that has implicitly propelled the description from the beginning. Having repeated the name of Jesus Christ incessantly at the opening of this letter, Paul has devoted himself to walking his reader into what that name entails, the *ways* of the person who bears that name in our world. This is why when Paul switches to the passive voice in his expression of the fuller knowledge that will come to him as one who has been fully known (**when I was a child . . .**), he should be understood to be holding out an invitation to understand love in terms of a *passivum divinum*. It is precisely this divine dimension of love that is incapable of being retranslated into a relationalist conception of inter-human love.

It is really only in the expression of 13:12, **but then we will see face to face**, that Paul's discussion of love reaches the point of no return, falling inevitably into the gravitational well of overtly Christological language. Though "no one has ever seen God" (1 John 4:12), the divine countenance has come to shine on the human race in the form of the incarnate Son, whose face Paul has seen on the road to Damascus (Acts 9:27) and whose redemptive work he describes as a transformation into his image (>15:49). The condition of Paul's being able to conceive of this future face-to-face encounter with the Lord is the dim version of that perception that has already dawned on humanity, the witness of Christ's appearance that has been given to the church. The One encountered in the present is none other than the one that was and is and is to come, and yet for now his face can be seen only indirectly.

At this point our train of argumentation can be turned around: it is precisely because Paul is speaking of love that he is allowed or even compelled to speak of God in a language that does not directly invoke the name of God. God is the *source*, not a mere pinnacle of love; love is defined in relation to its origin in God and its power to draw creatures into it. We believe that contemporary debates on the possibility, necessity, and viability of God-talk have much to learn from the way that Paul has presented his discussion of love with its movement of ever greater transparency towards the divine. At first he simply describes the phenomenon of love by characterizing it through reference to a number of its features named in adjectival form—love is patient, love is kind, and so on. As the description unfolds, however, the adjectival mode of describing love's *features* gives way to verbs that characterize what love *does*: love rejoices, love bears, believes, hopes, and endures. As already noted, the presentation of love as a center of agency moves it closer to a personalized account, most obviously when the verbs used are ones that we associate with human agents rather than with impersonal causal effects.

Since every such list of features will be necessarily selective, those features drawn together in Paul's list can be expected to point to particular people who exemplify in particularly vivid ways Paul's presentation of love's ways. In good company with a number of other commentators we note that the characteristics of love that Paul names do work well as a description of his own apostolic persona. If we attend to Paul's own understanding of the exemplarity of his apostolic persona as anchored in the exemplarity of Christ himself—"imitate me, as I am imitating Christ" (1 Cor 11:1)—we begin to grasp that his overall strategy in this chapter is to present what looks to be a inner-worldly account of love in a manner that allows it to become ever more transparent towards the divine, a transparency that is eventually wholly dissolved into a Christological ascription.

A methodological characterization of the gentle way in which Paul has been preparing his readers to follow him in this progression could be put this way: a descriptive account of the phenomena of love has been presented that has been increasingly laced with language open to a divine dimension that is finally anchored in the person of Jesus Christ. The sequence of this transitioning remains instructive for our contemporary debates about the utility of direct and indirect God talk. It is because Paul drives his account of love towards the embrace of Christ, the one who alone can perfect love, that we can see why he cannot so easily be assimilated to the translationist agenda of liberal theologies. Translationist approaches tend happily to follow Paul's first move to present a descriptive account of love as increasingly transparent towards the spiritual dimension—love-talk being understood as a secret form of God-talk. What is characteristic of such accounts is their insistence that the two dimensions remain in constant interplay and can be mutually retranslated into each other at any time. Consequently, such approaches must finally reject the unidirectionality employed by Paul with its culmination and termination in a univocal Christological identification of love. Whereas translationist theologies are based on a *principle* of incarnation (which allows for an infinite series of incarnating and de-incarnating), Paul drives his portrayal of love *into the arms of* the incarnate One (so offering us grounds and criteria from which discernments can be made about genuine love on the one hand and mere semblances of love on the other).

Despite his earlier censure of the Corinthians for their deployment of hierarchical accounts of the relations between believers (>2:6–8, 12:21–26), in 13:11 Paul allows for a certain delimited sense in which child-to-adult accounts of maturation are meaningful in Christian theology. The Apostle's account of progression from partial and immature knowledge to maturity is immediately protected from misunderstandings by the relativizing feature named in 13:12. In this life even the "mature ones" can only **see in a mirror, dimly,** in comparison to what will be the case when **we will see face to face**. In the context of the Corinthian yearning for higher knowledge Paul is inviting them to embrace a type of maturity that is incomplete at its best and that can only be willingly received by those travelling the way of love. Such an account of maturation bars all claims to completeness, either of being or of knowledge: **Now I know only in part; then I will know fully, even as I have been fully known.** With this final move the quest to progress from immaturity to maturity—which had become such an obsession among the Corinthians—is sharply downgraded as the central goal of the Christian life. Whether we are childish or mature, Paul insists, our knowledge and gifts remain incomplete, but **then**, in the future when fullness has come, **we will see face to face**. Two implications follow. First, what counts as knowledge here is an interpersonal knowing of proximate presence, as emphasized in the Hebrew concept of *yadaʿ* (ידע) with its connotation of the physical and intimate knowing of sexual embrace. To see face to face is to know directly and physically, person to person. When such knowledge is of *God*, it is a knowing that cannot be had without our being transformed, remade from beings whose existence is shaped by shame and alienation into those who can stand aright before the Creator and Judge of all creation.

The connection of this "knowing" discourse with the topic of love now becomes crystal clear, because to know *this* One necessitates our being elevated to at least glimpse a knowing of ourselves as God knows us, **as I have been fully known**. Because God is the One who alone fully embodies love, the transformation that is required in order to stand face to face with this One must begin with the transformation of our ways of knowing into ones that are entirely shaped by love—which is how God sees us. This is why the promise that we will one day see face to face must be understood as a promise of the ongoing work of the three persons of the Trinity. To this end Chrysostom adduces what we think is an apt concluding textual connection: "*For what person knows a man's thoughts except the spirit of the man which is in him? So also no one comprehends the thoughts of God except the Spirit of God* (1 Cor 2:11). Even Christ says that this knowledge is his alone, saying, *Not that any one has seen the Father except him who is from God; he has seen the Father* (John 6:46)."[23]

As the bond of love between Father and Son it is the Spirit who keeps them face to face. It was the Spirit who descended bodily as a dove who embodied the light of God's face shining on the Son as the beloved one at his baptism (Mark 1:10 par.). Conversely, Jesus's cry of dereliction on the cross (Mark 15:34; Matt 27:46) names the experience of the hiddenness of God's face. Believers can therefore only confess **love never fails** as a statement of trust that the love of the Father has not and will not fail in bringing the Son by the power of the Spirit back into face-to-face relation, moving mountains, or rolling away stones, in order to do so.[24]

Abiding in the Love of the One

> **[13] And now faith, hope, and love abide, these three; and the greatest of these is love.**

The main theme of this chapter has been the ways of love with the faith and hope that intertwine it. Though distinct from faith and hope, Christian love can never be separated from them.[25] Only because God is faithful to his creatures and because love is finally measured against the One who loves can God's desire to bring humans into relationship be affirmed as the grounds for human hope for an **abiding** love. Humans are time-saturated contingent creatures, ever growing and changing. Their abiding can only rest within the truth established by God's faith, hope, and love for his creatures, a love determining his acts of faithfulness to creatures that are other than himself. It is *God's* faith, hope, and love in us that finally constitute the condition of our continuing at all, and this faithfulness alone ensures they will abide.

This again is not an affirmation that may be reversed to form a thanksgiving to a God who "believes in us all" (as Forrest Whitaker is reputed to have claimed in an Oscar award speech). Because God's faith, hope, and love are foundational, and our abiding in it is a receptive

---

23. Chrysostom, Homily 34, PG 61:288–89, in JK, 225.

24. It is this insistence on God's acts as defining our sense of who God is that leads Robert Jenson to write the line that has come to define his work: "God is whoever raised Jesus from the dead, having before raised Israel from Egypt." Jenson, *Systematic Theology*, 1:63.

25. Kierkegaard, *Works of Love*, 255–56.

activity, our human loving can only be a form of being co-opted by God's love. Stated negatively, to not love another person is to have fallen from *God's* love for them.[26] To not **hope all things** is to fall from the true and real that never falls, and hence ends up being **nothing** (13:2). When each of us looks in the mirror we can as yet only see a multiplicity, we among the masses, we among the one Christ. We now only see Christ in the world dimly. But when we see him face to face we will see in his face the whole richness of the multitudes who have made up his body—an image we can comprehend only if we have encountered the power of his loving face to transfigure our neighbors and render them lovable. In *this* seeing the desires of faith and hope find love's object, and it is precisely as they take on this form that love is the greatest.

---

26. Ibid., 300–302, 304.

1 Corinthians 14

Distinguishing Private and Public Edification

> ¹Pursue love and strive for the spiritual gifts, and especially that you may prophesy. ²For those who speak in a tongue do not speak to other people but to God; for nobody understands them, since they are speaking mysteries in the Spirit. ³On the other hand, those who prophesy speak to other people for their upbuilding and encouragement and consolation. ⁴Those who speak in a tongue build up themselves, but those who prophesy build up the church. ⁵Now I would like all of you to speak in tongues, but even more to prophesy. One who prophesies is greater than one who speaks in tongues, unless someone interprets, so that the church may be built up.

Glossolalia, or "speaking in tongues," has long embarrassed Christian readers and continues to do so in many quarters. This sense of embarrassment is corroborated by the conspicuous neglecting or downplaying of the topic in a number of contemporary commentaries. This observation suggests the importance of beginning with an honest assessment of our own sense of distance from (or for some: proximity to) the Apostle's interest in this phenomenon. Later in the chapter Paul assumes that were an outsider to stumble into an glossolalic event of worship, the visitor's first question would be, "Are they out of their minds?" (14:23). For most Christians in the so-called developed world who engage with this material, this question seems perfectly reasonable. What does this reaction tell us about the common sense that we bring to the text? Must modern Christians consider themselves as in some sense much like the observer of the early Christian church that Paul calls ἰδιώτης (*idiōtēs*), the "outsider" or "uninitiated," who are unable to comprehend speaking in tongues?

The way Paul depicts the *idiōtēs* in this chapter might be approximated by using the imagery of the anthropologist first entering the inner sanctum of a tribal ritual, who tries to come to grips with the bewildering mix of *fascinosum* and *tremendum* that befalls one in the face of an esoteric religious cult. The reference to "primitive" religious rites is intended to draw attention to the reality that for most contemporary Western believers glossolalic worship is presumed to be a historically distant phenomenon. It is a hard sensibility to shake, despite our awareness of the well-publicized fact that the Pentecostal churches constitute the fastest growing branch of current Christianity. Given this odd disjunction between the mass of new converts who are enthusiastically embracing tongues-speaking churches and those feeling a sense of bewilderment about the phenomenon (and may never had a significant experience of this type of ecstatic Christian worship), in approaching this chapter we must be especially aware of our tendencies to read it in a way that unthinkingly seeks to justify our own respective cultural, religious, or liturgical patterns. This tendency is already evidently displayed in the choices of translators down through the ages. To take one example, some translators attempted to eliminate the confusion this chapter causes by simply rendering the Greek for prophecy as "preaching."[1] While such moves allow the chapter to be incorporated into a tame cessationist faith that is content to affirm that the days of such "wonders of the Spirit" has passed, they also evade the chapter's core challenge, we would suggest.

A not unrelated way to evade the challenge of this chapter is to assume a narrative of the development of Christian worship that takes a charisma-driven phase to have been necessary to get the early church community off the ground as well as a subsequent crystallization of this order into more stable and properly organized institutional forms.[2] Whether this story is told with a sense of regret or relief, what it shares with the cessationist reading is the assumption that the wheel of history has definitively turned away from a worship culture in which glossolalia was to have a non-embarrassing significance. The widespread influence of these approaches helps to explain the unease with this chapter that is dominant among modern Western Christians in indicating the reasons people no longer concern themselves with expressions of early Christian life and worship that have been superseded.

But to defend our modern unease with the more embarrassing features of this chapter in such way, will only anesthetize us readers to the message Paul offers in this chapter, that "God is not a God of disorder, but a God of peace" (14:33). Paul's argument, as we shall attempt to demonstrate, is diametrically opposed to the presumption that peace can be

---

1. Phillips, *New Testament in Modern English*, 344–46. This translation rests on a long tradition, as represented by Cyril of Alexandria: "Prophesying must mean simply this: the ability to interpret the prophecies." Cyril, *Homily* 34, PG 61:288–89, in JK, 230. This tradition is also taken up in Calvin: "Prophesying does not consist in the simple or mere interpretation of scripture, but also includes the knowledge for making it apply to the needs of the hour, and that can only be obtained by revelation and the special influence of God." Calvin, JC 288.

2. This position was influentially expounded by Harnack, *History of Dogma*, bk. I ch. III. §7.3 (214–17).

subsumed within any order-disorder dichotomy. This is why we think that the most pregnant theme in this chapter is revealed when asking how Paul's appeal to the Corinthians can be understood as instituting peace rather than implementing order.

While significant types of order can indeed be implemented by decreeing the form to which all must accede, peace can only be achieved as Christians discover the unity that exists between those who must eventually constitute it. Peace therefore must be understood as an order different in kind from the order enforced by the issuance of decrees because it will only emerge through the mediation of a kind of third agency that transcends the invested interests of the parties involved. Peace can neither be decreed nor produced by procedures. This is why we will see Paul depicting peace as that order which only the Holy Spirit can "set up" by promoting the articulated consent and mutual embrace of the parties that it has liberated from a state of antagonism. Peace, as the Apostle understands it, is a relationship characterized by the mutual recognition of all the participants of what each has to contribute to the wider whole. This recognition is the basis of the harmony of the whole body, strengthened by the bonds of love. Having set up these themes in chapters 12 and 13, the Apostle now elaborates them further in chapter 14 by again attending to concrete questions about how different roles are properly negotiated within the gathered worship of the church. With remarkable dexterity he shows how the order of peace can be discovered within what must have appeared a rather unwieldy and even chaotic worship celebration. But at the same time Paul wishes to ensure that the order of peace must not be so rigid as to quench the Spirit's right to intervene at any time. Because divine peace in worship is a dynamic state, it can only be sustained by remaining ever open to both the disruptive judgments and consolations that characterize the work of the Holy Spirit.

The return to practicalities in this chapter is encapsulated in the question of 14:26: **what should be done then?** We think it plain that Paul expects every believer to be a prophet. The term **prophecy** has a wide semantic range in contemporary English not unlike its definitional breadth in the biblical traditions. Scriptural examples of prophesying range from interpreting dreams (Num 12:16, Dan 5) and seeing visions (Num 12:6–8) to the announcing the divine word (Exod 7:1–2), which appears to be the key constitutive feature. Working within this wider semantic field, Paul's first move is to indicate that prophecy is fundamentally a phenomenon of verbal interaction led by the Spirit. Thus prophecy is the paradigmatic spiritual gift for Paul in that through it the church is constituted and reconstituted as a "prophethood of all believers," a position following naturally from his earlier emphasis on the monarchy of the Spirit (>11:3). At the same time, what is to be understood as a general phenomenon characteristic of the *church as a whole* is also formally represented by a distinct *role* within the church's polity. It appears that the vocation of this specific role of prophets in the church is precisely to draw attention to the general phenomenon of prophecy as a key mark of the church. This we find suggested in Paul's express wish that every believer prophecy: **I would like all of you to speak in tongues, but even more to prophesy**. In this sense the **all** (πάντες/*pantes*) of 14:24 means "every"; anyone can be called to prophecy at any time.

Prophecy among the saints, does however, take a specific form for Paul. It is consistently and tightly married to the concern for *oikodome* that has been his constant refrain in these chapters: that, **those who prophesy build up the church**. In wishing all believers to enter into their prophetic gifts, the Apostle imagines in 14:24-25 how powerful the church would be if this universal prophethood were fully manifest: **if all prophesy, an unbeliever or outsider who enters is reproved by all and called to account by all . . . that person will bow down before God and worship**. We understand Paul to be imagining here a living body of reciprocated spiritual gifts as he has depicted it in some detail in chapter 12, a body constituted by the mutual exchange of gifts (>12:4-7) as allocated by the Spirit to each believer (>12:8-11). Paul draws the Corinthians' attention to the reality that a church in which prophecy already exists is ripe for constructive encouragement to bring it to even fuller expression. To anticipate the conclusion of the chapter, this suggests that Paul's final exhortation that **all things should be done decently and in order** must be interpreted in terms of the order of the exchange of the Spirit's gifts depicted in chapter 12. In other words, an ordered church is rightly called "prophetic" because it articulates and is an artifact of the work of the Spirit, and something else than church is achieved when orders are imposed by successfully exerting some control of "mind over matter."

Somewhat disconcertingly for Christians unfamiliar with charismatic worship, the Apostle shows no desire to do away with the unsettling and in a sense even anarchic power of the Spirit.[3] He does, however, want this power channeled through speech, and especially intelligible speech. The aim of this focusing is to insist that prophetic speech always be a servant of the Holy Spirit whose overturning and surprising continually challenges the merely human social inertia of the gathered church but ever does so as a work of divine love for the community. Christians are constantly learn-

---

3. As we use it the term "anarchy" denotes the unexpected and often disturbing breaking of expected social norms, and is not in the first instance a theory of statecraft, though our position does have implications for a Christian understanding of the state. See Ellul, *Anarchy and Christianity*.

ing anew what it means that the Spirit's overturning interventions are acts of love. This is a truth that must be learned in life with the Spirit because these liberative acts are also interruptive, challenging seemingly comfortable patterns of human relationship that are in reality denuding. Paul insists that the Corinthians **strive for the spiritual gifts, and especially that you may prophesy** because it is through these prophetic utterances that the unexpected and uncontrollable work of the Spirit on human lives remains visibly and audibly present to the whole church. The concern to guard the productively interruptive power of the Spirit underlies Paul's interest in distinguishing between the phenomena of tongues and prophecy as well as his plea for the Corinthians to pursue **love** precisely through striving for spiritual gifts as embodied in **prophecy**.

Both prophecy and tongues are forms of speech that receive and display the anarchic, overturning, and remaking power of the Spirit. But prophesying stands above *glossolalia* because it channels the unsettling power of the Spirit by directing it to the upbuilding of believers. In this chapter Paul can therefore been seen as extending his discussion of love from chapter 13. Here he is showing how charismatic phenomena are the highest form of love because they allow the believers to continue their training in the *sui generis* sociality that the Spirit fosters. Chapter 14 thus parallels chapters 13 and 12 in explicating love as *oikodome*, the difference being that in chapter 13 love is explicated in Christological language while in 12 and 14 the same love is given a layered elaboration in terms of the Spirit's modes of forming Christian life. The aim of this loving work of the Son and the Spirit is that those who come into contact with such love through the church will **bow down before God and worship him, declaring, "God is really among you"** (14:25).

Although strange forms of ecstatic speaking have characterized the Christian church from the very beginning (Acts 2:1–18, 10:4–46), in the Corinthian context speaking in tongues had a more direct link to the not so distant pagan past of most believers. In the cults of that time and place ecstatic speech represented a claim to the immediate presence of the deity, which the priest(ess) and worshippers were understood to receive by ceding control to the spirit realm. It is safe to assume that it was their background in pagan ecstatic forms of worship that allowed the Corinthians both to recognize glossolalia and to prioritize this one particular gift of the Spirit over others.[4] Given this pagan context it is remarkable that Paul seems to

---

4. "At the most highly developed [Greek] oracles the god spoke through the mouth of a man or woman. Such was the method at Delphi, which is typical of all inspirational oracles. The prophetess spent several days in purificatory preparation and then entered into a trance, during which she heard the consultant's question. Her answer, no doubt

both embrace and reshape the Corinthians' excitement about this spiritual gift.[5] It is noteworthy, first of all, that he describes himself as far from an outsider to the phenomenon—**I speak in tongues more than all of you** (14:18)—particularly given his background in a synagogue that would not have proven a nurturing environment for enthusiastic liturgical sensibilities.[6] At the same time the Apostle states categorically that his own ecstatic practice has a properly circumscribed role within the context of Christian worship and is "grounded" in its being properly practiced primarily at home in private devotion. It is an opening that well serves the overall arc of the chapter with its call for glossolalic practice in the Corinthian public assembly to grow beyond its characteristic incomprehensibility by being paired with interpretation.

Before proceeding to trace the chain of the argument in this early part of the chapter, however, we would like to pause to draw special attention to the astonishing fact that Paul does not simply quash a practice that resembles and is probably influenced by pagan practices, but unambiguously embraces the ecstatic forms of Corinthian prayer. This embrace is yet another example of Paul exemplifying the love that he has previously characterized as "bearing all things" (13:7). Only what has been embraced can also be transformed. The demand that cultural dispositions and preferences be deposited on the

---

unintelligible to the untrained auditor, was interpreted by the attendant priests and transformed by them into intelligible verse or prose." Cary and Knock, *The Oxford Classical Dictionary*, 624.

5. As Dunn observes, with the local cultic context in mind Paul's treatment in this chapter should be understood as developing distinctions that did not typically exist in the ecstatic religions. "[T]here is no real boundary line between 'translation' and 'interpretation'—as is confirmed by the semantic range of (*di*)-*ermeneuein* within the biblical Greek itself (see II Macc. 1:36; Job 42:18 (17b); Lk. 24:27). Moreover, the more we recognize Hellenistic influence on Corinthian glossolalia, the more seriously we have to consider the basic meaning of the word in wider Greek thought—viz., 'to interpret, expound, explain'. In particular, the relation between 'glossolalia' and 'interpretation' so closely parallels . . . the 'prophecy of inspiration' and the 'prophecy of interpretation' that it becomes difficult to deny a close equivalence of function between, for example, the prophet who interpreted the utterances of the Pyhia at Delphi and the interpreter of tongues at Corinth." Dunn, *Jesus and the Spirit*, 247.

6. Levison has recently substantiated that the relatively peripheral movements within first century Judaism that did embrace prophetic utterances of some type in gathered worship all represent attempts to stretch the boundaries of their own non-ecstatic Jewish worship traditions by incorporating Greco-Roman understandings of ecstatic utterance, and in ways that were far from uncritical (*The Spirit in First Century Judaism*). In distinction from these other first-century Jewish ecstatics, what is remarkable about the work Paul is doing in this chapter is how critically he is engaging with contemporary Greco-Roman sensibilities, even if his criticisms are implicit rather than explicit.

way into church is not genuinely Christian, as voices from the Afro-American tradition of worship especially have insistently reminded us.[7] Paul's approach to the Corinthian practice of glossolalia thus resonates with the negotiations that had to be undertaken by missionaries in colonial contexts about whether instruments such as African drums are appropriate in Christian worship.[8] Paul appears completely unthreatened by the reality that he does not have to teach the Corinthians glossolalic worship, which they might have first encountered in pagan cults;[9] he seeks instead to channel into the waters of *oikodome* what he considers the genuine gifts the Corinthians bring to gathered worship. This refusal to denounce their ecstatic worship as syncretistic paganism allows the Apostle to avoid the cardinal mistake so often made by colonial missiologists (>9:19–23).

In teasing out what is to be retained and what is to be repudiated in their current worship practices, Paul draws on the traditions of Israel's prophets who saw the Spirit's work as gathering the "riches of the nations" to Christ (Isa 60). We therefore again read Paul in this passage to be modelling the cultural sensitivity he has urged on the Corinthians in matters of dress (11:4–16). Being under the rule of the Spirit makes it continually necessary to discern proper and improper trajectories in cultural currents. It would have been too easy a solution for Paul to request of the Corinthians to simply give up their ecstatic gifts; instead he wanted them to learn to discern how these very gifts are transformed when being bound to the good of others. Such a binding is not native to the religious phenomenon of ecstatic utterance but is very much intrinsic to the kenotic love displayed on the cross. Christians must understand themselves as inevitably bringing cultural dispositions into public worship. And Paul would not have them be embarrassed about this reality so long as they have confidence that the

---

7. Jennings, *The Christian Imagination*, esp. ch. 2. Commenting on the eighteenth-century Jesuit missionary to Peru, José de Acosta Porres, Jennings concludes that his mission practices show him to be "cut off from a simple Gentile remembrance that would enable a far more richly imagined possibility of movement toward faith from within the cultural logics and spatial realities of Andean life. That is to say, he is cut off from active remembering that he and his people were also 'like the Indians.' . . . this would have meant embodying a generosity of spirit that was sorely lacking in his assessments of native practices" (98).

8. Some contemporary accounts of the place of African drumming in the discovery of social order and the synchronization of human society with the harmony of the natural world sound remarkably similar to the non-orchestrated and non-scripted discovery of the order that the Spirit imparts to the ecclesial body that Paul sets out in 1 Corinthians 12. See Arnaut, "Africans Dance in Time," 252–81.

9. This is not a historical claim *per se*, but is an entailment of the claim that communities of worship shape individual's powers of judgment. See Wannenwetsch, "Ecclesiology and Ethics," esp. 60–62.

gospel will unfailingly conform everything to the rule of the Spirit and show willingness to have their cultural habits bent, broken and remade.

A clear structural distinction sets the parameters for Paul's redirection of the glossolalic practices of the Corinthians: **Those who speak in a tongue do not speak to other people but to God; ... On the other hand, those who prophesy speak to other people**. The description of this difference is followed by a further qualification that **Those who speak in a tongue build up themselves, but those who prophesy build up the church**. This qualifying judgment allows Paul to rank the two gifts in a clear order of priority: **One who prophesies is greater than one who speaks in tongues**. Far from being a concealed debasement of the relatively lesser gift (which Paul himself practices and recommends) this re-prioritization within the relation between private and public glossolalia serves to index the appropriate place of this gift within an overall public order characterized by the Spirit's rule. In this order the individual function of each gift is to be strictly directed to the overall goal of upbuilding the church.

In engaging the Corinthians on this theme Paul anticipates a perennial tension in Christian history between those who would emphasize the significance of private edification (the building up the Christian self) and those who would prioritize public worship (the building up the church). The significance of the line Paul treads in the early stages of this dispute will become more apparent if we consider a riposte the Corinthians might have offered to his prioritization of public worship: "You say our uninterpreted glossolalic worship is not community oriented, but we do take mutual consolation and encouragement from being part of this extraordinary and exciting gathering." In the sanctification theory of Friedrich Schleiermacher, whose account remains extraordinarily influential in modern Protestantism up to this day, we encounter a theoretically elaborated version of this same argument. The church is edified in gathered worship, Schleiermacher explains, through the power of mature individual religious consciousness that must of necessity share its energy and insights with others, and in so doing inflames the piety of those around them.

> Fellowship is demanded by the *consciousness of kind* which dwells in every man ... [and] is accomplished through the fact that everything inward becomes, at a certain point of its strength or maturity, an outward too, and as such, perceptible to others. Thus feeling, as a self-contained determination of the mind ... will ... purely in virtue of the consciousness of kind, not exist exclusively for itself, but becomes an outward, originally and without any definite aim or pertinence, by means of

> facial expression, gesture, tones, and (indirectly) words; and so becomes to other people a revelation of the inward. This bare expression of feeling, which is entirely caused by the inward agitation... does indeed at first arouse in other people only an idea of the person's state of mind. But, by reason of the consciousness of kind, this passes into living imitation; and the more able the percipient is... to pass into the same state, the more easily will that state be produced by imitation.[10]

In other words, even when it is not expressed through loving verbal exhortation, the community members with "higher" religious consciousness will provoke among the less developed the aspiration for a similar level of heightened devotion.

In positioning those with "higher" religious consciousness at the core of group unity Schleiermacher must emphasize the formative role of emulative behavior. In our view his account rests on a dual assumption that is theologically problematic. First, it assumes that a competitive relation is constantly at play between fellow believers; and second, it presupposes that this underlying spirit of competitiveness leads to an irresistibly stimulating effect of "the strong" (in Paul's terms) on the "weak" leading to the maturation of "the weak." As the play on Paul's very different account of the relation between the spiritually "strong" and the "weak" already signifies, the Apostle's account of mutual (not unilateral) edification is very different in kind from any model that, like Schleiermacher's, rests on the psychological mechanisms of mimetic desire in which "elite" representatives of spiritual maturity are expected to catalyze the edification of the social body as a whole."[11] We think Paul would therefore have been unimpressed by this "resonance model" of inter-Christian edification, which yields an account of the church as essentially a gathering of individuals who have found being together especially productive for their individual faith. In our view Paul inverts all such individualized accounts in this passage by explicating the processes of the edification of believers in terms that draw attention to the genuinely public and so political nature of the Spirit's gifts.

---

10. Schleiermacher, *Christian Faith*, §6, 27, emphasis in original. The earlier version of this position is developed in *On Religion*, "Fourth Speech—Association in Religion, or Church and Priesthood."

11. For reasons already discussed (>7:16), ours is not a principled rejection of any role for mimetic learning in the Christian life, but we do harbour what Herdt (in *Putting on Virtue*) pejoratively calls "hyper-Augustinian" reservations about giving mimesis too central of a role in Christian formation, reservations that extend from over against Schleiermacherian Protestantism to Aristotelian/Thomist/MacIntyrian virtue theories.

A linguistic detail from 12:3 forces us to clarify what is at stake in choosing to prioritize either individual faith or the public word in a theology of the gifts: **those who prophesy speak to other people for their upbuilding and encouragement and consolation.** Where the NRSV connects the expression of prophesying and its desired outcome of **upbuilding, encouragement and consolation** with the particular preposition **for their**, the Greek contains no such preposition, instead linking the three nouns with the verb as direct accusative objects. While the literal rendering "speaking upbuilding, encouragement, and consolation" is linguistically awkward, it does offer an important theological insight. The act of prophetic speech is not validated solely by its outcome, that is, the extent to which it succeeds in effecting a change in someone else's religious consciousness, to use Schleiermacher's terms. To "speak consolation" is itself an objective event, a loving act ventured within the world of human relations, whether or not a recipient actually receives that word as comfort (or perhaps as unsettling).

This relative independence of the prophetic word of a measure of success (as presupposed in Schleiermacher's account of spiritual stimulation) is one of the features that make it necessary to understand prophetic utterance according to the rationale of *public* expression. Whereas the model of the "rubbing off" of higher states of religious consciousness in some individuals on lesser such states in other individuals remains caught in the paradigm of private edification (irrespective of whether it is happening in the home or in a congregational meeting), Paul's account of prophecy in the church is inescapably tied to an understanding of worship as a public affair. While there are aspects and spaces in the Christian life in which Schleiermacher's stimulus-edification-model has some mileage—in family life, for example, where the role model of parents has a rather immediate effect on children—the sphere of public worship is not such a place. Instead of being under the stimulus received through the religious consciousness of others, the believers are under the *direct* stimulus of the divine word. Prophecy is the paradigmatic gift through which the public character of the church assembly is highlighted. Every individual believer, whether possessed by a higher or a lower religious consciousness, is *equally* treated (and in deed in need of such treatment) to the "stimulus" of the divine word. It is precisely in this sense that prophecy is a gift of the community, rather than of the individual who exerts it.

We can understand his move here as parallel to Paul's earlier explanation of why the Corinthians have misunderstood the Eucharist in framing it according to the standards of the private patron's function (>11:20–22). There the Corinthians misunderstood the point of communion when separating the ritual from the meal that they ate as their ἴδιον δεῖπνον (*idion deipnon*), their individual respective meals; and here, in their glossolalia-dominated worship service they equally fail to perceive the reality of the Spirit as an agency devoted to building up the church, rather than merely emanating through an assortment of private religious revelers who might find the presence of other spiritually minded individuals edifying. Significantly, this public-private dichotomy will also turn out to be the key for unraveling Paul's later puzzling refusal of speech to women in worship.

The Apostle's way of ensuring that acts of worship are genuinely edifying for the body as a whole is to designate the proper place of glossolalia as the believer's "private intercourse" with God. It gains admission to public worship only when it is accompanied by the interpretation that makes it accessible as an act of love to the whole congregation. Moreover, Paul takes pains to indicate its subordinate status within his own economy of desire: **in church I would rather speak five words with my mind, in order to instruct others also, than ten thousand words in a tongue** (14:19). If it is to retain a role in public worship, ecstatic prayer needs first to be deprivatized, that is, transferred into articulate, comprehensive, and so properly public speech. One way of understanding this move in conceptual terms is to say that even the most intimate individualistic and "religious" features of Christian life must be made serviceable to the word. When we take this observation seriously it also becomes clear why taking glossolalia, worship, spirituality or piety as general religious phenomena present in many religions (including Christianity) is, theologically speaking, yet another way of resisting the genuine work of the Spirit. Within the parameters of Paul's discussion, what matters is not a presence of any such "spiritual" phenomena that can be taken to be indicating the presence of the spirit; what matters is the Holy Spirit's particular mode of operation to work with and transform any such "spiritual" phenomenon into a means of upbuilding the distinct body of Christ.

It is by no means incidental that Paul associates his capacity to **benefit you** with the requirement to be speaking **to you**. There is no hint here that Paul trusts the force of his religious personality to implicitly or inarticulately stimulate or infect the Corinthians with his vision of the Christian faith. This is why his explicitly insisting on the necessity of addressing the Corinthians in verbal terms can be understood as, once again, signaling the kenotic form of Paul's apostolicity, which never attempts to rise "above" the linguistic and cultural conditions of intelligible human speech. His emphasis on articulacy here should be understood as an implicit critique of any understanding of religion that sanctions incomprehensibility, whether through reliance on sheer resonance ("wave stimuli") or other models of edifying sublime experience. We find this point confirmed by the way in which Paul envisions the "effect" of genuine Christian worship on the uninitiated or odd visitor. What he expects to happen to this visitor is to have an *articulate* witness evoked from them—**"God is really among you"** (14:25)—rather than a bare sense of excitement or the naked wish to repeat the experience of participating in an ecstatic event. By emphasizing the regular home of glossolalia in private devotion Paul does not eviscerate the Spirit of anarchic power in worship; but he does expose the unique vulnerability of this form of worship and why some of its forms need to take shelter in the sphere of private devotion. If untamed in public, ecstatic expressions tend to generate a complex of mutually reinforcing stimuli that not only can get out of hand, but can be emotionally stimulating in ways that all too easily lend themselves to manipulation by worship leaders. But manipulation is antithetical to the gospel, as Paul has already emphasized from the outset of his communication with the Corinthians (>1:17).

Since social masses are by definition ponderous and slow to move, introducing shared ecstasy is one of the most effective ways to reduce their inertial weight. The common description of ecstatic prayer as "uplifting" points to its capacity to suspend that which normally keeps us grounded—the reflexivity that looks on one's self from the outside, so to speak, positioning us in the world as rational and responsible agents. Glossolalia circumvents this reflexivity by embracing immediate intercourse with God without the self-observation of the mind (**my mind is unproductive** [14:14]). Paul assigns this intimate moment to the more protected private sphere because he understands that public worship would corrupt it by exposing it to the forces of mass stimulation.

Paul's advice is not, therefore, that of the Puritan, who insists that being "out of one's mind" is always and by definition immoral ("be not drunk" serving as a favorite proof text). Nor is it the Stoic message that Christians should always be in control of their minds. The Apostle clearly embraces and values certain ways of being "beyond control," but he insists that such abandon not be courted in contexts in which it would render its practitioners dangerously vulnerable. Glossolalic worship is, of course, not the only socially organized forum in which self-reflexivity is lowered by intent, and such social spaces remain attractive, not least for their promise of interpersonal immediacy. The drinking culture of the public house, for instance, turns on the desire for the type of enjoyable social intercourse that lowered inhibitions enable. In such spaces we can allow others access to sides of ourselves that our inhibitions normally keep us from sharing. Less traditional cultural forms also tap into this promise of immediate interpersonal connection that it implicitly offers. The intimacy offered by the combination of "spirits" and social forms is, for example, prominently displayed in the contemporary rave culture, which, not by accident, thrives on designer drugs with names like Ecstasy. The rave culture offers us one of the purest examples of such uninhibited communal abandon precisely by virtue of its characteristic combination of ecstatic social connection with overwhelming sound that deafens speech. It is a tragic indictment of the lack of intimacy many experience in Western churches today that the intimacy on offer in the pub and rave scenes, which only mimic the true intimacy of the body of Christ, remain such potent rivals despite the shadows of destructive behaviors that accompany them in which such intimacy is exploited, from theft to rape, or its side effects, drug- and alcohol-induced death.[12] Given that Spirit-infused speech is depicted in scripture as confusingly similar to substance-infused patterns of communication (Acts 2:13; Eph 5:18), we can see why Paul wishes to avoid other kinds of exploitation by confining all instances of this vulnerable state to the home, not only glossolalic but also that induced by ingested substances (11:22).

Though Paul does rank private glossolalia below public prophesying by emphasizing the higher value in public worship of the upbuilding of the social body, he stops short of any suggestion that the private upbuilding of the self must be considered selfish. Though a lesser good, he still affirms it as a good worth seeking. What then are the positive effects on the individual Paul clearly indicates with the statement **Those who speak in a tongue build up themselves**? *How* is private glossolalia edifying? Given the priorities Paul has established thus far, whatever edification this practice offers can only be different in mode but not in kind from the edification available to the whole church.

These questions provide a way into theological reflection on a topic that has received little if any discussion in the many strands of the exegetical tradition that have read this verse as merely a concession[13] or who move on after admitting incomprehension of a gift that is supposed to be upbuilding "in some mysterious way."[14] Ernst Käsemann pulls together the most common answers by reference to Romans 8. This linkage generates the suggestion that glossolalia is edifying to the individual because it allows her to express her solidarity in suffering with the broken creation that awaits the redemption of their Lord. It is a line of interpretation that Käsemann assumes accurately

---

12. We find most of the attempts to respond to this criticism by making churches more "rave like" or emotively potent noticeably deficient in their awareness of the public and collective nature of Christian worship as well as their articulateness about the role played by the spiritual gifts. For one description of the issues at stake, see Lindenbaum, "The Pastoral Role of Contemporary Christian Music."

13. Calvin, JC, commenting on verse 4, 287.

14. Hays, RBH, 234.

reflects Paul's *theologia viatorum*. For this reason he resists interpretations that link this passage with Paul's reference to speaking in the "language of angels" in 13:1, which Käsemann thinks will only tempt believers down the path of a *theologia gloriae*.[15] Though Käsemann's significant exegetical connections will have to be addressed in any complete theological account of the edification offered in private glossolalia, the antithesis he employs is unnecessary in our view as needlessly narrowing complementary ways in which the edifying nature of glossolalia might be understood.

Paul's characterization of ecstatic prayer as speaking **to God** provides the initial, and in our judgment decisive, hint about how glossolalia can be understood to draw believers into the realm of inner divine communication: the Spirit speaks in the believer to Father through the Son. The immediacy of this experience can be understood as a proleptic experience of the heavenly communication that characterizes eschatological existence.[16] In this vein the gift of glossolalia is *ek*-static in the sense of drawing the one who prays out of the circle of ambiguity that otherwise characterizes the situation of speaking to God. Here human weakness finds its needed strength, for "we do not know how to pray as we ought, but the Spirit himself intercedes for us with sighs too deep for words" (Rom 8:26).[17] To understand the Spirit as mediating the inner divine communication is also a clarification of the identity of the God to whom we pray, for as Paul has previously made explicit, "No one understands the thoughts of God except the Spirit of God" (2:11).

That "no [human] one understands" the words of glossolalic prayer is not in principle a cause for embarrassment, even if in certain circumstances it might become an embarrassment, as when it is undertaken in public worship but not met by an outspoken interpretation. This human incomprehensibility of glossolalic prayer is best seen as consoling, because it lifts the burden of our justified suspicion that we cannot pray without projecting our desires onto God, as Feuerbach has so sharply taught us, or without falling into the temptation to moralistically abrade ourselves and

---

15. Käsemann, *Perspectives on Paul*, 132-37.

16. "Paul thus characterizes the glossolalist as holding a secret conversation with God (he speaks to God—14:2); the subject matter is the eschatological secrets known only in heaven; so presumably the language used is the language of heaven (see Rev. 14:2f.)." Dunn, *Jesus and the Spirit*, 244.

17. "[H]ere we may draw on Rom. 8:26-8, even though that is not talking about gossolalia as such. *He who experiences glossolalia (or wordless groans) experiences it as effective communication with God.* The prayer which he finds himself unable to utter the Spirit utters through him, giving him the sense of communing with God, the confidence that God knows his situation and needs better than he does himself..." Dunn, *Jesus and the Spirit*, 245.

anyone in earshot. If Paul characterizes glossolalia as prayer **to God** he is not merely stating the obvious, but is identifying a particular type and contextualization of prayer that alone can be assured it is actually speaking to God. Its certainty is drawn from the experience of relief from the motivational ambiguity that frequently besets Christian prayer, both in public and in private, and does so by radically redirecting and reconfiguring the rational reflexivity that normally supports our self- and other-consciousness.

If we understand the particular edification of private glossolalia as the relocation of the one who prays into the inner divine communication we can then return to embrace Käsemann's insight about how in glossolalia the believer may participate with the sigh of all creation. To be part of the heavenly converse *as a human* is to be simultaneously situated with those who pray in that other appropriate place for humans: as a creature among creatures. The one who prays is thus "displaced" from him- or herself, not into some no-place such as the state of nirvana, but into the overlapping places where we belong, both God's own communication *and* firmly into creation. Paul allows for glossolalia in public worship instead of relegating it completely to the private realm because he understands the church to be the material place where this dual sense of displacement-replacement is genuinely at home. As the vestibule of heaven, the church is the earthly place where believers can trust they will be drawn into that transfiguring divine communication that renders them fully creatures.

Furthermore, the immediacy that glossolalia enables and represents suggests that it can also be understood as a kind of primal language like that which develops between a newborn and his or her mother. It has often been observed (frequently dismissively), that speaking in tongues resembles the babbling of a pre-linguistic infant. We are also reminded of the fact that in the Hebrew the word for spirit, *ruakh* (רוּחַ), is a feminine noun. Mothers often "enter" the babbling of infants so that a sort of "private language" develops between mother and child as a unique codification of nonsense tones and syllables particular to this relationship. However nonsensical from the viewpoint of developed language, such pidgin or proto-language is signally important for the infant in laying the foundations for articulate language to later develop in preparing and fostering in the newborn the affective confidence to venture the linguistic experimentation necessary for the formation of all other human relationships.[18]

If the gift of glossolalia resembles such a primal maternal relationship for the one who prays, there must be a genuine place within the Christian

---

18. Few have thought more theologically about this connection than Jean Vanier. See his *Community and Growth*, ch. 1.

faith for the relationship with "my sweet savior" that has been the special emphasis of pietistic strands of Christianity. The personal affective bond that marks an individual's attachment to the Good Shepherd who calls every single one of his sheep by his or her own name must not be denounced as in principle individualist or romantic. The caveat we overhear in Paul's discussion is not uttered against the affective nature and corresponding expression of the personal relationship with God. It is, however, more specifically meant to ensure that believers understand that the body of Christ is not simply an aggregate of individuals who widen or project their private devotions into a social space. What the Apostle wishes them to take to heart is that the church as a public *sui generis* is configured precisely the other way around: not as an extension of the private realm, but as a transformation (here: through interpretation) of the patterns that "edify" the individual (glossolalia) to serve the edification/upbuilding of the social body. In both cases the upbuilding in view can only be an effect of the Spirit's agency at work, never something that can be produced by the good performance of the one who prays and prophecies.

This resistance to an anthropocentric reading of edification helps us to make sense of several aspects in Paul's argument. The power and primal character of the glossolalic experience explains why it is so tempting to conflate this private edification with the sum total of the Christian faith. The powerful consolation it offers easily generates fantasies of remaining in this maternal womb forever, and who would want to leave behind the intimate moment of immediate connection of the divine "understanding without words"? Given the notorious human tendency to yearn to regress into the maternal womb Paul's exhortation that the Corinthians must **not be children in your thinking ... but in thinking be adults** emerges with a new force of intelligibility. When the desire for immediate converse with God is indulgently pursued, even to the point of elaborating it as a skill displayed in public, a dangerous undertow is put in motion. Those given what is seen to be the otherworldly "skill" of tongues, like children who have just acquired a new skill, are indulged in their desire to have everyone look at them as they perform it—a bizarrely staged use of an otherwise beautifully infantile form of speech. To withstand this undertow Paul first urges the Corinthians to understand the role played by thought and explicit communication in organizing public ecstatic experience, and then urges them to consider more deeply how their gifts might be deployed in tandem with intelligible language for the benefit of the whole church.

Immediate Ecstasy and Mediated Speech

> ⁶Now, brothers and sisters, if I come to you speaking in tongues, how will I benefit you unless I speak to you in some revelation or knowledge or prophecy or teaching? ⁷It is the same way with lifeless instruments that produce sound, such as the flute or the harp. If they do not give distinct notes, how will anyone know what is being played? ⁸And if the bugle gives an indistinct sound, who will get ready for battle? ⁹So with yourselves; if in a tongue you utter speech that is not intelligible, how will anyone know what is being said? For you will be speaking into the air. ¹⁰There are doubtless many different kinds of sounds in the world, and nothing is without sound. ¹¹If then I do not know the meaning of a sound, I will be a foreigner to the speaker and the speaker a foreigner to me. ¹²So with yourselves; since you are eager for spiritual gifts, strive to excel in them for building up the church.

In 14:6–12 Paul offers a raft of new distinctions with which he aims properly to orient Christian prophetic speech. The basic criterion he wishes to explore is how such speech will **benefit you**. The two metaphors from the world of musical instruments he uses to illustrate the parameters of this criterion emphasize ways in which the distinctiveness of sound can be understood as the condition of intelligibility. To grasp the theological point Paul is making about the nature of this distinctiveness, however, requires a closer look at how his analogies are actually functioning. The first problem Paul addresses of the **flute or the harp** needing to **give distinct notes** is not meant to suggest a defect in the musical instrument but their being badly played. **How will anyone know what is being** played if someone just breathes into a flute or plucks random strings on a harp? Technically speaking, we hear a single tone as pure (as a perfectly pitched C note, for instance) not because it is made up of a single frequency but because the blend of frequencies that constitute its sound cover a limited spectrum and can therefore be heard as a single tone. The human ear's ability to hear such a note as distinct depends not on homogeneity but on the *narrowness* of a given frequency band. If I simply lean with my forearms onto a piano's keyboard, I have played a large number of entirely distinct notes, but what the ear hears is only noise. Our creaturely ability to perceive sounds as distinct rests on the physiological capacities of the perceptive organs and the limits of our mental processing abilities. We hear noise when overwhelmed by too many frequencies hitting the ear at once.

With this phenomenon of aural distinction in mind it becomes more obvious that when Paul compares the indistinctness of sounds produced by an unskilled person playing a musical instrument with the Corinthian worship in which all simultaneously speak in tongues, he is showing that the core problem with the Corinthian cacophony is tonal sequence rather than merely the identifiability of specific sounds. This emphasis is marked with a question, **how will anyone know what is being played?** In other words, the ultimate test of the distinctiveness to which Paul is drawing our attention here is not the recognition of the *instrument* but in the recognition of the *tune*. The critical problem for the church is to identify *which* and *whose doxologies* are being sung in each sound that makes itself heard in the ecclesial assembly.

Paul's second example, of the **bugle**, further emphasizes that the issue at stake is recognition according to the criterion of purpose. The "for what" criterion is therefore the core issue in this example. **Who will get ready for battle?** The focus of Paul's discussion of distinct sound is in neither case on comprehensibility per se (to be able to identify the language or content of ecstatic speech), but rather its capacity to position its recipients according to the purpose of the type of speech represented in prophesying: to make the congregants ready to receive God's own word through the mouth of the prophet. Paul's choice of the metaphor of the bugle's call to battle is perhaps doing double work here, not only as an example of a musical instrument that is well known for the clear notes it (ideally) makes, but also one whose purpose makes it carry some traditional theological resonances; the *ecclesia audiens*, after all, is no other than the *ecclesia militans*. The purpose of prophetic speech is always also a preparation of the congregation for the battle that is the Christian life. We see that the hearing with which Paul is principally concerned is not reducible to comprehensibility when he explains that it is a listening for the inspiration of the Spirit that allows judgments to be made about words which may be comprehensible on their own and yet do not serve the upbuilding that is central work of the Holy Spirit (>12:1–31). This is why Paul calls it a **speaking into the air** when glossolalia in gathered worship is not accompanied by articulate interpretation. The expression nicely indicates that the appropriately "upward" referent of glossolalic speech will be dissipated into the ether if not properly oriented toward human recipients for their **benefit**. "Lost in the air" would then suggest such words disappear not as though leaving no mark at all, like words never uttered, but as lost in the more important sense of never having found a recipient who responds properly to the battle call.

Considering the happy case when glossolalic utterances have been interpreted and their meaning made comprehensible, we must resist the temptation to understand this according to the logic most prominently found in (post)modern theories of the aesthetics of reception: where it would be assumed that the act of transmission is constitutive for the establishment of meaning in the first place. In such theories what *really* matters is not the playing but the work of interpretation. This is a temptation to which the translators of the NRSV appears to have succumbed in translating 14:11 as **if then I do not know the meaning of a sound**. The Greek word that this translation renders as "meaning" is δύναμις (*dynamis*): a power that specifies purpose through a recognizable and distinctive form. The *dynamis* of a prayer of thanksgiving, uttered in glossolalic fashion, is here assumed by the Apostle to lie in the utterance itself. It is possessed of the power to be what it is meant to be: a prayer of thanksgiving, recognized as such by the one who prays as well as by the receiver (speaking **to God**). What is lacking in the context of public worship when others hear the utterances but are not given an interpretation is not "meaning" but "upbuilding." They might be able to perceive the utterances according to their purpose (as thanksgiving), but since they cannot know what it is thanks is being given for, they remain in a critical and lamentable sense outside of its power. Hence Paul's verdict: **For you may give thanks well enough, but the other person is not built up** (14:17).

If then I do not know the meaning of a sound, I will be a foreigner to the speaker and the speaker a foreigner to me (14:11). According to the Apostle, publicly to revel in (uninterpreted) glossolalic delights that are meant for private devotion amounts in the end to an embodied denial of the reality of the church as a reconciled community of brothers and sisters and "fellow citizens" in God's new *politeuma*. Paul's insistence on articulate forms of expression in public worship is thus to be understood as his way of attending to the reality of the church as a communion of saints who must not be turned into foreigners again: every activity that effects such as misrepresentation of belonging and allegiance must be kept at bay.

Though Paul privileges the home as the appropriate site for glossolalic gifts he does not simply ban it from the gathering of the worship service. Only because some individuals, along with their interpreters, display glossolalic gifts in gathered worship can believers gain a proper understanding of how glossolalia builds up even in private. In reality there exists no "private Christian self" that could be built up in isolated devotion. The self that is being built up even in individual devotion can only be the *ecclesial* self, a self whose growth will be inextricably related to the upbuilding of the church. Thus our previous investigation of how glossolalia that "nobody understands" (14:2) can nevertheless build up the individual (14:4) becomes intelligible as an imaginative exploration of what Paul explicitly and repeatedly describes—the intrinsic linkage of each spiritual gift to the upbuilding of the whole body of Christ.[19]

The relation between glossolalia and prophecy has now been set out in a manner that exposes their underlying unity: both foster a type of intimacy that heightens affective bonding. Prophesying is commended on the basis of its encouraging, consoling, and upbuilding nature, as a work that builds affective communal bonds in a manner very like the intimacy with God that individual glossolalia in the home properly serves (>12:26). This is not an unexpected result, given that Paul understands the private and public forms of this gift still to be the gifts of the same Spirit. Their undeniable structural differences remain formally subordinate to the primal commonality of their source. Whereas the intimacy given in the gift of glossolalia does not include other people, the superiority of the gift of prophecy lies in its extension of that intimacy to bind the church community together. The most fundamental structural difference between them, then, lies in the respective ways in which each gift negotiates immediacy and mediacy. Whereas glossolalia is characterized by the inarticulate immediacy of speech while needing to be mediated in a public setting through interpretation, with prophecy it is the other way around. As a phenomenon of articulate speech, it is by definition a form of mediation: the act of bringing across the divine word to human audiences, the particularities of which need to be accommodated in the manner of speech. But as we have observed, prophecy is at the same time the form of speech amongst all such forms that also claims an unheard of level of immediacy: that of being a direct divine address whose most striking characteristic is not needing or even allowing for interpretation.

The gifts received in the Church, whether glossolalia, or **revelation or knowledge or prophecy or teaching** are all inseparable from a dual demand: to modulate speaking in whatever ways are necessary to acknowledge the distinct receptivity of the hearer, a labor Paul has constantly commended and displayed in his own kenotic forms of address (>1:17), and to adjust the respective form of speech to the distinct ways in which God wishes to communicate through any such mode.

---

19. We can now see more clearly that the "paradox of self-love" that so complicated readings of chapter 13 for an earlier generation of modern Christian ethicists is in part due to not having accounted for Paul's own account of the problem. For Paul the problem of learning to love myself as an individual is in fact the problem of discovering myself as one whose truth is to be discovered within the matrix of the love of Christ for his body (see >13:2).

Desiring vs. Coveting Spiritual Gifts

> [13]Therefore, one who speaks in a tongue should pray for the power to interpret. [14]For if I pray in a tongue, my spirit prays but my mind is unproductive. [15]What should I do then? I will pray with the spirit, but I will pray with the mind also; I will sing praise with the spirit, but I will sing praise with the mind also. [16]Otherwise, if you say a blessing with the spirit, how can anyone in the position of an outsider say the "Amen" to your thanksgiving, since the outsider does not know what you are saying? [17]For you may give thanks well enough, but the other person is not built up. [18]I thank God that I speak in tongues more than all of you; [19]nevertheless, in church I would rather speak five words with my mind, in order to instruct others also, than ten thousand words in a tongue.
>
> [20]Brothers and sisters, do not be children in your thinking; rather, be infants in evil, but in thinking be adults.

In 14:15 Paul suggests a conceptual distinction that poses a real problem for the interpreter: **I will pray with the spirit, but I will pray with the mind also**. This terse statement is more difficult to understand than it might at first appear, as in 14:14 the Apostle has just set up what appears to be an intrapersonal distinction: **For if I pray in a tongue, my spirit prays but my mind is unproductive**. While the anthropological nature of the distinction between mind and spirit is clear here, it is less obvious whether the mention of the same distinction in the following verses remains on this same plane. Some interpreters seem to assume that the anthropological rationale extends through the following few verses, as when Thiselton, for example, translates "with the mind" as "in the inner depths of my being." But this is to dismiss as theologically relevant the fact that Paul uses no possessive pronouns here. Instead, he speaks only of praying τῷ πνεύματι/τῷ νοΐ (*tō pneumati/tō noi*), "in or through spirit/mind." An anthropological reading might take Paul to be emphasizing the straightforward point that when believers pray they ought to pray with every part of their being, but to take this route is to complicate the activity of prayer that should be phenomenologically perceptible to the one who prays.

To extract ourselves from this tangle we need to come to grips with how, precisely, the mind might be described as being involved in an activity that is defined as a relinquishment of cognitive control. If the involvement of the mind is reduced to a gatekeeper's role and is engaged only enough to know that what follows will be cognitively uncontrollable, it becomes difficult to fathom why it matters so much to the Apostle that he prays *tō noi*, "in mind." If, therefore, an anthropological reading of the whole section seems finally to disintegrate, a reading that perceives a shift of referent from **my spirit** in 14:14 to "in spirit" in 14:15 to be a deliberate reference to God's Holy Spirit, suggests itself as worthy of more detailed consideration.

The problem this alternative reading immediately presents, however, is that Paul's insistence that the believer's mind accompany his spirit apparently renders the Holy Spirit herself mindless. It appears that we will need to find a way of reading this passage that will allow the anthropological level of analysis to be theologically infused. For example, when Paul characterizes praying in a tongue as an activity that keeps the mind **unproductive,** a literal rendering of the Greek ἄκαρπός (*akarpos*) would be "fruitless." In this case the engagement of the mind must mean something more than that interpretation renders glossolalia rationally comprehensible. What is at stake here in the encouragement to pray **in the mind** must transcend the understanding by the one who prays of what is prayed; it must entail the engagement of the mind in order to further the understanding of *others*. We thus detect in Paul's use of the language of fruitful-/fruitlessness a theological hint that turns us back towards his concern for the *oikodome* of the whole body. Bearing in mind that fruit must be more than a flower, we understand the Apostle to be pointing to a use of that gift in public that transcends the mere attracting of attention towards providing actual sustenance for other believers.

It seems to us that the key that opens the door to this theological understanding of the anthropological distinction between mind and spirit is provided in 14:13: **Therefore, one who speaks in a tongue should pray for the power to interpret.** Only because he understands interpretation to be a divine gift as *distinct* from praying in tongues can Paul emphasize in this way that it should be explicitly prayed for.[20] If understanding were given with the ecstatic prayer itself, its articulation in comprehensible speech to others would be simply a condescending act along these lines: "The spiritual understanding of my inarticulate prayer that I have already been given, I will now explain to you." The understanding, however, that is given *tō noi* positions the interpreter of the spiritual prayer as making a genuinely communicative act in which all participants are understood to be equidistant from the Spirit's cognitive inspiration.

---

20. "For Paul . . . interpretation of tongues is a charisma, an inspired utterance, not simply some form of rational discernment—how one could rationally discern 'mindless utterance' is a puzzle in itself: 'there is no dictionary of glossolalia' . . . Perhaps he simply assumed, or encouraged the assumption for the sake of good order, that whatever inspired utterance in the vernacular followed the 'tongue,' that was the interpretation." Dunn, *Jesus and the Spirit*, 248, quoting Delling, *Worship*, 33.

The Hebrew term for "word," *dabar* (דָּבָר), contrasts with the Greek *logos* in that the former is presumed always to be embodied. In Greek usage the *logos* was essentially a disembodied idea that might take on embodiment as a sometimes necessary embarrassment corresponding to the ephemeral and changing material predicament of human existence.[21] Paul mentions three forms of speech in the spirit—**prayer, praise** and **blessing**—all of which he indicates should be done **with the mind also**. This reveals how much Paul was steeped in the Jewish *dabar* tradition. Whereas from the perspective of Greek *logos* philosophy, the mind would be assumed to be automatically involved as, in fact, the originator of any word, the outward expression of which might be comprehensible or not to others, Paul's Hebrew background makes him equate the word with the *utterance*—as embodied in an act of speech. This is why for the odd case of inarticulate speech, it must be added as a request for what is otherwise taken for granted in human speaking: the involvement of the mind. But as we noted above, the Apostle does not consider the absence of reflectiveness that characterizes glossolalia as a form of immediate intercourse with God a deficiency in itself. It is only within a public setting in view that the involvement of the mind becomes necessary, precisely for the sake of comprehensibility to others (first) and oneself (second).

The question, therefore, is how we are to understand the **but** that precedes the **also** in verse 15. The description Paul offers of the problem that arises when spirit and mind are not linked in prophetic utterance illumines his understanding of the three forms of speaking in the Spirit: **if you say a blessing with the spirit, how can anyone in the position of an outsider say the "Amen" to your thanksgiving, since the outsider does not know what you are saying?** We have already indicated why it makes sense for Paul to acknowledge that it is quite possible for the initiated to grasp the *forms* of prayer that go on in various glossolalic utterances. But insofar as this same understanding is not available to the uninitiated or unbelieving bystander, the form itself, the sheer physical performance of unintelligible speaking looms as threatening behavior (14:23), and for this Paul censures their utterance; **For you may give thanks well enough, but the other person is not built up.** Paul requests that blessing with the spirit be accompanied by an interpretation so that the outsider may **say the "Amen" to your thanksgiving**. Once again the aim is not simply the seeker-sensitive comprehensibility of the word, its translation from physical reality into mental comprehension,

---

21. "The dominant meaning of *Logos* is ,'declaration' (*apophansis*); the word makes its contents known. That the Logos (sic) does this in audible words, by being spoken, is therefore secondary and can be wholly disregarded" Bultmann, "The Concept of the Word of God," 292.

but its thankful embrace as a fruit of a happening of words that reveals divine presence. Not only in the sheer givenness of glossolalic utterance, but also in the very way it is spoken out, must it be evident that **"God is really among you"** (14:25).

In line with most contemporary translations, the NRSV suggests that Paul speaks in tongues **more** than the Corinthians in terms that are "probably quantitative rather than qualitative; possibly both."[22] The Greek, however, offers us a more inviting possibility in reading literally, "I thank God more than all of you [that] I talk in tongues." The formulation can be read as an expression of Paul's self-understanding as one who is more genuinely grateful than the Corinthians for the gift of glossolalia, precisely as he understands and values its theological significance rather than marveling in its spectacular features or the reputation that it brings. An "adult" relation to glossolalia (14:20) is characterized not only by being able to practice it but by also by having an appropriate awareness of its effects on others. It is just this reflection that leads Paul here to express gratitude towards the divine giver for the missiological potency of tongues instead of focusing on the personal edification he has received in having been given it.

We are now in a position to understand why Paul's desire that the Corinthians **earnestly desire spiritual gifts** presents an alternative to their desire for spiritual powers that Paul criticized in the first chapters of this letter (3:1–3). For two reasons we find it appropriate that the Apostle has left this entreaty until he has explained what he means by spiritual gifts. If spiritual gifts are understood as personal possessions conceived within the grammar of competitive acquisition, it would be most accurate to say that the Corinthians *covet* the gifts because each wants them *for himself*. Paul's careful elaborations in this chapter have now revealed why covetousness displays a fundamental misunderstanding of the very nature of the gifts. Hence the second reason why he can only now urge them to **earnestly desire spiritual gifts**: the spiritual gifts as he has defined them are by definition not for the individual but *for the church*, and therefore cannot be coveted but are more truthfully described as desired. This earnest desire lays itself open to discover the acts of love toward the body that must be given form by the Spirit. It is the Spirit who answers the openness of Christians desirous for gifts by using them to build up the body of Christ.

---

22. Barrett, CKB, 321.

Manufactured Comprehension vs. Gospel Understanding

> ²¹ In the law it is written, "By people of strange tongues and by the lips of foreigners I will speak to this people; yet even then they will not listen to me," says the Lord. ²² Tongues, then, are a sign not for believers but for unbelievers, while prophecy is not for unbelievers but for believers. ²³ If, therefore, the whole church comes together and all speak in tongues, and outsiders or unbelievers enter, will they not say that you are out of your mind? ²⁴ But if all prophesy, an unbeliever or outsider who enters is reproved by all and called to account by all. ²⁵ After the secrets of the unbeliever's heart are disclosed, that person will bow down before God and worship him, declaring, "God is really among you."

As theologically attuned modern commentators have not failed to notice, Paul's quotation of Isaiah does not seem to flow smoothly within the overall drift of his argument: **"By people of strange tongues and by the lips of foreigners I will speak to this people; yet even then they will not listen to me"** (Isa 28:11–12). The quotation also raises questions about which version of the Isaiah passage Paul is quoting. Together these textual problems have generated an incredible range of proposals, from the suggestion that the verse is being presented as a citation that Paul thinks the Corinthians have illegitimately taken as a slogan[23] to readings that position it as the heart of the concentrically developed argument of the whole chapter.[24]

At first glance the parallels between the passage and Paul's argument in this chapter seem rather superficial, stating the obvious that in both contexts, Isaianic and Corinthian, the authors are dealing with people who do not comprehend the phenomenon of **strange tongues**. But if we attend to the respective reasons for this incomprehension in both cases, we notice that the differences are greater than the commonalities. In Isaiah it is speech that is in principle comprehensible—words spoken by foreign invaders that are presented by Isaiah as divine words of judgment—that is rendered miraculously incomprehensible by the hardening of the hearts of the people of Israel who have refused to listen to their own prophets. In the Corinthian worship, by contrast, the issue is speech that is in principle incomprehensible and needs to be made comprehensible through interpretation. It is our suggestion that staying with the twists and turns of Paul's unfolding argument will reveal that the quotation from Isaiah is indeed connected directly

---

23. The representatives of this position are surveyed in Peppiatt, *Women and Worship*, ch 5.

24. Bailey, *Paul through Mediterranean Eyes*, 394–95.

to the discussion of glossolalia and prophecy, by way of a totally unexpected connection. As we will try to demonstrate, for Paul, both uncomprehended forms of speech are ones that have been divinely aimed at preparing its addressees for repentance (14:25).

In 14:21–25 Paul develops a description of two different ways of "doing tongues"—one a precursor of judgment (as when God's patience is exhausted and he must draw on foreigners to utter his prophecies) and the other a sign of new life. A telling semantic shift in Paul's usage of the language of "sign" in 14:22 draws our attention to this distinction. There he switches from foreign tongues as a sign displaying the judgment on those who do not believe to an understanding of foreign languages as a sign that distinguishes divine favor and presence with believers.[25] This suggests that the attraction of the seemingly odd Isaiah passage for Paul lies in its reference to the role of strange tongues in the coming Day of Judgment. By deploying this quotation in the course of his discussion of glossolalia Paul implicitly warns the Corinthians that if the church lets tongues take the lead in gathered worship without being closely accompanied by interpretation (14:19), then it is entirely appropriate for the outsider to unwittingly don the prophetic mantle in declaring to the church that **you are out of your mind** (14:23, see 14).

The judgment that normally hangs over the nations now threatens a church that has childishly turned tongues from a gift intended for individual upbuilding into its inverse, performances that stand as a sign of a self-enclosed individualism even when enacted right in the middle of the gathered congregation. The prophetic speech for which Paul exhorts the Corinthians to **earnestly strive** thus *discloses* what Paul has already called a "proof from power" (>4:20) that evokes confession in those who witness it. The proliferation of the "mere talk" that Paul has already set up as the antithesis of the proof from power indicates that a message is afoot in the Corinthian church that has been intelligibly articulated but is not a servant of the Spirit's communicative power. It is in this way that the "mere talk" of some Corinthian believers parallels the "normal" talk of the nations, and articulation of "strange" languages becomes a medium for the divine confrontation of the wayward that God wishes to accomplish through all believers (14:24).

While Paul presses for articulate interpretation in the practice of Christian worship he still holds that glossolalia can be of significance for the odd visitor being won over by the gospel.[26] The point is that this desir-

---

25. "We cannot make a decision about how we will interpret the word 'sign' without making a corresponding decision about Paul's use of 'unbeliever' and 'believer.'" Peppiatt, *Women and Worship at Corinth*, 123.

26. The scenario we imagine resembles the one ventured by Bailey. "Picture the

able result cannot be directly attributed to the mere comprehensibility of the utterances in worship. The power of the gospel alone has the capacity to make the visitor comprehensible to herself: **the secrets of the unbeliever's heart are disclosed** (other translations having "reproved" or "convicted"). By slightly shifting one of the familiar strands of interpretation of this passage,[27] we understand this disclosure not as in the first instance the exposure of the person's sin, but as a recognition of who she is before God—a troubled yet free creature within the grand scheme of God's wild and beautiful world as exposed by proximity to the prophetic annunciation of the redeemed community. We understand the emphasis we have laid on the positive role played by the worshipping community in the conviction of the unbeliever to be an important but often overlooked aspect of Augustine's account of his conversion.

> While [Ponticianus] was speaking, Lord, you turned my attention back to myself. You took me up from behind my own back

---

following scene: An inquirer and an unbeliever attend a worship service of the Christian assembly in Corinth. The prophets give their messages. Old Testament texts are presented as fulfilled in the life and ministry of Jesus. The cross and the resurrection are discussed. 'Precept on precept' are presented. The unbeliever is still not convinced. It is all quite rational, even though delivered with passion. The inquirer has heard various religious enthusiasts present their views and said enquirer is still not convinced. Then one of the prophets finishes his remarks and suddenly, out of nowhere, a speaker in tongues starts praying. When the speaker is finished, a third party translates the prayer. The tongues speaker was not raging out of control. He or she waited until the prophet was finished and only then began his or her Spirit-filled, incomprehensible prayer language. The unbeliever is startled and amazed. He has never heard anything like this in his life. There was no emotional build up with song, dance, drums, sacrifice and exciting music to work the crowd into a frenzy. The strange yet attractive incomprehensible words seemingly came out of nowhere. Then, also mysteriously, a second person translates those words into rational speech. Something is going on that the unbeliever cannot explain. Perhaps—just perhaps—God is present and speaking to this gathering of Christians in this private home. Has the divine touched earth, asks the unbeliever? The *inquirer* is accustomed to such things. This is not a sign for him. He is eager to focus on the message of the prophets, respond with his *amen* and reflect on what it means for his life. The *believers* are deepened in their faith by those same prophetic messages. But for *unbelievers* this strange Spirit-filled language is indeed a sign pointing to a divine reality beyond the veil. As Paul affirmed, tongues are a 'sign for unbelievers,' while prophecy is a 'sign for believers.'" Bailey, *Paul Through Mediterranean Eyes*, 402–3.

27. "The unbeliever is reproved . . . not because the prophet pronounces judgment on him either in his secret, unexpressed opinion of him, or in what he actually says in explicit terms, but because, when he listens, his conscience accepts its own judgment through what is taught. He is judged because he goes down into the depths of his own being, and after examining himself, he comes to a realization of what he is like, a knowledge which was denied him before . . . His conscience is stirred so that he knows his sins which were hidden from him before." Calvin, JC, 299.

> where I had placed myself because I did not wish to observe myself (Ps 20:13), and you set me before my face (Ps. 29:21) so that I should see how vile I was ... And I looked and was appalled, but there was no way of escaping from myself. If I tried to avert my gaze from myself, his story continued relentlessly, and you once again placed me in front of myself; you thrust me before my own eyes so that I should discover my iniquity and hate it. I had known it, but I deceived myself, refused to admit it, and pushed it out of my mind. But at that moment the more ardent my affection for those young men of whom I was hearing, who for the soul's health had given themselves wholly to you for healing, the more was the detestation and hatred I felt for myself in comparison with them.[28]

Augustine's articulation of the dynamics of his own conversion helps us to see the role played by material, articulate and embodied presence of the redeemed community as well as its source in the divine working that we think Paul is suggesting. Repentance gains its compelling intelligibility to individual unbelievers when what must be left behind to join this divine movement for the first time becomes concretely tangible.

Modern church movements that have attempted to render Christian worship more accessible to outsiders are certainly to be commended for taking seriously Paul's question, **If ... an outsider or unbeliever enters ... will they say ... ?** But one of the dominant responses to this question has been to emphasize comprehensibility as the sufficient answer to this problem. The pairing of the assumption that complete comprehensibility is desirable with the wish to lower the barriers presented to the outsider entering the church has led to paring Christian worship down by asking what concepts or practices contemporary unbelievers might find strange or off-putting. This chapter in Paul's epistle should be seen as challenging such approaches in its presumption that no one can be brought to comprehend herself in truth if the language that confronts her is deliberately cleansed of any element of "strange tongues."

This is why it is critical to attend to the implications of Paul's refusal to iron out everything that is not immediately comprehensible in Christian worship. The effect of his insistence on interpretation is, paradoxically, permanently to preserve room for literally strange tongues. According to the rationale of "lowering the comprehensibility threshold," tongues stands out as the paradigmatic representative of the incomprehensible aspects of Christian worship that need to be avoided for being embarrassing at best

---

28. Augustine, *Confessions*, VIII.vii.16–17, 144–45.

and irrational at worst. In this light we begin to see how protecting of the space for glossolalia in the congregation has the effect of protecting an essential aspect of almost every form of Christian speech, including prophesying, teaching, and confessing, which can never be entirely shorn of performative moments that remain beyond immediate comprehensibility. Far from being an embarrassment, for Paul these unintelligible or not-yet comprehensible elements reveal in a uniquely important way the ongoing need for the mediation of the Spirit who leads us into truth (>2:13–16).

Important distinctions will need to be made, of course, between mere comprehension, the mind's ability to assemble meaningful combinations of individual signifiers in an uttered expression, and understanding in which the wider and deeper implications of an utterance are grasped. I may perfectly well have comprehended something you have said and yet still not understand what you are suggesting or want from me. It is one thing to comprehend the confession *ex maria virgine*, "born of the virgin Mary," as a feature of the nativity stories but quite another to understand and embrace that confession in a manner that illumines one's own existence.

Our criticism of attempts by the contemporary churches to lower the barriers to entry for unbelievers should therefore not be read as expressions of principled resistance to attempts to render Christian worship more comprehensible. Updating the language of worship and streamlining liturgical practice may well be undertaken to facilitate the understanding of the gospel. But Paul's treatment of glossolalia indicates that there can be no strategy capable of rendering everything in the Christian faith comprehensible. Any genuine purchase on the Christian gospel will be won only in embracing both comprehensible and incomprehensible dimensions of the reality that is life with the Trinitarian God—in confident faith that comprehensibility will come over time to dawn on that which currently seems to us incomprehensible (>13:12). Hence it would be equally misguided to marvel in and seek to preserve in principle any incomprehensible aspect of Christian faith and worship. What matters instead is being and remaining attuned to the *trans*-comprehensibility of the Christian faith. What is inviting about the gospel is neither "refreshing simplicity" nor "marvelous complexity"; the gospel beckons as and when the disclosive God is active in its address.

The Dynamism of the Prophetic Spirit

> [26]What should be done then, my friends? When you come together, each one has a hymn, a lesson, a revelation, a tongue, or an interpretation. Let all things be done for building up.

> ²⁷If anyone speaks in a tongue, let there be only two or at most three, and each in turn; and let one interpret. ²⁸But if there is no one to interpret, let them be silent in church and speak to themselves and to God. ²⁹Let two or three prophets speak, and let the others weigh what is said. ³⁰If a revelation is made to someone else sitting nearby, let the first person be silent. ³¹For you can all prophesy one by one, so that all may learn and all be encouraged. ³²And the spirits of prophets are subject to the prophets, ³³for God is a God not of disorder but of peace.
>
> (As in all the churches of the saints, ³⁴women should be silent in the churches. For they are not permitted to speak, but should be subordinate, as the law also says. ³⁵If there is anything they desire to know, let them ask their husbands at home. For it is shameful for a woman to speak in church. ³⁶Or did the word of God originate with you? Or are you the only ones it has reached?)
>
> ³⁷Anyone who claims to be a prophet, or to have spiritual powers, must acknowledge that what I am writing to you is a command of the Lord. ³⁸Anyone who does not recognize this is not to be recognized. ³⁹So, my friends, be eager to prophesy, and do not forbid speaking in tongues; ⁴⁰but all things should be done decently and in order.

As Paul turns to offer more concrete guidance to the Corinthians on the practicalities of Christian worship (**What should be done then, my friends?**), he offers them more than baldly practical instructions. From the outset he assumes a scenario—**When you come together, each one has a hymn, a lesson, a revelation, a tongue, or an interpretation**—that articulates no less than what we might call Paul's theology of political worship. The instruction that **each one** be allowed to represent to the whole political body a particular ministry to which he or she is called, turns everyone into a full citizen of the church polis.²⁹ More specifically, the Apostle again describes the criterion of each person's contribution as geared toward the *bonum commune* of the church polis: **Let all things be done for building up**.

It bears repeating that in an age in which only men were considered capable of having speaking roles in public discussions about how the political body was to be ordered, it was a revolutionary move of the highest order for Paul to characterize Christian worship as a sort of *agora* in which

---

29. As Aristotle puts it in his *Politics*, a citizen is "best defined by one criterion, a man who shares in the administration of justice and in the holding of office" (1274b, 32–36).

everyone, men *and* women had the right to take the floor and have his or her contribution heard (>11:11–12). Given the revolutionary nature of this new reality, not only of universal suffrage in the church but also of the role played by speech in sustaining it, Paul's emphasis on the need for certain speakers to silence themselves must appear troubling. The call for silencing appears in relation to three distinct scenarios. In 14:28 those are summoned to be silent in church who might have a tongue but no one to interpret; in 14:30 the one is summoned to silence who is confronted with a more immediate revelation; and in 14:32 a summons to be silent is addressed to women of the Corinthian church. While the reasons for Paul's response to the first case scenario will by now have become apparent given his arguments to this point in the chapter, the latter scenario especially remains perplexing, as it only in this case (and in this case only) the addressees seem to be a general group of people—women.

If the Apostle is in fact silencing a group, women, there are good theological reasons to be troubled. As Dietrich Bonhoeffer was quick to observe in the midst of the Confessing Church struggle, the silencing of entire groups of Christians in worship is fundamentally anti-Christ, such as when German Christians of the Nazi era cited this verse to defend the silencing of Jewish pastors. To this attempt Bonhoeffer responded, "Either we consider this admonition as legally binding [1 Cor. 14:34], in which case it still does not say anything about Jewish Christians' keeping silent in the churches, or we do not consider it legally binding, that is, women also are allowed to speak in the churches, in which case there is no possibility of forbidding Jewish Christians to speak as a matter of principle."[30] While it should be obvious that no less than the integrity of the gospel is at stake in this apparent silencing of all women in worship, we suggest it best to take a step back before tackling this perplexing passage straight away. It seems to us helpful to attend to the logic of Paul's sequence of instructions to silence by approaching them through the lens of the second scenario. This will help alleviate at least some of the perplexities presented by the third case, which have haunted Christian interpreters and communities down through the centuries.

Let two or three prophets speak, and let the others weigh what is said. If a revelation is made to someone else sitting nearby, let the first person be silent (14:29). The scenario in which a limited number of prophets speak, with others weighing or actually judging (διακρινέτωσαν/ *diakrinetōsan*) what has been said, displays a fine-tuned interplay in which the congregants understand their political power in a manner that allows

---

30. Bonhoeffer, *Sanctorum Communio* (DBWE 1), 429.

the ultimate authority to rest with the Spirit. The political subtlety of this portrayal of Christian worship is further demonstrated by how the appeal to silence in 14:30 is positioned. The one offering prophetic speech is expected to allow anyone the prerogative of interruption if he or she is given a revelation. Here we see Paul describing a spiritual order in which the ordering principle (two or three, one after the other) actually rests on a principle of interruptability! In principle no one bearer of a spiritual gift is warranted in commanding all authority in the moment of utterance. On these grounds the notion of spiritual order will always entail an emphasis on "spiritual" over "order," as the Spirit can never be captured within any given structure or routine.

It would be impossible and pastorally unwise were we to assume that the two principles of order and interruption ought to be subsumed into a single overriding one that could guide decisions about how to structure the life of the church in its internal and external affairs. No "balance" should ever be sought between the two if their power to mutually challenge and unsettle settled configurations produced by the respective other is to be preserved. This would include attempts such as specifying a limited time and place for the interruptive dimension of the Spirit within a given order as we find, for example in the principle of the *proprium* in the worship of "liturgical" churches.[31] And anyone who has had any sustained exposure to charismatic or "spontaneous" forms of popular worship can attest how a reckoning with this disruptive character of the Spirit will inevitably lead to domesticate it in some sort of regularity, which might be far from any formality and perhaps only consist in training worshippers to routinely respond to the predictable urge—"it's time now for another spontaneous interruption."

In the worship Paul describes there is no glossolalia without interpretation, no prophetic speech without others who judge it, and neither of these are without the need sometimes to be silenced by an intervention of the revelatory Spirit. Spiritual order of this type can never be entirely comfortable as it situates the church this side of eternity in a risky business marked by the need to interpret, judge, discern, and interrupt time and again.[32] Precisely

---

31. *Proprium* and *ordinarium* are terms that distinguish parts of the liturgy that stay the same (the stable elements being called *ordinarium*) or change according to the liturgical season (the dynamic elements being called the *proprium*). This nomenclature for liturgical ordering, it should be added, is intended to allow specific and limited moments for both principles, and thus should be understood as an acknowledgment of the need for a principle of "interruption" of the ordinary on a regular basis. What can be said with certainty is that the nomenclature was not instituted as an expression of the Weberian sensibility that whatever interventions the Spirit may have in stock will need to be absorbed into an ecclesial institutional form.

32. Augustine was a master of pneumatic preaching and his sermons display a

because this is never comfortable, the desire to escape the vulnerability that comes with reliance on the Spirit is never far away in Christian churches. Such attempts may include setting up ecclesiastical offices responsible for settling or, in Paul's sense, bringing to a halt the cycle of spiritual utterance, prophecy and discernment, and new utterance, through a final word or ultimate judgment. Paul, however, shows no desire to overcome the wildness of the Spirit. What he urges on the church is to become sensitive to unscripted interventions in order to develop that particular discernment that can perceive whether they are in fact upbuilding or not (14:32). Such a church will be continually if subtly remade by its sensitivity to the need to reconfigure its orders both as a result of having listened to this interruptive Spirit in the past and to remain open to these interventions in the future (14:26).

God is a God not of disorder but of peace (14:33). We have seen the Apostle describing in some detail why the fine-tuned interplay of all the charismata, in both their mutual upbuilding and challenging, must be understood as the crucial aspect of the peace that characterizes Christian worship (>ch. 12). This peace has an order, a "Spirit-order," and it is this order alone—not any humanly constructed order, however apparently "spiritual"—that properly displaces the disorder brought about by the Corinthians' perennial temptation to covetousness and their predilection for ecstatic manifestations. We consider it vital, therefore, to understand the expression **as in all the churches of the saints** to belong with the previous phrase (**God is not a God of disorder but of peace**) rather than with the

---

remarkable ability to course correct according to the leading of the Spirit. One sermon, for instance, is redirected by a miracle of healing that happened at the cathedral at Carthage while he was preaching, and on multiple occasions he displays a remarkable faithfulness to the lectionary in preaching on an entirely different passage than he had prepared after a lector had read the wrong passage before he mounted the pulpit. See *City of God* XXII.8 and Boyd-MacMillan, "The Transforming Sermon." Afro-American homiletics, with its understanding of call and response, offers a particularly clear example of liturgical form that finely balances the stable forms of worship but in a way that is structurally open to and expectant of the interruptions of the Spirit in the congregation. One notable feature of such services is the role played in them by repetition, which allows space for interruptions and in effect calls for clarifications and interjections of fresh insight. Bonhoeffer develops this emphasis on the role of repetition in awaiting the Spirit, and the promise of such waiting in his meditations on Psalm 119. "How could I ever walk along the long path of this psalm and begin it ever anew, how could I not tire of these unceasing repetitions, if God had not shown me that each of his words is full of undiscovered and unfathomable wonders?" Bonhoeffer, "Meditation on Psalm 119, 1939–1940," in *Theological Education Underground, 1937–1940* (DBWE 15), 520. Homiletic traditions characterized by preaching that unleash a torrential flurry of new thoughts, in contrast, essentially deny the opportunity for the congregation to break in.

one that follows (**women should be silent in the churches**).³³ This is to read it as a description of the *type* of unity to be expected among all churches that are gathered by the same God. To do otherwise, as do a majority of modern translations that render the expression **as in all the churches** as an amplifier of the injunction **women should be silent in the churches**, leads to the theologically dubious addition of parenthesis around verses 14:33a–36 in an attempt to soften the impact of these verses that appear to offend modern sensibilities about gender equality.

The bracketing of these verses to suggest they are interpolations or quotations of the position of Paul's opponents is lamentable in preventing us from considering that Paul's call to silence might be a case-specific command and so might be theologically rather more promising than embarrassing. If we take 14:33b to be rounding up verse 33 rather than opening up verse 34, a reading becomes possible that could be glossed, "As in all churches, the God of peace rules, so be it in the Corinthian church." This is to understand 14:34 as the specification of the general rule that all Christian churches observe a Spirit-ordering for a specific case that has arisen in the Corinthian community. The general assertion is thus framing Paul's ensuing injunction to a particular congregation (and not "all churches") that "women should allow for silence" (14:33b, Thiselton's trans.).

As in 11:4–15, where Paul discussed the tendency of the Corinthian women in the church to break local decorum in their mode of visual appearance ("letting their hair down"), here he describes a parallel aspect of the women's over-enthusiastic embrace of their new right of full citizenship in the church polis: in this case the right to take the floor and have their voices heard via prophetic speech. Again we think it plausible to imagine that women who had never before known full citizen's rights (the Jewish synagogue, like the Greek polis, also enforcing "women be silent" as a rule³⁴) would have been tempted to exult in their newfound freedom by gladly taking the floor and not easily relinquishing it. This could have been true for both women acting as prophets or as those weighing or sifting other prophets' speech by, for instance, interrogating others in a ceaselessly interruptive manner.³⁵

Lest this assumption be read as reinforcing the familiar gender stereotyping of women as the more loquacious sex, in our view such a phenomenon would also have been a very understandable response to the stifling

---

33. Many commentators through the centuries have opted for this reading, see Aquinas and Calvin.

34. Bremen, *The Limits of Participation*.

35. Wendland, *Die Briefe an die Korinther*, 132.

scope of patriarchal primacy at this time. In the face of the disruptive power of the Spirit the main alternatives to the rule of the Spirit of peace would have been all-or-nothing arrangements: either the reinscription of the rule of the *pater familias* over all others,[36] or the codification of the antitype to that rule as established in some sub-cultural spheres, such as the cult of prophetesses, in which a dominant female plays a structurally parallel role to a ruling male. Because for Paul both arrangements represent the rule of one inescapable framework of order standing against disorder neither arrangement can qualify as a representation of the dynamic peace of God. Such orders are of the type that can be instituted and maintained by assertions that subordinate parties return to their place. In both the patriarchal sphere and the realm of the priestess cults there are in principle no alternations of speakers or power relations and therefore by definition any overturning of expected hierarchy represents a disorder to be quashed.

Given these considerations, we are now in the position to propose that the silence to which the Corinthian women are called by the Apostle cannot be based on a general assertion of gender subordination, but expresses for a local context the implications of the genuinely universal rule (**in all the churches of the saints**) of spiritual interruption of spiritual speech. As culturally understandable as it might be for women who have not been allowed a voice in public for so long to now erupt in a ceaseless stream of expression or interrogation, even for them Paul's central rule still applies: **If a revelation is made to someone else sitting nearby, let the first person be silent** (14:30). The reproach **women should be silent** (14:34) needs therefore to be understood not as being addressed to women in general but specifically to those unwilling to yield the floor to others, whether male or female, and who instead keep talking or interrogating, while themselves brooking no interruption.

It is the arrogance of such a posture that prompts Paul to press the barbed questions of 14:36: **Or did the word of God originate with you? Or are you the only ones it has reached?** In the church no one has the right to claim to be the only one God's word has reached. It is the question of the origin of the word of God that most explicitly indicates that Paul is addressing a local problem rather than offering a universal ruling on gender

---

36. Peppiatt is right to note that in the Corinthian context, if men were enforcing the rule of silence, this reinscription of patriarchal habit would most likely have been promulgated in the clothing of religious elitism. "[Paul] is totally uncompromising with the puffed-up Corinthian men who are convinced that they are right on the grounds that they hear from God and are more spiritually gifted than Paul. They are rich, reigning, and boastful, whereas Paul and his companions were a dishonored spectacle to men and angels." Peppiatt, *Women and Worship at Corinth*, 136.

relations. Do **you** (Corinthian women) propose to step out of the universal rule of Jesus Christ? If our reading is sound, in the historical setting of the Corinthian church it is the women in particular who needed to be silenced for quenching the Spirit and its particular order by, ironically claiming a type of *pater familias* right of final authority that allows no interruption. They needed to be silenced not because they disrupted order, but because they disrupted a specific form of peace. The high irony embodied in many conservative churches today is the precise inversion of this configuration. Having abandoned the early broad-based *polis* of prophetic speech Paul is setting out here, in which women's voices were not only included but by their inclusion one of the most visible features of the new politics of the church, many self-proclaimed "biblical" churches today deploy this very text in order to rule out in principle the Spirit's disruption occurring through the voices of over half the congregation.

The distinctive order of peace that Paul calls forth for Christian worship demands not only the spiritual disruption of unspiritual order but also the overturning of unspiritual disruption by spiritual order. This peace is therefore properly understood as a *dynamic* state that can be neither captured nor routinized in its ability to shift and accommodate new social engagements. Paul's prime concern in all passages on silence in this chapter is for a spiritual hierarchy that points to the sovereignty of the Spirit over and against every form of order or disorder. As we have seen, this rule applies both to cases in which unspiritual speech is disrupting the order of the service (the persistent and ceaseless interrogation) and to cases of unspiritual claims to the right to uninterrupted speech—"magisterial" or patriarchal claims to hold the final say in matters of judging prophetic speech.

This line of interpretation overcomes the need to make either 14:31 or 35 the generalizable key to this discussion. There is no need definitively to pronounce on whether the women in Corinth were disrupting the order of service by undisciplined interruption or rather by an over-enthusiastic embrace of their new role as prophets and judges of prophets to yield a culture of monologue insensitive to the role of interruption. Either case would represent a breach of the order of peace that we have described above. Even if their questions were good ones, or their monologues had good content, both breached the order of the service by overshooting the bounded nature of the Spirit's endowment of peace.

Because the order of peace is, like any order, given definition by its boundaries, the Apostle now once again takes up the language of decorum—**For it is shameful for a woman to speak in church** (>11:5-6). In this case some women's speech could be called shameless to the extent that a genuine right—to both prophetic speech and interruption—was being exploited by over-use. This also suggests why Paul returns to the language of decorum, as "shameless" indicates a loss of sense for social measure (>11:22). The suggestion to **let them ask their husbands at home** is Paul's practical solution to recalibrate the Corinthians' sense of measure on this point (for *both* male and female). One way to preempt the temptation to refuse to be silent when the Spirit calls somebody else to take the floor is to use the private sphere, with its ample supply of time, to deal with any "surplus" questions that may be creating pressures to speak without measure in gathered worship.

Paul's admonition **Let them ask their husbands at home** cannot, therefore, be an injunction drawing on a presumed principled gender hierarchy. The weight of the suggestion is practical, in precisely the same vein as Paul's suggestion in chapter 11 that the wealthy believers "eat at home." In either case he recommends a measure aimed at making sure that public worship is not compromised by private indulgence (>11:34). In a practical pinch, and in the absence of a Christian equivalent to the rabbinic institution that was available to Jews for answering theological questions, Paul drafts husbands in to play something like this role. Paul's pastoral advice is essentially, then, "Yes, it is permissible to quench your hunger, and yes it is fine to ask questions and to speak out. But if it cannot be done in a measured way in public worship (taking its measure from the peace of the overall setting that it is to serve), then use the resources available in the private sphere to appropriately fulfill those needs."

As convincing as we hope our line of interpretation has been, a potential disruption to its logic must still be addressed. Having stressed a case-specific reading of **let the women be silent** that reflects the particularities of the Corinthian situation, Paul's rather blunt reference to the law in 14:34 (**as the law also says**) appears to demand a more principled understanding of **they are not permitted to speak, but should be subordinate**. The abrupt manner in which this reference to the law is introduced has typically called to commentators' minds (both ancient and modern[37]) the book of Genesis in its portrayal of the sequence of creation in which the woman is created subsequently to the man (Gen 2:20-24) or is said to be made subservient to the man as an implication of the fall (Gen 3:16). In this vein Paul's reference to the law could be understood according to the well-known pharisaic

---

37. Origen takes a slightly different tack to arrive at the same conclusion, and is consistent in following this logic by refuting all the passages in the Old Testament that appear to depict women prophesying in the gathered assembly. Origen, *Homilies*, JTS 10 (1909), in JK, 239-40. The most influential contemporary reassertion of principled gendered hierarchy based on Genesis is found in Piper and Grudem, *Recovering Biblical Manhood and Womanhood*, esp. chs. 3, 6.

deployment of the creation narrative to ground a principled female subordination. This line of interpretation would mean taking Paul to be drawing on his pharisaic upbringing and its assumptions about ontologized gender hierarchy in a manner that we find to be in some tension with his more nuanced pastoral summons to equality under the Spirit's rule.

As widespread as the assumption is that can be found all over ancient and modern commentaries, that the law Paul is referring to here must be the passages in Genesis that are taken to undergird female subordination, we think it worth considering the possibility that Paul's reference to the law in 14:34 is not to Genesis but to the passage from Isaiah that Paul has quoted only a few verses before, in 14:21: **"By people of strange tongues and by the lips of foreigners I will speak to this people; yet even then they will not listen to me," says the Lord.** This reading assumes that when Paul uses the term "law" he does not mean only the five books of Moses but includes the prophets, the "book of the twelve."[38]

As we noted above, modern commentators feel that this quotation does not seem to fit into Paul's earlier argument, let alone this present one. However, on the basis of the reading we have developed to this point, the quotation from the prophetic book appears almost shockingly to the point and also reinforces our contention that this passage is not essentially concerned with gender. The passage from Isaiah on which Paul draws comes in a chapter devoted to an exposition of God's impending judgment on Israel. This judgment is addressed in particular to the elite, the priests and prophets. Isaiah portrays them as a breed of rather strange ecstatics: "Woe to the proud crown of the drunkards of Ephraim, the priest and the prophet reel with the strong drink . . . they err in vision, they stumble in giving judgment" (Isa 28:1, 7). Not only are the bearers of spiritual ministry in Israel perverting their genuine office and right to ecstatic utterances by substituting bottled spirits for the Spirit, but they are also characterized by a strong sense of pride: "To whom will he teach knowledge, and to whom will he explain the message? Those who are weaned from the breast? For it is precept upon precept, precept upon precept, line upon line, line upon line, here a little there a little" (Isa 28:9-10). The drunken "proud crown" of Israel refuse to be interrupted in their ways and go as far as mocking the forms of teaching through which divine wisdom is instilled in the people: the step by step, letter by letter teaching that the Spirit deems fitting for the respective state of maturity of the recipient. Very perceptively, Luther's German translation does not translate but transliterates the Hebrew expression of 28:10a: "*Tsaw latsaw tsaw latsaw, qaw laqaw qaw laqaw*" (צַו לָצָו צַו לָצָו קַו לָקָו קַו לָקָו). Luther

---

38. Watson, *Paul and the Hermeneutics of Faith*, ch 2.

obviously wished his non-Hebrew readers to pick up the hint here that the proud and drunken priests had reduced themselves to babbling, and in the context of our interpretation of 1 Corinthians 14 the phonetic allusion to glossolalia is hard to overlook.

The verse Paul cites to the Corinthians is thus contextualized in the book of Isaiah by a striking portrayal of religious ministries that yield to unspiritual substitutes for the genuine source in God's Spirit. In their mockery of Israel's mode of spiritual instruction as childish, the priests of Israel appear as an antitype to Paul who summons the Corinthians to overcome their childish way of coveting the spectacular among the gifts of the Spirit. Both the over-enthusiastic childish Corinthians and the drunken pseudo-grownups of Ephraim need, according to Paul, to hear the divine judgment that in Isaiah comes in the form of interruption by foreigners speaking in their respective languages in the manner that the priests have just mocked as childish. Amazingly, given the circumstances that we have seen Paul addressing in Corinthian worship, the word of the Lord that the foreigners speak to the drunken priests of Israel offers them a form of rest that they obviously do not possess: "The Lord will speak to this people, to whom he has said, 'this is rest, give rest to the weary, and this is repose'" (Isa 28:11b–12). The condition of the God of Israel's reign of peace is again the silencing of the proud speech that otherwise staves off this divine interruption by way of mockery. Isaiah's invocation of rest does indeed make reference to the primal history, not to the creation of woman from man, but to the seventh day that interrupts the sequence of divine creation and so opens a repose that breaks into human activity, inviting all humankind, male and female, into the genuine presence of God and one another.

Having sought to demonstrate how the law to which Paul appeals to explain the silence he enjoins on the women of Corinth is best explained with a proxy quotation of Isaiah, we are now in a better position to understand the sort of claim Paul is making in 14:37–38: **Anyone who claims to be a prophet, or to have spiritual powers, must acknowledge that what I am writing to you is a command of the Lord. Anyone who does not recognize this is not to be recognized.** What is in need of recognition (14:38) is not simply or primarily Paul's apostolic authority, but more precisely the rule of the Spirit as a rule geared to oikodomeic peace. Those who are "not to be recognized" are by implication specifically those who resist this spiritual order by failing to be silent at spiritually appropriate moments. Even in the exercise of the gifts of prophecy that Paul wishes the Corinthians to eagerly pursue (14:39), discernment will need to be made between types of prophesying that recognize the order of the Spirit of peace and those that do not. As Douglas Harink aptly summarizes, "'Be subordinate' is not the gospel adjusting itself to the existing order; rather, it is the gospel itself immediately taking resident aliens, slaves and wives *beyond* the existing order [by] radically contextualizing and relativising the so-called reality of the existing orders within the greater reality of the truth, governance and care of Jesus Christ."[39]

It would take us too far afield to survey the long and winding reception history of Paul's argument for more silence in the Corinthian church, but we cannot leave our interpretation without at least a few hints as to where it locates us in the wide and often wild stream of commentators' remarks on Paul's verdict. A particularly suggestive note comes from Luther who, in his *Table Talks*, comments on a letter that the bishop of Meissen wrote to Elisabeth of Rohlitz and in which he quoted 1 Corinthians 14:34 in order to silence her. As a widow of the Earl of the region, Elisabeth had initiated certain changes in religious arrangements within her domain and the bishop had charged her with overstepping her authority, claiming that it was his alone. Elisabeth, Luther reports, wrote back that while she agreed the measures were within the bishop's sphere of responsibility, she had advanced the changes in view of the welfare and salvation of her subjects. After reporting on this interchange Luther comments that he intended to write her the words of Psalm 45:1, "My tongue is like the pen of a ready scribe," adding the interpretative comment, "If they are unwilling to listen to men, they will need to listen to women and allow children to speak up."[40]

While this situation is not an exact parallel to what is going on in Paul's Corinth, the similarities remain striking. Here we have someone who wishes to silence another member of the church and does so by borrowing the apostle's authority and the authority of office to decree that women should be silent in the church. We also have the other who does not agree to silence but keeps interfering, as well as a third theological commentator who quite against the cultural instincts of the time (and to a certain degree his own) commends the woman's resistance against the bishop's attempts to silence her. He does so by quoting the law and locating her and her story within God's story, ultimately to make the point that whoever becomes the bearer of the ministry of either speaking authoritatively in religious matters or judging what others have said, what counts above all else is that God's word finds the good pen of a ready scribe, allowing a word to be publically uttered that exposes attempts to still the movement of the Spirit.[41]

---

39. Harink, *1&2 Peter*, 87.

40. Luther, *Luthers Epistel-Auslegung*, 195, quoting *Tischreden* III, 633, lines 25ff., translation ours.

41. The most that can be said in defense of the Bishop of Meissen is that he has the full authority of St. Thomas Aquinas behind him. The commentary of Thomas on

How does our interpretation situate us in the debates between egalitarians and complementarians that are especially heated in conservative English speaking evangelicalism? We happily welcome insights from modern feminist/egalitarian quarters as they have helped us to better appreciate the particularities of the Corinthian situation, in which a key aspect of the patriarchalism of their culture was suspended, leading to an enthusiastic demonstration of their newfound liberty. Through their work we have also come to appreciate how modern scholarship has been over-determined by masculine ideals that have obscured the high profile of women in early Christianity.[42] At the same time, we also commend the zeal with which defenders of complementarianism wish to rescue the passage as genuinely Pauline and integral to the logic of this epistle.[43] As our exegesis has demonstrated, it is theologically fruitful to take 14:33b–36 as genuinely Pauline. The liberating insight for us is that the interpretative rule in reading these passages need not be imported from outside scripture, whether from modern canons of the absolute equality of the sexes or pharisaic interpretations of original created gender inequality. Paul can be read as offering his own interpretive keys in the course of his argument *within* this chapter. Thus, rather than taking **let women be silent** as a generalizable rule or order for all the churches, we understand Paul's rule as, "everyone should be silent, including women, when a revelation arrives."

Having opened the chapter with an exhortation to love, Paul has proceeded to demonstrate how love establishes a pneumatic order in which structure and disruption are held together in a dramatic union, a union aptly called peace. This is to reconceive peace not as the balancing of various interests, an equilibrium achieved between differing priorities among congregants, but an ever-ready *expectancy* for the Spirit's interruptions of judgment and grace through the ordering of prophetic activity. Paul has now laid the groundwork to end with a more overt and succinct exhortation

---

these verses (sections 879–81) offers us an essentially complete catalogue of the arguments used to ban female speaking in church: women are to be silent because they (Eve) "spoke once and subverted the entire world"; he cites 1 Cor 11:5 as a proof that women are to be subservient to men in Christian worship and makes this an ontological subjugation ("their function"); he says they are "deficient in reasoning," quotes Aristotle "who says in his *Politics* that corruption of rule occurs, when the rule comes to women," claims women are naturally more prone to feeling shame, and "if therefore they ask and dispute in public, it would be a sign of shamelessness, and this is shameful to them"—which he also takes to ban them from being lawyers.

42. Schüssler Fiorenza, "Women in the Pauline Churches," 203–26.

43. Peppiatt surveys the long list of interpreters who have offered interpolation theses regarding 14:33b–36 (*Women and Worship at Corinth*, 108–11), and Carson draws together the most important problems with such attempts in *Recovering Biblical Manhood and Womanhood*, 141–42.

to this order of peace under the Spirit's rule. Within this rule true worship generates worship, as the example of the outsider who is won over by the prophetic character that Christian worship displays. The person who experiences the genuine *dynamis* of worship will be brought to **declaring "God is really among you!"** The Greek word for declaring, ἀπαγγέλλω (*apangello*), oscillates between "testifying" and "proclaiming." Indeed, if the outsider says "Amen" to the church's thanksgiving (14:16), she is by this very token becoming part of the thanksgiving herself.

By way of conclusion, three claims that Paul makes in this chapter have become clear, claims that raise questions for us about our contemporary conceptions and practice of worship. First, Paul is not offering a blueprint for Christian worship in all times and places. But neither is it possible to read his description of worship in ancient Corinth, in all its glossolalic richness, as simply a precursor that has been superseded by Christianity's progress toward the hegemony of intelligible speech in worship. Considering Paul's engagement with the Corinthians in this chapter from within the liturgical habits we have inherited forces us to consider anew what the challenges might be that other forms of Christian worship present to us. On the basis of the *una sancta*, the unity of the church under the rule of the one Spirit of peace, the particularity of other churches' practices should stand as a continuous challenge to the certainties we harbor in our own tradition of worship, and definitely bars us from the always tempting quest to define a single liturgical formulation or era as the pinnacle of Christian worship.

We say this on the assumption that Paul is not offering us here a fixed pattern of worship to be emulated in all times and places, but rather a more fundamental insight into the sort of questions we need to ask if our worship is to remain attentive and subordinate to the Spirit of peace. Though it will look differently in every time and cultural configuration, this peace can only be sustained through the activity of theological questioning and practical discernments that can never cease. To ask then how the Corinthians "are us" in the light of this chapter does not mean to ask whether we worship in a context in which glossolalia is practiced, but to ask: what are *our* prideful forms of holding onto the powers of interruption or judgment? Where are our own temptations to translate our public worship into the modes and codes of our private devotion? How are we resistant to being interrupted by the interference of the Spirit? It may not be an overly loquacious group of prophetesses with which we have to reckon but any number of all too familiar contemporary malformations: an autocratic pastoral team, a woodenly inflexible liturgical form, a fetish for comfort in worship, or the insistence of political correctness that does not allow for interruption.

1 Corinthians 15

> But someone asks why Paul has deferred, or put off, to the end of this letter, a subject which deserved precedence over everything else.[1]

> Once he has finished teaching about spiritual gifts, Paul moves on to the most important subject of all, the matter of the resurrection.[2]

> Clearly, Paul has saved the weightiest matter for last—as any good teacher would do.[3]

> Hence, the end of the Epistle is also its beginning, its principle that supports and actuates the whole, because it is not only a termination, but the end.[4]

As the material argument of the epistle draws to a close, we think it best immediately to give away our most striking finding about chapter 15. As we investigated its content and placement we became increasingly uncomfortable with what has become the default reading—that this chapter offers a grand finale to the letter. As the epigraphs above suggest, Paul is often seen in this chapter as leaving behind the lowlands of messy moral problems he has discussed in previous chapters for the heights of this celebratory hymn to the resurrection. From here, we imagine, he has found safe high ground from which all the quagmires that have just been navigated can be surveyed. What we have been surprised to discover in chapter 15 instead is an Apostle keen to continue in the mode of kenotic pastoral care, patiently returning to the series of concrete problems and questions put to him by the Corinthians.

In one sense this chapter is a mere continuation of his characteristic pastoral posture, as indicated by his moving from a discussion on disorder in Christian worship in chapter 14 to take up yet another problem afflicting the church in Corinth: that "some" were denying a core Christian

---

1. Calvin, JC 312.
2. Chrysostom, *Homily* 38, PG 61:321–23, in JK, 243.
3. Hays, RBH 252.
4. Barth, *Resurrection of the Dead*, 115.

doctrine, the resurrection. Along with this seemingly new issue, it is obvious that Paul is still dealing with the very same Corinthians who have provoked his exhortations in the previous chapters. His engagement with them in chapter 15 moves to reveal a previously invisible unity running through the variety of problems he has dealt with up to this point: the Corinthians' refusal of death.

Only from the perspective provided to us by the resurrection does the remarkable diversity of "cases" through which Paul has labored in chapters 1–14 start to emerge as animated by this most paradoxical form of the death-drive. What underlies the remarkable variety of problems in Corinth is an underlying spiritual problem that not only united the Corinthians, but also unites them with us: the desire to have newness of life without embracing death. The newness of life that comes with the gospel Paul has to offer can only come via the radical erasure or death of one form so that a new one can come into being. The real issue of this chapter, then, is not to establish once and for all the immortality of the human being nor even the first-century resurrection of the God-man. Rather, the pastoral thrust of this intervention aims to overcome the Corinthians' unwillingness to die into a new life, an unwillingness oddly expressed through a certain way of discussing the resurrection that the Apostle briskly unmasks for what it is—a foolishness from which they need to sober up (15:34–35). The new life that Paul sets before them can only begin when the Corinthians give up their belief that the Christian life can be had without any genuine break with their former self-identifications. Grasping the differences between continuous changes and sharp breaks in the course of human existence will therefore be the key to understanding this chapter. Accounts of the resurrection that are marked by a denial of its being a radical break can take manifold forms—not only the blunt declaration that life after death is impossible or non-existent, but also by spiritualizing death and resurrection as one smooth transition into a higher form of life that leaves behind not only the pain of dying, but also the embarrassments that come with living the life of what Paul calls a "psychic animal" (15:44–45).

As he opens this chapter Paul initially appears only to be censoring a minority that happened to have "intellectual problems" with the concept of the resurrection. The way that he then widens the discussion of dying and rising with Christ, however, suggests that the resurrection-deniers only offer him an occasion to more sharply articulate a concern that has been dominant in the letter from the very first chapter (1:17–18). Given the various ways in which Paul has had to draw the Corinthians' attention to their failure to embrace the *cruciformity* of Christian existence, it is little wonder that they found the concept of the resurrection to offer them a particularly strong springboard from which the problem of the crucifixion could be overleapt. Attracted to the heavenly life resurrection promises, they remained repelled by the suggestion that in order to enter this new life they would need first to submit to the embarrassment of dying in a cruciform life. The Corinthians resisted dying to old pagan habits such as visiting prostitutes (ch. 6) and patron-style hosting of table fellowship (ch. 11). They likewise refused to die to their self-centered spiritual ambition, as evidenced by their boasting (ch. 3), gift-hoarding (ch. 12), and factionalism (ch. 1). Each of these situations Paul took to indicate a deficiency of trust in the reality of the resurrected as one who forever bears the marks of the cross. The alternative directions Paul gives to the Corinthians in each of these contexts we find to be aptly encapsulated in his claim here that, **What you sow does not come to life** unless it dies (15:36, >11:33-34).

It is only against the backdrop of the Corinthians' enduring refusal to embrace a cruciform life that we can understand the Apostle's employment of the strongest language to rebuke them: Fool! It is a rebuke that appears rather rude given the apparent innocuousness of the questions he thereby repudiates: **How are the dead raised? With what kind of body do they come?** (15:35). To modern ears these sound like the most reasonable of questions and we instinctively sympathize with believers who would wrestle with them—as indicated by their continual appearance in pastoral contexts and theological treatises ever since. Rather than allowing ourselves to dismiss this apparent lack of pastoral sensitivity in Paul's rebuke, we do better to begin by asking what sort of posture is displayed in these questions that the Apostle finds so counterproductive. Our suggestion is that the more alert we become to this posture, the more we will begin to understand why it was a pastoral necessity for Paul to respond to them in the most confrontational terms.[5]

We are set off in the right direction if we ask what question has been precluded by Paul's refusal of the two questions in verse 35. He does not keep us waiting and in the very next verse singles out that the alternative question most worth asking: "What you sow does not come to life unless it dies." In analyzing this response we will follow the lead suggested by the opening of Bonhoeffer's 1933 Christology lectures who asks us to begin by distinguishing "what" and "how" questions from "who" questions.[6] Paul, we will suggest, is highly sensitive to all exclusions of the "who" that should mark all Christian talk about resurrection. Taking this route will allow

---

5. "[A]s he proceeds he warms to the task, bares his head, and shouts..." Chrysostom, *Homily* 38, PG 61:321-23, in JK, 244.

6. Bonhoeffer, "Lectures on Christology," in *Berlin, 1932–1933* (DWBE 12), 301-8.

us to discover Paul's rebuke to be intelligible as an act of resistance to the Corinthians' exclusive focus on "how" and "what" questions. Paul sees their obsession with the technicalities of bodily resurrection[7] to be a barrier to their engaging the question on which their very salvation turns, that is, *who* they will have to become in order to inherit the life of the resurrection, and *whose* resurrection is in view when they use this language.

Scripture and Resurrection: Mutual Vindication

> [1] Now I would remind you, brothers and sisters, of the good news that I proclaimed to you, which you in turn received, in which also you stand, [2] through which also you are being saved, if you hold firmly to the message that I proclaimed to you—unless you have come to believe in vain.
> [3] For I handed on to you as of first importance what I in turn had received: that Christ died for our sins in accordance with the scriptures, [4] and that he was buried, and that he was raised on the third day in accordance with the scriptures, [5] and that he appeared to Cephas, then to the twelve. [6] Then he appeared to more than five hundred brothers and sisters at one time, most of whom are still alive, though some have died. [7] Then he appeared to James, then to all the apostles. [8] Last of all, as to one untimely born, he appeared also to me. [9] For I am the least of the apostles, unfit to be called an apostle, because I persecuted the church of God. [10] But by the grace of God I am what I am, and his grace toward me has not been in vain. On the contrary, I worked harder than any of them—though it was not I, but the grace of God that is with me. [11] Whether then it was I or they, so we proclaim and so you have come to believe.

If, as we have suggested, we take verse 36 to display the central theme of this chapter, Paul's opening move to situate his discussion as a treatment of a very early Christian credal formula (15:3b–5) appears to be a way to boost the punch that will accrue to a line in the creed to which the Corinthians had not yet sufficiently attended: the statement that **he was buried**. Burial as the external seal of physical death must have seemed an especially

---

7. In terms of Aristotle's scheme of the four causes, these questions belong to the class of inquiries into material (what) and formal (how) causes, and so "technical" in relation to inquiries into original and final causes. Aristotle, *Metaphysics* 5,1013a.

embarrassing aspect of the gospel story to those who conceived of Christian existence as a process of purely spiritualized dying and rising.[8]

With the phrase **Now I would remind you** Paul emphasizes that he is not introducing anything new under this heading. What he has to say will be neither a novel teaching nor an entirely new departure from the sequence of topics discussed in the letter. The Greek term for "reminding" (γνωρίζω/ *gnōrizō*) indicates a drawing to conscious awareness of something that has already been known but which is now appreciated from a fresh perspective.[9] The traditional credal formula Paul quotes is then marked out as common Christian knowledge with the phrase **which you in turn received**. Interestingly, the Corinthians' relation to this core Christian testimony is denoted with a spatial term, as Paul speaks of the εὐαγγέλιον (*euangelion*), the **good news**, in which **you also stand**. The formulation "in which" is a literal translation of the Greek ἐν τῷ (*en tō*). It is best not to follow Thistleton's rendering of this expression as "on which you have taken your stand." The significance of the difference between such a "foundational" rendering and a spatial rendering emerges when we see how each alternative frames the subsequent lines that must be followed through Paul's further delineations of the believer's relation to this gospel.

The first is Paul's insistence that the Corinthians **hold firmly to the message that I proclaimed to you**. Here the task is to clarify what it is that Paul believes must be held firmly. Thiselton translates the object of this

---

8. Given the paucity of historical data we are skeptical of attempts to argue for any definitive rendition of the Corinthian beliefs Paul is refuting here. On the basis of the configuration of Paul's response to their misunderstandings about the resurrection, we have come to imagine (with the majority of contemporary historical critics) that their beliefs overlapped in some way with those of the Hellenistic Jewish writer Philo. The following passages provide a flavor of his theology and expose his key terminology, so providing us with a useful foil for exposing how Paul's (somewhat similar) conceptual language differs from thoroughly Hellenized Jewish thought: "[The 'heavenly man'] is the worker and the guardian, i.e. he remembers what he has heard and practices it, whereas the moulded [or 'earthly'] man neither practices nor keeps the virtues; he is merely introduced to their precepts by the generosity of God, but will soon be exiled from virtue . . . The body . . . is evil by nature and treacherous to the soul. This, however, is not evident to all, but to God alone and to those whom God loves . . . It is only when the mind occupies itself with higher things and is initiated into the mysteries of God that it judges the body evil and hostile . . . The philosopher . . . in love with the Beautiful which dwells within him, devotes himself entirely to the soul, taking no account of the body, which is to him a dead thing. His one concern is that this evil and dead thing should do no harm to the soul . . . When, O my soul, will you fully comprehend that you bear a dead thing? Will it not be when you have become perfect and are worthy of rewards and crowns? For then you will be a God-lover and not a body-lover." Philo, *Allegorical Laws*, quoted in Murphy-O'Connor, JMO, 246-47.

9. Rienecker, *Sprachlicher Schlüssel zum Griechischen Neuen Testament*, 388.

clinging as the "*substance* of the gospel," the NRSV as the "*message* that I proclaimed," and the German ecumenical translation as the "*literal* wording." These are all amplifications of the Greek, which simply reads *logos*, "word." As we have already seen and emphasized many times in our reading of this letter, Paul's Hebraic understanding of the word as a living address renders meaningless the game of parsing which aspects represent the substance and which the dispensable accident of this gospel. If the *logos* to which Paul insists his readers hold firmly is understood as some eternally true idea, to "hold firmly" to it will mean to preserve that idea without adulterating it; but if the *logos* that one must firmly hold is a personal reality, this can only be accomplished through an ongoing encounter with this reality sustained by hope and trust. On this reading what Paul extols here is a posture of the whole human being characterized by total reliance on the promissory character of the living incarnate word.

This opening emphasizing of the importance of remaining within the enscripturated tradition[10] lends gravitas to Paul's warning in 15:2b: **unless you have come to believe in vain**. Following the lines set up by his previous translation decisions ("on which you stand"/"substance"), Thiselton renders εἰκῇ (*eikē*, "in vain") as "without coherent consideration." This reading suggests the Corinthians had not sufficiently distinguished substance from peripheral matters and were thus unable to give "informed consent" to their credal affirmations. But in the light of our understanding of the phrase "holding firmly" as not only an intellectual operation but an expression of all one's faculties and powers, Paul's warning takes on the widest possible existential scope. For the Apostle, if a believer does not hold to the gospel with every fiber of her being, she will be lost in spite of any initial attraction to the word.

The seriousness with which Paul couches his "reminder" of the tradition *in* which Christians stand by quoting the creed into which they have been literally immersed in the baptismal font is mirrored later on in the chapter when he speaks of Christians as "the most pitiful of people" (15:19) if there be no resurrection of the dead. Again we are confronted with what looks like overblown and offensive language as pastorally inadvisable as his retort to their seemingly innocent technical questions about the resurrection ("Fool!"). Ought there not be some scope for discussing the merits of a kind of religious pragmatism that considers the healthy effects of belief in general? Surely there is some inherent value in sensing direction, forgiveness,

---

10. "Notice how Paul adduces Scripture as his strongest proof, for there is no other enduring way of preserving our doctrine and our faith than the physical or written Word, poured into letters and preached orally by him or others." Luther, "1 Corinthians" (1533), in LW 28:76-77.

consolation, and compassion, all of which come with faith irrespective of whether the hope in Christ's resurrection is warranted or not?[11]

To ask again why the Apostle does not appear willing to entertain such considerations leads us into a more accurate understanding of the type of argument he is pursuing in this chapter. What is already plain is that this argument presumes the utmost trustworthiness of the scriptural witness. The sole but all-sufficient reason to pity the Christian "pragmatist" who takes the Christian faith as a good thing whether or not resurrection has happened is that, if there is no resurrection, **We are even found to be misrepresenting God, because we testified of God that he raised Christ—whom he did not raise if it is true that the dead are not raised** (15:15). As Luther recognized, "it is impossible for the apostles to be false witnesses of God; otherwise God would not be faithful and could not be God."[12]

For Paul the whole discussion about dying and rising is essentially determined by, and determinative for, the trustworthiness of Christian tradition as testified in scripture. This is apparent throughout a chapter in which arguments "according to the scriptures" feature prominently, and appeals to scripture's authority "as it is written" are regularly repeated (15:3-4, 27, 45, 54-55). The strategy of repeating quotations from scripture is a key aspect of Paul's decision to "remind" his brothers and sisters (15:1) of that in which they stand together. The "in which" formulation signals that there is no outside vantage point from which the trustworthiness of the gospel could be assessed, perhaps by way of historical verification of the factuality of the resurrection,[13] or by scrutinizing the empirical evidence that resurrection-like psychological transformations have occurred. The one trustworthy location from which this question can be examined is

---

11. Barth picks up a comment by an earlier commentator (Bousset) expressing what we label a pragmatic account of the resurrection: "Paul proceeds to an assertion [15:19] which we cannot approve and follow. We are rather of the opinion, however firmly we hold with Paul the hope of eternal life, that, even if there should be no hope of eternal life, a life faithful to the spirit of Jesus and spent in sacrifice would stand higher and be even happier than a life passed in undisturbed sensuality!" (*The Resurrection of the Dead*, 167–68). We are tempted to respond that such Christian pragmatism could only plausibly exist in the context of a safe and untroubled bourgeois life (paralleling the experience of the wealthy in the upper strata of the Roman Empire), in which political structures and cheap labor can be trusted to take care of the essential conditions of life, leaving religion with the job of supplying the extra "spiritual" benefits. How different must it be for someone who has "fought with wild beasts at Ephesus" and is "facing death every day" or indeed, the church of the martyrs in which the willingness to give up one's life would render the question as to whether the resurrection is a reality or a vain idea a far more pressing concern.

12. Luther, "1 Corinthians" (1553), LW 28:96.

13. Barth, *The Resurrection of the Dead*, 142ff.

occupied only by those content to remain inside the word and discover the truth it reveals from within.

In this context it is also worth paying attention to the fact that the credal formulation that Paul quotes as one he has "received" itself twice includes the explicit expression **according to the scriptures**. This phrase is not offered here as supplementary evidence of facts as "already foretold by the prophets"—evidence that needed to be tested by way verification through eyewitness. The expression is repeated because the claim that **Christ died** for our sins can only be known on the basis of trusting the scriptural witness. No other means is available for establishing *this* meaning of the historical fact of Jesus's death on the cross. The references to scripture in the traditional formula's account of the resurrection must therefore be understood not as providing "evidence" for the resurrection but as a constitutive part of it. The resurrection is a salvific event that once and for all times reveals the nature of God as faithful to his promises and, as a result, his goal for all history in the glory of the new creation.

Near the end of this chapter Paul more fully demonstrates what his argument from the trustworthiness of the word entails. His statement that **When this perishable body puts on imperishability, and this mortal body puts on immortality, then the saying that is written will be fulfilled: "Death has been swallowed up in victory"** (15:54) seems to indicate that the fulfillment of the scriptural promise is more important for Paul than any sensational vision of risen bodies. For the Apostle there is a virtuous reciprocity that is fundamental to the relation between scripture and resurrection. He maintains, on the one hand, that understanding the resurrection depends on scriptural witnesses, in continuity with the gospel account of Jesus's opening the eyes of the disciples on the Emmaus road by explaining the scriptural passages about the suffering and dying of the Son of Man (Luke 24:13–27). Even doubting Thomas eventually is lead to believing without the empirical evidence he first sought (John 20:24–29).

At the conclusion of his reflections on the resurrection, though, Paul offers an exciting reversal of that dependency—the resurrection is also a vindication of the trustworthiness of the word of God! His final argument is that it is only **when this perishable body puts on imperishability** (15:54) that the scriptural promise of an eventual killing of death itself will be fulfilled. In this circular argument from scripture the trustworthiness of scripture is presented as the tried and true ground on which the belief in the resurrection rests, while at the same time awaiting its final testing and confirmation through the resurrection of all flesh yet to come. It almost seems as if Paul senses the offensiveness of this circular line of argument and tries to soften it by mentioning the verification that the large number of eyewitness might confer, naming **Peter and then the Twelve**, and ending with himself **last of all** (On Paul as apostle in 15:8–9, >1:2–3). Even this apparent "added evidence," however, only stands once we have understood that only the scriptures can establish saving faith in a Christ who not only died, but died **for our sins**. Believing in the resurrected one as **raised on the third day** will only be possible **according to the scriptures**, since outside of the scriptural witness there would have been no reason to see any significance in the number of days Jesus was buried. Even the post-resurrection appearances that Paul mentions will only become intelligible if they are read as having happened **according to the scriptures**, since Christ could only be seen *as* the resurrected one by those invested with the specific messianic hope imbued by Israel's prophetic tradition.

The resurrection thus stands precisely at the point at which an enscripturated hope is most obviously indispensable, since it is the divine act most foreign and repellant to all our experiences of sensory perception. "I feel and see that I and all men must rot in the ground," comments Luther, "but the Word informs me differently, namely, that I shall rise in great glory and live eternally."[14] In the meditation on Hans Holbein's painting of Jesus being taken down from the cross that lies at the heart of his novel *The Idiot*, Fydor Dostoyevsky powerfully depicted the core of this problem.

> In the picture the face is terribly smashed with blows, swollen, covered with terrible, swollen and blood-stained bruises, the eyes open and squinting; the large, open whites of the eyes have a sort of dead and glassy glint. But, strange to say, as one looks at the dead body of this tortured man, one cannot help asking oneself the peculiar and interesting question: if such a corpse (and it must have been just like that) was seen by all His disciples, by His future chief apostles, by the women who followed Him and stood by the cross, by all who believed in Him and worshipped Him, then how could they possibly have believed, as they looked at the corpse, that that martyr would rise again? Here one cannot help being struck with the idea that if death is so horrible and if the laws of nature are so powerful, then how can they be overcome? How can they be overcome when even He did not conquer them, He who overcame nature during His lifetime and whom nature obeyed, who said *Talitha cumi!* and the damsel arose, who cried *Lazarus come forth!* and the dead man came forth?[15]

---

14. Luther, "I Corinthians" (1553), LW 28:71.
15. Dostoyevsky, *The Idiot*, 391–92.

The examples from botany that we will later see Paul using to clarify some aspects of the resurrected life must not be read as attempts to "naturalize" the resurrection on the assumption that since if even seeds are resurrected, resurrection must be all around us every day. Rather than naturalizing resurrection, these examples illustrate how trust in scripture has direct epistemic consequences, one of which is to withstand a re-naturalizing of elements of nature that have become means of salvation for Christian believers. To paraphrase Luther: when Christians begin to question the trustworthiness of the word, as some have done, then water becomes just water, and baptism is invalidated, bread and wine are no longer the Eucharist, and all the divinely instituted ordinances dissolve, from church offices to marriage and secular governance.[16]

Only if we grasp the significance of the trustworthiness of scripture in Paul's argument, with its basis in the prophetic confidence that God's word cannot fall, can we appreciate that Paul is not here taking anything resembling the realist position in later philosophical controversies over the *universalia*, in which it was assumed that an ontological priority obtained of universal concepts over the concrete entities that they define (*universale ante rem*)—despite the apparent proximity to this position that might be suggested by the phrasing of 15:13-16: **If there is no resurrection of the dead, then Christ has not been raised**. Paul might here be taken to be endorsing the argument that, "first you must believe in the general concept, the idea of resurrection, before you can hope to experience the resurrection (of Jesus or your own) as an instantiation of that idea." The opposing philosophical position would have it that, "only since Jesus has been raised from the dead can we speak of resurrection as a generic concept, the conditions of which might then be discussed to discover whether they might pertain to the rest of humanity."

It is only when we allow our puzzling through such questions to drift away from the scriptural anchor that we found to be essential to Paul's argument that we are condemned to oscillate between these conceptual polarities, an oscillation that has fueled the long string of controversies over the *universalia* down through the ages.[17] Whether taking our starting point from the resurrection of Jesus or the resurrection of all flesh, as soon as we recognize that both are already grounded "according to scripture" the decisive authority for thinking is located outside of the conceptual scheme that has given rise to the controversy about *universalia* in which the general idea must validate the concrete instantiation or particulars must be adduced

---

16. Luther, "1 Corinthians" (1553), LW 28, 77–78.
17. Pasnau, *Theories of Cognition*.

in order to prove the existence of general truths. In the absence of a trustworthy divine word, neither Jesus's resurrection on the third day nor the resurrection of all on the last day can be independently established nor can they validate one another.

Pitiful Christians

> **[12] Now if Christ is proclaimed as raised from the dead, how can some of you say there is no resurrection of the dead? [13] If there is no resurrection of the dead, then Christ has not been raised; [14] and if Christ has not been raised, then our proclamation has been in vain and your faith has been in vain. [15] We are even found to be misrepresenting God, because we testified of God that he raised Christ—whom he did not raise if it is true that the dead are not raised. [16] For if the dead are not raised, then Christ has not been raised. [17] If Christ has not been raised, your faith is futile and you are still in your sins. [18] Then those also who have died in Christ have perished. [19] If for this life only we have hoped in Christ, we are of all people most to be pitied.**

Verses 12–19 form a discrete epicycle of the argument of the chapter and offer a discussion of the various aspects of the misery in which believers would be left in the hypothetical situation that there were no resurrection. The shift in personal pronouns throws up an interpretative difficulty we believe to be easily resolved. Even though it is a particular group, **some of you**, who occasion Paul's turning to the theme of resurrection, the predominant **us** and **we** language as well as the occasional use of the second person (15:17) indicate that Paul is in fact addressing the whole Corinthian church. Every Christian, he says, regardless of his or her philosophical opinion about the possibility of resurrection from the dead, will be left in vanity (15:14), futility (15:18) and a pitiful state (15:19) if the Christian claim about a coming general resurrection is untrue. For the Apostle, it is not those who doubt the resurrection who must be said to render **in vain our proclamation**; rather, if the resurrection is not a reality it is God himself who is nullifying their faith by misleading them through the resurrection promises of scripture: **We are even found to be misrepresenting** (ψευδομάρτυρες/*pseudomartyres*, lit. pseudo-witness) **God, because we testified of God that he raised Christ—whom he did not raise if it is true that the dead are not raised.**

An unstated background claim is implicated here, namely, that in the resurrection God was vindicating both Jesus's life and proclamation (Rom

1:4). Throughout Jesus's ministry he had been shadowed by ambiguous and often accusatory witnesses, culminating in the testimony that led to his death as a political subversive and blasphemer. This cloud of human witnesses continually raised troubling questions about which power(s) Jesus actually represented. In the same way that the resurrection was the Father's vindication of the Son's proclamation, so will it be with the proclamation of the apostles. It too must await God's final seal of verification, which still must come through resurrection—this time through the resurrection of all human flesh.[18] That all Christian proclamation must expect that its ultimate verification can only come through God's bringing new life for all flesh puts it in an irreducibly vulnerable position. This is why witness and vindication are always tied together, concretely. Theologically speaking, witness, whether scriptural or embodied in Christian life and teaching, is a reality which can only be divinely vindicated, and in no other way.[19] As Paul has made unambiguously clear in previous chapters, specific demands are placed on the form of Christian witness by the intrinsic vulnerability of the Christian proclamation that must await its final verification at the final resurrection. The vulnerable gospel to which this witness points must be articulated through an intentional foregoing of all attempts at self-verification by the witness, whether through rhetorical means of power, accompanying signs, or practical syllogisms that point back to the efficacy of this proclamation in the form of conversion counts and church growth charts (>1:17, 9:19–23).

Verse 19 appears to deviate slightly from the reasoning Paul has employed in the preceding verses of this section in that it seems not implausible to assume it applies in a more specific way to the same group mentioned in 15:12, those who say **there is no resurrection of the dead**. It is conceivable that such views might have been part of Philo-style claims to have access to the reality of the "heavenly man" independent of the earthly aspects of human life. From such a position it would make good sense to speak of hope in Christ **in this life only**. By claiming a purely spiritual and immediate access to divine realities through their relationship to Christ, self-proclaimed elite members of the congregation could well have claimed a right to look down on less enlightened fellow Christians. From the perspective of such "spiritualists" the unenlightened would appear **pitiful** for being concerned with the merely "earthly man" and clinging to an inferior hope in Christ centered on the afterlife and the compensations it might offer them there for what they were lacking in the here and now. If 15:19 is

---

18. Pannenberg, *Jesus—God and Man*, 53–87.
19. Baan, *The Necessity of Witness*, chs. 1–2.

aimed at such a specific group or attitude, then its wording (**we are of all people most to be pitied**) would see Paul turning the tables on them by explicitly including the self-proclaimed elite in the general statement that *we* are the most pitied of all people, if *their* highlighted claim was true that there was no resurrection of the dead.

Granting that a Philo-type version of mind-over-matter dualism could plausibly be assumed to have existed in some form in the Corinthian church is not to suggest that the significance of Paul's retort is exhausted by reference to this one historical group. Attending to the continuing force of Paul's apostolic voice we may well also hear it to be addressing contemporary versions of hope in Christ **in this life only** such as a Christian pragmatism that rests content with a hands-on Christianity. Today such a Christian attitude often strikes a modest pose in its willingness "do without" the never-ending quest for and quarrel with all these metaphysical presuppositions so beloved by apologetic Christianity over the centuries.[20] Pragmatist Christianity rests on the assumption that good works are more effectively motivated by an optimistic attitude about the prospect of changing this world for the better as opposed to the "quiescent" beliefs about heaven as a better place. Christian pragmatists assume that the moral vision they have learned from Jesus will foster an "elevated" if not literally resurrected life for themselves and others (>1:22–27).[21] Given the argument we have just traced, we understand Paul to be offering a lively endorsement of the this-worldliness of this pragmatic version of Christian hope, but even more passionately to be questioning (if not "pitying") its presumption that its dispensing with the hope of material resurrection for all can actually be lived out in a world constantly threatened by death.

Queuing for Heaven

[20] But in fact Christ has been raised from the dead, the first fruits of those who have died. [21] For since death came through

20. One of the more influential versions of this position was promulgated by Francis Schaeffer, who held that if Christians gave up the law of non-contradiction, they had in effect given up the Christian gospel. In his scheme Christian witness turned on the reestablishment of a unified concept of reality only achievable for those who adhere to the law of non-contradiction. See *The God Who Is There*, ch. 1.

21. In 1884 Leo Tolstoy offered the two most obvious modern versions of this argument in his *My Religion: What I Believe*, ch 8. He suggests that the doctrine of personal resurrection encourages an individualist self-absorption with *my own* reward which all too nicely combines with an understanding of the *scale* of the future reward to sap Christians of any real desire to invest in the things of the kingdom that really matter in this life.

a human being, the resurrection of the dead has also come through a human being; ²²for as all die in Adam, so all will be made alive in Christ. ²³But each in his own order: Christ the first fruits, then at his coming those who belong to Christ. ²⁴Then comes the end, when he hands over the kingdom to God the Father, after he has destroyed every ruler and every authority and power. ²⁵For he must reign until he has put all his enemies under his feet. ²⁶The last enemy to be destroyed is death. ²⁷For "God has put all things in subjection under his feet." But when it says, "All things are put in subjection," it is plain that this does not include the one who put all things in subjection under him. ²⁸When all things are subjected to him, then the Son himself will also be subjected to the one who put all things in subjection under him, so that God may be all in all.

The opening negation of 15:20, νυνὶ δὲ (*nuni de*), not only marks a strong caesura with the previous verses, but also points to a marked shift in argumentative genre. The consideration of the implications of the hypothetical assumption that there was no bodily resurrection now gives way to a section in which the reality of the resurrection is specified along the lines of what appears to be a straightforward sequence of events through which it will occur. The translations **But in fact** (NRSV) or "In reality, however" (Thiselton), both nicely convey that in these verses Paul does not engage the philosophical challenge of arguing toward a conclusion by weighing various hypotheses in order to offer the most plausible purchase on reality. Instead of "testing" the pro- and anti-resurrection hypotheses Paul simply takes the resurrection as a given. What might appear at first glance as a fideist gesture of asserting a truth without seeking evidence in fact rests, as we have seen, on the verification that Paul has just explained can only come through the trustworthy word of the scriptural tradition. Although Paul does not explicitly add the formula "according to the scriptures" to his claim about the reality of the resurrection in 15:20, that **in fact Christ has been raised from the dead, the first fruits of those who have died**, the scriptural fundament of this premise becomes obvious in the following verses in which it is argued that **all will be made alive in Christ,** just as **all die in Adam**. It is on the basis of this scriptural framework with its reliance on Genesis 2–4 and its portrayal of the first human being through which death has come into the world (15:21) that the Apostle can now set up the parallelism between the first and the second Adam that will organize much of the remaining argument in the chapter.

Because the Adam-Christ pairing is also prominent in Paul's letter to the Romans, a brief consideration of its more elaborate presentation there will give us a clearer sense of how the Apostle is deploying this pairing in 1 Corinthians. "Therefore as sin came into world through the one man and death through sin, and so death spread to all men because one man sinned . . . yet death reigned from Adam to Moses, even over those whose sins were like Adam, who was the type of the one to come" (Rom 5:12, 14).

This is a complex pairing and is in fact comprised of two parallelisms that, confusingly, also parallel each other: first, between Christ and the first Adam, who Paul in Romans 5:14 calls the "model" for Christ, and second, between Christ as second Adam and all other sons and daughters of the first Adam. This paralleling of parallels presupposes a theological distinction within Adam: as "first of creatures" and, after the fall, the "first of sinners." The second aspect of the first Adam is what the theological tradition has called the "old Adam" in every human being. This distinction between the first and the old Adam will be important to keep in mind in the subsequent discussion because it corresponds to yet another distinction that it is necessary to make if we are to understand the account of death Paul is offering in this chapter. Like Adam, we too face two distinct aspects in the phenomenon of death. We encounter it as a first enemy, a spiritual separation from God, as well as the last enemy, the cessation of bodily life.

Given the ease with which we drift into a speculative mode that will quickly begin to imaginatively fill in the rather plain "schedule" that Paul gives of the order in which the resurrection will occur, it seems advisable consciously to resist this temptation by investigating instead the theological significance the Apostle associates with the resurrection sequence. The formulation in 15:23, for instance, suggests that the first to follow Christ into his resurrected life will be **those who belong to Christ**, leaving open the question as to whether this is spoken of those who have passed away or are still alive. The close parallel passage in 1 Thessalonians 4:13–18, however, takes a unambiguous position in this question: "and the dead in Christ will rise first" (1 Thess 4:16). This understanding of those who are still alive on the day of Christ's second coming falling into line behind the deceased saints in the heavenly procession stands in contrast to the intuitive assumption that those who see Christ coming on the clouds would be the natural candidates to be first reunited with him. The fact that this is not the order Paul envisions again hints at the point that Paul will with increasing insistence emphasize in this chapter: that those who have gone "through death" are at the front of the queue for the new uninterrupted life with Christ. Apart from this theologically motivated reinforcement of the unity of cross and resurrection, this sequential order of the resurrection need not be taken to suggest any hierarchical relation among the resurrected. The pastoral motivation for Paul's delineation of eschatological events is made abundantly clear in the parallel discussion of 1 Thessalonians 4. This schedule, Paul says there, is offered so that the Thessalonian believers could "comfort one another with these words" (1 Thess 4:18) that culminate in their shared hope that "we shall always be with the Lord" (1 Thess 4:17).

Paul does not foreground these pastorally minded concerns in 1 Corinthians and instead moves on to offer a wider picture of the cosmic relevance of the resurrection. In this more expansive treatment he explains that resurrection not only creates a new situation for the dead but also for death itself. To resurrect all flesh from the dead is in effect to destroy **the last enemy**, as **death** is characterized in 15:26. The first century resurrection of Jesus Christ is thus both the initial impact as well as the main transmission line for what Paul describes in 15:27 as the final **subjection of all** things under Christ's feet, the reign of Christ being completed only when he will have **put all his enemies under his feet**. This direct citation of Psalms 110:1 and 8:7 not only indicates the Christological reading of the Psalter characteristic of the earliest Christians but also demonstrates that for Paul the rule of Christ is political in nature, as it is in the royal psalms. This political horizon of Christ's rule also explains Paul's additional linkage of the resurrection of the dead with Christ's destruction of **every ruler and every authority and power**. After the Fall all political rule has been characterized by the troubling substrate of its power sources as being both from God's benign institution of government (Rom 13) on the one hand, and from the last enemy, on the other. In its punitive prerogative, political rule implicitly banks on the threat of death as the secret catalyst for every punishment to be effective in a world in which fear is the most powerful motivational resource.

Reading these verses as describing the progression of Christ's *political* rule over the nations affirms that the intermediate institutions of divine rule will be handed back to the Father. Indeed, in the *eschaton* there will be no need for the institutions and roles that mediate divine rule in the history of humankind—"neither marriage nor giving in marriage," nor political rule, nor priesthood.[22] The biblical witness also indicates that the mediating institutions provided by God's good providence often also take on a sinister autonomy. When fueled by schemes of human self-affirmation and self-justification these good gifts of the creational order degenerate to becoming demonic taskmasters, or in biblical language, "principalities and powers."[23]

---

22. Both major magisterial reformers draw attention to this political interpretation of 15:34 in their commentaries on this passage.

23. See Barth, *CD* 4/4:213–33, and Prather, *Christ Power and Mammon*. It should also be noted that the biblical use of "principalities and powers," though certainly

These demonic authorities and powers swell the ranks of the "enemies" under threat of destruction by the enemy of death since their whole existence is ordered to the annihilation of humans.[24]

The next item on Paul's resurrection sequence list is a fitting consummation of this defeat of the powers of death, the handing over of the kingdom of the Son to the Father: **When all things are subjected to him, then the Son himself will also be subjected to the one who put all things in subjection under him** (15:28). We think it important not to overlook the significance of "handing over" as an interpersonal act that is described here in reciprocal terms. The rule the Son hands back to the Father at the finale of the events of the resurrection is precisely what the Father handed over to the Son at its beginning, which Paul nicely summarizes in another letter: "God has highly exalted him and bestowed on him the name above every name, that at the name of Jesus every name should bow, on heaven and on earth and under the earth" (Phil 2:9–10). Once again and finally the resurrected One will demonstrate that despite the cosmic scope of his reign he remains eternally the crucified one who did not take his high position by theft.

This inner-trinitarian reciprocity also explains the eschatological moments in the gospels when Christ appears as he will in the end, as the one who "did not count equality with God a thing to be grasped, but emptied himself" (Phil 2:7). Because this vision of political rule and its handover is tied to the missions of the divine persons in creation we are well advised not to speculatively read them back into God's hidden inner-trinitarian relations, perhaps in a monarchical fashion, since the concluding statement to this section **that God may be all in all** must be understood as a statement about the Trinity and not about the Father exclusively. The **all** includes the entirety of creation and history, which eventually will be *in* God, thereby restored and perfected according to the original divine purpose. The God who will be all in all is a Trinity with an inter-divine life that in the resurrection will be perfectly brought together with the world God has made to "be like us" (Gen 1:26; see 1 Thess 5:10), which will then at long last have been made entirely fit for that role.

While the resurrection of Jesus Christ has already brought about the dethroning of the principalities and powers, the final stripping of their absolute claims to sovereignty and unreserved allegiance will only be revealed in its full scale by the ending of all human reign. Having long been the hidden ruler of the universe, Jesus Christ will then emerge into full visibility as

---

entailing this pejorative aspect in most instances, can also have a more neutral meaning, in which the creational aspect still reverberates. See Bertschmann, "Bowing before Christ—Nodding to the State?"

24. The fathers and modern exegetes typically emphasize this latter reading.

the cosmocrator. It is on this basis that Paul spots the logical parallelism in which the destruction of the last enemy, death, entails the overthrow of all other authorities and powers. While a dethroning of death according to its spiritual power already occurs in each and every baptism as a dying and rising with Christ, the future resurrection of all flesh will make this dethroning visible and complete, and then "death will be no more" (Rev 21:4).

The Practicalities of Fighting Death

> [29] Otherwise, what will those people do who receive baptism on behalf of the dead? If the dead are not raised at all, why are people baptized on their behalf?
> [30] And why are we putting ourselves in danger every hour? [31] I die every day! That is as certain, brothers and sisters, as my boasting of you—a boast that I make in Christ Jesus our Lord. [32] If with merely human hopes I fought with wild animals at Ephesus, what would I have gained by it? If the dead are not raised, "Let us eat and drink, for tomorrow we die." [33] Do not be deceived: "Bad company ruins good morals." [34] Come to a sober and right mind, and sin no more; for some people have no knowledge of God. I say this to your shame.

If in the last section we saw Paul exploring how the hypothesis of the nonexistence of resurrection inflects the activities of daily life, in these verses he reverses the direction of travel to display why resurrection is necessary for some human practices to be intelligible or sustainable. On the surface the two examples adduced—**baptism on behalf of the dead**[25] and Paul's own risking of his life in "reckless" missionary endeavors (**I fought with wild animals at Ephesus**)—appear to have little in common. The disparity between an apostle's missionary activities and a marginal Christian ritual to which

---

25. This type of vicarious baptism on behalf of the deceased members of one's own household was presumably undertaken on the occasion of the believer's own baptism. If so, it becomes intelligible as a kind of retrospective extension of the well attested pattern in which the *pater familias* is baptized together with his whole household as depicted in Acts 16:15, 33. Such baptisms might well have been performed in Corinth, including by those who denied the resurrection of the dead. Wendland therefore suggests that by raising this example Paul is highlighting the unintelligibility of a common practice when resurrection is denied in principle. Although the Corinthian spiritualists would likely have found this vicarious act attractive to the degree that they were aware of the powerlessness of *pneuma* and *gnosis* to afford salvation beyond the individual, Paul only had to remind them of the fact that any spiritual effects of baptism had to be inseparable from the actual dying that each beneficiary could not avoid eventually undergoing. Wendland, *Die Briefe an die Korinther*, 150.

Paul points while keeping a certain distance (as practiced by **those people**) makes them an unlikely pairing as argumentative aids. We have already hinted at one conceptual link, in that Paul appears to present both cases within the logic that has become prominent in the later doctrinal tradition under the label *lex orandi-lex credendi*. This theological principle derives from cases in which an ongoing practice, such as prayer, is taken to have a normative significance for the casting of doctrinal propositions.[26] In this sense we see Paul here finding a credal affirmation—resurrection from the dead—confirmed for its coherence with an established liturgical practice: that of vicarious baptism of the deceased. A further underlying commonality between the two examples the Apostle is indicating is that both arise on the margins of the sphere of death and can be characterized as activities in which Christians confront that enemy with spiritual weapons.[27] When Paul characterizes his enemies in Ephesus as wild animals and not, say, as jealous or ill-meaning fellow human beings, it is obvious that he understands his mission as nothing less than spiritual warfare, which would be both futile and unsustainable if fought **with merely human hopes**.

Having brought the resurrection of the dead into view as a presupposition that needs to be assumed if patterns of church life and apostolic ministry are to be intelligible and sustainable, it now becomes more apparent why 15:33b, **"Let us eat and drink for tomorrow we die,"** is the appropriate antithesis to that logic of resurrection. This quotation describes the practical attitude that follows from the assumption that human life is perfectly intelligible and sustainable without a coming bodily resurrection. Despite the fact that the line "let us eat and drink for tomorrow we die" had by that time almost certainly become a popular motto (having passed into common coinage from a comedy of Menander), Paul is not necessarily quoting it in order to characterize the Corinthians' attitude. What we have so far discovered about Corinthian culture rather suggests that Paul quotes this motto as an ironic challenge to their assumption to be able to take on the "heavenly man" without dying in the body. This would have Paul responding: "Well, if the dead are not raised, you'd just as well join the culinary society, and let everyone see how fatally disengaged you've become from your bodily life."

---

26. In this approach it is assumed that prayer and theology should necessarily be in harmony with, or even in a generative relationship to, the language used in the liturgical formulas of the worshipping congregation. Wannenwetsch, *Political Worship*, 80–85

27. "I once asked William Stringfellow if he believed in the resurrection. He replied in the affirmative. So I asked him what he meant. He stated simply, 'Phil Berrigan being arrested in front of the Pentagon.' I understood this to mean: Phil Berrigan acted without regard to the possible harm to his reputation, personal injury, or the threat of lengthy imprisonment—various metaphors signaling the power of death." Scott Kennedy, page 5 of unpaginated foreword to Stringfellow, *A Second Birthday*.

The punch of such an ironic retort would then display how their disdain for the bodiliness of human existence in fact exposes them as full participants in the base world they despise others for not yet having transcended.

It is equally possible that some of the Corinthians were indeed espousing a hedonist lifestyle as part of a spiritualist construal of their existence, which would fit seamlessly with visiting prostitutes or enthusiastically letting their hair down in worship. In that case Paul's summons to **come to a sober and right mind** would represent a twofold challenge aimed at the physical level of liquor-induced stupor as well as at the intellectual stupefaction caused by spiritual self-indulgence. In either case the key to Paul's retort lies in his locating the shamefulness of this behavior (**I say this to your shame**) not in a moral deficiency ("don't drink and drive") but in their defective or distorted "theo-logy." We should notice that it is not the Apostle shaming them; he is merely bringing their self-induced shame to light. Their shame is that they have no real **knowledge of God.** In the context of a discussion of resurrection what is most likely being indicated here is that specific embarrassment that "enlightened" spiritualists would feel about a deity who has *literally* gone through bodily interment and resurrection. Embarrassments about such a "materialist" conception of God were common at the time. Examples can be found in Plato's presumption that gods must be immutable to be consistent with the requirements of logic as well as in Aristotle's concept of the unmoved mover, reliant as it is on a disembodied nature, since all material bodies are by definition subjected to the one originating cause that set all material things in motion.

Irrespective of the degree to which the Corinthians' embarrassing behaviors were explicitly or implicitly informed by particular Greek philosophical traditions, Paul is flying in the face of the essentially undisputed sensibilities of his age by emphasizing that the Christian God is indeed just the sort of entity rejected by all of these philosophies: a God who bodily dies and rises. If he is not, Paul insists, and if we discard the bodily resurrection and the exaltation associated with the biblical hope for resurrection, we will inevitably end up chasing various surrogates for resurrection that take the form of ersatz transcendent states. In this vein, even the eating and drinking habits that embody the belief in "no resurrection" are marked by a moment of intense near-transcendent abundance that make them hard to relinquish. There is an ironic mimicry of the hope associated with the resurrection in the attractiveness of a good party that holds out the pseudo-eschatological promise to overcome anxiety and act as the social lubricant that can ensure a "good time" (>14:1–5).

The surrogate dimension of such forms of life has been aptly characterized as yet another form of spiritual death by Dietrich Bonhoeffer in his exposition of the first chapters of the book of Genesis. According to his reading in *Creation and Fall*, the fact that the tree of *knowledge* is the tree of *death* signifies that human beings after the fall live under the reality of death in this life by being condemned to live by their own account of good and evil. No longer able to live "with God" as the genuine source of that knowledge, they are still bound to live "before God." "To be dead means to-have-to-live."[28] With this language of living death Bonhoeffer is pointing toward a compulsive vitalism, the inescapable tyranny of having to live for the mere sake of being alive. Such a "spiritual death" takes form precisely as a living out of our physical lives in a manner so completely self-referential that it becomes equivalent to being separated from the wellspring of all life, God.[29] By introducing this new notion of spiritual death Paul prepares us not to miss his transition into a discussion of death that will transcend the aspect he has so far emphasized, the simple cessation of earthly life.

Will I Be "Me" in the Resurrection?

> [35] But someone will ask, "How are the dead raised? With what kind of body do they come?" [36] Fool! What you sow does not come to life unless it dies. [37] And as for what you sow, you do not sow the body that is to be, but a bare seed, perhaps of wheat or of some other grain. [38] But God gives it a body as he has chosen, and to each kind of seed its own body. [39] Not all flesh is alike, but there is one flesh for human beings, another for animals, another for birds, and another for fish. [40] There are both heavenly bodies and earthly bodies, but the glory of the heavenly is one thing, and that of the earthly is another. [41] There is one glory of the sun, and another glory of the moon, and another glory of the stars; indeed, star differs from star in glory.
>
> [42] So it is with the resurrection of the dead. What is sown is perishable, what is raised is imperishable. [43] It is sown

---

28. Bonhoeffer, *Creation and Fall*, 91.

29. In making this point Bonhoeffer deploys some of the distinctions we indicated at the outset of this chapter as necessary for understanding Paul's ecclesially and interpersonally oriented account of death and new life in Christ, distinctions that use the language of the Philo-like spiritualist to very different ends. "Self-centered love constructs its own image of other persons, about what they are and what they should become. It takes the life of the other person into its own hands. Spiritual love recognizes the true image of the other person as seen from the perspective of Jesus Christ. It is the image Jesus Christ has formed and wants to form in all people." Bonhoeffer, *Life Together* (DBWE 5), 44. For more detailed discussion of this theme, see Brock, "On Becoming Creatures."

> in dishonor, it is raised in glory. It is sown in weakness, it is raised in power. ⁴⁴It is sown a physical body, it is raised a spiritual body. If there is a physical body, there is also a spiritual body.

The sowing/seed metaphor used by Paul in 15:36–37 throws up a genuine interpretive challenge. The matter would be relatively straightforward had Paul simply said "your bodies are like bare seeds that cannot come to life unless they die, which is why there can be no transition from the *bare* seed into the full form, say of a tree, or even a seedling." The complicating factor is Paul's combination of active sowing language with passive seed language. What seems to be proposed with the sowing language is that there is some call being presented to those who live in their bodies to invest some sort of work in their dying. What contribution, if any, Paul asks, can we make in our lives in the here and now to the determination of the future form of life into which we will grow? Given the uniformity of his emphasis in this letter that the faith of the Corinthians be understood as a partaking in "the work of the Lord" (15:58), Paul cannot be proposing here that an emphasis on the resurrection should yield Corinthian confidence that eventually *their* **labor is not in vain** (15:58, echoing 15:10, >3:6–9). The difficulty for the interpreter, then, lies in how to understand the labor of sowing. Is the suggestion that this investment be directed at the human body by attending in a disciplined way to its physical needs? Or is Paul suggesting an investment that extends to the spiritual level? Paul's answer to the latter question is a clear no. The investment of labor that sowing indicates will never transcend the risk of dropping seeds in the ground in the hope that they will "rise again." It is always a sowing of what remains **perishable**, **weak**, and physical (15:42–44). In Paul's view the Corinthians have confused matters here by assuming sowing to be an active investment in their own spiritual development that can be trusted to play a decisive role in determining the "eternal" form that their lives would subsequently take. For the Apostle this is the equivalent of hoping to produce a fully-grown tree straight out of a seed.

Paul's theological reasoning becomes palpable if we attend to the grammar of his seed metaphor and note how differently it functions from modern biological accounts that assume a continuous morphological transition of living seed into a seedling.[30] Paul's theological point is apparently a

---

30. Paul obviously needed to make his point by drawing on commonly accepted ancient assumptions about the genesis and development of biological life. Theories of the spontaneous generation of life out of death or putrefaction (such as fleas out of dust, maggots out of rotting meat or tapeworms within other animals) had been common in

re-presentation of Jesus's teaching that, "unless a grain of wheat falls into the earth and dies, it remains just a single grain; but if it dies, it bears much fruit" (John 12:24; see Mark 8:35 and par.), a teaching that he links to the language of "bearing the cross" (Matt 10:37–38, Luke 14:26–33). The emphasis in this New Testament usage of the metaphor is therefore quite obviously on the need for the seed actually to *die*.

This reading is confirmed when we turn our attention to the imperative formulations Paul uses further on in the chapter, such as, **For this perishable body must put on imperishability**. It is the perishability of the physical substance we know as the body that allows us to count on the thoroughness of the processes we know as decay to so break it down that there will eventually be no body left that could put on imperishability. If then the putting on of imperishability is going to be possible, the perishable body will need to be entirely recreated. In the same way that a "bare" seed disappears in turning into a stem, roots and leaves, the perishable human is in need of recreation. The continuity of the identity of the recreated human being with the perishable human being must be thought of as remaining "hidden" in God's own remembering. The seed metaphor must therefore be understood on the grounds of the *analogatum,* the actual phenomenon of the physical body that completely decomposes *post mortem*, which then determines how we read the *analogans*, in this case, the seed imagery.

We are now prepared to grasp the full force of 15:38, which Paul introduces with **But** (δὲ/*de*) **God gives it a body as he has chosen**. It is an expression in which several intertwined emphases are simultaneously set out.

"*God* gives it a body, as *he* has chosen": it is the investment of God and not of the sower that determines the eventual form of existence each body will take.

"God *gives* it a body": that this transformation is a new act of the Creator is also emphasized, resulting in a genuine *kaine ktisis* rather than suggesting a smooth process of evolving form.

"God gives *it* a body": the new form is *of* the created physical body that is not annihilated in the transformation. Paul thus affirms that some continuity and recognizability must be presumed between the created and resurrected bodies, lest the new creation appear a complete undoing and

---

the West from the time of Greek thought (see Aristotle's *History of Animals*, Book I) and were taken up without modification in Christian thought (see Augustine's comment on Gen 1:20, "Let the waters bring forth abundantly living things" in his *Literal Meaning of Genesis*). These theories were only subjected to sustained questioning from the seventeenth century by experimental scientists. They were definitively dispatched by the famous mid-nineteenth-century experiments of Louis Pasteur. We must, therefore, resist the impulse to "Pasteurize" Paul.

1 Corinthians 15

denial of the first creation. It is not precisely specified, however, in what this continuity consists.

"God gives it a body as he has *chosen*": the way in which the new form affirms the old is one that God finds fitting, and emerges from a sovereign act of divine willing.

This set of assumptions converge in the affirmation that the continuity between perishable individual humans and their recreated forms is substantial enough to warrant our speaking of the person at the other end of the resurrection transformation as the one who we knew before death. This continuity is not, however, located in any one feature of the first Adam that would be presumed to prevail in the resurrected life since it depends solely on God's own remembering (Heb. *zakhar* [זָכַר]: "What is man, that you are *mindful* of him" [Ps 8:4]).

Such a reading protects us against the recurrent temptation in the Christian tradition to identify in the fabric of the human being an *ens continuum*, an "enduring part," destined to and capable of carrying a continuous human identity. One of the most popular proposals has been to posit an immortal soul assumed to have some "storage capacity" for carrying personal memory. Less attracted to the notion of a soul, moderns have gravitated toward assuming that ineradicable features of human "personality," or even particular bodily configurations should be understood to characterize the irreducible "self" that must endure if we are to be recognizable on the other side of the resurrection transformation. What is true, however, for all proposals of these types: the way the answer is formulated to the quest for an *ens continuum* exposes how each approach assumes characteristic processes of the transformation/transition that is resurrection.

What now becomes obvious is that the search for a continuum is bound to end in a denial of the necessity for the seed really to die. Continuum accounts of the resurrection thus evacuate it of its transformational potency. This is why it is not surprising for Paul to have taken up the stripping motif (taking off/putting on) as a way of resisting notions of transformation that substitute the language of dying with the presumably more sanitary language of purification. When "dying" is conceived in these more soothing terms we can be sure that the corresponding account of "resurrection" will also be cast as a mere stripping away of contaminated outer layers that are taken to be at minimum peripheral accoutrements of an inner core that, once it is freed of the ballast of "earthly things," can freely rise to the heights of the new existence.

The question of *post mortem* recognizability has understandably been a recurrent question among Christians through the ages, expressed in the worries of the bereaved about whether they will recognize and be recognized by their loved ones in the eschatological community.[31] Such questions have sprung up afresh in more recent debates in a younger branch of theology concerned with disability.[32] These debates revolve around the question of what the perfecting of human existence could mean for the identity and recognizability of those who find themselves with serious physical and mental impairments in this life. Will the divine recreation in the resurrection not amount to the practical erasure of a person's personality and identity, if the body at stake is one whose legs never walked, ears never heard, or mind never formed a word?

Two of the dominant ways this question has been answered by modern Christians are prefigured in a reported conversation between Karl Barth and his theologian friend Heinrich Vogel, sparked by the latter's firm hope for his crippled daughter eventually to be able to dance around the Lamb's throne in the resurrection. To Vogel's expression of this desire Barth responded that what needed to be changed in the eschaton was not the physical configuration of the body of Vogel's daughter but rather "our" perception of it as somehow not quite up to the standard that God intended for his creation.[33] Given what we have discovered in Paul's discussion so far in this chapter, Vogel's assumption that his daughter would still be recognizable as his daughter while being healed to be "like everyone else" appears to place limits on God's "choosing" of the form in which his daughter should be resurrected. The effect of this limitation of God's authority to choose his own way of ensuring the continuity of the created and resurrected body is the projection of worldly standards of physical completeness or normalcy onto the imagination of resurrected life. Barth's answer thus seems theologically more appropriate in not preempting God's choice while at the same

---

31. This concern has manifested especially in discussions about the beginning and the end of life, from questions about malformed and aborted births to worries about whether God can reassemble bodies dismembered by wild animals or lost at sea. See Augustine, *City of God* XVI.8, XXII.14, 20.

32. This line of questioning was reopened by Eisland's *Disabled God*. Yong (quoting Gaventa and Coulter) offers a poignant example of the practical form this question takes in that literature: "'Will I be retarded when I get to heaven?' The parents answered that she would not. There would be no sickness, no pain. Everyone would be perfect. To this she responded, 'But how will you know me then?'" Yong, *Theology and Down Syndrome*, 259.

33. "And, he added, the final revelation of the truth and meaning of this life will involve a radical reordering of prevailing cultural values: '*she* will sit at the head of the table, while we—if we are admitted at all—will have to sit right down at the other end.'" The interchange is reported in a number of slightly differing accounts, and the quotation above is as related by Wood, following Barth biographer Busch, in "This Ability," 392–93.

time assuming that all of us need to have our standards of perception transformed about what counts as acceptable.

Yet one consideration remains that does not appear in Barth's reply: the communal aspect of the resurrected life. Queries about the continuity of the recreated individual human form with its earlier perishable form are unresolvable if we confine our investigation to each individual body per se. A properly theological inquiry will need also to ask after the place of individual human bodies *among other bodies* in the new creation, an aspect of resurrection that the apostolic tradition has characterized in social terms as the "new humanity" (Eph 2:15). Having said this, we are also aware that we must not too quickly jump to an alternative construction in which a social account of the eschatological life is taken to render obsolete questions about the continuity of individual identity, which would again risk projecting the politically correct resistance in some quarters to an "individualized eschatology."

Given these opposing alternatives, it seems best to allow Paul to take us on the "detour" indicated by his strangely expansive usage of the notion of the body in 15:39-41. Here the language of "bodies" that is applied to seeds is also used to link and distinguish heavenly and earthly entities as well as a whole range of bodies made of other types of flesh. The imagery of the teeming bodies that populate the firmament, with their power to pull and repel other bodies, reminds us of one of the principle features of bodies: given their physical nature, they must relate to one another tangentially, each excluding the other from the space that it exclusively occupies. As physical entities, bodies naturally rival each other. This feature of physical existence has become a central problematic engaging the attention of modern political philosophers, who tend to be focused on the problem of managing this rivalry so that it does not erupt into warfare.[34] The way the debates have unfolded in modern political thought has made it obvious that no political arrangement is capable of doing without some sort of physical boundaries such as fences, walls, or borders to mark the need in a fallen world for constant social reconfigurations of the body in and amongst the many bodies.

In the context of this dominant modern political tradition it strikes us that the church in Paul's construal is understood precisely as *a* body, within which physical boundaries are no longer needed to preserve that separation that allows fallen society to continue to exist without breaking down. This alternative picture of political space already emerged in chapter 11 as part of Paul's description of a church that was rightfully addressed with the line,

---

34. Wannenwetsch, "Owning Our Bodies?," 50-65.

"when you come together *en ekklesia*..." We saw in our discussion of that chapter that to speak of the bodies of the faithful as congregating "in" the church at a time in history when no church buildings existed demands an understanding of the church as *itself* a spatial body (>11:18, 33–34). As this specific kind of body the church does not exist *in* space,[35] but rather *offers* space in a manner that invites human bodies into a new kind of atmosphere. In this atmosphere the drawing and repelling power that each individual exerts as a physical body becomes intertwined to form a larger entity not unlike a planetary system in which the gravitational forces that each individual body exerts and experiences (such as our sun and its planets) come into a harmony that can be identified as a discrete entity occupying a specific, definable space. Since the body of Christ is a creature of a non-bounded entity, the Holy Spirit, which operates like the "wind, that blows wherever it pleases" (John 3:8), we cannot (as in modern political theories) extrapolate from mechanical pictures of bodies as governed solely by their physical inability to inhabit the same space in order to understand the real physicality of this peculiar political body.

Revisiting the Barth-Vogel discussion on the form and perception of disabled human life in the resurrection, we can now say with more precision what we find lacking in both approaches to the question of how we will be recognizable to each other in the eschaton. In light of our considerations about the unique spatial character of the church, the problem with Vogel's vision is his refusal to reckon with the new atmosphere in which the resurrection is not just the reconfiguration of human physical traits, but also *remakes human perceptions* of what is beautiful about human bodies and personalities (>12:12–13). For Paul the new atmosphere that is constitutive of the space that is the church is one in which *eros* is transfigured, that form of reception that responds to the attracting and repelling powers of other bodies. In this light Vogel's imagination appears to be captive to the *eros* of the first Adam that cannot but perceive beauty and perfection according to the aesthetic standards that have become dominant in one particular cultural configuration.[36] Barth seems to have understood that his friend did not

---

35. To say that the church does not exist *in* space is not to suggest that it does not *occupy* space, which of course it does, in the form that Bonhoeffer would call an organization, or American Christians would call the church of "parking lots and potlucks" (Hauerwas), that is, as a taxable entity that owns property. In this sense the church is very much like a physical body with exclusive use of physical spaces. Where there is a church in *this* sense, there cannot be a synagogue, mosque, or indeed, a gambling hall: the problem is not to acknowledge the church's existence as organization, but to take this way of existing as being determinative of the scope of its existence as that transformed physicality which exists not *in* another but *as* another atmosphere.

36. "The man who cannot view the whole is offended by what he takes to be the

allow for a deep enough transformation of all humans in the resurrection, including all our standards of perception. And yet Barth's request for a transformed aesthetics will remain underdeveloped as long as the linkage of the motto "the last will be first" is not shown concretely to *reconfigure the sociality* of the ecclesia. As a divinely constituted body, the new aesthetics that the resurrection promises is not one that exists only over the temporal horizon but is in fact the source of the new atmosphere already at work in the church. Here this new atmosphere is creating an entirely different *order of sociality* characterized by the disruption of the old Adam's sense of repulsion at some people's bodies and minds (>12:21–26).

The new relational spatiality that is the church models the new humanity in in its reshaping of the polarity between the individual and the collective. The old Adam remains trapped in this polarity, as testified by the notorious inability of political organization through the ages to freeze the pendulum that constantly swings between collectivist and individualist political theories. By contrast, to be drawn into the body of Christ is to be opened to one another in a manner that both protects individuals from having their individuality submerged into the group, and dissolves their reasons to protect themselves from being swallowed into what is "normal" for the group. In short, the "recognition worry" of disabled and other people assumed to be not-normal people might be better phrased thus: "If you cannot love us today, what makes you think you would love us if we were *different, healed* or *better*?"

Paul has firmly resisted any suggestion that in the act of raising and recreating dead bodies God embarks on a project of total erasure and reinvention, some sort of "creative destruction" that wipes away all that went before in order to replace it with something totally different.[37] The death that the Apostle believes Christians must embrace *includes* the immolation of all images of normality and all those loves that bar us from receiving others as

---

deformity of a part; but this is because he does not know how it is to be adapted or related to the whole" Augustine, *City of God*, XVI.8, 709.

37. Amos Yong has been most consistently and theologically engaged in the discussion of how those with disabilities will be changed in the resurrection, in sustained dialogue with this chapter of 1 Corinthians. Yong, *Theology and Down Syndrome*, ch. 9. In order to do justice to the worry of the disabled that they will lose their identity in the resurrection, following the theology of Gregory of Nyssa, he proposes a progressive ameliorative process of healing. Rapid transformations are minimized in this account of the resurrection in order to make space for a maximal view of the ultimate change that will happen to individuals over time. By privileging the idea of the soul as the form of the body, and by then understanding the soul's growth in knowledge as infinite, he imagines the body to be infinitely plastic, thus coming close to a "physicalist" inversion of the Corinthian "spiritualist" position in which the soul's death and resurrection was thought to be minimally destructive of either physical or spiritual essence.

"members of one another." By virtue of being members of the body of Christ and hence "of one another" (Rom 12:4) the faithful receive a **spiritual body** only when they have sown their **physical body** into the *death* of Christ. The faithful are resurrected out of this death both in this life and in the life to come. To be saved is to be baptized into a body made for relationship, and to be undergoing the transformation into persons being made capable of such relationship once again.[38] The demand to embrace the death of self-imagination in order to be raised into the body of Christ only avoids being an identity-destroying tyranny when it remains tied to the confession that the God who resurrects is no other than the God who creates. Our bodies and intellects do and will make "sense" in the resurrection not because they stay the same, but because they die to the forms of relationship that keep humans from being fully incorporated into the peaceable communion of the body of Christ.[39]

Two Deaths, Two Resurrections

> [45]Thus it is written, "The first man, Adam, became a living being"; the last Adam became a life-giving spirit. [46]But it is not the spiritual that is first, but the physical, and then the spiritual. [47]The first man was from the earth, a man of dust; the second man is from heaven. [48]As was the man of dust, so are those who are of the dust; and as is the man of heaven, so are those who are of heaven. [49]Just as we have borne the image of the man of dust, we will also bear the image of the man of heaven.
>
> [50]What I am saying, brothers and sisters, is this: flesh and blood cannot inherit the kingdom of God, nor does the perishable inherit the imperishable.

A longer train of thought is opened in 15:45 that is structured around conceptual parallels that Paul builds up to deepen and specify what is at stake in the contrast between the first and second Adam. While the main dualities he uses to articulate this contrast seem rather self-explanatory (from earth/

---

38. "Someone, in the body, desires to see his friend, in the body. He knows that he lives far away, with a many days' journey in between. In his spirit he has already gone ahead, and when he arrives in body, then he feels what a burden he carries. The weight of the flesh is not able to obey the will [to fellowship, we would add] as speedily as anticipated... But when it is a *spiritual body*, about which it has been said, *It is sown a natural body and rises a spiritual body* [15:44], what ease, what swiftness, what obedience to desire it will show!" Augustine, *Sermon* 163.7, 10–12, PL 38:892–95, in JK, 279.

39. See Brock, "Autism, Care, and Christian Hope," 7–28.

from heaven), in this verse he introduces a highly complex pairing that demands further consideration: **The first man, Adam, became a living being** [ψυχὴν ζῶσαν/*psychēn zōsan*]; **the last Adam became a life-giving spirit** [πνεῦμα ζῳοποιοῦν/*pneuma zōopoioun*]. While both Adams are described using the same root for "life," *zoe*, Christ is not characterized as having a different type or intensity of life, but rather according to the generative power of his existence as life-*giving*.[40] The other lexical pair, *pneuma* "spirit," and *psyche*, were introduced earlier by the Apostle to distinguish the body of the first Adam as *psychic* in distinction from its form in the resurrected life as *pneumatic* (15:44). It is Paul's characterization here of Christ as **life-giving spirit** that has propelled our insistent resistance to any reduction of the biblical term "spiritual" to an anthropological trait like the psyche or any other human faculty. In biblical language, "spiritual" denotes the quality by which the whole human being—as a living embodied entity—is determined by its nervous connection with the font of all life, God (Ps 36:9).

In distinction from the sequence of events presented in 15:23–26, the repetition of the term **first** in 15:45–47 is not meant to suggest a temporal succession. It is likely that the Corinthians assumed they knew who they were on the basis of an understanding of who the first Adam was, because only on such assumptions could they believe themselves capable of going beyond this first Adam in this life. A reading in which the first Adam is superseded by the second is ruled out because incapable of accounting for the emphatic contrast with which Paul opens 15:46: ἀλλ (*alla*, **but**). By emphasizing that it is not the spiritual but the natural ("psychic") that comes first the Apostle is apparently correcting a Corinthian assumption that it is possible to access the life of the second Adam by somehow laying aside the natural reality of the first Adam. Paul categorically refuses any such claim by emphasizing in verse 49 that Christians can aspire to no more than to bear *both* images, of the second and **also** the first Adam.

A conceptual difficulty makes the series of parallelisms that Paul offers in this section particularly difficult to grasp. While he seems to be operating on the basis of a simple juxtaposition of the first and second Adam, the logic of his argument does not become theologically intelligible without the introduction of a third character, the "old Adam." Paul does in fact introduce this old Adam elsewhere, in the chapter on baptism in Romans 6 for

---

40. "If He is no longer active in the world, as He must needs be if He is dead, how is it that He makes the living to cease from their activities, the adulterer from his adultery, the murderer from murdering, the unjust from avarice, while the profane and godless man becomes religious? If he did not rise, but is still dead, how is it that He routs and persecutes and overthrows the false gods, whom unbelievers think to be alive, and the evil spirits whom they worship?" Athanasius, *On the Incarnation* V.30, 61.

instance, which facilitates his articulation of the duality that accompanies the Christian's being simultaneously united with Christ in his death as well as in his "newness of life" (Rom 6:4): "For if we have been united with him in a death like his, we will certainly be united with him in a resurrection like his" (Rom 6:5). When in the following verse Paul then mentions the old Adam, the parallelism he deploys explicates the relation of the old Adam to the first Adam: "We know that our old self (παλαιὸς ἡμῶν ἄνθρωπος/ *palaios hēmōn anthrōpos*, the "old human being") was crucified with him so that the sinful body might be destroyed and we might no longer be enslaved to sin" (Rom 6:6).

Since these Adams are not two persons but two aspects of the same person, the interpretative difficulty lies in the challenge of understanding their inner relation, marked as it is by *both* distinctiveness *and* inseparability. The first Adam will eventually die, and this death will entail the destruction of the body, but this post-lapsarian death is distinguishable though not separable from that reality of sin that tragically circumscribes the life of the old Adam. It is on these grounds that Paul speaks of the destruction of the "sinful body." His earlier reference to baptism into Christ's *death* and *burial* (Rom 6:3-4) also indicates, further, that this "first" or spiritual death can and should be understood as a being rendered "dead to sin" (Rom 6:11). Thus there is a decisive meeting with death *within* this life that the "second" physical death can only consummate. The death of the seed put into the ground, the death that cannot be sanitized by transformational views, is the death that the first Adam must die specifically *as* the "old" Adam. The Christian life in its fullness only becomes intelligible as a life lived as sinner and saint, *simul iustus et peccator*, if grasped according to this twofold image that it bears of the first and the second Adam. Contrasting starkly with the Corinthians' desire for spiritual immediacy, with this imagery the Apostle insists that Christians never seek to graduate to a spiritual plane beyond the reach of all that being the first Adam entails, the salvific necessity of dying to the old Adam's economy of desire and the creature's suffering of physical death.

When these two inseparable aspects of the creature are not distinguished (the "first" and "old" Adam), it becomes impossible properly to distinguish the two aspects of death that we have labeled physical and spiritual. And without this distinction it will be next to impossible to resist re-naturalizing accounts of death that render it a "necessary" feature of life.[41] A tradition of seeing the Fall as a necessary emancipation from tutelage that

---

41. For a more detailed account of the dual aspect of death in the light of contemporary debates on the "ethics of dying," see Wannenwetsch, "From *Ars Moriendi* to Assisted Suicide," 428–40.

extends from Philo to Hegel, which centers on a narrative about the necessity of humanity growing beyond original innocence, has recently re-emerged in some feminist discourses that offer psychologized readings of the fall.[42] In such accounts "death" is read as the breaking of the paternalist deadlock, an awakening to the realities of human life lived in autonomy. In contrast to such readings Paul never depicts death as a "pathway" to enlightenment: it always stands as a "living sign" of the fatal futility of the rebellion of the human creature against being "merely" dust, an ironic reminder that we are ever daughters and sons of that first Adam who, like him, resist the tutelage of the eternal God (>2:13–16). The polemical intent of the first/second polarity is reinforced in 15:50 in the Apostle's insistence that **flesh and blood cannot inherit** the kingdom of God. In their refusal to be "sown in weakness" the Corinthians and all who follow in their footsteps are revealed as heirs of the first Adam with no intrinsic right to inherit anything of the second Adam's **kingdom of God**. The man of dust inherits by right only the serpent's kingdom of dust, and through incorporation into the second Adam alone can we inherit his kingdom (Gen 3:14–15).

Having outlined Paul's account of the "dual Adam," it is worth noting the way in which the impossibility of separating the first Adam from the old parallels and illumines how both aspects of death can be experienced in close proximity. The death of the old Adam, which must precede physical death, can prepare the way for or foreshadow the experience of it—and paradoxically the traffic can also flow the other direction. Reflecting on his own impending physical death, William Stringfellow found himself face to face with its tyrannical nature, which only became apparent when death drew so near that it seemed to have gained a complete sovereignty over a life of constant pain:

> It is, so to speak, only then and there—where there is no equivocation or escape possible from the fullness of death's vigor and brutality, when a man is exposed in absolute vulnerability—that life can be beheld and welcomed as the gift which life is. In "that" singular affection for life death is transcended in a way in which dominion is restored to man in his own life and his relationships with the rest of creation.[43]

Stringfellow's observation highlights the capacity of proximate physical death (whether threating one's own life or that of a loved one) to trigger a breakthrough in relation to spiritual death. The opposite scenario can be

---

42. Bechtel, "Rethinking the Interpretation of Genesis 2.4b—3.24"
43. Stringfellow, *Second Birthday*, 67.

glimpsed in those mental and emotional states that characterize the yearning for suicide. What brings people to seek a premature physical death can in many cases be described as a practical and visible embrace of the death that already lives in them, of faith, hope, and love. This is the reason why in most cases moral frameworks that seek to ascribe blame to or acquit someone of the act of suicide can never do theological justice to the sheer desperation that befalls people who have lost all faith, love or hope.[44]

Changed in the Lord's Work

> [51] Listen, I will tell you a mystery! We will not all die, but we will all be changed, [52] in a moment, in the twinkling of an eye, at the last trumpet. For the trumpet will sound, and the dead will be raised imperishable, and we will be changed. [53] For this perishable body must put on imperishability, and this mortal body must put on immortality. [54] When this perishable body puts on imperishability, and this mortal body puts on immortality, then the saying that is written will be fulfilled: "Death has been swallowed up in victory." [55] "Where, O death, is your victory? Where, O death, is your sting?" [56] The sting of death is sin, and the power of sin is the law. [57] But thanks be to God, who gives us the victory through our Lord Jesus Christ.
>
> [58] Therefore, my beloved, be steadfast, immovable, always excelling in the work of the Lord, because you know that in the Lord your labor is not in vain.

The Greek term used in 15:51 for **changed** (ἀλλαγησόμεθα/*allagēsometha* emphasizes yet again the outcome of a *divine* action of transformation, in that the adjective *alla*, "other," lays emphasis on our being "othered" in the resurrection. We find in this a confirmation of our earlier point that what is at stake in this change cannot be a mere transition in which some *ens continuum* endures because this is a trans*form*ation—a divinely orchestrated change reaching all the way to the roots of our being. Luther notes that this change of form also involves a trans*location*: "Suddenly we are removed from table or bed or from our work, as we happen to be walking, standing, sitting, or lying, so that we are dead and alive again in a moment, changed in every way, and soaring up in the clouds."[45] Paul does not deploy the Greek notion of metamorphosis here, since, as Luther also notes, this aspect of the

---

44. See Bonhoeffer's discussion of suicide in *Ethics* (DBWE 6), 196–203.
45. Luther, "1 Corinthians" (1553), in LW 28:200.

1 Corinthians 15

change of form that accompanies human transformation has been directly addressed in 15:38–42.

A translocation is being envisioned here that will occur **in a moment, in the twinkling of an eye**. This moment, Kierkegaard influentially noted, "is not properly an atom of time but an atom of eternity. It is the first reflection of eternity in time, its first attempt, as it were, at stopping time."[46] Paul's use of a standard apocalyptic trope signaling the divine arrival, **the trumpet will sound**, indicates that the theologically significant aspect of this moment "in between" time and eternity is the suddenness of its arrival. Unlike any "process" that must unfold over a period of time, this divine arrival is not one that emerges through a sequence of steps; in this, our re-creation is utterly unlike our first creation.[47] In emphasizing the resurrection as a divine "moment" Paul reinforces his emphasis that the victory over death that is the resurrection is one that is entirely *given* to the faithful; this triumph we have not won and has only become ours **through our Lord Jesus Christ** (15:58). This victory cannot be received in a triumphalistic posture, as Bonhoeffer noted, because the **victory** over death that is given to believers is in fact only a sign that they have gladly welcomed *Christ's* victory.[48] God **gives us the victory** through **our Lord Jesus Christ** (>9:18).

The joyful notes in this acclamation of a triumphant divine victory must be held together with the concluding exhortation that follows immediately in 15:58 that what Corinthians (then and now) need to embrace is not victory but death. To say that death has been **swallowed up in victory** is to indicate that death is not only inevitable, but is now actually *possible*. More specifically, a truly human dying has after the fall only been *made* possible once again for human beings through the victory that is resurrection: only now can humans embrace death in hope. The constant brushes with martyrdom characteristic of the patristic age brought this point luminously before them:

> There is proof of this too; for men who, before they believe in Christ, think death horrible and are afraid of it, once they are converted despise it so completely that they go eagerly to meet it, and themselves become witnesses of the Savior's resurrection

---

46. Kierkegaard, *Concept of Anxiety*, 88.

47. Augustine contrasts the twinkling of an eye motif with the "length of time that it takes for a human being to develop from the beginnings in the womb to the last dust of the grave." *Sermon* 362.13–17, PL 39:1619–22, in JK, 278.

48. Bonhoeffer, "Communion Homily on 1 Corinthians 15:55, Sigurdshof, Remembrance Sunday, November 26, 1939," in *Theological Education Underground, 1937–1940* (DBWE 15), 487.

from it. Even children hasten thus to die, and not men only, but women train themselves by bodily discipline to meet it.[49]

Without (hope in the) resurrection death cannot be embraced for what it is—gateway to eternal life for sinners redeemed—and will be embraced only by those who invest it with its own quasi-salvific power as one last heroic expression of human autonomy, a sacrifice of the self for a higher good, or some other form of the attempt to stave off the "senselessness" of the physical death of all living things.[50] If it is true to say that death makes resurrection possible simply as its precondition, it is also true in the substantial Christological sense: that we can only "really" die if we die "into" the reality of resurrection. The **sting of** *this* **death**, it is important to emphasize, **is sin** and not the physical process of dying. If physical dying itself were understood as death's sting then we would be compelled forever to battle being sown in weakness, dishonor, and decay. The kenotic humiliation of the old Adam would be rendered impossible. Only those who are prepared spiritually to die, that is, to die to this pride of wanting to be more than the seed of weakness and decay, can also genuinely embrace their physical death as human beings comprised of body *and* soul.

We end our discussion of this chapter by returning to our initial conundrum—how death can be something that we both passively suffer and must actively undertake. Understanding the precedence of divine working in the transformation of the human being has helped, first, to see why Paul stretches the metaphor of "putting on" to its breaking point, and has reminded us of the futility of all quests for an *ens continuum*. The believer's embrace of Christ's victory over death is a labor that must be patiently and continually undertaken through day-to-day practices in which the humiliation that is dying is embraced.[51] Because this labor of discipleship must be formed by the truths that have been handed down in the scriptural tradition, the Apostle characterizes this labor as an active receptivity, calling Christians to **be steadfast, immovable** in their adherence to the Word of God. Only so will they be **always excelling in the work of the Lord**, the work associated with transformative, kenotic, up-building service to others, **because you know that** [only] **in the Lord your labor is not in vain**.

49. Athanasius, *On the Incarnation* V.26, 57.

50. Hauerwas, "Sacrificing the Sacrifices of War," ch. 5.

51. "Although it does not require it, baptism prepares Christians for the death of the martyr.... As sacrament, baptism gathers the individual body into the corporate body of the church, a community whose politics is rooted in another way than that which predominates in the world. If this other way is lived clearly and plainly it will stand as a witness; and as such it can and sometimes will provoke a response among the nations that attempt to annihilate it as a rival." Hauerwas, *Approaching the End*, 61–62.

It might be tempting to read this emphasis on *your* labor as a ringing call to human willing, perhaps understood as an active engagement in self-mortification, of "dying to self." But putting the emphasis in this way threatens to overturn Paul's whole discussion at the last minute by forgetting that individual sanctification and the labors of faith do not serve the end of personal growth as a goal in itself, but are always oriented by an ecclesial horizon and the divine working. While embracing death is a kind of labor that demands the active engagement of the will, the labor that Paul enjoins here is in the first place the work of upbuilding the community and proclaiming the gospel. It is true that in the course of that work, mortifications will be demanded that should be embraced rather than evaded (>9:19–27); the old Adam does have to die, and this dying does not happen without Christians willing to participate in their transformation. But there is no "killing of the self": there can only be an embracing of the death into which we are baptized by Christ (Rom 6).

In the context of his discussion of the resurrection in this chapter Paul should be read as denying the Corinthian belief that their own efforts could ever determine the shape their transformed life will eventually take (15:38). Instead the Apostle offers to the Corinthians (and so to us) a gospel in which the precedence of divine grace alone will ensure that the labors will not be fruitless. Just as the Apostle has witnessed that "*his* grace toward me has not been *in vain*" (15:10) so too can the Corinthians embrace a confident hope that **in the Lord** *their* labors will also not be **in vain**. Having previously indicated the many physical and interpersonal sufferings the Apostle has undergone for those to whom he preaches Christ crucified (not least, the Ephesian "beasts," 15:32), Paul can justly say that for the sake of *oikodome* "I worked harder than any of them." To this he adds, once again making his emphasis unmistakable, that it was "not I, but the grace of God that is with me" (15:10). It is this death-embracing hope for resurrected life, actively welcomed in this life and the life to come that "we proclaim, and so you have come to believe" (15:11).

1 Corinthians 16

Traveling as Carrying Generosity

Having rounded up the body of the letter with the magisterial treatment of the resurrection in chapter 15, the Apostle concludes with a string of apparently unconnected practical and logistical details that through the centuries have sparked far more discussions about the situational background they assume than serious theological investigation. If there is anything our time spent with this letter has taught us to expect, however, it is that even when, or *especially* when, Paul is discussing "mere" practicalities he does so in a thoroughly theological fashion. A precedent has by now been well established that warrants our expectation that theologically significant insights will pepper his discussion of such mundane affairs as organizing a collection, making travel plans, and greeting past, present, and future visitors.

Today most of us are well used to travelling, visiting other places, greeting each other and so on. But precisely because of that familiarity, we must not forget how radically different the material conditions are under which we do so from those at the time of Paul's travels. We hop on a plane and take a taxi to a conference center where we "bump into" people that we greet in passing, perhaps taking the time to linger a little longer over a cup of coffee before heading back to our hotel room. Visiting in the first century was a far more exposed venture, both in terms of time and financial investment. It was thus extremely costly and, in addition, had to be made without the comforts of modern hotel culture. As Paul reminds the Corinthians in his later letter, this often entailed great personal risk (2 Cor 11:25–27). The prodigious investment that was so evidently entailed in traveling a great distance was counterbalanced by the burdens one would lay on that host's hospitality, at whose mercy one would remain if staying on for a time. To be "stuck with each other" for a longer duration as host and guest thus demanded a much fuller "reception" of each other, with all the complicated physical and psychological baggage any extended stay inevitably entails.

Keeping in mind the large investment of time and patience ancient travel required allows us to see already in Paul's discussion of travel plans the unifying thread of the chapter: the theme of *recognition*. There is a dual aspect to this recognition that offers us an insight into the significance of the collection Paul is organizing (16:1:4). Genuinely recognizing a visit means to grasp *who* they are that are visiting and *what* they bring. Paul wants to establish that the collection is a journey in which not only the Corinthians' money but more importantly their gratitude is carried to the Jerusalem church. His elaboration of this chapter's central theme of recognition as a "carrying of gratitude" gives us a deeper insight into the affective dimension of Paul's concluding comment, that the visiting Corinthians have "refreshed my Spirit" (16:18) by representing to him the bond of love that the congregation has for him.

We also need to bear in mind the ecclesial significance of the visits Paul is discussing in this chapter. Such visits between fellow Christians could never be private affairs, since the visitors were always representing a sending church to their host, who, in turn, represented the host church to their visitors. Because only very wealthy people would have had the resources to make long journeys with prolonged stays on private funds, almost all such inter-ecclesial visiting had to be of an ambassadorial type: the visitor was sent by a congregation for a time and provided for in a way that freed him from other duties and the need to make a living. Within this representational understanding of visitation, the Christian visitor would not merely stand for the one particular local sending church, but would also represent in his arrival the visiting of the wider body of Christ as a whole.

A glimpse of how such ambassadorial representation works is provided by a modern-day parallel from the period of the iron curtain. After the post-WWII partitioning of Germany into Western democratic and Soviet-ruled eastern parts, German congregations, both Protestant and Catholic, established a comprehensive network of partnerships between individual local churches on either side of the wall, links fostered through mutual visits over decades. Since these partnerships were established on an essentially random basis, without drawing on any previously established geographical or interpersonal commonalities, it was clear that the visits by delegations from a local church were, in a sense, a visit of the one universal church to a given local community. Though the visitors were able to utilize modern modes of travel, Soviet-style travel agencies and border policies in the east did everything they could to ensure these visits were cumbersome and embarrassing. Thus no one involved or looking on could mistake such visits for private recreational or tourist trips.

This said, there was one feature of these visitations in partitioned Germany that had not been present for Paul: their ecclesial partitioning into individual church traditions that had been established much earlier and that had nothing to do with the political East-West schism of the twentieth century. In Paul's days, long before the great ecclesial schism between

East and West, there could be no confusion that an ecclesial visitor came as a representative of the ecumenical church to the local church, thereby concretely displaying the church's unity. The post-schism churches of our time, in contrast, tend to see themselves as having "relationships" with other churches or join "networks" between churches. This is why today we must stretch to see beyond the limits that our denominationally fractured forgetfulness places on our imagination if we are to recover a greater sensitivity for what ecclesial visiting meant when the church was still united. To this end we have found patristic writers for whom the unity of the church was still a living reality to be especially illuminating readers of this chapter.

Since unlike previous chapters this chapter does not unfold a cumulatively building argument, we have felt free to explain the organizing logic of the chapter, which can be identified in certain themes (such as recognition) or sensitivities (such as those for the political matrix of the exercise of authority), by beginning with the two apparent summary verses in the middle of the chapter, 16:13–14. Taking seriously that chapter 16 is the conclusion of a letter, our interest is in investigating the points at which themes discussed earlier in the epistle are echoing and in some case being extended in its concluding paragraphs. Our reading, then, aims to conclude by trying to bring the substance of the whole letter more clearly into view.

On Reading Other People's Mail

> [13] Keep alert, stand firm in your faith, be courageous, be strong. [14] Let all that you do be done in love.

The language of these two verses is highly generalized in a chapter otherwise concerned with specific and concrete issues. As a result 16:13–14 seem somehow lost on first glance, interrupting as they do an otherwise obvious progression of Paul's comments on the travels and whereabouts of specific individuals. Casting aside the temptation to skip over or offer a platitudinous reading of these verses as a moral spine stiffener,[1] we must attempt to discover what, precisely, the challenge is that they put to every commentator. Three of the main interpretative options had already been

---

1. To further indicate why we find ourselves to be in particularly strong reliance on patristic interpreters of this chapter, we quote just one example to illustrate how quickly modern scholars tend to be content with rather underdeveloped comments on this passage. Bailey: "The final call to love provides a fitting conclusion to the homily. . . . awaiting the resurrection is not enough. They are to be engaged. The final appeal, to do everything in love, relates to the letter as a whole, not only to the final essay." *Paul Through Mediterranean Eyes*, 480.

discovered by the church fathers Theodoret, Origen, and Chrysostom. Theodoret presents us with what could be called a "moral message" reading: "Paul writes **be watchful** on account of the deceivers, and **stand firm** and **be courageous** because of his hearers' open adversaries. For the pious were being persecuted by the impious."[2] We have labeled this a "moral message reading" because Theodoret's comment rests on a moral contrast between "the" pious and "the" impious, which does not explain but merely reiterate the imperatives "be watchful" or "be courageous." The basic message that comes through in this reading can be paraphrased as, "whenever you are under attack by any adversaries, remember that Paul's writings contain all the moral virtues you will need to overcome them."

Origen, in contrast, does not look to these verses for a moral message but for the "message of scripture," the ontology behind specific concepts that are being offering here. By linking the main terms of these verses with passages from other books in the Bible, intra-canonical linkages are made through which these central terms can be conceptually defined: watchfulness, being firm, being courageous. Seeking to clarify the respective ontological meaning of the terms Paul is deploying here, Origen aims to generate distilled "biblical" definitions of each term, ready to be applied by every Christian in all circumstances. For example, he proposes that watchfulness be understood as the watchfulness of the soul in all times and places. This yields the conclusion that, "all that you do be done in love" (16:14) be understood thus: "It is characteristic of beginners to act out of fear, but the mature act out of love."[3]

Chrysostom's aim is not unlike Origen's, as he is also seeking clarity about the precise meaning of the terms Paul is using here. But unlike Origen, he does not go down the route of conceptually harmonizing the canonical materials but instead investigates how these terms function specifically for Paul. If this search for a "functional Pauline definition" is to bear fruit, he must pay close attention to the context of these verses in Paul's presentation in this chapter as well as to the chapter's location within the argument in the entire letter. With these textual contexts in view, he suggests the following:

> In saying these things, Paul appears to give a warning, but actually he is accusing them of laxity. Thus, he says, **be watchful** because they are sleeping, **stand firm** because they are tottering, **be courageous, be strong** because they have grown soft, **let all that you do be done in love** because they are factious. The phrase **be watchful, stand firm** is directed at the deceitful;

---

2. Theodoret, *Commentary*, PG 82:372, in JK, 288.
3. Origen, *Homilies*, JTS 10 (1909) 51, in JK, 289.

the phrase **be courageous** is directed at the schemers; and to those warring factions that try to tear everything in pieces he addresses the clause **Let all that you do be done in love,** *which is the bond of perfection* (Col 3:14), the font and root of everything good.[4]

It is Chrysostom's approach that most closely resembles the one we have followed throughout the letter. In this vein, we will continue in this chapter by seeking echoes of arguments developed earlier in the letter that illuminate the use of the terms in 16:13–14, as undefined as they are in that immediate context. Such a hermeneutic positioning suggests that we best approach this chapter with questions like, "**Watch out**—but for what danger?" "**Stand firm in your faith**—against which forces of resistance?" "**Be courageous, be strong**—but for what purpose?" On our reading of these spare verses, Paul is not invoking general virtues or offering a "get serious" moral broadside, but is expressing the warning that what he has asked the Corinthians to do in previous chapters, and what he is asking them yet to do in this chapter, *these things* will be impossible without genuinely watching and exhibiting faithful courage.

For example, the implications of the bare imperative to **watch** become clearer when we recall Paul's discussion in chapter 14 in which Christian worship is portrayed as sustained by a particular watchfulness for the operating patterns of the Holy Spirit. The summoning to **stand firm in your faith** becomes readily explicable when we recall the rousing call to bravely face dying and being remade that Paul lays out in such detail in chapter 15, beginning as it does with the specific injunction that the Corinthians hold firmly to this faith in which they stand (15:1–2). If we bear in mind the political struggles that reverberate through the whole letter we can see that when Paul summons the Corinthians to be **courageous, be strong**, he is preparing them to make the momentous, mortifyingly humiliating step of greeting each other with a holy kiss (16:20). Offering one another such a holy kiss could not have come lightly given the internal tribulations and factional battles that plagued the Corinthian church. Thus to face such an embrace would have called for a particular courage and strength as well as a willingness to die to self that they were not able to generate in themselves, but which needed the help of the wider church as represented by the Apostle. **All the brothers greet you** is therefore not only a friendly introduction to the summons to greet one another with a holy kiss, but details the material condition that will be necessary for the Corinthians to heed that advice.

---

4. Chrysostom, *Homily* 44, PG 61:374–75, in JK, 288.

As we draw our commentary to a close it is worthwhile reflecting briefly on the nature of both our commonality with, and divergence from, our co-readers in the ancient church. Our working strategy has always begun with a prolonged period of sheer exposure to the original texts, attempting to find Paul's line of argument through each chapter before directly engaging with other commentators' works. The aim has been to discover in each chapter a particular argumentative dynamic to illuminate the Apostle's core theological and pastoral concerns that run through the whole train of his communication with the Corinthians. When our sense of the coherence of the respective chapter under consideration has become sufficiently clear the subsequent stage of comparing our readings with those of the exegetical tradition old and new inevitably has revealed greater and lesser agreements with the voices of those who have preceded us in their engagement with these texts as scripture.

Our engagement with the three patristic writers we have just discussed again demonstrate what we have repeatedly found to be the case: that our affinity or lack thereof with various commentators certainly does not line up according to any neat modern-pre-modern division. The particular fondness that we developed for the exegesis of Chrysostom over that of Origen, for example, is not neatly mapped with simple historical or geographical labels. As displayed in our resonance with Chrysostom in this chapter, we have found ourselves most closely in synch with theologians and exegetes who not only inquire directly into what Paul is saying, but also into what he *does* in each case with what he is saying. Having spotted a potential connection between our sense of what Paul is doing and that of a traditional commentator we have then typically allowed them (in this case Chrysostom) to educate us further along the line of coherent reasoning as fellow travelers. In this joint travelling we are pushed, in turn, to become more precise in our understandings of how what we are doing differs in approach from other main approaches such as the ones represented in this chapter by Theodoret and Origen. It is thus what they help us to *see* in the biblical text that draws us to certain interpreters, not any interest in constructing a list of those we consider our favorite or the "best" exegetes in the abstract.

Exercising Authority Together

> ¹Now concerning the collection for the saints: you should follow the directions I gave to the churches of Galatia. ²On the first day of every week, each of you is to put aside and save whatever extra you earn, so that collections need not be taken

> when I come. ³And when I arrive, I will send any whom you approve with letters to take your gift to Jerusalem. ⁴If it seems advisable that I should go also, they will accompany me.

The detail with which Paul discusses the collection taken in the churches of Macedonia for the mother church in Jerusalem indicates that it meant a great deal to him. We would therefore be underplaying the breadth and theological nature of his interest in the collection if we understood it simply as a response to the relatively greater poverty of the church in Jerusalem. As Paul explains in 2 Corinthians,

> For the rendering of this service not only supplies the wants of the saints, but also overflows with many thanksgivings to God. Through the testing of this ministry you glorify God by your obedience to the confession of the gospel of Christ and by the generosity of your sharing with them and with all the others, while they long for you and pray for you because of the surpassing grace of God that he has given you (2 Cor 9:12–14).

The collection is more than a response to evident financial need, and as such is similar to the temple tax that Jews all over the globe were to contribute to the still-functioning temple. As the passage from second Corinthians shows, in Paul's eyes the core aim of the collection is to demonstrate the unity of the church that is, prior to any monetary exchange, God's gift to his people. This is why he urges the Corinthians to gather a gift so that an emissary might "carry away your generosity to Jerusalem" (Barrett's delightful translation of 16:3). Fundamentally then, the collection is not merely to be the gift of some*thing*, but a material gift in which the Corinthians are investing nothing less than *themselves*. The Greek term for what is being sent is χάρις (*charis*), "grace," and suggests that the NRSV has underplayed the force of Paul's point with the translation **taking your gift**. As it joins with other churches in this effort, the collection sends a signal from Corinth to the Jerusalem mother church that she is esteemed like a beloved great-grandmother—who not only symbolizes the unity of the whole family but also provides the concrete occasion for the scattered members of the family to tangibly experience what they are to each other: one family. Apart from such occasions that are provided through the grandmother's role as their "forum," when they gather, for instance, for a ninetieth birthday party where cousins meet cousins for the first time and old acquaintances are renewed, the reality of being one family threatens to remain a rather abstract piece of knowledge for them that could easily fade over time and spatial distance.

The detailed instructions Paul gives for the mechanics of collecting and delivering this gift to the mother church again display a fine sense for the political reality of the church and strongly echoes his earlier portrayals of the interplay of *charismata* and ministries, whether in Christian worship (chapter 14) or in the decision-making processes in the church as a whole (chapters 5–6). While Paul has shown himself willing to give instruction, the way he describes the procedures for the collection displays a desire to honor the Corinthians in their own authority. So, for example, in suggesting to **send** the messenger or messages **to Jerusalem** along with the collection, the Apostle stresses that he is happy to do so by sending them with **any whom you approve**. In 16:4 Paul uses a similarly vague formulation (**If it seems advisable that I should go**) that reflects and expresses his hope that he and the congregation might together discover a jointly agreeable solution.

In the fourth century the monks at Hadrumetum in North Africa desired to hear in Paul's willingness in 16:14 not to exercise his own authority an example to be emulated by monastic superiors: "let those in authority over us merely instruct us in what we ought to do and pray that we may do it. But let them not rebuke us if we fail to do it." "On the contrary," Augustine critically responded, "the teachers of the Church, the apostles, did all these things: they said what was to be done, they offered rebuke if it was not done, and they prayed that it might be done."[5] Augustine is quite obviously uncomfortable granting that Paul's apostolic authority might be hostage to what others decide or advise even as he grants that apostolic authority is nevertheless confirmed through recognition by others. At the same time the monks at Hadrumetum were also onto something when they noticed that Paul does not in fact command here the details of how the collection is to be carried out.

The argument might well have been avoided had both sides of this forth-century debate better understood the role played by political authority in Paul's relation to the Corinthian church. For Paul to request that the Corinthians make preparations for a collection but to do so in a manner that grants them authority in how it will proceed is not to limit or undermine the apostle's authority, as the monks suggest, nor does it have to be justified as only appearing on a surface level to be a negotiation of authority, as Augustine's reply seems to entail. Both Paul and the Corinthians are being granted real authority here by the nature of the Lord's apostolic commission to Paul, which, as we have often seen in the course of the letter, represents a specific *form* of political authority. We will only fully comprehend the nature of this "communal authority," built as it is on respect for the different purposes

---

5. Augustine, *On Rebuke and Grace* 5, PL 44:918–19, in JK, 289.

and degrees of authority that resides in different members of the body and their respective ministries, when we pay attention to the theological dimension that makes the Apostles various forms of address intelligible, including those he holds intentionally vague.

Staying with the Gospel's Enemies

> ⁵I will visit you after passing through Macedonia—for I intend to pass through Macedonia— ⁶and perhaps I will stay with you or even spend the winter, so that you may send me on my way, wherever I go. ⁷I do not want to see you now just in passing, for I hope to spend some time with you, if the Lord permits. ⁸But I will stay in Ephesus until Pentecost, ⁹for a wide door for effective work has opened to me, and there are many adversaries.
>
> ¹⁰If Timothy comes, see that he has nothing to fear among you, for he is doing the work of the Lord just as I am; ¹¹therefore let no one despise him. Send him on his way in peace, so that he may come to me; for I am expecting him with the brothers.
>
> ¹²Now concerning our brother Apollos, I strongly urged him to visit you with the other brothers, but he was not at all willing to come now. He will come when he has the opportunity.

Paul's presentation of his travel plans is full of relativizing terms positioned very similarly to his descriptions of the decision-making processes he suggests ought to support the collection. Vague phrasing is deployed to describe his intended visit with them and its duration; **perhaps** and **you may** and **wherever**. The theological reason behind this vagueness becomes apparent in 16:7b, **if the Lord permits**. Again Chrysostom gets to the nub of the matter: "He does not speak with certainty so that, if what he said should not happen, he might have an excuse—namely, that he had spoken indefinitely, and the power of the Spirit was leading him wherever it wished and not where he himself wanted."[6] Once again Paul encourages the Corinthians to understand themselves as active agents needing courage and strength while insisting that Christians understand their true agency as operating in the mode of response to the work of God that plays the far greatest role in determining the course of events (>9:20a).

---

6. Chrysostom, *Homily* 43, PG 61:370–72, in JK, 285.

If Paul is vague about the eventual outcome of his plans because he constantly bears in mind the Spirit's sovereignty over any human strategy, he is nevertheless clear about his desire to come and stay with the Corinthians for an extended period: **I do not want to see you now just in passing**. His outspokenness about this desire puts him in the vulnerable position of depending on their welcome, and we take this intentional gesture to put himself at their mercy as yet another way in which he displays the concreteness of his kenotic approach to proclaiming the gospel. Having expressed this wish in writing reveals Paul's affective attachment to this special community. As sternly as he has rebuked them at times, it is now as we approach the end of his letter impossible to think of these rebukes as having been uttered in the self-protective mode that communicates, in essence, "this is what you get from me, take it or leave it." Nor is this expressed desire to linger a veiled threat, as Pelagius reads 16:8 effectively to be communicating that, "there are many things to correct in you—just as a doctor tarries where many people are sick."[7] When we read Paul's expression of desire for a lengthier stay as a genuine statement of affection, his very last line of this long and winding letter, **My love be with all of you,** starts to look much less like a routine parting formula. The careful detail evident in the discussion of the collection has allowed us to appreciate, once again, how much of his intellectual capacity and emotional energy the Apostle has invested in a letter that he wishes to be recognized as love's investment from beginning to end.

To preach the gospel in this kenotic and truth-committed fashion does, however, travel by way of judgment. Paul's intent to stay in Ephesus for a while longer testifies to this duality, given his explanation for why the stay is needed. We take it to be significant that the explication Paul offers for the prolonged stay is given not only in the first part of his statement—**for a wide door for effective work has opened to me**—but also in the second part: **and there are many adversaries.** Resistance to the gospel is just as much an opportunity for it to show its power as is the welcome of its message. It is thus the *coincidence* of grace and judgment that Paul discerns as an occasion for the gospel and a sign of the nearing eschaton. Had he been experiencing only resistance the discerning thing would have been to follow the advice to shake their dust from his feet (Matt 10:14, par.). If on the other hand his preaching had achieved nothing other than smooth and easy success the Apostle would have had good reason to worry about the authenticity of his mission, whether it was actually serving a divine word with the power of a two-edged sword (Heb 4:12, Rev 1:16).

---

7. Pelagius, *Commentary*, Souter 227, in JK, 284.

It is precisely because he senses that the acceptance of and resistance to the gospel in Ephesus are both of high amplitude that Paul finds reason to hope that the judgment and grace characteristic of the day of the Lord is afoot and that his witness will somehow be able to serve the divine disclosure of hearts (>14:25). Chrysostom proves particularly sensitive to the theology displayed in the reasons Paul gives for staying on in Ephesus: "The devil never gets angry except when he sees many of his instruments snatched away."[8] Desirous of being neither a successful builder of big churches nor a clean-up agent,[9] Paul, as we understand his aim in staying, rests content to remain a witness and servant in the fracas that God is stirring up in Ephesus. The Apostle knows that his most precious reward in such moments is simply to be present to witness the gospel gathering a community around itself, an event in which he feels himself privileged to have a role (>9:18). Whatever the personal cost, Paul understands that he must linger at such points of contest because such moments are the nursery of apostolic relationships (>11:19)—an insight whose accuracy has been so richly attested for this case by the subsequent story of the Ephesian church.

We understand Paul's interest in an extended stay with the Corinthians as a further expression of his kenotic service to them and kairotic hope for them. Given the problems in their community, the Apostle was surely not mistaken that such a stay would be hard work for him. But as in Ephesus, Paul also knows that there is no substitute for directly facing the resistance that the gospel provokes, and he is ready to undertake yet again this act of vulnerable love for the Corinthians. But since he cannot yet be present in person he is sending Timothy into this dangerously complex situation of resistance and grace. In doing so his concern for Timothy shines through in the intensity of his admonitions to the Corinthians that they **see that he has nothing to fear among you** with the telling addition that no one should **despise him**. For Timothy to be received as Paul suggests he should, depends, it seems, on a prior condition: that peace descend on a community riven by contentious factionalism and no doubt tempted to rancor against the bearer of a letter of substantial correction. If Paul's negative injunctions protecting Timothy are to be heeded, the spiritual transformation towards which Paul has labored so hard to direct the Corinthians will

---

8. Chrysostom, *Homily* 43, PG 61:370–72, in JK, 285.

9. Pelagius offers the former view, Calvin the latter. "With you I must tarry, even spending the winter—there are many things to correct in you—just as a doctor tarries where many people are sick." Pelagius, *Commentary,* Souter 227, in JK 284. "It is, therefore, as if he said: 'by prolonging my stay here a little longer I shall do a lot of valuable work, whereas, if I were not on the spot, Satan would do a very great deal of damage.'" Calvin, JC, 353.

have to occur. This Spirit alone can bring the political harmony and mutual service that will allow them to **send him** [Timothy] **on his way in peace**. Paul has signaled his willingness to do the hard work of introducing the Corinthians to this peace in all its relational dynamism by indicating his desire to come and stay for a long while, but what is most interesting is the way in which he expects his time in Corinth to be appropriately drawn to a close: **so that you may send me on my way**. The overriding aim of his various modes of investment in the life of the Corinthian church—in person, through his emissaries, and with his letter writing—is to teach them not only to live together in peace but also to be able to take leave in peace. In both moments of interaction the task is to discover and display the form of life that conforms to the rule of God's Spirit.

The relational language in which the main theme of this chapter is embedded, the language of recognition, appears negatively in the injunction **let no one despise him**. This language of recognition also gives shape to Paul's commendation of Timothy, who carries a letter from him that was bound to inflame the tensions already present in the community. Notice that instead of saying "you mess with him, you mess with me," the Apostle tries to make sure that the Corinthians recognize Timothy as someone with his own distinctive role in the **work of the Lord**. The Apostle intimates that Timothy is far more than Paul's functionary, thus liberating the one who has carried his letter also to give his own interpretation of the writer's intentions, as needed. Paul clearly hopes that this letter will nourish reconciliation and catalyze a response from the Corinthians, so that Timothy will be able to return to him with a letter that not only speaks about but literally embodies the reconciliation that will be needed if their communication is to remain open.

Given Paul's overall emphasis that the Corinthian church seek unity and single-mindedness, it is all the more remarkable that he does not conceal a clash of wills between himself and Apollos. As much as he **earnestly** urged **Apollos** to join the party of ambassadors, Apollos would not go (Paul's word choice here emphasizes the innocence of his urging, >12:31; 14:1, 39). Yet what appears to be a clash of wills in which Paul has been bested is revealed on further investigation to be something much more significant. What the NRSV translates **but he** [Apollos] **was not at all willing to come now** does actually not have the pronoun "he" as grammatical subject in the Greek. It literally reads, "and not at all was there the will that he would come now." Barrett proposes a straightforwardly theological reading: "It simply was not God's will that he should do so now." Here again (as in 16:4), Paul seems intent to semantically conceal the agency at work in this decision, as though he was hinting at the theologically decisive moment in which human wills align with God's. In specifying that it is the temporal element that is the lynchpin that will eventually resolve the dispute (**not now, but when an opportunity arises**) Paul is apparently suggesting that a three-dimensional solution to an apparent clash of human wills ought to be expected as something that will arise when all parties embrace the divinely appointed timing, the *kairos*. There is no need here to enter debates about whether God's will is abstractly beyond all human wishing or can be trusted in principle to fall into alignment with human willing. We understand instead Paul to be suggesting here that what is paramount is to look for the convergence of wills *in time*—a convergence that will be worked out in the ebb and flow that makes up temporal difference and sequence. The stalemates so characteristic of human willing can and will dissolve in God's right time.

Refreshed by Present Believers

> **¹⁵Now, brothers and sisters, you know that members of the household of Stephanas were the first converts in Achaia, and they have devoted themselves to the service of the saints; ¹⁶I urge you to put yourselves at the service of such people, and of everyone who works and toils with them. ¹⁷I rejoice at the coming of Stephanas and Fortunatus and Achaicus, because they have made up for your absence; ¹⁸for they refreshed my spirit as well as yours. So give recognition to such persons.**
>
> **¹⁹The churches of Asia send greetings. Aquila and Prisca, together with the church in their house, greet you warmly in the Lord. ²⁰All the brothers and sisters send greetings. Greet one another with a holy kiss.**

We now move to the discussion Paul placed after the paraenesis in 16:13–14 that we discussed at the outset of this chapter, in which the *cantus firmus* of the whole letter is presented in succinct form: "Let all you do be done in love." After this interjection Paul continues rather incongruously to discuss the entourage that will accompany his letter on its way back to the Corinthians. Apollos will not participate, but Timothy will, and now also **Stephanas** and his group are mentioned in addition. The Apostle introduces his request to the Corinthians to **give recognition to such persons** and that they put themselves **at the service of such people** by drawing attention to the fact that they were **the first converts in Achaia**. In contrast to the direction suggested by the NRSV translation, the fathers noticed that the Greek for **first converts** (the ἀπαρχή/*aparchē*) signals more than a temporal distinction and so is best understood as an invocation of the biblical imagery of the "first fruits" that have been offered up from this region to God. This framing of the matter is reiterated when Paul commends them not only for being first, but for their service, their **works and toils**.[10] As a recognition of their service Paul urges the Corinthians to put themselves at the service of such servants and all who are like them, using a Greek term he has used before in the letter: ὑποτάσσησθε (*hypotassēsthe*) that literally translates, "you for your parts, *subordinate yourselves to such men*" (translation Barrett). It is safe to assume that, given their designated status as the first fruits of the region, Stephanus and his household had been converted by Paul himself in the initial wave of missionary success that also birthed the church in Corinth.

There appears to be some diplomacy at work on the Corinthian side in the choice to send Stephanus to Paul during a season of difficult communication. This would also suggest further that Paul's expression to **rejoice at the coming of Stephanas and Fortunatus and Achaicus** may be taken as a mark of the particular affective bond that he would have enjoyed with these the first fruits of his earliest mission in Corinth. On the basis of the comfort Paul receives from this personal bond, Barrett's reading of the relative explanatory clause as "because they have supplied what you could not do for me" appears an unnecessarily bitter comment implying that, "For all the reasons I might be cross with the Corinthians, at least the presence of my private friends is consoling."

Though grammatically possible, the more likely and theologically more profound translation is offered by the NRSV: Paul rejoices in the coming of the three Corinthian emissaries **because they have made up for your absence**. In rejoicing in their presence Paul testifies to the fact that there is in the end no substitute for the physical presence through which fellow Christians actually "embody" to each other the church as a whole (>1:4–9, 9:18). These comments also indicate why Paul understands his letters as a *substitute* for communication in the flesh, since written texts, taken on their own, can easily open up a distance that will inevitably be filled by misunderstandings. With insight that would serve us well in the age of the comment box flame-war and the accidental incineration of friendships through prematurely sent or misjudged e-mails, Paul is aware that if his letters are not to be disastrously derailed by miscommunication they need to be accompanied by ambassadors in the flesh: an entourage of fellow workers who can go some way to ensure that the message as a whole comes through, as

---

10. "This is no small compliment, to be the first to come to Christ . . . the **firstfruits** are necessarily better than the rest since they are the first offerings to God . . . Not only did they genuinely believe, as I said, but they also demonstrated deep piety, mature virtue, and an eagerness to help the poor . . . " Chrysostom, *Homily* 44, PG 61:375–76, in JK, 290.

they know the author would have it. Apparently not even in the early church could Christians really pull off the feat of "just me and my Bible"—communication not embedded in ecclesial relationship.

But how, precisely, are we to understand the processes of believers being **refreshed** by the presence of other believers that Paul is describing here? Refreshment is what we physically experience as something entering our body and quickening it, restoring its energy levels. To call something refreshing is not primarily to designate it as being pleasant to the taste, but to point to its effectiveness in restoring our bodies—*re*-freshing them. It is this restorative aspect that has such strong metaphorical resonances with human interrelations. Just as meeting an old school friend brings back all sorts of memories that may well be sentimental and nostalgic, it can nevertheless be refreshing in reconnecting us with the places and sources that exuded newness and vitality.

The psalmist draws on the metaphorical universe of refreshment to describe God's revivifying the believer; "He leads me beside still waters, and restores my soul" (Ps 23:2). This theological framing suggests that when Paul speaks of his visitors having refreshed him, he is not nostalgically recalling the glory days of his early missionary success; rather, he is experiencing these visitors as a divine reaffirmation of his apostolate by way of the physical reconfirmation that their presence embodies that he remains their Apostle. This visit facilitates Paul's recollection of the clarity of the Lord's leading in the conversion of Stephanas as well as displaying how fruit bearing that divine work has proven to be in the meantime. Precisely like the poet of the twenty-third psalm, Paul is refreshed because in his visitors he is reconnected with the source of the one relationship that truly refreshes. It is a refreshment that does not simply recharge Paul's "batteries" but refits him for the service of the gospel, the power of which the presence of Stephanas again makes visible to his eyes. This account of the contours of Paul's refreshment explains what would otherwise be quite an odd claim, that **they refreshed my spirit** as well as yours.

With the statement **All the brothers and sisters send greetings** Paul paves the way for the Corinthians to understand the meaning of the crucial injunction that immediately follows: **Greet one another with a holy kiss**. A substantial circle of greetings from churches and their individual members are now presented that it is reasonable to assume the Apostle has received in person: **The churches of Asia send greetings. Aquila and Prisca, together with the church in their house, greet you warmly in the Lord.** The passing on of greetings from specific local churches and specific individuals indicates that when he writes All **the brothers and sisters send greetings** Paul concludes with a gesture very like the one with which he opened the letter. In either case he addresses the Corinthians as part of the universal communion of saints, holy and blameless in God's sight with the whole of the church (>1:2, 10). If this is who they are before God and the eyes of the many believers of all the churches, the Corinthians have neither reason nor excuse not to **Greet one another with a holy kiss**. It is a formulation that gracefully exposes the interpersonal conflicts in the Corinthian church to the eyes of the worldwide church in a manner that lowers the barrier for their entry into peace by making the disputes that divide them seem in the larger scheme of things petty and insubstantial—if not morally then at least in proportion to the weight of glory that radiates towards them from the greetings of the whole communion of saints.

Saying Goodbye to Paul

> ²¹I, Paul, write this greeting with my own hand. ²²Let anyone be accursed who has no love for the Lord. Our Lord, come! ²³The grace of the Lord Jesus be with you. ²⁴My love be with all of you in Christ Jesus.

The mention of the **holy kiss,** the "anathema," and the "maranatha" in such quick succession, all of which were likely parts of the eucharistic celebration, reveals Paul's assumption that his letter would be read in the context of the Corinthians' liturgical gathering. The anathema formula **Let anyone be accursed who has no love for the Lord** sounds to modern ears like a shockingly and uncharacteristically harsh pronouncement,[11] but as we have seen, Paul is repeating here a gesture he has made at least twice already in this letter. Instead of understanding this anathema as a threatening gesture as have many commentators, including Chrysostom,[12] we have suggested reading it as again a part of the form taken by his love for them, in this case as a *particulum exclusivum*. To the extent that love is the prime marker of the very being of the church (**let all you do be done in love**), a love that mirrors and transmits the love of the trinity, to have **no love for the Lord** would be coterminous with positioning oneself outside of the church and the blessings it receives from her Lord. There are many things that Christians are not supposed to do, and Paul has taken great pains to discuss a whole variety of them in this letter. But unlike any of those behavioral aspects of the Christian life that are susceptible to being corrected, to not love the Lord

---

11. It was also apparently common in the early church. See *Didache* 9:5.

12. "With this one word **accursed** he makes them all afraid—those who were making their members the members of a prostitute, those who offended their brothers by eating food offered to idols . . . " Chrysostom, *Homily* 44, PG 61:376–77, in JK, 292.

is quite accurately described as the one thing constitutive of self-exclusion, a reality that Christians should take seriously by "handing these people over to Satan" (>5:5) and "not recognizing" them (>14:38).

The exclamation **Our Lord, come!** dates to the early days of the Aramaean-speaking church, and can either mean "our Lord has come," or be pronounced in the adhortative mode as in the NRSV rendering. Some modern translations simply transliterate the term "maranatha" and in so doing hint at the core expression of the letter's final greeting in the form of the pairing of anathema and maranatha. We understand this pair to express the binary of life stances put before everyone by **the grace of the Lord Jesus Christ**. Those who cry "maranatha," are taking up a life characterized by "watching" for the arrival of the eschatological day of the Lord, the *kairos* in which grace and judgment ("anathema") descend to reveal, expose, and convert human hearts (>16:13). Thus an invocation that calls to watch and pray, "Come Lord!," is legitimately paired with a statement of faith in the judgment that always accompanies grace. It is the waiting for this day, watching for what the Spirit will do, that defines what it means to be firm in faith, courageous and strong.

Paul verifies his **love** that is **with all of you** by writing a greeting **with my own hand**. As indicated in Gal 6:11, when Paul writes with his own hand, it should be understood as "something unusual, and [indicates] a particular stress of feeling," as Charles Hodge nicely puts it.[13] As chapter 13 has also made abundantly clear, Paul sees his entire ministry as an expression of **grace in Christ Jesus**. As one whose action is **in** love, Paul, through the display of his care for the Corinthians, makes visible why one who understands himself as judged, enlivened, and now writing in love, can begin his parting words with a rebuking of those who reject love (**If anyone does not love the Lord** . . .).

We end our journeying with Paul with a final reflection on our procedure. As we noted in our discussion of 16:17, we must appreciate the substantial investment made by the Corinthians to have sent several higher profile members of their congregation to Paul, carrying a letter or number of letters to which we have seen Paul responding. Given the factionalism of their church, the political wisdom of sending a whole number of ambassadors, representative of the respective parties, is certainly patent. But what is especially important about these small travelling groups in our view is the fellowship they would have had while travelling from Corinth to Paul in Ephesus. The ambassadors' intimate knowledge of their home church would have inspired them to discuss various aspects of their communal life during

---

13. Hodge, *1 & 2 Corinthians*, 372.

their travels together, including ways of explaining the Apostle's intent when facing the resistance they could expect to meet upon returning to the bosom of the Corinthian community. This fellowship is extended and complexified when Paul sends back a whole entourage with his letter comprised not only of Stephanas and his group but also Timothy who, Paul explicitly notes, "is my beloved and faithful child in the Lord" and who is "to remind you of my ways in Christ Jesus as I teach them everywhere in every church" (4:17). There is no doubt some political wisdom in Paul's move to combine "their" ambassadors with "his" man, but once again the more significant point seems to us the accompaniment of the written letter with a living letter—a fellowship of ambassadors/interpreters who could not only tell the Corinthian church of the Apostle's condition but could also attest to his authorship of the letter.[14] This is another reason why Paul's admonition to receive Timothy is so directly stated, for in this situation to receive the envoy is to receive the one who has sent him, and, as we see elsewhere in the New Testament, to reject the envoy is to reject the sender.[15]

During the course of our research we have come to sense a palpable parallel to this situation in our own way of approaching Paul. We have taken the questions of the church in our day to the Apostle, and, as a fellowship of interpreters, have labored to carry what we have heard of his message back to our readers in the form of a commentary. Though certainly at times demanding quite a bit of extra investment as well as the discomforts that accompany extended close proximity, our traveling together towards Paul and back to the churches of our day has often prompted discoveries not available to either one of us on our own. Through the practical difficulties of having to travel in order to spend time together and to find suitable spaces for the extended physical co-presence we found necessary for our interpretative fellowship, the experience of co-authoring this commentary had a palpably refreshing side for us that we came to see somewhat like the refreshment that Paul describes the visits as having had for him.

Two pairs of eyes are better than one, it is often said, and we discovered in the course of our exegetical labors that this familiar observation was far more important than we had expected. As our ways of preparing for our joint sessions evolved, a habit also emerged of opening our working periods by confessing the ways in which each of us felt close to and repelled by the Paul we were each encountering in each chapter. In sometimes rather dramatic ways we discovered through this practice how difficult it is to

---

14. See Mitchell, "New Testament Envoys," 641–62.

15. "I have written something to the church; but Diotrephes, who likes to put himself first, does not acknowledge our authority." 3 John 9.

understand one's own vantage point realistically and sufficiently. To take an illustrative example, the issues associated with traveling and visiting that we found central for our consideration of this chapter only came into view once we queried our easy assumption that we knew what Paul means in discussing the practice of traveling and visiting fellow Christians—easy, of course, only as long as not queried by a fellow traveler. It was a line of questioning that allowed us to work toward discerning how our own vantage points, biases, and reading habits might facilitate or obstruct our reading of Paul. As our engagement with this last chapter in the epistle reminded us once again, in the attempt to discern such personal vantage points we are not only dealing with our respective private dispositions and instincts but are actually representing to each other different and sometimes conflicting ways and traditions of being church.

Often our travelling toward and with Paul entailed discussions of the predicaments of our respective church traditions and contexts. As we discovered in ever richer detail the implications of Paul's kenotic approach to the Corinthians, we also came increasingly to understand our labor of doing so as an expression of love for our own churches. We have been able to continue on such a long journey sustained by the confident hope that Paul is still *our* Apostle. Hope provides the energy for such a journey, the hope that if we tarried with his words Paul would receive us in reciprocal love that we expected sometimes to include rebuke and correction. And in God's gracious time Paul did indeed appear. Having been ourselves braced and refreshed by rediscovering Paul as our Apostle numerous times in the course of our fellow travelling, we were enabled again and again seriously to consider how we might "carry away his generosity" back to our churches. Such talk between emissaries will always remain an essential component of the churches' calling to stay in personal contact with each other. But they will be able to do so only as a form of continuous listening to the living witness of the Apostle, a voice that has not been cut off by the death in the flesh of our brother Paul.

Bibliography

Adair-Toteff, Christopher. *Fundamental Concepts in Max Weber's Sociology of Religion*. New York: Palgrave Macmillan, 2015.

Aquinas, Thomas. *Summa Theologiae*. Translated by Fathers of the English Dominican Province. 2nd rev. ed. 20 vols. London: Burns, Oates & Washbourne, 1912–42.

Aristotle. *The Politics*. Edited and translated by Ernest Barker. New York: Oxford University Press, 1962.

Arnaut, Karel. "Africans Dance in Time: Kinaesthetic Praxis and the Constructing of a Community." *Cultural Dynamics* 1 (1988) 252–81.

Athanasius. *On the Incarnation: The Treatise De incarnatione Verbi Dei*. Translated and edited by a religious of C.S.M.V. Crestwood, NY: St. Vladimir's Seminary Press, 1993.

Augustine. *The City of God against the Pagans*. Translated and edited by R. W. Dyson. Cambridge: Cambridge University Press, 1998.

———. *Confessions*. Translated by Henry Chadwick. Oxford: Oxford University Press, 1991.

———. *On Genesis: A Refutation of the Manichees; Unfinished Literal Commentary on Genesis; The Literal Meaning of Genesis*. Translated by Edmund Hill. Edited by John E. Rotelle. New York: New City, 2002.

Baan, Ariaan. *The Necessity of Witness: Stanley Hauerwas's Contribution to Systematic Theology*. Eugene, OR: Pickwick, 2015.

Badiou, Alain. *Saint Paul: The Foundation of Universalism*. Translated by Ray Brassier. Stanford: Stanford University Press, 2003.

Bailey, Kenneth E. *Paul through Mediterranean Eyes: Cultural Studies in 1 Corinthians*. London: SPCK, 2011.

Barrett, C. K. *First Epistle to the Corinthians*. 2nd ed. London: Adam and Charles Black, 1971.

Barth, Karl. *Church Dogmatics*. 4.4: *Lecture Fragments*. Translated by Geoffrey W. Bromiley. Edinburgh: T. & T. Clark, 1981.

———. *The Resurrection of the Dead*. Translated by H. J. Stenning. London: Hodder and Stoughton, 1933.

Bayer, Oswald. *Martin Luther's Theology: A Contemporary Interpretation*. Translated by T. H. Trapp. Grand Rapids: Eerdmans, 2008.

Bechtel, Lyn M. "Rethinking the Interpretation of Genesis 2.4b—3.24." In *A Feminist Companion to Genesis*, edited by Athalya Brenner, 77–117. Sheffield: Sheffield Academic, 1993.

Beecher, Henry Ward. *Yale Lectures on Preaching*. Second Series. New York: Fords, Howard & Hulbert, 1900.

Bertschmann, Dorothea. "Bowing before Christ—Nodding to the State? Reading Paul Politically with Oliver O'Donovan and John Howard Yoder." DPhil thesis, University of Durham, 2012.

Black, Michael. "The Theology of the Corporation: Sources and History of the Corporate Relation in Christian Tradition." DPhil thesis, Oxford University, 2008.

Bonhoeffer, Dietrich. *Berlin, 1932–1933*. Edited by Larry L. Rasmussen. Translated by Isabel Best and David Higgins. DBWE 12. Minneapolis: Fortress, 2009.

———. *Creation and Fall: A Theological Exposition of Genesis 1–3*. Edited by John W. de Gruchy. Translated by Douglas Stephen Bax. DBWE 3. Minneapolis: Fortress, 1997.

———. *Life Together; Prayerbook of the Bible*. Edited by Geffrey B. Kelly. Translated by Daniel W. Bloesch and James H. Burtness. DBWE 5. Minneapolis: Fortress, 1996.

———. *Sanctorum Communio: A Theological Study of the Sociology of the Church*. Edited by Clifford J. Green. Translated by Reinhard Krauss and Nancy Lukens. DBWE 1. Minneapolis: Fortress, 2001.

———. *Theological Education Underground, 1937–1940*. Edited by Victoria J. Barnett. Translated by Victoria J. Barnett et al. DBWE 15. Minneapolis: Fortress, 2012.

Boring, M. Eugene, Klaus Berger, and Carsten Colpe, eds. *Hellenistic Commentary to the New Testament*. Nashville: Abingdon, 1995.

Boyd-MacMillan, Ronald. "The Transforming Sermon: A Study of the Preaching of St. Augustine, with Special Reference to the *Sermones ad populum*, and the Transformation Theory of James Loder." PhD diss., University of Aberdeen, 2009.

Bremen, Riet van. *The Limits of Participation: Women and Civic Life in the Greek East in the Hellenistic and Roman Periods*. Amsterdam: J. C. Gieben, 1996.

Brock, Brian. "Autism, Care, and Christian Hope." *The Journal of Religion, Disability, and Health* 13 (2009) 7–28.

———. "Dischipelschap: Waarom het volgen van Jezus betekent dat ik mijzelf moet vergeten [Discipleship: why following Jesus means forgetting myself]." In *Dischipelschap: Een theologische peiling*, edited by Huibertus de Leede and Herman Paul, 29–52. Zoetermeer: Uitgeverij Boekencentrum, 2016.

———. "On Being Creatures: Being Called to Presence in a Distracted World." *International Journal of Systematic Theology* 18 (2016) 432–52.

———. "Praise: The Prophetic Public Presence of the Mentally Disabled." In *Blackwell Companion to Christian Ethics*, edited by Stanley Hauerwas and Sam Wells, 139–51. 2nd ed. Malden, MA: Wiley-Blackwell, 2011.

———. *Singing the Ethos of God*. Grand Rapids: Eerdmans, 2007.

———. "Theologizing Inclusion: 1 Corinthians 12 and the Politics of the Body of Christ." *Journal of Religion, Disability, and Health* 15 (2011) 351–76.

Brock, Brian, and Stephanie Brock. "The Disabled in the New World of Genetic Testing: A Snapshot of Shifting Landscapes." In *Theology, Disability, and the New Genetics: Why Science Needs the Church*, edited by John Swinton and Brian Brock, 29–43. London: T. & T. Clark, 2007.

Brock, Brian, and John Swinton, eds. *Disability in the Christian Tradition: A Reader*. Grand Rapids: Eerdmans, 2012.

Bultmann, Rudolph. "The Concept of the Word of God in the New Testament." In *Faith and Understanding*, edited by Robert W. Funk and translated by Louise Pettibone Smith, 286–312. London: SCM, 1969.

BIBLIOGRAPHY

Calvin, John. *The First Epistle of Paul the Apostle to the Corinthians*. Translated by John W. Fraser. Edited by David W. Torrance and Thomas F. Torrance. Grand Rapids: Eerdmans, 1960.

———. *Institutes of the Christian Religion: 1541 French Edition*. Translated by Elsie Anne McKee. Grand Rapids: Eerdmans, 2009.

Cary, Max, et al., eds. *The Oxford Classical Dictionary*. Oxford: Clarendon, 1949.

Chauvet, Louis Marie. *Symbol and Sacrament: A Sacramental Reinterpretation of Christian Existence*. Translated by Patrick Madigan and Madeleine Beaumont. Collegeville, MN: Liturgical, 1995.

Collins, Raymond F. *First Corinthians*. Sacra Pagina 7. Collegeville, MN: Liturgical, 1999.

Conzelmann, Hans. *1 Corinthians: A Commentary on the First Epistle to the Corinthians*. Translated by James Leitch. Philadelphia: Fortress, 1975.

Delling, Gerhard. *Worship in the New Testament*. Translated by Percy Scott. Philadelphia: Westminster, 1962.

Dillon, Brian. *Tormented Hope: Nine Hypochondriac Lives*. London: Penguin, 2010.

Dix, Gregory. *The Shape of the Liturgy*. London: A. & C. Black, 1945.

Dostoyevsky, Fyodor. *The Idiot*. Translated by David Magarshack. London: Penguin, 1955.

Dunn, James G. *Jesus and the Spirit: A Study of the Religious and Charismatic Experience of Jesus and the First Christians as Reflected in the New Testament*. Grand Rapids: Eerdmans, 1997.

———. *The Theology of Paul the Apostle*. Grand Rapids: Eerdmans, 1998.

Eisland, Nancy. *The Disabled God: Toward a Liberatory Theology of Disability*. Nashville: Abingdon, 1994.

Ellul, Jacques. *Anarchy and Christianity*. Translated by Geoffrey W. Bromiley. 1991. Reprint, Eugene, OR: Wipf and Stock, 2011.

Fitzmyer, Joseph A. *First Corinthians: A New Translation with Introduction and Commentary*. New Haven: Yale University Press, 2008.

———. *1 Corinthians*. The Anchor Bible. Garden City, NY: Doubleday, 1976.

Forbes, Christopher. *Prophecy and Inspired Speech in Early Christianity and Its Hellenistic Environment*. Tübingen: Mohr Seibeck, 1995.

Frei, Hans. *The Eclipse of Biblical Narrative: A Study in Eighteenth and Nineteenth Century Hermeneutic*. New Haven: Yale University Press, 1980.

Furnish, Victor Paul. *The Theology of the First Letter to the Corinthians*. Cambridge: Cambridge University Press, 1999.

Garland, David. *1 Corinthians*. Baker Exegetical Commentary on the New Testament. Grand Rapids: Baker, 2003.

Gundry-Volf, Judith M. "Beyond Difference? Paul's Vision of a New Humanity in Galatians 3:28." In *Gospel and Gender: A Trinitarian Engagement with Being Male and Female in Christ*, edited by Douglas A. Campbell, 8–36. London: T. & T. Clark, 2003.

Habermas, Jürgen, and Niklas Luhmann. *Theorie der Gesellschaft oder Sozialtechnologie: Was leistet die Systemforschung?* Frankfurt: Suhrkamp, 1971.

Hamann, Johann Georg. "Aesthetica in nuce." In *Writings on Philosophy and Language*, translated and edited by Kenneth Haynes, 60–95. Cambridge: Cambridge University Press, 2007.

Harink, Douglas. *1 & 2 Peter*. London: SCM, 2009.

Harnack, Adolf. *History of Dogma*. Translated from the 3rd German edition by Neil Buchanan. New York: Dover, 1961.

Hauerwas, Stanley. *Approaching the End*. Grand Rapids: Eerdmans, 2013.

———. *Sanctify Them in the Truth: Holiness Exemplified*. Edinburgh: T. & T. Clark, 1998.

———. "Sacrificing the Sacrifices of War." In *War and the American Difference: Theological Reflections on Violence and National Identity*, 53–70. Grand Rapids: Baker, 2011.

Hays, Richard. *First Corinthians*. Interpretation: A Bible Commentary for Teaching and Preaching. Louisville: John Knox, 1997.

Herdt, Jennifer. *Putting on Virtue: The Legacy of the Splendid Vices*. Chicago: University of Chicago Press, 2008.

Hodge, Charles. *Commentary on 1 & 2 Corinthians*. Edinburgh: Banner of Truth, 1974.

Jennings, Willie James. *The Christian Imagination: Theology and the Origins of Race*. New Haven: Yale University Press, 2010.

Jenson, Robert. *Systematic Theology*. Vol. 1, *The Triune God*. Oxford: Oxford University Press, 1997.

Johnson, Kelly. *The Fear of Beggars: Stewardship and Poverty in Christian Ethics*. Grand Rapids: Eerdmans, 2007.

Kant, Immanuel. "Groundwork of the Metaphysic of Morals." In *Practical Philosophy*, translated and edited by Mary J. Gregor. Cambridge: Cambridge University Press, 1996.

———. *Religion and Rational Theology*. Translated and edited by Allen Wood and George Di Giovanni. Cambridge: Cambridge University Press, 1996.

Käsemann, Ernst. *Perspectives on Paul*. Translated by Margaret Kohl. London: SCM, 1971.

Kierkegaard, Søren. *The Concept of Anxiety: A Simple Psychologically Orienting Deliberation on the Dogmatic Issue of Hereditary Sin*. Edited and translated by Reidar Thomte and Albert B. Anderson. Princeton: Princeton University Press, 1980.

———. *Works of Love*. Edited and translated by Howard Hong and Edna Hong. Princeton: Princeton University Press, 1995.

Kieślowski, Krzysztof. *Trois couleurs: Bleu* [Three colors: Blue]. MK2 Diffusion/ Miramax, 1993.

Kim, Yung Suk. *Christ's Body in Corinth: The Politics of a Metaphor*. Minneapolis: Fortress, 2008.

Kittel, Gerhard, ed. *Theological Dictionary of the New Testament*. Translated and edited by Geoffrey W. Bromiley. Vol. 3. Grand Rapids: Eerdmans, 1965.

Kovacs, Judith L., trans. and ed. *1 Corinthians: Interpreted by Early Christian Commentators*. The Church's Bible. Grand Rapids: Eerdmans, 2005.

Levison, John R. *The Spirit in First Century Judaism*. New York: Brill, 1997.

Lietzmann, Hans. *An die Korinther I-II*. Tübingen: J. C. B. Mohr (P. Siebeck), 1969.

Lindemann, Andreas. "Die Kirche als Leib: Beobachtungen zur 'demokratischen' Ekklesiologie bei Paulus." *Zeitschrift für Theologie und Kirche* 92 (1995) 143–46.

Lindenbaum, John. "The Pastoral Role of Contemporary Christian Music: The Spiritualization of Everyday Life in a Suburban Evangelical Megachurch." *Social & Cultural Geography* 13 (2012) 69–88.

Luther, Martin. *D. Martin Luthers Werke: Kritische Gesamtausgabe.* 61 vols. Weimar: Hermann Bohlaus Nachfolger, 1883–1983.

———. *Luther's Works.* Edited by Jaroslav Pelikan and Helmut T. Lehmann. American ed. 55 vols. St. Louis: Concordia Publishing House; Philadelphia: Fortress, 1955–86.

———. *Martin Luthers Epistel-Auslegung.* Vol 2, *Die Korintherbriefe.* Edited by E. Ellwein. Göttingen: Vandenhoeck & Ruprecht, 1968.

Macaskill, Grant. *Union with Christ in the New Testament.* Oxford: Oxford University Press, 2013.

Marion, Jean-Luc. *God Without Being: Hors-Texte.* Translated by Thomas Carlson. Chicago: University of Chicago Press, 1991.

McClendon, James W., Jr. "Narrative Ethics and Christian Ethics." *Faith and Philosophy* 3 (1986) 383–96.

Mitchell, Margaret. "New Testament Envoys in the Context of Greco-Roman Diplomatic and Epistolary Conventions: The Example of Timothy and Titus." *Journal of Biblical Literature* 111 (1992) 641–62.

Monteith, W. Graham. *Epistles of Inclusion: St Paul's Inspired Attitudes.* Guilford: Grosvenor House, 2010.

Murphy, Francesca Aran. *1 Samuel.* Brazos Theological Commentaries on the Bible. Grand Rapids: Baker, 2010.

Murphy-O'Connor, Jerome. *Keys to First Corinthians: Revisiting the Major Issues.* Oxford: Oxford University Press, 2009.

Nygren, Anders. *Agape and Eros.* Translated by Philip S. Watson. London: SPCK, 1932.

O'Donovan, Oliver. *The Desire of the Nations: Rediscovering the Roots of Political Theology.* Cambridge: Cambridge University Press, 1996.

———. *The Problem of Self-Love in St. Augustine.* New Haven: Yale University Press, 1980.

O'Donovan, Oliver, and Joan Lockwood O'Donovan. *From Irenaeus to Grotius: A Sourcebook in Christian Political Thought.* Grand Rapids: Eerdmans, 1999.

Outka, Gene. *Agape: An Ethical Analysis.* New Haven: Yale University Press, 1972.

Pannenberg, Wolfhart. *Jesus, God and Man.* Translated by Lewis L. Wilkins and Duane A. Priebe. 2nd ed. Philadelphia: Westminster, 1977.

Pasnau, Robert. *Theories of Cognition in the Later Middle Ages.* Cambridge: Cambridge University Press, 1997.

Peppiatt, Lucy. *Women and Worship at Corinth: Paul's Rhetorical Arguments in 1 Corinthians.* Eugene, OR: Cascade, 2015.

Phillips, J. B. *The New Testament in Modern English.* London: William Collins, 1960.

Piper, John, and Wayne Grudem, eds. *Recovering Biblical Manhood and Womanhood: A Response to Evangelical Feminism.* Wheaton, IL: Crossway, 2006.

Prather, Scott Thomas. *Christ, Power and Mammon: Karl Barth and John Howard Yoder in Dialogue.* London: Bloomsbury T. & T. Clark, 2013.

Radcliffe, Timothy. "Paul and Sexual Identity: 1 Corinthians 11:2–16." In *After Eve: Women, Theology and the Christian Tradition,* edited by Janet Soskice, 62–72. London: Collins, 1990.

Rees, Geoffrey. *The Romance of Innocent Sexuality.* Eugene, OR: Cascade, 2011.

Reynolds, Thomas E. *Vulnerable Communion: A Theology of Disability and Hospitality.* Grand Rapids: Brazos, 2008.

Ricoeur, Paul. "Toward a Hermeneutic of the Idea of Revelation." In *Essays on Biblical Interpretation*, edited by Lewis S. Mudge, 73–118. Philadelphia: Fortress, 1980.

Rienecker, Fritz, ed. *Sprachlicher Schlüssel zum Griechischen Neuen Testament*. Giessen-Basel: Brunnen, 1977.

Roberts, Alexander, and James Donaldson, eds. *The Ante-Nicene Fathers*. 10 vols. Reprint. Peabody, MA: Hendrickson, 1994.

Robertson, Archibald, and Alfred Plummer. *A Critical and Exegetical Commentary on the First Epistle of St. Paul to the Corinthians*. New York: Scribner, 1911.

Schaeffer, Francis. *The God Who Is There: Speaking Historic Christianity into the Twentieth Century*. Downers Grove, IL: InterVarsity, 1968.

Schleiermacher, Friedrich. *The Christian Faith*. Translated and edited by H. R. MacIntosh and J. S. Steward. 2nd ed. Edinburgh: T. & T. Clark, 1928.

———. *On Religion: Speeches to Its Cultured Despisers*. Translated by John Oman. New York: Harper & Row, 1958.

Schüssler Fiorenza, Elisabeth. "Women in the Pauline Churches." In *Feminism and Theology*, edited by Janet Martin Soskice and Diana Lipton. Oxford: Oxford University Press, 2003.

Sloterdijk, Peter. *God's Zeal: The Battle of the Three Monotheisms*. Cambridge: Polity, 2009.

Stout, Jeffrey. *Democracy and Tradition*. Princeton: Princeton University Press, 2004.

Stringfellow, William. *My People Is the Enemy: An Autobiographical Polemic*. 1964. Reprint, Eugene, OR: Wipf and Stock, 2005.

———. *A Second Birthday: A Personal Confrontation with Illness, Pain, and Death*. 1970. Reprint, Eugene, OR: Wipf and Stock, 2005.

Stuart, Elizabeth. "Love Is . . . Paul." *The Expository Times* 102 (1991) 264–66.

Taylor, Joan E. "The Woman Ought to Have Control over Her Head because of the Angels." In *Gospel and Gender: A Trinitarian Engagement with Being Male and Female in Christ*, edited by Douglas A. Campbell. London: T. & T. Clark, 2003.

Thistleton, Anthony. *First Corinthians: A Shorter Exegetical and Pastoral Commentary*. Grand Rapids: Eerdmans, 2006.

Tolstoy, Leo. *My Religion: What I Believe*. Translated by Huntington Smith. Guildford, UK: White Crow, 2009.

Vanier, Jean. *Community and Growth*. London: Darton, Longman and Todd, 2007.

Wannenwetsch, Bernd. "Affekt und Gebot: Zur ethischen Bedeutung der Leidenschaften im Licht der Theologie Luthers und Melanchthons." In *Passion, Affekt und Leidenschaft in der Frühen Neuzeit*, edited by Johann Anslem Steiger, 1:203–15. Wiesbaden: Harrassowitz, 2005.

———. "Creation and Ethics: On the Legitimacy and Limitation of Appeals to 'Nature' in Christian Moral Reasoning." In *Within the Love of God: Essays on the Doctrine of God in Honour of Paul S. Fiddes*, edited by Anthony Clarke and Andrew Moore, 198–216. Oxford: Oxford University Press, 2014.

———. "The Desire of Desire: Commandment and Idolatry in Late Capitalist Societies." In *Idolatry: False Worship in the Bible, Early Judaism and Christianity*, edited by Stephen Barton, 315–30. London: T. & T. Clark, 2007.

———. "Ecclesiology and Ethics." In *The Oxford Handbook of Theological Ethics*, edited by Gilbert Meilaender and William Werpehowski, 57–73. Oxford: Oxford University Press, 2005.

———. "From *Ars Moriendi* to Assisted Suicide: Bonhoefferian Explorations into Cultures of Death and Dying." *Studies in Christian Ethics* 24 (2011) 428–40.

———. "Head: Christianity Medieval Times, Reformation Era, and Modern Europe." In vol. 10 of *Encyclopedia of the Bible and Its Reception*, edited by Hans-Josef Klauck et al. Berlin: de Gruyter 2015.

———. "Owning Our Bodies? The Politics of Self-Possession and the Body of Christ (Hobbes, Locke, Paul)." *Studies in Christian Ethics* 26 (2013) 50–65.

———. "Plurale Sinnlichkeit. Glaubenswahrnehmung im Zeitalter virtueller Realität." *Neue Zeitschrift für Systematische Theologie und Religionsphilosophie* 42 (2000) 299–315.

———. *Political Worship*. Translated by Margaret Kohl. Oxford: Oxford University Press, 2004.

———. "Representing the Absent in the City: Prolegomena to a Negative Political Theology according to Revelation 21." In *God, Truth, and Witness: Engaging Stanley Hauerwas*, edited by L. G. Jones, R. Hütter, and C. R. Velloseo Ewell, 167–92. Grand Rapids: Brazos, 2005.

Watson, Francis. *Paul and the Hermeneutics of Faith*. London: T. & T. Clark, 2004.

Webb-Mitchell, Brett. *Beyond Accessibility: Toward Full Inclusion of People with Disabilities in Faith Communities*. New York: Church Publishing, 2010.

Wendland, Heinz-Dietrich. *Die Briefe an die Korinther*. Das Neue Testament Deutsch 7. Göttingen: Vandenhoeck and Ruprecht, 1980.

Williams, Sarah. *The Shaming of the Strong: The Challenge of an Unborn Life*. Colorado Springs: Life Journey, 2005.

Wood, Don. "This Ability: Barth on the Concrete Freedom of Human Life." In *Disability in the Christian Tradition: A Reader*, edited by Brian Brock and John Swinton, 391–426. Grand Rapids: Eerdmans, 2012.

Yong, Amos. *The Bible, Disability, and the Church: A New Vision of the People of God*. Grand Rapids: Eerdmans, 2011.

———. *Theology and Down Syndrome: Reimagining Disability in Late Modernity*. Waco: Baylor University Press, 2007.

Young, Frances M. *Brokenness and Blessing: Towards a Biblical Spirituality*. Grand Rapids: Baker, 2007.

Name Index

Adair-Toteff, Christopher, 2:80n5
Adam, 1:16, 2:112, 2:205–6, 2:215,
    2:218–23, 2:226–27
Agamben, Giorgio, 1:160, 1:161n28
Ambrosiaster, 1:4n6, 1:6n8, 1:10n17,
    1:22n34
Apollos 1:18, 1:20, 1:65, 1:74–75, 1:78,
    2:236, 2:239–40
Aquinas, Thomas, 1:81n7.9, 1:107n24,
    1:123n15, 1:131n27, 1:165n30,
    1:166, 1:206, 1:206n16.18, 2:34,
    2:34n12, 2:42–44, 2:46n30, 2:47,
    2:67, 2:142, 2:183n33, 2:189n41
Arendt, Hannah, 1:6n10, 1:217n40
Aristotle, 1:52, 1:209n23, 2:179n29,
    2:190n41, 2:195n7, 2:211,
    2:214n30
Arnaut, Karel, 2:156n8
Athanasius, 2:76n3, 2:221n40, 2:226n49
Atkinson, Tyler, 1:71n11
Augustine, 1:xvii, 1:xviinn2–3, 1:95–96,
    1:95n6, 1:96nn7–10, 1:117,
    1:137n2, 1:171, 1:171n3, 1:175,
    1:176n7, 1:198n7, 1:206,
    1:214n38, 1:222n45, 2:3,
    2:46n30, 2:89n14, 2:100, 2:133,
    2:142, 2:176–77, 2:181n32,
    2:214n30, 2:216n31, 2:219n36,
    2:220n38, 2:225n47, 2:235

Baal, 1:42n4, 2:36
Baan, Ariaan, 2:203n19
Bach, Johann Sebastian, 1:208
Badiou, Alain, 1:33n46, 2:129n4,
    2:133n8,
Bailey, Kenneth E., 2:36n17, 2:41n23,
    2:124n48, 2:128nn1–2,
    2:176n24, 2:175n26, 2:176n26,
    2:230n1

Banner, Michael, 1:74n14
Barnabas, 1:195
Barrett, C. K. 1:82n12.3, 1:83,
    1:83n14, 1:116, 1:116n6, 1:130,
    1:130nn24–25, 1:131–32,
    1:131n28, 1:143n13, 1:172n2,
    1:177, 1:181, 2:10n8, 2:21n18,
    2:22n19, 2:173n22, 2:234, 2:239,
    2:241
Barth, Karl, 1:30n44, 1:81n7, 1:213n35,
    2:44n26, 2:192n4, 2:198n11,
    2:207n23, 2:216–19,
Barton, Stephen, 1:7, 1:7n12, 1:25n40
Bayer, Oswald, 1:30n43, 1:153n20,
    1:221n44, 2:59n49, 2:67n52
Bechtel, Lyn M., 2:223n42
Beecher, Henry Ward, 2:106–7
Beethoven, Ludwig van, 1:208
Bennett, Jana, 1:134n30
Bertschmann, Dorothea, 2:208n23
Black, Michael, 2:134n12
Bonhoeffer, Dietrich, 1:11n19, 1:12n19,
    1:22, 1:22n36, 1:40n1, 1:54n16,
    1:68n6, 1:69–70, 1:70n8,
    1:72n12, 1:83n15, 1:84n16,
    1:91n2, 1:135n31, 2:64n51,
    2:118n45, 2:180, 2:182n32,
    2:194, 2:211–12, 2:218n35,
    2:224n44, 2:225n48
Boyd-MacMillan, Ronald, 2:182n32
Bray, Gerald, 1:35n50
Bremen, Riet van, 2:183n34
Brock, Brian, 1:ix, 1:x, 1:54n15, 1:64n3,
    1:80n6, 1:96n10, 1:115n5, 2:4n4,
    2:99n24, 2:116n42, 2:127n49,
    2:132n6, 2:138n14, 2:212n29,
    2:220n39
Bultmann, Rudolf, 1:12n20, 1:38,
    2:172n21

Name Index

Calvin, John, 1:45n9, 1:81n7, 1:98n11,
    1:117, 1:117n8, 1:120–21,
    1:120nn11–13, 1:126n17,
    1:128n20, 1:129n21, 1:130,
    1:131n26, 1:155n20, 1:175,
    1:202n13, 1:206, 1:206n19,
    1:222n45, 2:26n23, 2:29n7,
    2:46n31, 2:53, 2:133, 2:151n1,
    2:162n13, 2:176n27, 2:183n33,
    2:192n1, 2:238n9
Cary, Max, 2:155n4
Cephas, 1:18, 1:74–75, 1:196, 2:195
Cervantes, 1:127, 1:127n18
Chappell, Timothy, 1:212n29
Chauvet, Louis Marie, 2:57n45
Chrysostom, 1:20, 1:20nn29–30, 1:21,
    1:21n31, 1:22n35, 1:24n38,
    1:68n5, 1:81n7, 1:100n16,
    1:103n19, 1:104n20, 1:193,
    1:193n4, 1:202n13, 2:35n16,
    2:47, 2:100, 2:112n37, 2:114–16,
    2:147, 2:148n23, 2:192n2, 2:231–
    33, 2:236, 2:238, 2:241n10, 2:243
Clement of Alexandria, 1:64, 2:31–32
Cloe, 1:18
Collins, Raymond F., 1:47n11, 1:155n21,
    1:213n37, 1:223n47, 1:224n51,
    2:26n23, 2:30n8, 2:45n27,
    2:93n18,
Conzelmann, Hans, 1:10n16, 1:47n12,
    1:77n4, 1:81, 1:81n8.10, 2:26n23,
    2:30n9, 2:76n3
Crispus, 1:22
Cyril, 1:34n49, 1:45n8, 2:151n1

Dahl, Nils A., 1:53n14
Delling, Gerhard, 2:171n20
Deluz, Gaston, 1:211n28
Deming, Will, 1:140n9, 1:143n12,
    1:155n23
Descartes, René, 1:40
Dillon, Brian, 2:32n11, 2:112n36
Dix, Gregory, 1:104nn22–23, 2:49n38,
    2:104
Dolbeau, François, 1:202n13
Donatus, 1:4n6
Dorner, Isaak, 1:190, 1:191n1
Dostoyevsky, Fyodor, 2:140n15, 2:200

Du Boulay, Juliet, 1:104n22
Dunn, James G., 2:74n1, 2:77n4,
    2:89n13, 2:97, 2:155n5,
    2:163nn16–17, 2:171n20
Dysinger, Luke, 1:64n2

Eisland, Nancy, 2:216n32,
Elijah, 1:42n4
Elisha, 1:91n1
Elliot, Carl, 1:139n8
Elliot, Jim, 1:214
Ellul, Jacques, 2:153n3
Engberg-Pederson, Troels, 1:38n54
Eve, 1:16, 2:41n23, 2:112, 2:190n41

Fee, Gordon D., 1:200n10, 213n37
Fitzmyer, Joseph A., 1:94n4, 2:26n23
Forbes, Christopher, 2:37n20
Foucault, Michel, 1:212, 212n33
Fowl, Stephen E., 1:58n20
Frei, Hans, 2:2n1
Furnish, Victor P., 1:93n3, 2:86, 2:88n12

Garland, David, 1:13n22, 1:111n1,
    1:126n1, 1:137n3, 2:12n10,
    2:21n16–17, 2:34n12, 2:63n50,
    2:83n6, 2:111n34, 2:124n47,
    2:141n18
Garver, Eugene, 1:23n37
Girard, René, 1:183
Givens, Tommy, 1:33n47
Gooch, Paul W., 1:218n42
Goodrich, John, 1:197n6, 1:210n25
Goossen, Rachel Waltner, 1:132n29

Habermas, Jürgen, 2:96
Hadot, Pierre, 1:58n21
Hamann, Johann G., 1:30, 1:30n34
Handelman, Susan A., 1:56n19
Harink, Douglas, 2:188, 2:189n39
Harnack, Adolf, 2:80n5, 2:151n2
Hauck, 1:209n24
Hauerwas, Stanley, 1:v, 1:xi, 1:37n53,
    1:102n17, 1:198n8, 2:69n55,
    2:218n35, 2:226nn50–51,
Hays, Richard, 1:1n2, 1:9n13, 1:12,
    1:12n21, 1:18, 1:18n28, 1:45n7,
    1:91n1, 1:95n5, 1:104n21,

1:119, 1:119n9, 1:168n31,
1:192n3, 1:197n6, 1:201n12,
1:204n14, 2:10n8, 2:18n14,
2:27n4, 2:34n13, 2:44n25, 2:126,
2:162n14, 2:192n3
Heidegger, Martin, 1:7, 1:7n11, 1:212,
1:212n31
Heil, John Paul, 1:13n23
Heller, Kevin Jon, 1:213n36
Herdt, Jennifer, 2:158n11
Hodge, Charles, 1:27n42, 2:27n1, 2:244
Horrell, David, 1:103n18, 1:129,
1:129n22
Husserl, Edmund, 1:210

Ignatius of Antioch, 1:64, 2:11
Illich, Ivan, 1:xix

James, William, 1:34, 1:34n48
Jennings, Willie J., 1:217n41, 1:224n50,
2:117n44, 2:156n7
Jenson, Robert, 2:148n24
Jerome, 1:15n26, 1:137n2
Johnson, Kelly, 1:200n11, 2:114n38
Jones, Gregory L., 1:58n20
Julian, 1:113n3, 1:114–15
Jungmann, Josef, 1:104n22

Kant, Immanuel, 1:140n10, 2:23n20
Käsemann, Ernst, 2:85n9, 2:162–64
Kierkegaard, Søren A., 1:14n24,
2:140n16, 2:141n21, 2:148n25,
2:225
Kieslowski, Krzysztof, 2:133n7
Kim, Yung Suk, 1:36n51, 2:85n9
Kingsolver, Barbara, 1:194–95, 1:194n5
Kittel, Gerhard, 2:92n17

Lebron, Tim, 1:71n10
Levison, John R., 2:155n6
Lietzmann, Hans, 1:130, 2:141n17
Lindbeck, George, 1:188n14
Lindemann, Andreas, 1:211n27,
2:88n12
Lindenbaum, John, 2:162n12
Locke, John, 1:139n6
Longenecker, Richard, 1:1n1

Luther, Martin, 1:xvi, 1:xvin1, 1:15n25,
1:16n27, 1:40n2, 1:61, 1:64n1,
1:76–77, 1:76n1, 1:77n2,5,
1:108, 1:115, 1:115n4, 1:127n19,
1:153–54, 1:153n20, 1:161,
1:175, 1:175n6, 1:176n8, 1:182,
1:206n17, 1:207n21, 1:222,
2:51, 2:67, 2:76, 2:84, 2:112n37,
2:132–34, 2:138, 2:140, 2:187,
2:189, 2:197n10, 2:198, 2:200–
201, 2:224

Macaskill, Grant, 2:46n29
MacIntryre, Alasdair, 1:xviiin4
Malesic, Jonathan, 1:46n10
Marion, Jean-Luc, 1:175n5, 2:14n12
Martinez, Florentino G., 1:47n12
Martyn, J. Louis, 1:55n17
Maximus Confessor 1:37, 1:37n53
McCain, John, 1:188–89
McCarthy, David Matzko, 1:144n14
McClendon, James W. jr., 1:184,
1:184n12, 2:4n5
Melanchthon, Philipp, 1:81n7, 2:16n13
Merleau-Ponty, Maurice, 1:156nn25–26,
1:158n27
Miller, Colin D., 1:xviiin4, 1:38n55,
1:68n7
Mitchell, Margaret, 2:245n14
Monteith, W. Graham, 2:112n35
Moses, 1:195, 2:1–5, 2:11, 2:84n8, 2:88,
2:206
Murphy, Francesca Aran, 2:4n5,
2:104n30
Murphy-O'Connor, Jerome, 1:1n3,
1:153–54, 1:153nn17–19, 1:156,
1:180n9, 1:192n2, 1:200n9,
2:27n3, 2:45n28, 2:46n32,
2:50n39, 2:54, 2:55n44, 2:196n8

Nietzsche, Friedrich, 1:2, 1:36, 1:37n52,
1:212, 1:212n30.31
Novatian, 1:4n6
Nygren, Anders, 2:132n6

Oecumenicus, 1:45n8
O'Donovan, Oliver, 1:206n20, 2:90n14,
2:95n19, 2:132n6,

Origen, 1:10, 1:10n15.17, 1:37n53, 1:44n6, 1:45n8, 1:64, 1:77n3, 1:205n15, 1:213, 1:213n37, 1:216n39, 1:221, 1:221n43, 1:224n49, 2:7, 2:186n37, 2:231, 2:233
Outka, Gene, 2:132n6

Pannenberg, Wolfhart, 2:203n18
Pasnau, Robert, 2:201n17
Peppiatt, Lucy, 2:27nn4–5, 2:28n6, 2:34n15, 2:37n19, 2:39n22, 2:44n25, 2:174n23, 2:184n36, 2:190n43
Pfitzner, Victor, 1:224n51–52
Phillips, J. B., 2:151n1
Piper, John, 2:186n37
Plato, 1:24, 2:88n12, 2:211
Prather, Scott Thomas, 2:207n23

Qoheleth, 1:72

Radcliffe, Timothy, 2:37n18
Rees, Geoffrey, 2:42n24
Reynolds, Thomas E., 2:112n35
Rhees, Rush, 1:30, 1:30n45, 1:140n11
Richards, Ernest R., 1:1n1
Ricoeur, Paul, 2:130n5
Rienecker, Fritz, 1:124n16, 1:174n4, 2:196n9
Robertson, Archibald, 2:27n2
Rosenzweig, Franz, 1:55, 1:55n18

Schaeffer, Francis, 2:204n20
Schleiermacher, Friedrich D. E., 1:10n14, 1:179, 2:157–59
Schüssler Fiorenza, Elisabeth,
Serres, Michael, 1:130, 1:130n23
Severiano of Gabala, 1:222n46
Sloterdijk, Peter, 2:19n15, 2:142n22
Smith, James, 1:184, 1:184n12
Sosthenes, 1:1–3, 1:22
Spaemann, Robert, 1:139n5
Stephanas, 1:22, 2:240–42, 2:245
Stout, Jeffrey, 1:198n8, 2:128n3
Stringfellow, William, 2:117n43, 2:210n27, 2:223
Stuart, Elizabeth, 2:141n20

Stuhlmacher, Peter, 1:44n6, 1:60, 1:60n22
Swartley, Willard, 1:151n16

Taylor, N. H., 1:2n4
Taylor, Joan E., 2:30n9, 2:46n33
Tertullian, 1:137n2
Theodoret, 1:1n3, 1:68n4, 1:121, 1:122n14, 2:26, 2:231, 2:233
Thistleton, Anthony, 1:109n25, 1:112n2, 1:113n3, 1:138n4, 1:142–43, 1:160, 1:168, 1:168n32, 1:172, 1:174, 1:177, 1:182n10, 1:194, 1:202n13, 1:208, 1:208n22, 1:210n26, 1:222n44, 1:223, 1:223n48, 2:8n7, 2:22n19, 2:26n24, 2:50n39, 2:58, 2:62, 2:83, 2:100–101, 2:126, 2:141n19, 2:143, 2:170, 2:183, 2:196–97, 2:205
Timothy, 1:84, 2:236, 2:238–40, 2:245
Tolstoy, Leo, 2:204n21

Ulrich, Hans G., 1:xv, 1:xvi, 1:145, 1:213n34

Vanier, Jean, 2:112n35, 2:115, 2:164n18
Verhoef, Eduard, 1:1n3

Wannenwetsch, Bernd, 1:ix, 1:x, 1:3n5, 1:4n7, 1:21n32, 1:26n41, 1:71n10, 1:74n13, 1:82n11, 1:116n7, 1:119n10, 1:139n7, 1:156n24, 1:163n29, 2:14n11, 2:16n13, 2:34n14, 2:39n21, 2:48n37, 2:53n41, 2:57n46, 2:70n56, 2:97n22, 2:156n9, 2:210n26, 2:217n34, 2:222n41
Warren, Rick, 1:188
Watson, Francis, 1:109n26, 2:22n19, 2:187n38
Webb-Mitchell, Brett, 2:112n35
Weber, Max, 1:2, 1:224, 2:80n5, 2:181n31
Wendland, Heinz-Dietrich, 2:183n35, 2:209n25
Wiemer, Axel, 1:40n2
Williams, Sarah, 2:118n46

Witherington, Ben, 1:213n37
Wood, Don, 2:216n33

Yoder, John Howard, 1:132n29

Yong, Amos, 2:112n35, 2:216n32, 2:219n37
Young, Frances M., 2:112n35

Subject Index

Abortion, 1:188
Abstinence, 1:137, 1:137n3, 1:138, 1:142–44
Accountability, accountable, 1:75, 1:77–80, 2:59
Adultery, 1:127, 1:165, 1:205, 2:221n40
Adventure, 1:xxii
Aesthetics, aesthetical, 1:12, 1:176, 1:208–9, 2:128, 2:133, 2:168, 2:218–19,
Agency, 1:xiiin4, 1:3, 1:38, 1:66–67, 1:68n7, 1:116, 1:170, 1:177–79, 1:182, 1:186, 1:208, 1:213, 2:6–7, 2:18, 2:79, 2:81, 2:102–4, 2:123, 2:131, 2:146, 2:152, 2:160, 2:165, 2:236, 2:239
Alliance, 1:xxi, 1:73, 1:84, 1:215, 2:232
Anthropology, anthropological, 1:48, 1:127, 1:138, 1:171n1, 2:ix, 2:16n13, 2:73, 2:78, 2:150, 2:170–71, 2:221
Apocalyptic, 1:xviiin4, 1:47n12, 1:55n17, 2:225
Apology, apologia, apologetic, 1:109, 1:192, 1:198, 1:203, 1:215, 1:223, 2:204
Apostolate, 1:1, 1:2, 1:5–7, 1:44, 1:57, 1:78, 1:82, 1:84, 1:97, 1:190, 1:192, 1:196, 1:203, 1:210n25, 1:215, 1:221, 1:223, 2:105, 2:121, 2:122, 2:242
Apostolicity, apostolic, 1:xx–xi, 1:2, 1:5–8, 1:22–24, 1:43, 1:53, 1:56–59, 1:63, 1:66, 1:82, 1:86, 1:113, 1:137–38, 1:141, 1:145, 1:166–67, 1:192–93, 1:196–99, 1:210, 1:222, 2:28, 2:44n25, 2:53, 2:66, 2:73, 2:104, 2:121, 2:132,

2:136, 2:146, 2:160, 2:188, 2:204, 2:210, 2:217, 2:235, 2:238
Arbitration, 1:111–18, 1:120
Asceticism, ascetic, 1:50, 1:137–38, 1:190, 1:195, 1:211, 1:214
Authority
  apostolic, 1:xiv, 1:2–3, 1:5–8, 1:21, 1:53–62, 1:97, 1:146, 1:148–49, 1:159, 1:166–67, 1:196–98, 2:125, 2:188–89, 2:245n15
  of believers, 1:181–82, 1:185–88, 1:193, 2:21, 2:37n19, 2:45, 2:189, 2:233–36,
  of Christ, 1:34n49, 1:57, 1:150, 2:207
  of custom, 1:5–9, 1:29, 2:29–30, 2:33
  of Holy Spirit, 2:181, 2:185
  of law, 1:109, 1:115n4, 1:122, 2:89n14, 2:130
  of scripture, 2:198–201
  of spouse, 1:139–41, 2:39–41, 2:55–56
Authorship, 1:2, 1:6n9, 2:245

Baptism, baptismal, 1:4n6, 1:22–23, 1:91, 1:102–4, 1:110, 1:121–22, 1:155–56, 1:155n23, 1:177, 2:2–3, 2:12n10, 2:66, 2:87, 2:99, 2:148, 2:197, 2:201, 2:209–10, 2:221–22, 2:226n51
Belief, believe, 1:xvi, 1:5, 1:14, 1:33, 1:47, 1:47n12, 1:66, 1:68, 1:88, 1:127, 1:139, 1:167, 1:182, 1:184–85, 1:188, 1:220, 2:viii, 2:19, 2:21, 2:48, 2:66, 2:68, 2:106, 2:133, 2:137–38, 2:140, 2:142, 2:146, 2:175, 2:193, 2:195, 2:196n8, 2:197, 2:199, 2:201–2, 2:204, 2:211, 2:221, 2:225, 2:227, 2:241n10,

261

Subject Index

Belong, 1:18–19, 1:21, 1:25, 1:63, 1:65, 1:73–75, 1:122, 1:128, 1:135, 1:148, 1:151, 1:154, 1:168, 1:175n6, 2:32, 2:37, 2:76n3, 2:86, 2:91, 2:99–104, 2:107, 2:112, 2:131, 2:164, 2:168, 2:182, 2:195n7, 2:205–6
Bible, 1:xvi, 1:xviin3, 1:22n36, 1:68n6, 1:83n15, 1:135n31, 1:194n5, 1:195, 1:218, 2:vii–viii, 2:231, 2:242
Biblical, 1:xiii–xiv, 1:xviin2, 1:44, 1:48, 1:54–55, 1:60–62, 1:71, 1:74, 1:80, 1:88–89, 1:194n21, 1:108–10, 1:136n1, 1:158, 1:177, 1:198, 1:202, 2:vii–viii, 2:2–5, 2:13, 2:29, 2:40–41, 2:44n25, 2:46n34, 2:59, 2:80, 2:93, 2:112, 2:124, 2:126, 2:129, 2:139, 2:152, 2:155n5, 2:185, 2:207, 2:211, 2:221, 2:231, 2:233, 2:240
Boasting, 1:xviii, 1:1, 1:14, 1:37, 1:45n7, 1:72–73, 1:80, 1:83, 1:93–94, 1:102, 1:133, 1:203–5, 1:210n25, 1:215, 2:131, 2:135, 2:137, 2:139, 2:184n36, 2:194, 2:209
Body, bodiliness
    baptizing, 1:156
    biological, 1:29, 1:40n2, 1:213–214, 2:30–33, 2:42–4, 2:52, 2:75–76, 2:85–94, 2:111–13, 2:131, 2:137, 2:242
    flesh, 1:106–7, 2:35, 2:194–6, 2:199–200, 2:210–26
    healing of, 1:64, 2:205–6, 2:213–220
    human, 1:xiii, 1:xviin2, 1:97, 2:72
    owning one's own, 1:125–31, 1:135–36, 1:138–40, 1:142, 1:151–52, 1:221–22, 2:69–70
Body of Christ
    calling into, 1:9, 1:59, 1:176, 1:199, 1:213
    church as, 1:xviii, 1:xviin2, 2:10, 2:50
    and communion, 1:103–104, 1:108, 1:134, 2:17–18, 2:52, 2:56–60, 2:88
    conformity to, 1:93–97, 1:189, 1:216, 2:72
    discerning of, 1:64, 1:100–104, 1:116, 2:50, 2:60–66, 2:142
    dividing of, 1:25, 1:31–32, 1:57, 1:118–19, 1:122–25, 1:146
    pneumatic quality, 2:74, 2:79, 2:83–123, 2:92–95, 2:101–6, 2:117, 2:120–25, 2:156n8
    self-healing capacity, 1:xiii–xiv
    social essence, 1:50, 1:187, 2:94–99, 2:162, 2:165
    upbuilding of, 1:20–23, 1:166, 1:182, 2:160, 2:168–69, 2:171–73, 2:179
    universal, 1:74–75, 2:148–49, 2:228–29
Bread, 1:102–5, 1:108, 1:213, 2:2–4, 2:16, 2:18, 2:52–3, 2:56, 2:58–61, 2:99, 2:201
Building up (see also *oikodome*), 1:xix, 1:67, 1:109, 1:166, 1:171, 1:186–87, 2:19–20, 2:65, 2:135, 2:150, 2:153, 2:157, 2:160, 2:162, 2:166, 2:168, 2:173, 2:176 2:178–79
Buyer, buy, 1:16, 1:158, 1:162–64, 1:194

Canon, canonical, 1:xv, 1:23, 1:47, 1:62, 1:74, 1:117, 1:120, 2:42, 2:122, 2:130, 2:145, 2:190, 2:231
Casuistry, casuistic, 1:38, 1:99
Cartesian, 1:xvi, 1:40, 1:139, 1:157n25
Celibacy, celibate, 1:136–37, 1:137n3, 1:140n9, 1:141–43, 1:143n12, 1:149, 1:152, 1:155n23, 1:165, 1:197, 2:41
Chastity, chaste, 1:89, 1:136–37, 1:136n2, 1:141–142, 1:144, 1:146–56, 1:164, 1:166–68, 1:206
Child, 1:xviin2, 1:6n8, 1:8, 1:67, 1:77n3, 1:82, 1:85–86, 1:107, 1:133, 1:147, 1:152–53, 1:155, 1:155n23, 1:161, 1:218, 2:69, 2:116–17, 2:143, 2:145, 2:147, 2:164, 2:245
Chronos, chronological, 1:160–62, 1:167–68
Christology, christological, 1:40, 1:40nn1–2, 1:49, 1:54n16, 1:95, 1:213, 2:18, 2:41, 2:60, 2:85, 2:90, 2:145–46, 2:154, 2:194, 2:207, 2:226

Circumcision, circumcise, 1:147, 1:149, 1:151, 1:161
Coauthor, 1:xxi, 2:245
Commandment, 1:16, 1:114, 1:122, 1:148-49, 1:165, 2:130
Commentary, 1:ix-x, 1:xiii-xv, 1:xxi-xxii, 1:53-54, 1:61, 1:157, 1:201, 2:x, 2:84, 2:100, 2:114, 2:125, 2:189n41, 2:233, 2:245
Commodity, commodification, 1:20-21, 1:34n49
Communication, communicant, 1:27, 1:29, 1:39, 1:44-45, 1:53, 1:89, 1:104n23, 1:107, 1:122, 1:129-30, 1:132n29, 1:134-35, 1:157, 1:180, 1:186, 1:209, 1:218, 2:11n9, 2:43, 2:72-3, 2:75-6, 2:89, 2:91, 2:93, 2:95-6, 2:111-12, 2:116, 2:122, 2:130, 2:135-8, 2:161-4, 2:233, 2:239, 2:241
Community
　apostle's role in, 1:7-19, 1:197n6, 2:27-28, 2:139, 2:237-39, 2:245
　conflict in, 1:xviii-xix, 1:4-5, 1:18-22, 1:63-64, 1:67, 1:75-76, 1:86-87, 1:91-96, 1:169, 1:181, 2:53, 2:63, 2:105
　covenant, 1:9n13, 1:118-19
　discerning, 1:49-51, 1:53-57, 1:72n12, 1:78, 1:84, 1:98-106, 1:108-10, 1:167, 2:70 2:119, 2:176-77
　eschatological, 2:216
　eucharistic/baptismal, 1:133-34, 1:146, 1:156, 2:226-27
　of faith, 2:vii-viii
　gendered, 2:34, 2:43, 2:46
　kononia, 1:24-26, 1:30-31
　of peace, 2:72-74, 2:98-99, 2:168-69, 2:183
　pneumatic, 2:84, 2:91-95, 2:103, 2:111-13, 2:115-17, 2:132-33, 2:151-53, 2:157-59
　of service, 2:9, 2:13, 2:122-25, 2:129, 2:135, 2:142, 2:227
　unity of, 1:36-37, 1:112, 1:125, 1:187, 1:196-97, 1:210, 1:222-25, 2:17, 2:78-80, 2:86-87, 2:229
　virtual, 1:45n9, 1:84n16
Competition, competitiveness, competitive, 1:15, 1:20, 1:71, 1:141, 1:190, 1:214, 1:224-225, 1:224n49, 2:158, 2:173
Concession, 1:7, 1:15, 1:113, 1:116, 1:136-138, 1:141-143, 1:145-146, 1:165-166, 2:65, 2:162
Condescension, condescending, 1:xxii, 1:113, 1:119, 2:22, 2:171
Confession, confessional, 1:xvii-xviii, 1:17-18, 1:154, 1:156, 1:176-178, 1:183, 1:188-189, 2:vii, 2:56, 2:74-6, 2:98-9, 2:101, 2:108, 2:136-7, 2:175, 2:177-8, 2:220, 2:234
Conflict, conflicted, conflictual, 1:ix-x, 1:xii, 1:xix, 1:2, 1:2n4, 1:4, 1:6-7, 1:12-13, 1:16, 1:18-19, 1:25, 1:28, 1:30-31, 1:34, 1:37, 1:39, 1:42, 1:57, 1:112-113, 1:115, 1:151, 1:176n8, 1:213n37, 2:vii, 2:17, 2:29, 2:30, 2:88n11, 2:94-5, 2:243, 2:246
Conformation, conformity, conform, 1:xiv, 1:32-33, 1:72, 1:78, 1:93, 1:163, 1:175-176, 1:178-179, 1:184, 1:201, 1:212-214, 1:216, 1:223, 2:44, 2:93, 2:132, 2:143, 2:157, 2:239
Congregation, congregationalism, 1:xix, 1:xxi, 1:6, 1:8, 1:14, 1:57, 1:75, 1:85-86, 1:99-101, 1:109n25, 1:124-125, 1:144, 2:20, 2:34, 2:36, 2:38, 2:40, 2:42, 2:46, 2:48, 2:52, 2:54, 2:62-3, 2:77, 2:81, 2:106-9, 2:115, 2:125, 2:131, 2:159-60, 2:167, 2:175, 2:178, 2:182-3, 2:185, 2:203, 2:210, 2:229, 2:235, 2:244
Conscience, 1:70, 1:78, 1:116, 1:119-121, 1:169-170, 1:171n1, 1:173, 1:176, 1:176n8, 1:179-184, 1:186, 1:188-189, 1:206, 2:14, 2:19-26, 2:51, 2:61, 2:176n27
Convention, 1:xiii, 1:xviin3, 1:8, 1:53, 1:145, 1:197, 2:viii, 2:x, 2:29-30, 2:32, 2:87, 2:110-11, 2:116

Subject Index

Conversion, 1:xxii, 1:2–3, 1:7, 2:14, 2:44n25, 2:176–77, 2:203, 2:242
Conviction, 1:x, 1:xv, 1:xvii, 1:58–59, 1:157, 1:166, 1:183–84, 2:93, 2:176
Counsel, 1:15, 1:89, 1:114, 1:145, 1:161, 1:164–65, 1:205
Court, 1:7, 1:76, 1:79, 1:108, 1:111–17, 1:119–23, 1:125, 1:127, 1:218
Covenant, covenantal, 1:9n13, 1:33, 1:100n16, 1:123, 1:140, 1:155, 1:172, 2:41n23, 2:56, 2:59, 2:87–8, 2:91–92, 2:94–95, 2:113
Co-worker, 1:1, 1:66, 2:34n15
Creation, creator, create, creaturely
  of church, 1:7–8, 1:38, 1:84n16, 1:92, 2:100, 2:122–23, 2:133, 2:137–38
  of culture/cultural artifacts, 2:69–70, 2:107–12
  epistemological limits, 1:52, 1:138, 1:139n6, 1:157–58, 1:168, 1:172–73, 2:65–66, 2:166
  existence, 1:175–80, 2:40–41
  of faith, 1:43, 1:50, 2:vii, 2:3,
  God's investment in, 2:60–61, 2:144–45, 2:147–48, 2:199
  hermeneutic of, 2:21–23, 2:29
  power, spheres of, 2:17–19, 2:98
  reconciled creatures, 1:24, 1:72, 1:105, 1:152–53, 1:185, 1:216, 2:38, 2:162–64, 2:176, 2:206–8, 2:214–20, 2:222–24, 2:225
  of sexes, 2:41–48, 2:186–88, 2:190
  and time, 1:160–63
  wisdom, 1:29–31
Criticism, critic, criticize, critical,
  Apostle's, 1:xxii, 1:1n3, 1:10n17, 1:21, 1:26, 1:60–62, 1:80, 2:23, 2:32–34, 2:48–49, 2:52, 2:72–73, 2:118, 2:135–36, 2:141, 2:155, 2:173, 2:177–78
  contemporary cultural hermeneutic, 1:57, 1:77, 1:121 ,1:164–65, 1:189, 2:28, 2:62, 2:68–69, 2:81, 2:104–5, 2:167–68
  exegetical methodology, 1:xvi–xviii, 1:xx, 1:11, 1:40, 1:54, 1:88–89, 1:153, 1:155n23, 2:vii–x, 2:12, 2:196
  Jesus', 2:130
  of Paul, 1:45
  vs. theological thinking, 1:60–62
Cross, 1:13–14, 1:23–24, 1:26–31, 1:34–36, 1:41, 1:46, 1:95, 1:195, 2:22, 2:74n1, 2:98, 2:148, 2:156, 2:176n26, 2:194, 2:199–200, 2:206, 2:214, 2:241
Crucifixion, crucify, crucified, 1:xiv, 1:21–22, 1:25–26, 1:27n42, 1:29, 1:31–32, 1:35–37, 1:39–41, 1:42, 1:44, 1:45n8, 1:46–47, 1:53–54, 1:60, 1:80–81, 1:135, 1:151, 1:157, 1:214, 2:194, 2:208, 2:222, 2:227
Cruciformity, cruciform, 1:25, 1:27, 1:37, 1:41–42, 1:46–47, 1:53, 2:193
Culture, cultural, 1:xiv, 1:20, 1:47, 1:55–56, 1:58–59, 1:127, 1:130, 1:132–34, 1:137n3, 1:139, 1:189, 1:191, 1:194–95, 1:197, 1:204, 1:207, 1:211, 1:213–21, 1:224, 2:ix–x, 2:12, 2:27–37, 2:42–5, 2:48, 2:55, 2:64–71, 2:75, 2:107, 2:109, 2:112, 2:117–18, 2:151, 2:155–57, 2:160–62, 2:184, 2:189, 2:190–91, 2:210, 2:216n33, 2:218, 2:228

Decalogue, 1:16
Deism, deist, 1:46
Democracy, democratic, 1:21n33, 1:75, 1:198n8, 2:vii, 2:95, 2:229
Die, dying, 1:25, 1:180–81, 1:203–4, 2:6, 2:193–94, 2:196, 2:198–99, 2:205, 2:209–10, 2:213–15, 2:220, 2:222, 2:224–27, 2:232
Diet, dietary, 1:xix–xx, 1:124
Discernment, discern, 1:xv–xvii, 1:24, 1:27, 1:39, 1:50, 1:51–53, 1:55–57, 1:60, 1:63–64, 1:67, 1:69, 1:74, 1:83, 1:96–97, 1:99, 1:108, 1:119, 1:158–59, 1:162, 1:166–68, 1:193, 1:199–200, 1:217, 2:1, 2:11, 2:15, 2:28–29, 2:34, 2:37, 2:47, 2:50, 2:60–66, 2:70–71, 2:74, 2:78–79, 2:81–83, 2:95, 2:101, 2:111, 2:117, 2:119,

Subject Index

2:121–22, 2:125, 2:142, 2:147, 2:156, 2:171, 2:181–82, 2:188, 2:191, 2:237, 2:246
Discipline, 1:xvi–xvii, 1:23, 1:50, 1:61, 1:98n11, 1:99, 1:104, 1:104n21, 1:110, 1:138, 1:141, 1:143–44, 1:152, 1:190–93, 1:211–14, 1:216, 2:34n15, 2:45, 2:61, 2:185, 2:213, 2:226
Discovery, discover, 1:ix–x, 1:xiii, 1:xv–xvii, 1:xx–xxii, 1:1, 1:4, 1:7–8, 1:11, 1:14, 1:17, 1:30, 1:34, 1:51, 1:56, 1:58n21, 1:59, 1:61–62, 1:72, 1:88–89, 1:98, 1:104n22, 1:110, 1:118, 1:146, 1:151–52, 1:155, 1:157, 1:187, 1:198, 1:201, 1:211, 1:213, 1:219, 2:3–4, 2:79, 2:115–17, 2:119, 2:156n8
Dispute, 1:xviii, 1:6–7, 1:11–13, 1:19, 1:28, 1:50, 1:67, 1:74, 1:91, 1:111–14, 1:116–20, 1:126, 1:170, 2:11, 2:35, 2:37, 2:70, 2:82, 2:102, 2:157, 2:190n41, 2:211, 2:240, 2:243
Divorce, 1:34, 1:146–48, 2:94
Death, 1:29, 1:40n2, 1:69, 1:73–74, 1:81, 1:83, 1:100n15, 1:160, 1:176n8, 2:56, 2:60–61, 2:64, 2:66–69, 2:94, 2:144, 2:162, 2:193, 2:195, 2:198–200, 2:203–13, 2:215, 2:219–20, 2:222–27, 2:246
Doctrine, doctrinal, 1:xv, 1:xviii, 1:96, 1:161, 1:176–78, 1:183–86, 1:188n14, 1:205, 1:207, 1:224n49, 2:21–22, 2:29, 2:44, 2:47, 2:82, 2:86, 2:111, 2:193
Donatist, 1:4, 1:103
Doubt, 1:xvi, 1:40, 1:158n27, 2:25, 2:40, 2:109, 2:114, 2:154n4, 2:166, 2:199, 2:202, 2:238, 2:245
Dough, 1:93, 1:101–4, 1:103n18, 1:106, 1:108
Doxology, doxological, 1:9–14, 1:16–17, 1:19, 1:26, 1:38, 1:64, 1:79–80, 2:167
Duty, 1:70, 1:120, 1:140, 1:146, 1:206n19, 2:23n20

Eat, 1:xviii, 1:58, 1:64, 1:107–8, 1:124, 1:127, 1:170, 1:173, 1:176, 1:178, 1:180–83, 1:185, 1:204, 2:5, 2:16, 2:20–22, 2:24–25, 2:51, 2:53, 2:55–56, 2:60–2, 2:64–66, 2:71, 2:186, 2:209, 2:210
Ecclesia, ecclesial, ecclesiastical, 1:xviii, 1:xxi, 1:7–8, 1:15–16, 1:24–15, 1:37n53, 1:38, 1:60, 1:66, 1:69, 1:73, 1:76, 1:95–96, 1:99, 1:101, 1:105, 1:109, 1:111–17, 1:119, 1:125, 1:134, 1:216, 1:225, 2:ix, 2:34, 2:48, 2:50, 2:52, 2:54, 2:63, 2:79, 2:80, 2:95, 2:104, 2:113, 2:115, 2:122, 2:135, 2:156n8, 2:167–68, 2:181n31, 2:182, 2:212, 2:219, 2:227, 2:229, 2:230, 2:242
Ecclesiology, ecclesiological, 1:xx, 1:4n7, 1:35–36, 1:49, 2:18, 2:49, 2:50, 2:92, 2:98–99, 2:105–6, 2:109
Economy, economic, 1:15, 1:34, 1:54, 1:56, 1:73, 1:79, 1:124, 1:161–63, 1:179, 1:185, 1:207, 1:209, 1:210n25, 1:224, 2:40, 2:54, 2:97–8, 2:101, 2:142, 2:160, 2:222
Empiricism, empirical, 1:12, 1:14, 1:32, 1:97–98, 1:157n25, 2:123, 2:198–99
Epistemological, 1:27, 1:36, 1:54n16, 1:157
Epistle, epistolary, 1:xiv–xvii, 1:xx, 1:xxii, 1:1–2, 1:5, 1:8, 1:11, 1:16, 1:23, 1:35, 1:57, 1:62, 2:42n24, 2:140, 2:144, 2:177, 2:190, 2:192, 2:230, 2:246
Eschatology, eschatological, 1:xix, 1:23, 1:29, 1:82–83, 1:126, 1:161, 1:210–13, 1:210n25, 1:219, 1:222, 2:43, 2:46, 2:68, 2:163, 2:207–8, 2:211, 2:216–17, 2:244
Exegesis, exegete, exegetical, 1:xiii–xvii, 1:xx–xxi, 1:3n5, 1:44, 1:54, 1:58, 1:60–61, 1:73, 1:88–90, 1:99, 1:107n24, 1:111, 1:128, 1:130, 1:136, 1:145, 1:150, 1:158, 1:163n29, 2:vii, 2:2, 2:26, 2:39, 2:42, 2:125–27, 2:140, 2:162–63, 2:190, 2:208, 2:233, 2:245

Subject Index

Exousia, 1:124, 1:140, 1:181, 1:193, 1:196, 1:199, 1:222, 2:45
Experience, 1:xiii, 1:xv, 1:xvii, 1:7, 1:13, 1:26, 1:30, 1:34n48, 1:52, 1:61–62, 1:78, 1:91n1, 1:135, 1:139, 1:158, 1:160–61, 1:164, 1:169, 1:172–73, 1:176n8, 1:189–90, 1:208, 1:217, 2:2–3, 2:9, 2:15, 2:33–36, 2:56, 2:72, 2:74–75, 2:88, 2:109, 2:114, 2:116–17, 2:126, 2:129, 2:131, 2:141, 2:145, 2:148 2:151, 2:161–65, 2:198, 2:200–201, 2:218, 2:223, 2:234, 2:242, 2:245
Explanation, explain, explanatory
  of apostolic credentials, 1:7–8, 1:43, 1:56, 1:193, 1:196, 1:215, 1:222
  biblical verses, 1:45, 1:88, 1:136, 1:160–61, 1:166, 2:52, 2:126, 2:241–42
  of Corinthian misunderstanding, 2:159, 2:165, 2:173, 2:188
  intertextual, 1:xvi–xvii, 1:xxi, 1:109, 2:2–3
  of Pauline intent, 1:90, 1:93, 1:137n3, 1:154–55, 1:157, 1:163–64, 1:184, 2:237
  psychological, 1:172, 2:ix, 2:9, 2:16–17, 2:245
Ethics, ethical, 1:xviiin4, 1:xx, 1:4n7, 1:14, 1:38, 1:40n1, 1:50, 1:92, 1:94, 1:98–99, 1:106, 1:129, 1:135, 1:146, 1:166, 1:169, 1:189–91, 1:191n1, 1:209n23, 1:212, 1:212nn32–33, 1:213, 1:224, 2:1, 2:38, 2:124n48, 2:128, 2:130, 2:169n19, 2:222n41
Ethos, 1:xiv, 1:xviii, 1:6, 1:54n15, 1:64n3, 1:80n6, 1:92–94, 1:100–101, 1:103–4, 1:110, 1:114–15, 1:118, 1:120, 1:122, 1:127, 1:135
Eucharist, eucharistic, 1:64, 1:95, 1:100, 1:102, 1:104–5, 1:108, 1:110, 1:127, 1:134–35, 1:221, 2:11–12, 2:14–18, 2:25, 2:36, 2:49–53, 2:55–6, 2:58–62, 2:65–71, 2:85, 2:87–88, 2:99, 2:159, 2:243
Evangelism, 1:218–19

Excommunication, 1:77n3, 1:99–101, 1:102n17, 1:104
Existence, 1:3, 1:8–9, 1:29–30, 1:36, 1:40n2, 1:63, 1:71, 1:79, 1:94, 1:111–13, 1:117, 1:125, 1:128, 1:131, 1:135, 1:139, 1:150, 1:153, 1:155, 1:157, 1:162–63, 1:168, 1:173–75, 1:178–79, 1:181, 1:189, 1:196, 1:220–21, 1:223, 2:12, 2:36n16, 2:38, 2:52, 2:66–67, 2:70, 2:74, 2:76, 2:84, 2:86, 2:88n11, 2:91–92, 2:97, 2:100, 2:102, 2:113–14, 2:132, 2:137, 2:147, 2:163, 2:172, 2:178, 2:193, 2:196, 2:202, 2:208–9, 2:211, 2:214–18, 2:221

Faction, factionalism, 1:xiv, 1:xviii–xix, 1:1, 1:4, 1:6–7, 1:9, 1:12–14, 1:19–21, 1:23–25, 1:31–32, 1:34, 1:36, 1:46, 1:63, 1:65–66, 1:69–74, 1:76, 1:80, 1:188, 2:48, 2:50, 2:56, 2:59, 2:105, 2:194, 2:232, 2:238, 2:244
Faith
  acts of, 1:42n4, 1:100, 1:176n8, 1:214n38, 2:137–43, 2:227
  collectivity of, 1:9–10, 1:19–20, 1:119, 1:153–154, 2:vii–viii, 2:158–160, 2:165
  in error, 1:36, 1:50, 1:176, 2:151
  faithfulness, 1:77–81, 1:210n25, 1:212–14, 2:2, 2:10, 2:48, 2:58, 2:73, 2:94, 2:111 2:218–20, 2:230, 2:232, 2:245
  faithlessness, 1:15–16, 2:34
  formative power, 1:184–85, 1:189–91, 1:207, 2:91
  gift, 1:46, 1:49, 1:157, 2:81, 2:83–84, 2:133
  God's, 1:12–14, 2:6–8, 2:12–13, 2:15, 2:25, 2:40, 2:148, 2:199
  hermeneutic of, 1:59–60, 1:84, 1:99, 1:167, 1:175n6, 1:178–79
  hope and love, 2:142–49, 2:224
  in Jesus, 1:xx, 1:43, 2:114, 2:130–31, 2:202, 2:213, 2:244
  maturity of, 1:67, 2:19, 2:121, 2:156, 2:178

Subject Index

parents in, 1:73–74
in resurrection, 2:197–200
rule of, 1:xviii, 1:xii, 2:133
sin, opposite of, 2:25, 2:65
Family, familial, 1:ix–xi, 1:86, 1:118–19, 1:169, 1:172, 1:180–81, 1:187–88, 1:194–95, 2:34, 2:36, 2:69, 2:128, 2:159, 2:234
Father, fatherhood, fatherly, 1:xxi, 1:3, 1:5–6, 1:8, 1:14, 1:17, 1:21, 1:26, 1:28–29, 1:34n49, 1:43, 1:47, 1:75, 1:82, 1:85–88, 1:91–92, 1:94, 1:95, 1:173, 1:178–79, 1:194–96, 1:218, 2:39–41, 2:60, 2:76, 2:116–18, 2:121, 2:148, 2:163, 2:203, 2:205, 2:207–8
Fathers (Church), 1:21n32, 1:35, 1:45, 1:46n10, 1:61, 1:64, 1:74, 1:76, 1:136n2, 1:197, 2:31, 2:89, 2:208n24, 2:231, 2:240
Flight, flee, 1:90, 1:129, 1:131–35, 1:132n29, 1:150–51, 1:168, 2:13–15, 2:17
Freedom, 1:32, 1:78, 1:88, 1:94, 1:117, 1:134, 1:148, 1:151, 1:153n20, 1:167, 1:181, 1:183, 1:187–88, 1:190–195, 1:200–201, 1:203–7, 1:206n17, 1:209–11, 1:215–17, 1:219, 1:222, 2:10, 2:22, 2:26, 2:30, 2:36, 2:45, 2:68, 2:75, 2:131, 2:183
Friend, 1:x–xi, 2:9, 2:23–24, 2:34, 2:216, 2:218, 2:220, 2:242
Food, 1:16–17, 1:58, 1:63–64, 1:104–5, 1:124–26, 1:131, 1:169–70, 1:173, 1:176, 1:179–83, 1:185, 1:187–88, 1:191, 1:195–97, 2:1–2, 2:10–12, 2:14–17, 2:19–21, 2:23–24, 2:26, 2:52, 2:54, 2:60, 2:89, 2:94, 2:97, 2:243
Folly, fool, foolishness, 1:13–14, 1:23, 1:24, 1:26–29, 1:31, 1:32–33, 1:35–36, 1:51, 1:54, 1:71–72, 1:77n3, 1:81, 1:84–85, 2:22, 2:113, 2:120, 2:140, 2:193–4, 2:197, 2:212
Formation, 1:x, 1:40n1, 1:153, 1:184, 1:189, 1:211, 2:113, 2:158n11, 2:164

Fornication, 1:125–26, 1:128–31
Foundation, foundational, 1:65–68, 1:70, 1:78, 1:85, 1:87, 1:97, 1:129, 1:174, 1:188, 1:196, 2:84, 2:89, 2:95, 2:102, 2:114, 2:126, 2:148, 2:164, 2:196
Foundationalist, 1:33

Gift, 1:xix, 1:8–10, 1:12–16, 1:19–20, 1:28, 1:31, 1:38, 1:40, 1:48–49, 1:51–52, 1:75, 1:80–81, 1:84, 1:101, 1:134–35, 1:142–43, 1:156, 1:158, 1:164, 1:180n9, 1:208, 1:211, 1:214, 1:218, 1:224, 2:76–85
Gnosis, Gnosticism, gnostic, 1:13, 1:15, 1:24–25, 1:27–29, 1:46–47, 1:47nn11–12, 1:50–52, 1:57, 1:59–61, 1:73, 1:135, 1:143n12, 1:176, 1:186–87, 1:189, 2:209n25
Golden Calf, 1:71, 1:73, 2:11, 2:13
Gospel, 1:ix, 1:xvii–xviii, 1:10–11, 1:23, 1:26, 1:27n42, 1:28, 1:34n49, 1:36–37, 1:64, 1:69, 1:77n3, 1:85–86, 1:92, 1:101, 1:119n10, 1:147, 1:149, 1:185, 1:191–96, 1:198–211, 1:213, 1:215–24, 2:37–38, 2:41, 2:49, 2:56, 2:60, 2:63, 2:66–70, 2:73, 2:83–84, 2:108, 2:112–3, 2:130, 2:136–37, 1:157, 2:161, 2:174–76, 2:178, 2:180, 2:189, 2:193, 2:196–99, 2:203–4, 2:208, 2:227, 2:234, 2:236–38, 2:242
Grace, 1:3, 1:8–9, 1:11–12, 1:16–17, 1:25–26, 1:41, 1:53, 1:64–66, 1:105, 1:150, 1:153, 1:206, 1:220, 2:74, 2:88, 2:109, 2:136, 2:190, 2:195, 2:227, 2:234–35, 2:237–38, 2:243–44
Greed, greedy, 1:105–8, 1:121
Greeks, 1:31–33, 1:35, 1:54, 1:107, 1:160, 2:25, 2:85, 2:87–88, 2:91, 2:95, 2:97–98
Growth, 1:34, 1:65–66, 1:68, 1:152, 1:176, 1:183, 1:190, 2:9, 2:142–43, 2:168, 2:203, 2:219, 2:227,

Habit, habituation, habitual, 1:x, 1:xv, 1:xvii, 1:xx, 1:9, 1:15, 1:54, 1:55, 1:57, 1:76, 1:107n24, 1:110, 1:124, 1:132, 1:135, 1:147, 1:150, 1:153–54, 1:176, 1:179, 1:181, 1:184, 1:189–90, 1:201, 1:211–12, 1:214, 1:218, 2:10–11, 2:19, 2:29–30, 2:37, 2:43–44, 2:46, 2:51, 2:67–69, 2:72, 2:95, 2:119, 2:157, 2:184, 2:191, 2:194, 2:211, 2:218, 2:245–46

Heart, 1:xviin3, 1:xix, 1:38, 1:48, 1:76, 1:77n3, 1:79, 1:109, 1:175, 1:175n6, 1:184, 1:195, 1:217, 2:10, 2:14, 2:37, 2:53, 2:58, 2:83, 2:89, 2:92–93, 2:97, 2:109, 2:132, 2:133, 2:138, 2:140, 2:165, 2:174, 2:176, 2:200

Hellenistic, 1:13, 1:146, 2:11–12, 2:18–19, 2:44, 2:54, 2:66, 2:71, 2:75, 2:78, 2:88, 2:155, 2:196

Hermeneutic(s), hermeneutic, hermeneutical, 1:xiii–xvi, 1:44, 1:58–59, 1:60n22, 1:87, 1:89, 1:109, 1:109n26, 1:145, 1:184, 1:201–2, 1:211, 2:2–3, 2:32, 2:232

Heroic, 1:190, 1:193–95, 2:226

Historicist, 1:53

History, historical, 1:x, 1:xvii, 1:xx, 1:2, 1:11, 1:45–46, 1:47n12, 1:48, 1:53–57, 1:59–61, 1:67, 1:69, 1:94, 1:96, 1:112, 1:137n3, 1:143n12, 1:155n23, 1:168, 1:197n6, 1:201, 2:vii–x, 2:2, 2:5, 2:12, 2:14, 2:18, 2:27, 2:31, 2:34–35, 2:39, 2:43, 2:49, 2:54, 2:59, 2:61, 2:67, 2:69, 2:89, 2:95, 2:102, 2:111–12, 2:121, 2:126, 2:151, 2:156–57, 2:185, 2:188–89, 2:196, 2:198–99, 2:204, 2:207–8, 2:214, 2:218, 2:233

Homiletic, 1:xxi, 2:182n32

Homosexual, 1:112

Hope, hopeful, 1:xvi–xvii, 1:1, 1:11–12, 1:14, 1:26, 1:29, 1:34, 1:72–73, 1:79, 1:82, 1:84n16, 1:99–101, 1:118, 1:127–28, 1:131, 1:137, 1:144, 1:152, 1:154, 1:157, 1:163–64, 1:169, 1:175, 1:187, 1:191, 1:196–98, 1:202, 1:210–12, 1:222–23, 2:2, 2:8–9, 2:15, 2:25, 2:133, 2:140, 2:142–43, 2:148–49, 2:186, 2:197–98, 2:200–201, 2:203–4, 2:207, 2:211, 2:213, 2:216, 2:224–27, 2:35–36, 2:238, 2:246

Horizon, 1:xiii, 1:xx–xxi, 1:29, 1:46, 1:59, 1:74, 1:89, 1:95, 1:103, 1:106, 1:128, 1:144, 1:185, 1:210–11, 1:222n45, 2:48, 2:207, 2:219

Household, 1:21–22, 1:76, 2:209n25, 2:240–41

Husband, 1:128, 1:136, 1:139–41, 1:147, 1:152, 1:159, 1:165–66, 1:218, 1:221, 2:33, 2:39–40, 2:89, 2:179, 2:186

Idealism, idealist, 1:114, 1:157, 1:190

Identity, 1:3, 1:18–19, 1:56, 1:59, 1:93, 1:114, 1:219, 2:98–99, 2:101–2, 2:132, 2:163, 2:214–17, 2:219–20

Idol, 1:58, 1:71, 1:124, 1:169–70, 1:173–83, 1:185, 1:187, 1:189, 1:192, 1:204, 2:1, 2:13–16, 2:21, 2:24–26, 2:74–75, 2:97, 2:107–8, 2:110

Idolatry, idolater, idolatrous, 1:xviii, 1:19–20, 1:64, 1:69–73, 1:99n13, 1:105, 1:107, 1:121, 1:152, 1:189, 2:5, 2:12–15, 2:17, 2:19, 2:24–25, 2:69, 2:75, 2:107, 2:109

Imitation, imitator, 1:56, 1:85–86, 2:8, 2:25, 2:141, 2:146, 2:158

Immorality, immoral, 1:4, 1:91–92, 1:101, 1:105–7, 1:122, 1:128–30, 1:135–36, 1:141–42, 1:218

Indicative-imperative-scheme, 1:12, 1:38, 1:103

Individualist, individualistic, 1:9, 1:20, 1:22, 1:123, 1:135, 1:180, 1:210, 2:9, 2:41, 2:160, 2:165, 2:204

Infant, 1:63, 1:155, 2:164, 2:170

Intercourse, 1:137, 1:139, 1:141–42, 2:160–61, 2:172

Subject Index

Interpretation, interpretative, 1:xiii, 1:xv–xvi, 1:xx–xxii, 1:10–12, 1:30, 1:47n12, 1:49, 1:61–62, 1:67, 1:77, 1:80–81, 1:87–91, 1:105–6, 1:108, 1:110–11, 1:113–17, 1:129–30, 1:132, 1:141, 1:145, 1:162, 1:165, 1:174, 1:190, 1:196, 1:198, 1:200–203, 1:208, 1:210, 1:221–22, 2:vii–x, 2:2–3, 2:7–8, 2:21, 2:27, 2:37, 2:39, 2:41–42, 2:46, 2:62–63, 2:81, 2:97, 2:124–25, 2:128–30, 2:132, 2:136, 2:151, 2:155, 2:160, 2:162–63, 2:165, 2:167–69, 2:171–72, 2:174–79, 2:185–90, 2:202, 2:207, 2:222, 2:230, 2:239, 2:245

Intimacy, intimate, 1:87, 1:97, 1:129–30, 1:138, 1:140, 1:146, 1:193, 2:23, 2:35, 2:70, 2:72, 2:83, 2:147, 2:160–62, 2:165, 2:169, 2:244

Irony, ironic, ironical, 1:xxii, 1:2–3, 1:10, 1:16, 1:32–33, 1:36, 1:44–47, 1:45n7, 1:52, 1:81, 1:81n7, 1:82–85, 1:87–88, 1:97, 1:124, 1:134, 1:143, 2:11, 2:34, 2:50, 2:69, 2:107, 2:109, 2:124, 2:135, 2:185, 2:210–11, 2:223

Jew, Jewry, Jewish, 1:31–33, 1:33n46, 1:34n49, 1:35, 1:45n8, 1:47n12, 1:54–56, 1:56n19, 1:101n16, 1:108, 1:112, 1:146, 1:214, 1:216, 1:219–220, 2:vii, 2:25, 2:29, 2:30, 2:34–36, 2:44–45, 2:59, 2:85, 2:87–88, 2:91, 2:97–98, 2:138, 2:155, 2:172, 2:180, 2:183, 2:186, 2:196, 2:234

Judge, 1:xiii, 1:44, 1:58, 1:60, 1:67–69, 1:76–78, 1:77n3, 1:80, 1:89, 1:97, 1:105–6, 1:111–13, 1:116, 1:121, 1:150, 1:170, 1:187, 2:13, 2:16, 2:19, 2:24, 2:32–33, 2:47, 2:51, 2:61, 2:64, 2:68, 2:95, 2:147, 2:176, 2:181, 2:185, 2:196, 2:241, 2:244

Judgment, 1:8, 1:11, 1:15, 1:17, 1:24, 1:33, 1:36, 1:61, 1:64–73, 1:75–80, 1:77n3, 1:97–102, 1:105–6, 1:108, 1:112, 1:116–17, 1:121, 1:132n29, 1:133, 1:144–45, 1:152, 1:159, 1:165, 1:167–70, 1:222, 2:4, 2:11, 2:20–21, 2:23–25, 2:46, 2:53, 2:61–65, 2:67, 2:139, 2:152, 2:156–57, 2:163, 2:174–76, 2:182, 2:187–88, 2:190–91, 2:237–38, 2:244

Justice, injustice, 1:37, 1:88, 1:112–18, 1:120–26, 1:135, 1:145, 1:198, 1:200, S:113, 2:118, 2:128, 2:179, 2:219, 2:224

Justification, 1:xviiin4, 1:36, 1:38, 1:80, 1:94, 1:120, 1:122, 1:148, 1:153–56, 2:145, 2:207

Kairos, kairotic, 1:160–64, 1:166, 1:168, 1:189, 2:238, 2:40, 2:244

Kenosis, kenotic, 1:23–24, 1:27, 1:41, 1:44, 1:84, 1:157, 1:192, 196, 1:215, 1:218–19, 1:221–23, 2:156, 2:160, 2:179, 2:192, 2:226–28, 2:246

Kingdom, 1:8, 1:82–83, 1:85, 1:121–23, 1:160, 1:161n28, 1:162, 2:38, 2:97, 2:142, 2:204n21, 2:205, 2:208, 2:220, 2:223

Knowledge, 1:xiv, 1:xvi, 1:xviin3, 1:xxii, 1:2, 1:7, 1:9–10, 1:13, 1:19, 1:24–25, 1:28, 1:30n43, 1:39–41, 1:43–44, 1:46–52, 1:46n12, 1:47n12, 1:57, 1:59–63, 1:67, 1:72, 1:97–98, 1:169–73, 1:171n2, 1:176–89, 1:218n42, 2:2, 2:7–8, 2:13, 2:16, 2:20, 2:72–73, 2:81, 2:85–6, 2:88, 2:92, 2:121–22, 2:130, 2:134, 2:143–45, 2:147–48, 2:151, 2:166, 2:169, 2:176, 2:187, 2:196, 2:209, 2:211–12, 2:219, 2:234, 2:244

Labor, 1:xv, 1:1n1, 1:62, 1:65, 1:67–68, 1:104, 1:187, 1:195, 1:199–200, 1:202, 1:204, 1:208, 1:224, 2:54, 2:288, 2:169, 2:198, 2:213, 2:224, 2:226–27, 2:245–46

Lament, 1:95–96, 1:96n10, 1:201

Law, lawful, 1:xviii, 1:11, 1:36, 1:99n13, 1:100n16, 1:101–2, 1:109–12, 1:120n12, 1:123–24, 1:138, 1:142, 1:149, 1:151, 1:195, 1:198, 1:200n9, 1:202, 1:214–15, 1:218–20, 2:23n20, 2:28, 2:36n16, 2:38, 2:42–44, 2:46–47, 2:55, 2:67, 2:89n14, 2:90n14, 2:97, 2:128, 2:130, 2:174, 2:179, 2:186–89, 2:204n20, 2:224

Lawsuit, 1:111–19, 1:122–24, 1:123n15

Leader, leadership, 1:xix, 1:19–20, 1:26, 1:68, 1:70–76, 1:78, 1:187, 1:197, 1:201, 2:34n15, 2:79, 2:80n5, 2:93, 2:105, 2:108–9, 2:116, 2:120–21, 2:134, 2:140n15, 2:161

Legal, 1:xviii, 1:98, 1:111, 1:113–15, 1:117, 1:119–21, 1:125–26, 1:140, 1:188, 2:180

Liar, 1:129

Liberalism, liberal, 1:87, 1:93, 1:107, 1:133, 1:215, 2:vii, 2:ix–x, 2:19, 2:23, 2:69, 2:116, 2:144, 2:146,

Liberation, 1:72, 1:78–79, 1:127, 1:132, 1:144, 1:147, 1:176, 1:178, 2:30, 2:32, 2:35, 2:37

Libertarian, libertarianism, 1:50, 1:168, 2:26

Liberty, 1:124, 1:179–183, 1:191, 2:20–21, 2:23, 2:27n5, 2:133, 2:190

Linguistic, 1:xxii, 1:29, 1:42, 1:50, 1:86, 1:99–100, 1:163, 1:169, 1:217, 1:219–20, 2:ix, 2:8, 2:31, 2:49, 2:57–58, 2:62, 2:73, 2:134–35, 2:138, 2:159, 2:160, 2:164

Literal, 1:xviin3, 1:6n9, 1:17, 1:23, 1:27, 1:41, 1:72, 1:79, 1:85, 1:89, 1:90, 1:105, 1:116, 1:152, 1:160, 1:164, 1:167, 1:186, 1:202, 1:209, 1:217, 1:220

Literary, 1:xvi, 1:8, 1:53, 2:52, 2:58, 2:103, 2:143, 2:159, 2:171, 2:196–97, 2:4, 2:43, 2:67, 2:128, 2:130

Literature, 1:xviin3, 1:37n52, 1:101n16, 2:39, 2:77, 2:87, 2:216

Liturgy, liturgical, 1:ix, 1:70, 1:104n22–23, 1:156n24, 1:177–78, 2:17, 2:34, 2:37, 2:49, 2:54, 2:57–58, 2:60, 2:65, 2:105–6, 2:108, 2:151, 2:155, 2:178, 2:181–82, 2:191, 2:210, 2:243

Lutheran, 1:xxi

Malady, 1:xiii, 1:xvii, 1:xix

Management, managerialism, managerialist, 1:34, 1:39, 2:86, 2:106, 2:115,

Marriage, marry, 1:133, 1:136–38, 1:136n1, 1:140–46, 1:143n12, 1:148–50, 1:152–54, 1:155n23, 1:159, 1:161, 1:164–66, 2:37, 2:41–42, 2:94, 2:201, 2:207

Maturity, mature, immaturity, immature, 1:8, 1:16, 1:24, 1:44, 1:45n8, 1:46, 1:50–51, 1:63, 1:67, 1:176, 1:181, 1:183, 1:185, 1:189, 2:8, 2:18, 2:50, 2:106, 2:147, 2:157–58, 2:187, 2:231

Medicine, medical, 1:xix, 1:xx, 1:1n3, 1:64, 1:137n3, 2:11, 2:90, 2:96

Medieval, 1:xiv, 1:50, 1:115, 1:193, 1:206, 2:4, 2:44

Merit, meritorious, 1:193, 1:205, 2:100, 2:197

Method, methodological, 1:x, 1:xiii–xvi, 1:17, 1:35, 1:40–42, 1:53, 1:55, 1:57, 1:61, 1:73, 1:87, 1:89–90, 1:99, 1:108–9, 2:vii–vii, 2:126, 2:146, 2:154

Minister, ministerial, 1:34, 1:69, 1:75, 1:197, 1:200–202, 2:35, 2:42, 2:120

Ministry, 1:ix, 1:5, 1:34, 1:75–76, 1:192, 1:196, 1:197n6, 1:200–202, 1:213, 2:34–35, 2:43, 2:80–81, 2:104–5, 2:113–14, 2:120–25, 2:136–37, 2:176, 2:179, 2:187, 2:189, 2:203, 2:210, 2:234, 2:244

Misogynist, 1:xxi, 1:147

Mission, missional, 1:xix, 1:18, 1:43, 1:66, 1:82, 1:191, 1:194, 1:196, 1:199, 1:204, 1:207, 1:211–13, 1:215–17, 1:219, 1:221, 1:223–24, 2:41, 2:60, 2:73, 2:114, 2:120, 2:131, 2:156, 2:210, 2:237, 2:241

Subject Index

Missionary, 1:42, 1:56, 1:194–195, 1:200, 1:216–20, 2:156n7, 2:209, 2:241–42

Mourn, mournful, 1:25–26, 1:94–97, 1:95n5, 1:105, 1:158, 1:162–64

Moralize, 1:95, 1:108, 1:122, 1:128, 1:133, 1:200, 2:61, 2:100

Mystery, 1:xxii, 1:39, 1:47, 1:76, 2:11–12, 2:36, 2:224

Mystic, mysticism, mystical, 1:40, 1:47n12, 1:91, 1:91n1, 1:152

Name, 1:1, 1:3–4, 1:4n6, 1:6, 1:9, 1:16–17, 1:21, 1:21n33, 1:29, 1:35, 1:37n53, 1:46, 1:59, 1:73, 1:94, 1:97, 1:101, 1:105, 1:121–22, 1:124, 1:173, 2:3, 2:15, 2:34, 2:40, 2:53, 2:63, 2:68, 2:104, 2:113–14, 2:117, 2:121, 2:133, 2:139, 2:144–48, 2:162, 2:165, 2:208

Naming, 1:1–2, 1:4, 1:14, 1:94, 1:101, 1:107, 1:121, 1:143, 1:146, 1:160, 1:163, 1:212, 2:19, 2:200

Narrative, narrate, 1:xx–xxii, 1:14, 1:32, 1:34n49, 1:54, 1:56, 1:97, 1:191, 1:193–94, 1:209, 2:2–5, 2:13, 2:17, 2:41, 2:44, 2:59–60, 2:83, 2:112–13, 2:117, 2:129, 2:133, 2:141, 2:151, 2:187, 2:223

New Testament, 1:12n20, 1:101n16, 1:110, 1:154, 1:160, 1:172, 1:184, 1:193, 1:198, 1:209n24, 2:40, 2:77, 2:122, 2:124, 2:128, 2:214, 2:245

Nervous System, 1:xix, 2:93, 2:96, 2:118

Obligation, 1:12, 1:65, 1:203–5, 1:207

Offertory rite, 1:104n22

Oikodome (see also building up), oikodomic, 1:xix, 1:2, 1:18, 1:20, 1:24, 1:26, 1:49–50, 1:64, 1:95–96, 1:127, 1:146, 1:166, 1:182, 1:186, 2:20, 2:129, 2:153–54, 2:156, 2:171, 2:188, 2:227

Oikos, 1:165

Old Testament, 1:48, 1:72, 1:80, 1:98–100, 1:98n12, 1:100n16, 1:109, 1:172, 1:175, 1:202, 2:1–6, 2:10, 2:36, 2:47, 2:124–25, 2:128, 2:176, 2:186

Ontology, ontologize, ontological, 1:11n17, 1:12, 1:104, 1:140, 1:151, 1:153, 1:155n23, 1:165, 1:167, 1:177, 2:39, 2:42, 2:45–47, 2:103, 2:105, 2:111–13, 2:187, 2:201, 2:231

Organ, organic, 1:xix, 1:29, 1:126, 1:131, 1:141, 1:154, 1:156, 2:85–87, 2:90–92, 2:95–96, 2:206–9, 2:118

Organism, 1:xx, 1:29, 2:72, 2:90n15, 2:96, 2:98, 2:118

Owner, ownership, 1:125, 1:139–41, 1:144, 1:151–52

Pagan, paganism 1:20, 1:91–92, 1:106, 1:111, 1:116, 1:120, 1:153, 1:175, 1:179, 2:12, 2:14, 2:16–18, 2:35–36, 2:73–75, 2:104, 2:154–56, 2:194

Paraenesis, 1:3, 2:240

Paraklesis, 1:82, 1:85, 2:73

Parent, parenting, parental, 1:3, 1:8, 1:16, 1:61, 1:70, 1:85–87, 1:132–33, 1:155, 1:177, 2:1, 2:89n14, 2:159, 2:216

Parochialism, parochial, 1:18, 1:59, 1:72–73

Parousia, 1:159, 1:168

Passion, passionate, 1:14–15, 1:32, 1:95–96, 1:120, 1:142–45, 1:152, 1:159, 1:192, 2:7, 2:56, 2:67, 2:124, 2:128, 2:138, 2:186, 2:204

Pastor, pastoral, 1:xiii, 1:2–3, 1:37, 1:42, 1:92, 1:96, 1:161, 1:164, 1:166–67, 1:183, 1:188, 1:197, 1:206n19, 2:9, 2:25, 2:70–71, 2:101, 2:105–6, 2:108–9, 2:125–26, 2:180–81, 2:186–87, 2:191–94, 2:197, 2:207, 2:233

Patience, 1:xvii, 1:79, 1:184, 2:67, 2:143, 2:175, 2:228

Patriarchism, patriarchal, 1:58, 1:146–47, 2:27, 2:39, 2:41, 2:69, 2:184–85, 2:190

Patristic, 1:xiv, 1:10, 1:22n34, 1:45n8, 1:46n10, 1:61, 1:104, 1:193, 1:213, 2:112n37, 2:114, 2:225, 2:230, 2:233

Subject Index

Patron, patronage, patronize, 1:63, 1:197, 1:200–201, 1:204, 1:215, 2:51, 2:54–55, 2:59, 2:65–66, 2:69, 2:116, 2:119, 2:122, 2:159, 2:194

Peace, 1:xviii, 1:xix, 1:3, 1:8–9, 1:9n13, 1:27n42, 1:31, 1:119, 1:146–47, 1:152, 1:185, 2:24, 2:26, 2:28, 2:35, 2:70, 2:72, 2:78, 2:89, 2:94, 2:151–52, 2:179, 2:182–86, 2:188, 2:190–91, 2:236, 2:238–39, 2:243

Pedagogue, pedagogy, pedagogical, 1:xxi, 1:11, 1:16, 1:41, 1:82, 1:86–88, 1:95, 1:145, 1:183–84, 1:187, 1:224, 2:1, 2:6–10, 2:15

Perish, (im)perishable, 1:27–29, 1:27n42, 1:33–34, 1:44, 1:90, 1:184, 1:186, 1:210, 1:221–23, 2:199, 2:202, 2:212–15, 2:217, 2:220, 2:224

Phenomenology, phenomenological, 1:7n11, 1:144, 1:154, 1:156–58, 1:158n27, 1:163, 1:212, 2:78, 2:117, 2:170

Philosopher, philosophy, philosophical, 1:20, 1:24, 1:30n43, 1:30n45, 1:32–33, 1:56, 1:56n19, 1:58n21, 1:85, 1:130, 1:139n7, 1:140, 1:143n12, 1:157, 1:160, 1:165, 1:179, 1:205, 1:208, 1:211–212, 1:224n49, 2:9, 2:15–17, 2:23, 2:32, 2:36, 2:78, 2:172, 2:196, 2:201–2, 2:205, 2:211, 2:217

Pneumatology, pneumatological, 1:23, 1:49, 1:216, 1:220, 2:82

Political, 1:xviii, 1:1, 1:6n10, 1:19, 1:21n33, 1:23, 1:45n8, 1:69–70, 1:85, 1:91–94, 1:99–100, 1:102–103, 1:106, 1:118–119, 1:119n10, 1:121, 1:127–128, 1:145–146, 1:152, 1:162–163, 1:197n6, 1:225, 2:ix–x, 2:67, 2:72, 2:79–81, 2:85–98, 2:103–4, 2:106–7, 2:110, 2:113–14, 2:133, 2:140, 2:158, 2:179, 2:180–81, 2:191, 2:198, 2:203, 2:207–8, 2:217–19, 2:229–30, 2:232, 2:35, 2:239, 2:244–45

Politics, 1:xviii, 1:xix, 1:18, 1:70–71, 1:219, 1:225, 2:89n14, 2:91, 2:94, 2:185, 2:226

Porneia, 1:131–36, 1:141–42, 1:144–45, 1:148, 1:151, 1:163, 1:168, 2:14

Pornography, 1:132

Possession, possessiveness, possess, 1:2, 1:13n22, 1:20, 1:23, 1:27–28, 1:32, 1:37, 1:43, 1:46–47, 1:47n12, 1:49–51, 1:74–75, 1:84, 1:123–25, 1:133, 1:135, 1:139–41, 1:146, 1:158, 1:163–64, 1:168–69, 1:171, 1:173, 1:177, 1:180, 1:182, 1:185–86, 1:188, 1:211, 2:2, 2:8–9, 2:13, 2:22, 2:73, 2:75, 2:79, 2:84, 2:96, 2:102, 2:123, 2:131, 2:134–37, 2:141, 2:168, 2:170, 2:173, 2:188

Postmodern, postmodernity, postmodernist, 1:xiii, 1:xvi, 1:33, 1:35, 2:31

Powers (and principalities), 1:xviiin4, 1:99, 1:125, 1:133, 1:214, 2:9, 2:15–16, 2:44, 2:77–8, 2:82, 2:97, 2:130, 2:156, 2:173, 2:179, 2:188, 2:191, 2:197, 2:207–9, 2:218

Pragmatism, pragmatist, 1:32, 1:34, 1:34n49, 1:36, 2:197–98, 2:12, 2:198, 2:204

Praise, praiseworthy, 1:10, 1:10n17, 1:11–14, 1:16, 1:20, 1:30–31, 1:38, 1:55, 1:64, 1:76, 1:79–80, 1:84, 1:128, 1:205, 1:219n25, 2:4, 2:34, 2:83, 2:95, 2:108–9, 2:128–29, 2:137, 2:141, 2:170, 2:172

Prayer, 1:xv, 1:12, 1:37n52, 1:62, 1:64n2, 1:136–37, 1:142, 1:156, 2:24, 2:29–30, 2:34, 2:44, 2:108–9, 2:136, 2:155, 2:160–61, 2:163–64, 2:168, 2:170–72, 2:176, 2:210

Preach, preacher, 1:xviin2, 1:xix, 1:2, 1:23–24, 1:27–28, 1:45n9, 1:95–96, 1:152, 1:192–93, 1:201–2, 1:208–9, 1:211, 1:217–18, 1:222, 1:224, 2:31–32, 2:68, 2:100, 2:106–7, 2:114–16, 2:125–26, 2:151, 2:181–82, 2:197, 2:227, 2:237

Subject Index

Presence, 1:xv, 1:xx, 1:5–6, 1:8, 1:17,
1:29, 1:37, 1:41–42, 1:82, 1:91n1,
1:97–98, 1:135, 1:160, 1:164,
1:200n10, 1:219, 2:35, 2:45–46,
2:60, 2:113, 2:115–16, 2:118,
2:121, 2:147, 2:154, 2:160, 2:173,
2:175, 2:177, 2:188, 2:241–42,
2:245
Pride, prideful, 1:4, 1:32, 1:91, 1:93–94,
1:100–101, 1:104–5, 1:184,
1:186–87, 1:197, 1:206n19,
1:218, 1:224, 2:99–101, 2:115,
2:121, 2:133, 2:187, 2:191, 2:226
Prize, 1:13n22, 1:190, 1:195, 1:210n25,
1:213–14, 1:213n37, 1:218,
1:221, 1:222n45, 1:223
Proprietor, propriety, (non)proprietary,
1:139–41, 1:144–46, 1:151,
1:163, 1:168, 1:205
Prostitution, prostitute, 1:121, 1:125–28,
1:130–31, 1:134, 1:140, 1:146,
1:148
Psychology, psychological, 1:38, 1:41,
1:72–73, 1:82, 1:90, 1:120, 1:138,
1:144–45, 1:172, 1:184, 1:195,
2:15, 2:42, 2:106, 2:108, 2:158,
2:198, 2:223

Rationalism, rationalist, 1:31, 1:33–34,
1:140
Reconciliation, 1:18, 1:31, 1:35, 1:100–
101, 1:110–11, 1:113, 1:116–22,
1:124, 1:146, 1:179, 1:185, 2:28,
2:97–98, 2:239
Redeem, redeemer, redemption, 1:xxii,
1:16, 1:27n42, 1:37, 1:43,
1:55n18, 1:56n19, 1:179, 2:22,
2:28, 2:138–39, 2:162, 2:176–77,
2:226
Reformation, Reformer, 1:xiv–xv,
1:40n2, 1:43, 1:43n5, 1:45,
1:114–15, 1:153, 1:176n8, 1:184,
1:205–6, 2:15, 2:84–85, 2:207
Reign, 1:8, 1:56, 1:84, 1:145, 1:163,
2:38–40, 2:45, 2:66–67, 2:69,
2:82, 2:98, 2:112, 2:121, 2:184,
2:188, 2:205, 2:207–8

Remember, 1:172, 2:33, 2:51, 2:231
Reputation, 1:23–24, 1:91, 2:26, 2:137,
2:173, 2:210
Responsibility, responsible, 1:xvii, 1:34,
1:62, 1:69, 1:77, 1:98–99, 1:115,
1:118, 1:132, 1:140, 1:150, 1:152,
1:165, 1:167, 1:169–71, 1:179,
1:189, 2:viii, 2:x, 2:9, 2:32, 2:76,
2:93, 2:96, 2:104–5, 2:111, 2:161,
2:182, 2:189
Resurrection, 1:25–26, 1:40n2, 1:81n7,
1:126–28, 1:223, 2:40, 2:68,
2:176, 2:292–13, 2:216–20,
2:222, 2:224–28, 2:230
Retaliation, 1:122, 1:220
Revelation, revelatory, vxv, 1:xxii,
1:42–44, 1:46–47, 1:49, 1:51,
2:24, 2:79–80, 2:96, 2:151, 2:158,
2:166, 2:169, 2:178–81, 2:184,
2:190, 2:216
Reward, 1:xxii, 1:37n53, 1:65, 1:68–69,
1:190–91, 1:194–95, 1:198–200,
1:202–3, 1:205, 1:207–11, 1:215,
1:217, 1:222–24, 2:196n8, 2:204,
2:238
Rhetoric, rhetorician, rhetorical, 1:2,
1:8, 1:20, 1:23–24, 1:36, 1:41–42,
1:42n3, 1:58, 1:67, 1:71, 1:78,
1:83, 1:92, 1:106, 1:109, 1:112,
1:149, 1:181, 1:198, 1:203, 2:viii,
2:11, 2:15–16, 2:18, 2:21–2, 2:29,
2:47, 2:49, 2:55, 2:72, 2:87, 2:90–
91, 2:94, 2:102–3, 2:114, 2:128,
2:131, 2:136, 2:141, 2:144, 2:203

Sacrifice, sacrificial, 1:4, 1:28, 1:36,
1:57–58, 1:72n12, 1:102–3,
1:105, 1:123–24, 1:169, 1:173,
1:180, 1:182, 1:190, 1:193–96,
1:198, 1:203–5, 1:210–11, 1:215,
1:217, 2:16–17, 2:19, 2:22, 2:26,
2:140, 2:176, 2:198
Saint, 1:3–4, 1:9–10, 1:21n32, 1:33n46,
1:74, 1:74n13, 1:82, 1:90, 1:111,
2:84n8, 2:133, 2:136, 2:153,
2:168, 2:179, 2:182, 2:184, 2:206,
2:222, 2:233–34, 2:240, 2:243

Salvation, 1:26, 1:27n42, 1:29, 1:59, 1:64, 1:72, 1:80, 1:99–100, 1:153–55, 1:224, 2:2, 2:23, 2:83, 2:98, 2:189, 2:195, 2:201, 2:209

Sanctification, sanctify, 1:3–4, 1:9, 1:28, 1:37–38, 1:121–23, 1:153–56, 2:23, 2:157, 2:227

Scholastics, scholasticism, 1:38

Scripture, scriptural, 1:x, 1:xiv–xvii, 1:xxii, 1:16, 1:30, 1:38, 1:44–45, 1:54, 1:56, 1:58, 1:60–62, 1:77n3, 1:78, 1:80, 1:87–90, 1:94, 1:96, 1:114, 1:132, 1:145, 1:153, 1:158, 1:198, 2:viii, 2:3–4, 2:27, 2:29, 2:31, 2:43, 2:47–48, 2:82–83, 2:95, 2:108, 2:119, 2:126, 2:151–52, 2:190, 2:195, 2:197–203, 2:205, 2:226, 2:231, 2:233

Secret, 1:44, 1:45n7, 1:46, 1:46n12, 1:71, 1:77n3, 1:91, 1:107, 1:157, 2:146, 2:163, 2:174, 2:176, 2:207

Secretary, secretarial, 1:1n1

Self-control, 1:136, 1:138, 1:138n4, 1:142–44, 1:211, 1:213n37, 2:137, 2:161, 2:176

Servant, servanthood, 1:1, 1:5, 1:65–66, 1:76–78, 1:195, 2:24, 2:89, 2:121, 2:140, 2:153, 2:175, 2:238, 2:241

Sexuality, sexual, 1:xviii–xx, 1:50, 1:70, 1:91–92, 1:94, 1:98–99, 1:105–7, 1:121, 1:124–50, 1:131n27, 1:137n3, 1:140n11, 1:143n12, 1:144n14, 1:161, 1:164–66, 1:168, 2:5, 2:13, 2:28, 2:30, 2:35–38, 2:40–47, 2:70, 2:97, 2:128, 2:147

Shame, shaming, ashamed, shameful, 1:31–32, 1:81n7, 1:82, 1:85, 1:92, 1:94, 1:111–12, 1:119, 1:131, 1:183, 2:31, 2:39–40, 2:42, 2:55, 2:63, 2:68–69, 2:112–13, 2:147, 2:179, 2:185–86, 2:190, 2:209, 2:211

Sin, sinner, sinful, 1:4, 1:10n17, 1:11, 1:14, 1:16, 1:69, 1:71n10, 1:79, 1:88–89, 1:91, 1:96, 1:102n17, 1:106–7, 1:107n24, 1:109, 1:116, 1:118–19, 1:122, 1:129–31, 1:134, 1:144, 1:158–59, 1:166–67, 1:169, 1:180–81, 1:187–88, 1:194, 1:212, 1:214, 1:216, 2:viii, 2:1, 2:10, 2:15, 2:18, 2:25, 2:50, 2:59, 2:61, 2:97, 2:112, 2:176, 2:195, 2:199–200, 2:202 2:206, 2:209, 2:222, 2:224, 2:226

Skandalon, scandal, scandalous, 1:31, 1:91, 1:96, 1:119, 2:35, 2:46, 2:113

Slave, slavery, enslavement, enslaved, 1:86, 1:125, 1:132–33, 1:142–44, 1:148–49, 1:151, 1:151n16, 1:210n25, 1:214–16, 1:221–22, 2:35–36, 2:45, 2:54, 2:85, 2:87–88, 2:97–98, 2:189, 2:222

Slogan, 1:45, 1:126, 1:136n1, 1:146, 1:174, 1:179–81, 1:185, 2:11, 2:19, 2:21–22, 2:25–27, 2:44, 2:50, 2:174

Sociology, sociological, 1:19, 1:25, 1:90, 1:103, 1:201, 2:x, 2:17, 2:49–50, 2:80

Son, 1:xix, 1:9, 1:14, 1:17, 1:49, 1:94, 1:179, 2:39–40, 2:76, 2:113, 2:116–18, 2:121, 2:137, 2:145, 2:148, 2:154, 2:163, 2:199, 2:205, 2:208

Soul, ensouled, 1:64, 1:127–28, 1:152, 1:165, 1:199, 1:213, 1:224, 2:107, 2:132, 2:177, 2:196, 2:215, 2:219, 2:26, 2:231, 2:242

Steward, stewardship, 1:76–77, 1:209

Stoic, stoicism, stoicized, 1:120, 1:124, 1:143–45, 1:143n12, 1:147, 1:161, 1:168, 2:161

Strategy, 1:x, 1:xx-xxi, 1:39, 1:42, 1:73, 1:82, 1:87, 1:100, 1:148, 1:158, 1:161, 1:197n6, 2:3, 2:8, 2:11, 2:72, 2:97, 2:129, 2:146, 2:178, 2:198, 2:233, 2:237

Stumbling block, 1:xvii, 1:31, 1:54, 1:179–81, 1:185, 2:5

Suffer, 1:xx, 1:26, 1:65, 1:69, 1:84, 1:95–96, 1:115, 1:124, 1:130, 1:139, 1:224, 2:9–10, 2:15, 2:26, 2:74, 2:92, 2:94–95, 2:110, 2:113,

Subject Index

2:115, 2:118, 2:121, 2:141, 2:162, 2:199, 2:222, 2:226–27

Supererogation, supererogatory, 1:114–15, 1:115n5, 1:193, 1:195, 1:204–7, 1:206nn19–20, 2:134

Surprise, 1:xviii, 1:xxi–xxii, 1:57, 1:95, 1:146, 1:154, 1:161, 1:194, 1:200n9, 2:104, 2:109, 2:115, 2:119, 2:123, 2:192

Suspicion, 1:xvi, 1:106, 1:119, 1:193, 1:197, 1:201, 2:vii, 2:95, 2:107, 2:163

Teacher, 1:xv, 1:19–20, 1:28, 1:52, 1:75, 1:86–87, 1:147, 1:197, 2:1, 2:80, 2:119–23, 2:125, 2:141, 2:192, 2:235

Teleology, teleological, 1:126, 1:170, 1:212, 2:8, 2:50, 2:79, 2:100

Temple, 1:xix, 1:65, 1:69–71, 1:71n9, 1:107, 1:129, 1:135, 1:180, 1:182, 1:196, 2:35n16, 2:52, 2:75, 2:86, 2:234

Temptation, 1:6, 1:18, 1:35–36, 1:60, 1:70, 1:88–89, 1:106, 1:112, 1:131, 1:133, 1:135n31, 1:138, 1:166, 1:183, 1:187, 1:194, 1:219, 2:7–10, 2:14–16, 2:28, 2:67, 2:81, 2:104, 2:114, 2:131, 2:163, 2:168, 2:182, 2:186, 2:191, 2:206, 2:215, 2:230

Testimony, 1:9, 1:13, 1:60, 2:58, 2:95, 2:114, 2:196, 2:203

Therapy, 1:xiii–xiv, 1:xviii–xix, 1:106

Theologian 1:xviii, 1:53, 1:60, 1:117, 1:157, 2:ix, 2:28, 2:140, 2:144, 2:216, 2:233

Tolerance, tolerant, 1:xviii–xix, 1:94–95, 1:100, 1:102, 1:104–5, 1:133, 2:17–18

Transformation, 1:12, 1:25, 1:38, 1:156, 1:161, 1:186n13, 1:191, 1:212, 2:20, 2:145, 2:147, 2:198, 2:214–15, 2:219–20, 2:222, 2:224–27

Travel, traveler, 1:x, 1:xiv, 1:xxi, 1:114, 1:190, 1:194–198, 1:200, 1:203, 1:218, 2:69, 2:209, 2:228–29, 2:236–27, 2:245–26

Trinity, Trinitarian, 1:38, 1:42–43, 1:49, 1:51, 1:122, 1:178, 2:15, 2:40, 2:72–76, 2:82–83, 2:85, 2:97, 2:121–22, 2:142, 2:147, 2:178, 2:208, 2:243

Trust, trustworthy, entrusted, 1:xvi, 1:xvii*n*2, 1:14–15, 1:26, 1:51, 1:57, 1:76–77, 1:80, 1:82, 1:88, 1:131, 1:158, 1:167, 1:175, 1:175n6, 1:178, 1:184–85, 1:203, 1:205, 1:207, 1:218–19, 2:6–8, 2:10, 2:13, 2:30–31, 2:40, 2:60, 2:112, 2:140, 2:143, 2:148, 2:160, 2:164, 2:194, 2:197–99, 2:201–2, 2:205, 2:213, 2:240

Truth, truthful, 1:xix, 1:3, 1:5–6, 1:16, 1:19, 1:23–24, 1:28, 1:30, 1:32–33, 1:35–36, 1:49, 1:73–74, 1:79, 1:88, 1:98, 1:102–3, 1:105, 1:109, 1:133, 1:157, 1:164, 1:183–84, 1:206, 1:212, 1:212n32, 2:27n5, 2:29, 2:64, 2:73–74, 2:108, 2:139–41, 2:148, 2:154, 2:169, 2:173, 2:177–78, 2:189, 2:199, 2:202, 2:205, 2:216, 2:237

Unity, 1:xvi, 1:xviii–xix, 1:xxii, 1:1–4, 1:11, 1:16–19, 1:24–26, 1:28, 1:34–36, 1:66, 1:71, 1:96, 1:105, 1:115, 1:141, 1:149, 1:184, 1:189, 2:12, 2:18, 2:35, 2:50, 2:56–59, 2:71, 2:87, 2:91, 2:97, 2:109, 2:114, 2:118, 2:121–22, 2:152, 2:158, 2:169, 2:183, 2:191, 2:191, 2:193, 2:206, 2:30, 2:234, 2:239

Union, 1:9, 1:26, 1:127–28, 1:134, 1:152, 1:223, 2:12, 2:17, 2:60, 2:94, 2:110, 2:190

Virgin, virginity, 1:136n2, 1:142, 1:158–60, 1:167, 1:198, 1:205, 2:43, 2:44, 2:178

Virtue, 1:xviii*n*4, 1:37–38, 1:37n53, 1:38n54, 1:70, 1:106, 1:127, 1:141, 1:153, 1:189, 1:206, 2:7, 2:59, 2:78, 2:89, 2:104, 2:128, 2:133, 2:141, 2:157, 2:162, 2:196, 2:220, 2:231–32, 2:241,

Vice, 1:38n54, 1:106–8, 1:107n24, 1:121–22, 2:185
Victory, 1:214, 2:199, 2:224–6
Vocation, 1:xv, 1:2–3, 1:62, 1:141, 1:150, 1:152, 1:160, 1:165–67, 1:191, 1:193, 1:201, 1:206–7, 2:96, 2:113–14, 2:119, 2:121, 2:132, 2:139, 2:142, 2:153

Wait, await, 1:x, 1:xvii*n*2, 1:7, 1:9, 1:14–15, 1:24, 1:32, 1:44, 1:47, 1:79, 1:83, 1:125, 1:152, 1:164, 1:223, 2:28, 2:42, 2:55, 2:65, 2:70–71, 2:115, 2:162, 2:176, 2:182, 2:194, 2:199, 2:203, 2:230, 2:244
War, warring, 1:xviii, 1:6, 1:56n19, 1:83n15, 1:121, 1:139, 1:145–46, 1:151n16, 1:171, 2:28, 2:70, 2:232, 2:241
Weak, weakness, 1:5, 1:7, 1:12n19, 1:14, 1:19, 1:26, 1:31–32, 1:39–42, 1:57, 1:73, 1:81, 1:84, 1:96, 1:119, 1:167, 1:169–70, 1:173, 1:177, 1:179–89, 1:191, 1:192n3, 1:195, 1:197n6, 1:204, 1:215, 1:219–20, 2:9–10, 2:14, 2:21–22, 2:26, 2:61, 2:70, 2:89, 2:110, 2:112–13, 2:117, 2:158, 2:163, 2:213, 2:223, 2:226
Wife, 1:91–92, 1:94, 1:126–28, 1:136, 1:136n2, 1:139–41, 1:147, 1:152, 1:158–59, 1:164, 1:166, 1:195–98, 2:23, 2:33, 2:39, 2:89, 2:113
Wisdom, 1:20, 1:23–32, 1:25n40, 1:34–37, 1:39, 1:42–44, 1:45n7, 1:46, 1:47n12, 1:48–49, 1:51–52, 1:54, 1:57, 1:60, 1:71, 1:73, 1:79–80, 1:85, 1:133, 2:81, 2:86, 2:104, 2:196, 2:244–45
Wise, 1:20, 1:27, 1:31–32, 1:35, 1:37, 1:47, 1:71–72, 1:79, 1:81, 1:84–85, 1:111, 1:113, 2:26, 2:113
Witness, 1:x, 1:xvi, 1:4, 1:7, 1:28, 1:30, 1:48n13, 1:73–74, 1:84, 1:100, 1:118, 1:146, 1:156, 1:161, 1:164–65, 1:192, 1:199, 1:208, 1:223, 2:ix, 2:40, 2:46, 2:82–83, 2:116, 2:122–3, 2:139, 2:145, 2:161, 2:175, 2:198–200, 2:202–4, 2:207, 2:225–27, 2:238, 2:246
Word (God's), 1:x, 1:xv–xvii, 1:14, 1:23, 1:37, 1:51, 1:61–62, 1:145, 1:150, 1:172, 1:179, 1:191, 1:196, 1:200, 1:205, 2:76, 2:122–23, 2:125, 2:152, 2:167, 2:169, 2:179, 2:184, 2:188–89, 2:197, 2:199–202, 2:226, 2:237

Scripture Index

Old Testament

Genesis

1:20	2:214n30
1:26	2:208
2–4	2:205
2:20–24	2:186
3:1–18	2:112
3:7	2:112n37
3:14–15	2:223
3:16	2:186
4:16	2:113
4:26	2:113
6:2	2:47
8:1	1:172
11	2:110

Exodus

7:1–2	2:152
13:21	2:2
14:22	2:2
16:3	2:13
16:4–35	2:2
17:1–7	2:2

Leviticus

18:18	1:94
26:31	2:59n47

Numbers

11:5	2:13
12:6–8	2:152
12:16	2:152
20:2–13	2:2
21	2:5–6

Deuteronomy

17:7;12	1:99n13
19:19	1:99n13
21:21	1:99n13; 1:100n15
22:21;24	1:99n13
24:7	1:99n13
25:4	1:202
29:29	1:77n3

1 Samuel

8	2:104n30
19:18–20	2:133

2 Samuel

12:13	2:4

1 Kings

18	1:42n4

2 Kings

5:23–26	1:91n1

Ezra

10:6	1:95

Job

42:18	2:155

Psalms

1:1–2	2:127n49
1:3	1:64n1
8:4	2:215
5:13	

Scripture Index

Psalms (continued)

8:7	2:207
19:1–3	1:30
20:13	2:177
23:2	2:242
29:21	2:177
36:9	2:221
45:1	2:189
69:20	1:96
78:18	2:13
89:12	2:22n19
94:11	1:72
102:3	1:96
105:8	1:172
110:1	2:207
115	2:75
115:5	1:175
119	2:182n32
119:105	1:158
135:15–18	1:175

Proverbs

7:10	1:165

Ecclesiastes

1:2	1:72

Song of Songs

4:1	2:36n17

Isaiah

28:1, 7	2:187
28:9–10	2:187
28:11–12	2:174, 2:188
60	2:156
64:4	1:48

Ezekiel

44:20	2:45

Daniel

4:16	2:46n34
4:18	1:82
5	2:152
5:13	1:72
Joel 2:16	1:164

Amos

5:11–12	2:59n48
5:18;20	1:100n14
8:9–14	1:100n14

Habakkuk

2:18–19	2:75

New Testament

Matthew

5:3–4, 10–12	2:113
5:18	1:90
5:21–30	2:97
5:48	1:47
6:16	1:190
6:24	2:18
6:33	1:123
6:35	2:18
7:29	1:181
10:9–10	1:195, 1:200
10:14	2:237
10:37–38	2:214
16:4	1:8
18	1:112
18:15	1:118
18:17	1:118
19	1:207
19:21	2:67n52
22:30	2:46n34
22:37	2:132
22:37–40	2:129
23:11–12	2:113
26:22, 33	1:60
27:46	2:148

Mark

1:10	2:148
1:15	1:160
5:19	2:83
8:35	2:214
12:28–34	2:128

15:34	2:148	5:14	2:206
		6	2:221–2, 2:227
Luke		6:4–6	2:222
		6:11	2:222
1:72	1:172	7:16	1:23
2:4	2:83	7:20–23	1:138
10:35	1:206	8	2:162
14:7–14	2:113	8:12–15	1:23
14:26–33	2:214	8:26	2:163
19:8–9	1:206	12	1:96
23:29	1:164	12:1–2	1:186n13
24:13–27	2:199	12:1	1:82
24:27	2:155	12:2	1:74, 1:163, 2:62
		12:4	2:220
John		12:5	1:26, 1:88
		13	1:121, 2:207
3:8	2:218	14	2:22, 2:24
6:46	2:148	14:3–4	2:24
12:2–3	2:35	14:13	1:156
12:24	2:214	14:23	2:25
14:25	1:42n4	15:1	1:96
16:13	1:45	15:2	1:166
20:24–29	2:199	16:1	2:34
		16:6, 12	2:34
Acts		16:17	2:34
		16:23	2:54
2:1–18	2:154		
2:13	2:162	*1 Corinthians*	
2:44–46	2:53n41		
6	2:80	1	1:1–38, 1:84
6:1–7	2:122	1:1	1:1–3
9:27	2:145	1:2–3	1:196; 2:50, 2:132,
10:4–46	2:154		2:200, 2:243
15	1:221	1:2–4	1:3–8
16:14–15	2:34n15	1:4–9	1:9–16, 1:26, 1:64,
16:15, 23	2:209n25		1:79, 2:241
17	1:33	1:5–7	1:13–14, 1:19
17:21	1:33	1:7	1:14, 2:203
17:32	1:33	1:8	1:29
18:26	2:34n15	1:9	1:17, 1:19,
19:18–19	1:35	1:10	1:3, 1:17, 1:25,
20:34	1:206		2:243
21:9	2:34n15	1:11–12	1:18–21,
			1:761:211
Romans		1:13–16	1:21–23
		1:17	1:23–26, 1:209,
1:4	2:202–3		2:50, 2:136, 2:161,
1:20	1:30		2:169, 2:193
1:28	1:31	1:18–20	1:27–29
5:12	2:206	1:21	1:29–31

1 Corinthians (continued)

1:22–27	1:31–37, 2:12, 2:204
1:22–23	1:54
1:23—2:16	1:185
1:23	1:35
1:26	1:83
1:27–28	1:32, 1:38, 1:183, 2:113
1:28–31	1:37–38
2	1:39–62
2:1–5	1:39–43, 1:196
2:1	1:40, 1:46
2:2	1:xiv, 1:29, 1:38, 1:40, 1:43, 1:50, 1:77, 1:80, 1:214
2:6–8	1:44–48, 1:51, 1:57, 2:147
2:9–12	1:48–50
2:10–11	1:43, 2:148, 2:163
2:10–13	1:49
2:13–16	1:xiv, 1:51–53, 2:178, 2:223
3	1:63–75, 1:59
3:1–4	1:63–64
3:1	1:77
3:2	1:16, 2:169n19
3:5	1:81
3:5–9	1:1, 2:86
3:5–15	1:65–70
3:6–12	1:66, 213
3:8	1:67, 1:210n25
3:10–11	1:188
3:10–15	1:182, 2:86
3:11–13	2:138
3:13	1:78, 1:144, 2:62
3:14	1:210n25
3:16–17	1:70–71, 2:86
3:18–20	1:65, 1:71–72, 1:79
3:21–23	1:72–75
3:21	1:83
4	1:76–90
4:1–5	1:76–80
4:2	1:88, 1:210n25
4:3	1:192n3
4:5	1:79, 1:210n25
4:6–7	1:80–81
4:6	1:46, 1:89
4:8–13	1:81–85
4:8–9	1:3, 1:82–84, 1:87
4:9–16	1:7
4:10	2:11n9
4:10–12	1:5
4:13–14	1:82
4:14–21	1:xiv, 1:85–90, 2:1
4:15	1:75
4:20–21	1:2, 1:8, 1:83, 2:175
5	1:91–110, 1:112, 1:133
5:1	1:91–94, 1:106
5:2	1:94–96
5:3–5	1:97–102
5:5	1:77n3, 1:99, 2:244
5:6–8	1:102–5
5:6	1:122
5:7	1:38, 1:93
5:9–13	1:105–10, 1:204
5:11	1:93, 1:101, 1:106, 1:121–22
6	1:50, 1:111–37, 1:148, 2:32
6:1–6	1:111–13
6:4	2:120
6:7–8	1:113–21, 1:193
6:9–11	1:121–23
6:12	1:123–25
6:12–20	1:163
6:13–17	1:125–29, 1:181, 1:185, 2:52, 2:138
6:18–20	1:129–35
6:18	1:107, 2:14
6:19	1:38
7	1:50, 1:191, 1:136–68
7:1–6	1:136–42, 1:198
7:7–9	1:142–47
7:10–24	1:147–58
7:16	2:158n11
7:25–40	1:158–68
8	1:169–91
8:1–3	1:169–73, 2:20
8:1	1:67, 1:187

8:2	1:177–78, 1:187, 2:16	11:10–22	1:201
8:4–7	1:173–79	11:22	2:186
8:8–13	1:179–89, 1:218, 2:22, 2:138	11:11–12	2:180
		11:14–16	2:156
		11:17–19	2:48–50
8:8	1:180, 2:19	11:18	2:218
8:13	1:187, 1:204	11:19	1:7, 1:25
9	1:190–226, 2:29, 2:60	11:20–22	2:51–55, 2:15
		11:22	2:162
9:1–3	1:192–95	11:23–26	2:56–61
9:4–14	1:195–203	11:24–25	2:51
9:15–17	1:203–7, 2:136	11:27–32	2:51, 2:61–65
9:18	1:199, 1:206n19, 1:207–11, 1:223, 2:225, 2:238, 2:241	11:28	1:191, 2:61
		11:29	1:64, 1:108
		11:33–34	2:28, 2:42n24, 2:65–71, 2:186, 2:194, 2:218
9:19–23	1:214–21, 2:156, 2:203		
		12	1:38, 2:72–127, 2:167, 2:182
9:19–27	2:227		
9:20	1:216–17, 2:236	12:1–3	2:73–76, 2:159
9:22	1:211	12:2	1:xviin2
9:23	1:209	12:4–7	2:76–81, 2:135, 2:153
9:24–27	1:221–25		
10	2:1–26	12:4–13	1:97
10:1–5	2:1–5	12:7	2:84
10:1	2:73	12:8–11	2:81–85, 2:153
10:2–4	2:88	12:9	2:142
10:3–4	2:10–11, 2:99	12:12–13	1:211, 2:85–100, 2:218
10:1–12	1:55		
10:6	2:4–5,	12:12	1:213
10:6–10	2:5–6	12:14–20	1:224, 2:100–110
10:11–13	2:6–13	12:21–26	1:96, 1:220, 2:110–20, 2:14, 2:219
10:11	2:4–5		
10:12	2:11		
10:14–15	2:13–16	12:26	2:169
10:16–22	2:16–19	12:27–31	2:120–25
10:16	2:99	12:27	1:213
10:17	1:213, 2:11n9	12:27–29	2:43
10:23–30	2:19–24	12:28–30	2:80
10:30	2:26	12:31	2:239
10:23	1:124	13	1:90, 2:128–49
10:31—11:1	2:25–26	13:1–3	2:130–39
11	1:64, 1:108, 1:201, 2:27–71	13:1	1:175, 2:163
		13:1–13	1:64
11:1	2:146	13:4–7	2:139–42
11:2–16	2:27–48	13:7	2:155
11:3	2:122, 2:152	13:8–12	2:143–49
11:5–6	2:185	13:12	1:172, 2:178

1 Corinthians (continued)

14	1:221, 2:150–91
14:1–5	2:150–65, 2:211
14:1	2:124, 2:239
14:6–12	2:166–69
14:7	2:136
14:12	1:15
14:13–20	2:125, 2:170–73
14:21–25	2:174–78
14:26–40	2:178–91
14:29	1:44
14:34	2:42, 2:180,
14:33	2:28
14:38	2:244
14:39	2:239
15	1:128, 1:223, 2:67, 2:192–227
15:1–11	2:195–202
15:1–2	2:232
15:12–19	2:202–204
15:20–28	2:204–209
15:22–24	1:223, 2:40
15:29–34	2:209–12
15:35–44	2:212–20
15:45–50	2:220–24
15:51–58	2:224–27
15:49	2:145
16	2:228–46
16:1–4	2:233–36
16:5–12	2:236–40
16:13–14	2:230–33
16:15–20	2:240–43
16:21–24	2:243–46
16:21–24	1:xiv

2 Corinthians

1:3–7	1:26
1:8	2:73
2:9–10	1:44
2:15	1:28
5:20	1:82
9:12–14	2:136, 2:234
10:10	1:5
11:25–27	2:228, 2:228
11:29	1:96
12:10	2:22
13:5–7	1:223

Galatians

2	1:221
2:20	2:132
3:27	1:156, 1:160
3:28	1:213, 2:35, 2:97
5	1:49
5:18	1:23
5:22	1:141
6:2	1:218, 2:10
6:4	2:62
6:11	2:244

Ephesians

2	1:147
2:11–22	1:120
2:15	2:217
4:15–16	2:86
4:17	1:202
5:18	2:162
5:21	2:41
5:23	2:41, 2:86
5:24	2:41
5:30	1:128

Philippians

1:9	1:172
2:6–11	1:52
2:7	2:208
2:9–10	2:208
4:10–18	1:200

Colossians

1:15–20	2:18
1:18	2:86
3:14	2:232

1 Thessalonians

2:3–13	1:7
2:3–5	1:42n3
2:5	1:23
2:8–9	1:206
4	2:207
4:13–18	2:206
4:16	2:206
4:17	2:207

Scripture Index

4:18	2:207	*1 John*	
5:10	2:208	4:12	2:145
		4:16	2:145
1 Timothy			
2:12	2:42	*3 John*	
3:8–10	2:80	9	2:245
4:4	2:22		
Philemon		*Jude*	
8	1:82	8	2:47n35
Hebrews		*Revelation*	
4:12	2:237	1:16	2:237
11:4	1:57	14:2f	2:163n16
12:1	1:73	18:21–23	1:164
		21:4	2:209
2 Peter			
2:11	2:46n34		

www.ingramcontent.com/pod-product-compliance
Lightning Source LLC
Chambersburg PA
CBHW021654230426
43668CB00008B/619